The Freudian Robot

Nixon decided to bomb Cambodia and hide that decision from Congress, the computers in the Pentagon were "fixed" to create a double system of accounting—"one to keep the truth from the people, the other to tell the truth to the computer" (". . . Admiral and Computer," *New York Times*, August 14, 1973). The computers transformed the genuine strike reports about the 3630 recorded B-52 sorties in Cambodia and their bombing of a neutral nation into false reports about strikes in South Vietnam.[14] The US government officials who had access to the secret reports had to believe them because they came directly from the Pentagon's computers. Commenting on this war crime, MIT computer scientist Joseph Weizenbaum wrote: "George Orwell's Ministry of Information had become mechanized. History was not merely destroyed, it was recreated."[15] Those officials "did not realize that they had become their computer's 'slaves,' to use Admiral Moorer's own word, until the lies they instructed their computers to tell others ensnared them, the instructors, themselves" (Weizenbaum, *Computer Power and Human Reason*, 239). Gilles Deleuze and Félix Guattari would insist on a distinction here: "One is not enslaved by the technical machine but rather subjected to it." Subjection to the machine in a Foucauldian sense.[16] We will elaborate on the dangerous implications of this subjection and the human-machine entanglement later in the book.

In *Understanding Media*, McLuhan has suggested that "by continuously embracing technologies, we relate ourselves to them as servomechanisms. That is why we must, to use them at all, serve these objects, these extensions of ourselves, as gods or minor religions. An Indian is the servomechanism of his canoe, as the cowboy of his horse or the executive of his clock."[17] McLuhan's inversion of the master-slave relationship is provocative and contains some truths in it, but it nevertheless asserts a cybernetic (machine) view of human-machine relationship that puts his momentary nod to Zhuangzi and Heisenberg in a double bind.[18] For it is well known that cyberneticians have conceived of the central nervous system itself as a cybernetic machine like all other servomechanisms capable of maintaining equilibrium or homeostasis. Norbert Wiener, for example, would have

14. Seymour M. Hersh, "Wheeler Asserts Bombing Secrecy Was Nixon's Wish," *New York Times*, July 31, 1973; and Seymour M. Hersh, "Laird Approved False Reporting on Secret Raids," *New York Times*, August 10, 1973. For some of the key testimonies to the Senate Armed Services Committee, see Hersh's other reports in *New York Times* in the months of July and August 1973.

15. Weizenbaum, *Computer Power and Human Reason*, 239.

16. Deleuze and Guattari, *A Thousand Plateaus: Capitalism and Schizophrenia*, 457.

17. McLuhan, *Understanding Media*, 46.

18. Even the notion of double bind derives from the cybernetic theory of Gregory Bateson.

agreed with McLuhan, while Zhuangzi and Heisenberg would have found his mere inversion of a prosthetic view of human-machine relationship just as problematic as the straightforward instrumental view of machine. Clearly, McLuhan's critique of the technocratic civilization is contradicted by his enthusiastic endorsement of the cybernetics that has been the hallmark of that same civilization.

In that sense, McLuhan and many of his followers are still toeing the line of Confucius's disciple Zigong when they repeat ad nauseam that the physiological deficiencies of the human species are in need of prosthetic extension through technology. It is one thing to argue that the memory capacity of the human brain can be greatly extended by the increased power of a microchip computer and quite another to argue that the logic of the computer—and communication networks in general—is the same as the logic of the human psyche itself. In fact, the argument of technological prosthesis never works well in the latter case, especially in regard to cybernetic research. The prosthetic argument is actually an alibi for something more fundamental that has been going on since the mid-twentieth century, and this is the cybernetic conception of the human psyche as a computing machine.

In 1920, Raoul Hausmann—one of the foremost Dadaists of the twentieth century—made a curious sculpture and named it *The Mechanical Head: The Spirit of Our Age*. In the twenty-first century, this remarkable work could be renamed *The Freudian Robot* because it does seem to embody the spirit of our new millennium in all its essential aspects. Adorning the cover of my book, Hausmann's image of a mechanical head allows the reader to visualize and grasp some of the salient attributes of the Freudian robot discussed in the chapters that follow. The artist appears to have had an unusual premonition of what would happen to the human psyche under the technocratic regime of capitalist production when the mind grows increasingly attached to objects or prosthetic devices: a ruler, typewriter and camera segments, pocket watch mechanism, a crocodile wallet, and so on to fashion a machine head.

By the 1940s, we began to witness the first generation of cyberneticians arriving upon the scene when Warren McCulloch and Walter Pitts sought to demonstrate that psychic events follow the "all-or-none" law of communication circuits and constructed their formal neural nets isomorphic to the relations of propositional logic. In the early 1960s, AI scientists such as Kenneth Mark Colby and Robert P. Abelson began to develop their cognitive computer programs to simulate neurosis and paranoia. Marvin Minsky, founder of the MIT Artificial Intelligence Laboratory, attempted to derive cognitive models from computation; he calls himself a neo-Freudian. And there is also the untold story of Lacan, who closely followed the work of Norbert Wiener, Claude Shannon, and the cyberneticians of the Macy Conferences as he tried to rethink Freud and advance his own theory of the symbolic order. Where do all these developments add up? Can they tell us something new about the development of digital media that we do not already know? This book will show that there is a great deal more going on—politically, socially, and psychologically—than the perceived need to overcome human physiological deficiencies with technological prosthesis.

From the standpoint of Heisenberg, people and their machines are always mutually entangled in the pursuit of scientific knowledge. Quantum physics forces upon us the realization that "there are situations which no longer permit an objective understanding of natural processes, and yet use this realization to order our relationships with nature. When we speak of the picture of nature in the exact science of our age, we do not mean a *picture of nature so much as a picture of our relationships with nature.*"[19] Heisenberg further states that the previous division of the world into objective processes in space and time and the subjective mind in which these processes are mirrored—the Cartesian difference between *res extensa* and *res cogitans*—is no longer a valid starting point for understanding modern science. "The scientific method of analyzing, explaining, and classifying," says he, "has become conscious of its own limitations, which arise out of the fact that by its intervention science alters and refashions the object of investigation."[20] In other words, with quantum physics, method and object are no longer separated. With the coming of the Freudian robot upon the scene—where "the distinction between us and robots is going to disappear" or has already begun to disappear[21]—the redoubled simulacra of human-machine entanglement are bound to complicate Heisenberg's observation by bringing the extremely fraught neurophysiological and psychoanalytical dimension of that relationship into play.

These days, the public are bombarded with the prophecies of engineers and science fiction pundits who try to persuade us that we are on our way to becoming immortals through the implants and prosthetic extensions they will invent. Minsky, Hans Moravec, Ray Kurzweil, and others have

19. Heisenberg, *The Physicist's Conception of Nature*, 28–29.
20. Heisenberg, *The Physicist's Conception of Nature*, 29.
21. Rodney A. Brooks, *Flesh and Machines*, 236. My interpretation of the disappearance of the human-machine distinction is very different from Brooks's affirmative conception because he does not recognize the Freudian robot in this relationship.

announced that human beings will transcend biology in the near future. Kurzweil puts it symptomatically: "[A]s we move toward a nonbiological existence, we will gain the means of 'backing ourselves' up (storing the key patterns underlying our knowledge, skills, and personality), thereby eliminating most causes of death as we know it."[22] The familiar psychic defense mechanisms against the death drive that Freud identified long ago bring us face to face with the looming figure of the Freudian robot in Kurzweil and his colleagues. The return of the repressed may well lurk in the shadows of their updated myth of human transcendence in the manner of a pseudoreligion.

For this reason, I am convinced that the discovery of the Freudian robot promises a firmer and more critical grasp of the precarious nature of our networked society than can reasonably be accommodated by the human-machine competition theory (Hubert Dreyfus, John Searle, et al.) of what computers can or cannot do, or Donna Haraway's celebration of the cyborg, or the transhuman variety predicted by others. It seems to me that the idea of the cyborg or transhuman often obfuscates the political and psychic foundations of human-machine entanglement in the digital age more than it clarifies it. For Haraway, the cyborg is "a cybernetic organism, a hybrid of machine and organism, a creature of social reality as well as a creature of fiction."[23] And she is right to point out further that writing is preeminently the technology of cyborgs. But she goes on to assert that "[c]yborg politics is the struggle for language and the struggle against perfect communication, against the one code that translates all meaning perfectly, the central dogma of phallogocentrism. That is why cyborg politics insists on noise and advocate pollution, rejoicing in the illegitimate fusions of animal and machine" (176). This may sound empowering as far as the rhetoric goes, but as soon as we begin to reflect on the argument itself, it seems fraught with confusion and contradiction. What exactly is the discourse against which Haraway's cyborg politics is pitted? How does the cybernetic code which has always insisted on the fusion of animal and machine differ from the writing of cyborgs she advocates here? And from where does the political will of cyborgs issue forth? Until we figure out what kinds of psychic and political transformation remain open and available to cybernetics and

22. Kurzweil, *The Singularity Is Near: When Humans Transcend Biology*, 323. Brooks refuses to accept the techno-utopian myth of immortality. He points out that Kurzweil and Hans Moravec "have succumbed to the temptation of immortality in exchange for their intellectual souls." See Brooks, *Flesh and Machines*, 205.

23. Haraway, "A Cyborg Manifesto: Science, Technology, and Socialist-Feminism in the Late 20th Century," in *Simians, Cyborgs and Women: The Reinvention of Nature*, 151.

digital media, it is unlikely that Haraway's cyborg can do any better than become a Freudian robot and submit to the compulsion to repeat in the feedback loop of human-machine simulacra.

But ultimately, we ought to be concerned with the political consequences of an emerging society of Freudian robots, which is where American society is headed and attempts to lead the world. It is not for nothing that the sciences of robotics, artificial intelligence, and neurophysiology have served the defense and naval research programs so well and been generously rewarded with grants and taxpayer's money. In fact, many of their pundits do not feel any qualms about their participation in the imperial domination of the world and the universe.[24] Would democracy still have a substantial meaning for a society of Freudian robots who are consumed by the desire to control, militarily or otherwise, and are ultimately driven by the cybernetic unconscious?

This book examines the birth of the Freudian robot in the postwar Euro-American world order by looking at how information theory and digital media reframe the problem of the unconscious (sometimes dubbed "subconscious" by cynberneticians) between what I call human-machine simulacra. Digital writing is central to my analysis because the manipulation of (written) symbols in the computing machine is what makes digital media tick at the most basic level. For example, the introduction of the twenty-seventh letter into the English alphabet in 1948 was a significant event in the invention of digital media; inexplicably, this event has heretofore gone unnoticed in the studies of so-called New Media. Nor have we learned much about how Basic English and James Joyce's *Finnegans Wake* got into the experimental work of communication theory. As I try to bring Shannon back into conversation with James Joyce, Lacan with von Neumann, Freud with Minsky, and so on, the reader will learn a very different story about the making of digital media and those who made them happen.

This book is organized in six chapters that begin with an examination of the technology of writing. Chapter 1 begins by asking what constitutes the writing of digital media and where we are mostly likely to encounter

---

24. The majority of the AI researchers and cyberneticians who appear in this book have participated in such programs and benefited from such grants. Kurzweil has mentioned his own role in the five-member Army Science Advisory Group (ASAG) while discussing smart weapons in *The Singularity Is Near*, 330–35. One courageous dissenter I have come across is the late exiled German-Jewish scientist Joseph Weizenbaum at MIT, the famed inventor of the first mind simulation program, ELIZA. For Weizenbaum's scathing criticism of his MIT colleagues and technological messiahs whose work merely justifies military spending and masks real political conflicts, see Weizenbaum, *Computer Power and Human Reason*, 241–57.

it. These questions lead me to a systematic scrutiny of many of our presuppositions about the mind, machine, language, writing, symbol processing, and inscription technologies. My research reveals a number of significant conceptual lacunae in new media studies and modern literary theory; these lacunae have been responsible for what we do not see and what we have not been able to conceptualize in regard to digital media, namely, what I call the *techne* of the unconscious. The idea here is not to make psychoanalytical theory speak to the study of digital media but to explain how the *techne* of the unconscious got into the invention of digital media in the first place.

Chapter 2 provides a detailed historical analysis and technical explication of the twenty-seven-letter English alphabet to explain and analyze Shannon's invention of Printed English. Briefly put, Printed English is a mathematical refiguring of alphabetical writing as an ideographic system; it lies at the theoretical foundation of information theory. For this reason, our discussion of textuality, subjectivity, technology, and ideology in new media must proceed from an informed understanding of how Printed English has been the unacknowledged figure of the universal writing of imperial technoscience in the postwar decades. Under the mantra of digital media, all coding systems—in machine, language, neural networks, and genetic inscription—have been subsumed under a single unified and universal system unprecedented in the history of world civilization. This development prompts us to ask what is a universal symbol and how the universal symbol operates in digital media or, for that matter, in the book of life. The historical relationship between Basic English and Printed English is explored next to help explain how the Anglo-American empires of the mind came to be grounded increasingly in the politics of writing and communication technologies. The mind-testing games of Jung on the one hand and the cybernetic games adopted by information theorists and scientists at the Macy Conferences on the other are analyzed and compared to bring the nature of the psychic machine of postwar technoscience to light.

Chapter 3 reconsiders literary modernism by focusing on some of the most radical theories of language and writing that have emerged at the threshold of sense and nonsense. One of these views is grounded primarily in a mathematical figuring of alphabetical writing and a speculative treatment of the unconscious mechanism of language that is taken to function automatically like a psychic machine. James Joyce is among the first to intuit the statistical and psychic structure of alphabetical writing by pushing his experiment with "nonsense" word sequences to the extreme in *Finnegans Wake,* a work that Derrida has dubbed "a hypermnesiac machine." Joyce's work anticipated the stochastic properties of Printed English and helped Shannon set the limits of the entropy and redundancy rate of English prose. My reading seeks to reestablish some of the forgotten linkages among the radical theories and experiments across the disciplines, especially those bordering on nonsense and schizophrenia. Even as the modernist fervor subsided in the postwar years, the Bell Labs scientists continued to carry the surrealist experiments forward to generate automatic writing with an eye to producing computable verse and music and speculate about schizophrenia.

Chapter 4 focuses on the work of Jacques Lacan and his 1954–55 seminars. It proposes a new interpretation of Lacan's theory of language and the symbolic chain and his notion of the unconscious by investigating the intellectual provenance of French theory typically associated with this central figure. Lacan's reinterpretation of Freud must be significantly rethought in tandem with what he had learned about game theory, cybernetics, and information theory when these theories were systematically imported to France from the United States. The specific textual sources for Lacan's close reading of Poe's "The Purloined Letter" remind us that the general reception of Lacanian psychoanalytic criticism in the U.S. has been misguided due to our lack of familiarity with the scientific discourse of the time to which the French theorist was thoroughly exposed. This explains the popular misunderstanding of the Lacanian notion of language, his relationship to Saussure, and what Lacan means by the symbolic order. For instance, the ruse of writing espoused by John von Neumann and Oskar Morgenstern to generate strategic moves in game theory was taken up by Lacan to think about the function of the psychic machine of the unconscious. This psychoanalytical work provides us with some unusual insights about the cybernetic unconscious of the postwar Euro-American world order.

Chapter 5 examines the role of automata in psychoanalytic discourse by focusing on the problem of the Freudian uncanny. The accelerated advances in the technologies of animated pictures and automata have led many critics to return to Freud's original formulation. More importantly, robot engineers and computer game designers have begun to incorporate various ideas associated with the Freudian uncanny in their research programs as they investigate the emotional and cognitive impact of humanoid robots, automata, and social robots upon human beings. To grasp the full implications of automata for our understanding of the uncanny, we must reexamine the original point of contention between Freud and Ernst Jentsch and their contested readings of Hoffmann's "The Sandman." This work of reinterpretation aims to resituate the uncanny as the problem of human-automata relationship, whereby I hope to clarify the conceptual origins of the Freudian robot.

Chapter 6 suggests that the Freudian robot embodies the unconscious of our posthuman social structure. Raoul Hausmann's sculpture *Mechanical Head* is a sobering anticipation of the Freudian robot. Along with Shannon's *Ultimate Machine*, this work of art offers unparalleled philosophical insights on the death drive of the digital civilization. If the last stand of ideology lies in the engineering of the unconscious in the posthuman, it is important to raise the next question: Do we stand any chance to defend or counter-engineer against the new ruses of digital writing in the years to come?

1 Where Is the Writing of Digital Media?

> The two images, sound and visual, enter into complex relations with neither
> subordination nor commensurability, and reach a common limit insofar as
> each reaches its own limit. In all these senses, the new spiritual automatism
> in turn refers to new psychological automata.
>
> Gilles Deleuze, *Cinema 2: The Time-Image*

It is reasonable and convenient to assume that the digital media have the power to transform our ideas about writing, language, memory, consciousness, and social reality. The vast majority of scholarly studies and popular literature on new media readily prove the point. An equally reasonable but much more difficult task is to suspend that assumption for the moment and reflect on how the identity and role of writing itself has evolved significantly enough to make the invention of digital media possible in the first place. This chapter attempts the task by investigating the situation of writing in the digital revolution.

I have set out to document and interpret the remarkable evolution of alphabetical writing that took place at the crossroads of literature and science and has profoundly impacted both. This evolution has brought about the new media as we know them today just as much as it had inspired literary modernism in the early

1

decades of the twentieth century. Bearing in mind how alphabetical writing has become the symbolic sine qua non of both the literary medium and the mathematical medium in many regions of the world, we will explore how the transformation of this writing in recent history—what I mean by "writing" should not to be lumped together with "language" as a category or with any particular vernacular language—has led to the invention of digital media and furthermore to a contemporary civilization that theorists have variously characterized as postmodern, postindustrial, late capitalist, and so on. The question in the chapter title "where is the writing of digital media?" invites a critical examination of digital media and of what Deleuze grasped tentatively as "the new spiritual automatism."[1] I hope that this approach will help open up some new avenues of research and understanding with respect to the social and psychic makeup of contemporary digital technology.

There is no simple answer to the question of where one is likely to encounter the writing of digital media. Is it in the hardware or the software of the computer? Is it in the "hardware" of the brain or the "software" of the mind?[2] To raise these questions is to place a new demand on our knowledge of the role and identity of writing in relation to machine and to have a new understanding of digital media itself. The priority of the notion of writing does not imply an exercise in idealist speculation; on the contrary, the book begins by taking into full consideration a shared understanding among archaeologists and historians that writing was invented, first and foremost, as a material technology and that it has been one of the oldest surviving technologies we still practice. In fact, the technological essence of writing has turned out to be much more resilient in the making and dissemination of knowledge and information than the much touted powers of phonetic symbolism attributed by linguists and others to alphabetical and some nonalphabetical systems of writing. What is ultimately at stake—

1. Gilles Deleuze, *Cinema 2: The Time-Image*, 265–66.
2. The brain-mind duality of this formulation has shadowed the work of many contemporary neurophysiologists and cognitive scientists. Some have tried hard to leave the Cartesian theater behind and seek to ground animal consciousness in the functions and material processes of the brain's nervous systems, Daniel Dennett's *Consciousness Explained* and *Kinds of Minds: Toward an Understanding of Consciousness* being notable examples. But as Cary Wolfe has pointed out, Dennett's view of language is fundamentally dualistic as he takes language as something that can "represent rationales in a nervous system." This representationalist view "reinstalls the disembodied Cartesian subject at the very heart of his supposedly embodied, materialist functionalism." See Wolfe, *What Is Posthumanism?*, 36.

and what therefore must greatly concern us here—is none other than the changing face and psyche of civilization itself.

We begin, therefore, by questioning how the (world) civilization is doing these days. Is the future of a new spiritual automatism already in sight? Neither the description of the modern or postmodern condition nor the charting of capitalist and postindustrial developments from one stage to the next can adequately explain how the digital revolution happened the way it did and why it is impacting our lives at such multiple levels. The time is therefore ripe to reengage the notion of civilization and examine one of its most enduring and important technologies.

Why Civilization Matters

Civilization is unthinkable without writing.[3] This common sense is best captured by the characters *wenming* 文明 (Japanese pronunciation: *bunmei*), which the Chinese and Japanese—who share this transgraphic script but not each other's language—have adopted to translate "civilization." These two characters mean literally "illumination through written text(s)" or, literally, "text shines forth."[4] For a visual approximation of the same idea in today's mass media, let us consider the shimmering digits and codes that famously race across the opening frames of the film *The Matrix*. Symptomatically, the computer screen in that film shows no boundaries, as "a blinking cursor pulses in the electric darkness like a heart coursing with phosphorous light, burning beneath the derma of black-neon glass. The entire screen fills with racing columns of numbers. Shimmering like green-electric rivers, they rush at a 10 digit phone number in the top corner."[5] These racing columns of numbers appear to redraw the boundaries of nature and civilization and make them both new and strangely familiar. Over the past century, this notion of writing has expanded into all areas of knowledge and is even invading previously unknown areas of scientific

3. This consensus amongst the historians of writing does not deny the value of oral cultures but points to the emergence of social organizations of large, heterogeneous areas that depend upon mediated communication, such as writing. See Harold A. Innis, *Empire and Communications*.

4. The character *wen* 文 suggests "text," "writing," "texture," "traces," etc., whereas *ming* 明 borrows the combined strength of the sun and the moon to connote supreme brightness. It is interesting that Jacques Lacan, who studied Chinese, also dwelled on the character *wen* 文 as a sign of "civilization" in his 1971 seminar devoted to the discussion of "l'écrit et la parole" (Lacan, "L'Écrit et la parole," 87). For my detailed analysis of Lacan's concept of writing in relation to the cybernetic machine, see chapter 4.

5. Larry and Andy Wachowski, *The Matrix: The Shooting Script*, 1.

research and technology to help "illuminate" genetic engineering, cybernetics, neuroscience, and so on.

Inasmuch as writing has been the oldest and one of the most enduring technologies we know, the characters *wenming* 文明 assert the technological core of civilization more manifestly than does the Latin root of the English word "civilization," since the former puts emphasis on the *wen* or "written text." Keeping these cross-cultural references in the back of our minds, we may now embark on our course of discovery to find out how the technology of writing has evolved to become what it is for digital media. What philosophical truths does this changing technology deliver to help us make sense of the digital revolution? By the same token, will the digital revolution throw new light on the theory of writing?

Bernard Stiegler remarks: "The informatization of knowledge is only possible because informatics, as a technique for recording, reading, and diffusing of information, is a kind of writing."[6] This is true, but we must press further and ask what kind of writing. From clay tablets to microchips, the technology of writing has always involved at least a twofold physiological process of preparing material surfaces on which signs or codes are to be inscribed and of coordinating the human motor skills (or prosthetic robot arms) required for making the inscription. This does not mean that writing is necessarily a visual medium, and in fact our common view of writing as an arrangement of visual signs on a surface can be very limiting. For instance, the six-dot matrix of marks known as Braille is one of the formal mechanisms that rely on spatial rather than visual arrangement.[7] Moreover, this book demonstrates that writing has been entangled with numerical symbols since its early invention, and traces of their co-origination are easier to document than any particular visual representation of early speech across ancient civilizations. With the arrival of informatics and computer technology, writing has further penetrated the biomechanics of human speech to such an extent that sound (including speech) becomes a translation of text or an artifact of AI engineering—a notable example being TTS (text to speech) synthesis—rather than a visual representation of speech.[8] What we need today is a global and inte-

---

6. Bernard Stiegler, *Technics and Time, 2: Disorientation*, 108.

7. For a powerful argument about writing as an organization of graphic space rather than visual surface, see Roy Harris, *Signs of Writing*, 45.

8. Text-to-speech conversion is a branch of artificial intelligence that deals with the computational problem of converting written text into linguistic representation. This is one of the areas where the relationship between writing and speech can be fruitfully investigated for both engineering and theoretical purposes. See Richard Sproat, *A Computational Theory of Writing Systems*.

grated concept of writing that is simultaneously historical and theoretical to guide us toward a richer knowledge of these extraordinary processes. And for good reason, we also need to incorporate numerical thinking and discrete analysis into the theory of writing, especially with respect to alphabetical writing systems.

Postmodernity and New Media

Scholars of postmodernity have provided comprehensive analyses of the ways in which postwar socioeconomic developments and information technology have transformed advanced societies in late capitalism. One of the hallmarks of such transformation they point to is the storage and retrieval of a colossal amount of electronic information, including digitized written and printed records, in data banks, libraries, museums, archival centers, and global communication networks. From the time Jean-François Lyotard proposed the idea of "computerized society" in the 1970s to characterize the kinds of technological breakthroughs that were taking place in advanced societies, not only has the digital revolution happened and taken hold, but the momentum it generated has swept across every corner of the world and brought about the networked globe we inhabit today.[9] The effect of the digital revolution upon social life has been variously compared to the introduction of the printing press or photography into early modern Europe but is widely acknowledged as being more powerful and irreversible than anything human society has experienced before. This is largely due to the fact that "the computer media revolution," in Lev Manovich's idiom, "affects all stages of communication, including acquisition, manipulation, storage, and distribution; it also affects all types of media—texts, still images, moving images, sound, and spatial constructions."[10] These totalizing and universalizing processes indicate how much the technology of writing has developed to reshape modern life and the future of humanity with vast implications for planetary and interplanetary ecology.

Reflecting on the history of digital technology, Manovich, the author of *The Language of New Media*, shows us that the outcomes of these accelerated developments over the past few decades actually represent the convergence of two separate trajectories. One trajectory concerns the invention of the modern digital computer that performs calculations on numerical data faster than the mechanical tabulators and calculators it has replaced.

9. Jean-François Lyotard, *The Postmodern Condition: A Report on Knowledge*, 3.
10. Lev Manovich, *The Language of New Media*, 19.

The other involves modern media technologies that allow images, image sequences, sounds, and text to be stored on photographic plates, film stocks, gramophone records, and so on. The effective synthesis of these developments has led to the translation of all existing media into numerical data accessible through computers. The outcome is the new media through which graphics, moving images, sounds, waves, shapes, spaces, and texts all become computable at the digital level. Manovich identifies five principles whereby the new media organize these computable data. These are numerical representation, modularity, automation, variability, and cultural transcoding (20). All five principles undoubtedly bear on the central aspects of digital media examined in this book, and a number of them are also shared by writing and print media in general. The first principle—numerical representation—receives special attention in this chapter because it implies the indispensible notion of "discrete unit," which has provided the universal conceptual basis for digital technology.

In mathematics, a discrete unit is considered indivisible and is opposed to the continuous. A thing, an individual, or a symbol may qualify as a discrete unit when that unit cannot be further divided without losing its identity. Individuals are treated as discrete units by population census and are computed as data in that sense, but continuous lengths or waves must first be converted into discrete units, such as time series, to be computed in digits. For the purpose of the machine's processing of symbols, printed letters and numerals are regarded as discrete units whereas handwritten symbols are not, such as the letter B on the left (Fig. 1).[11] A detailed discussion of this technical distinction and other distinctions in chapter 2 should help clarify the importance of this theoretical point.

One question that the numerical principle of digital media has raised for us is why modern media technologies must rely on discrete units in order to generate data. Manovich alludes to a number of historical circumstances such as the Industrial Revolution, the assembly line, the standardization of types and fonts in the publishing industry, the standardization of image dimension and temporary sampling rate in cinema, and so on. These are undoubtedly important dimensions but the numerical representation of discrete units also involves a certain kind of abstract thinking and algorithmic manipulation that needs to be explained as well. Interestingly, instead of going to modern mathematics for an answer, Manovich

11. See Leonard Uhr and Charles Vossler, "A Pattern-Recognition Program that Generates, Evaluates, and Adjusts Its Own Operators," 253.

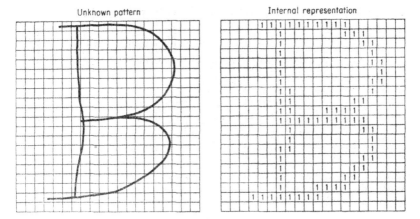

Figure 1. Continuous handwritten letter B versus its digital conversion into discrete symbol as a 20 × 20 matrix. From Leonard Uhr and Charles Vossler, "A Pattern-Recognition Program that Generates, Evaluates, and Adjusts Its Own Operators," in Edward A. Feigenbaum and Julian Feldman, eds., *Computers and Thought* (New York: McGraw-Hill, 1963), 253.

turns his attention to semiotic theory and the human language as a natural ground for discrete analysis, the evidence being that we speak in sentences and a sentence is made up of words and a word consists of morphemes, etc. Roland Barthes's definition of language is cited to show that "language is, as it were, that which divides reality (for instance, the continuous spectrum of the colors is verbally reduced to a series of discontinuous terms)."[12] After setting up the parallel between language and digital media, Manovich quickly adds that "the discrete units of modern media are usually not units of meanings in the way morphemes are" (29). Namely, the difference lies in the perceived disjuncture between symbol and meaning. Chapter 3 addresses the question of symbol and meaning in digital media, since the identity of discrete unit is the focus here. Note that Manovich's conceptualization of the discrete leaves "writing" out of the picture, and what he says about language and linguistic representation cannot but get him into a certain philosophical quandary: if language is made up of units of meaning that divide reality—a hypothesis more often asserted than proven—what reality or unreality do the discrete symbols of digital media divide?

12. Manovich, *The Language of New Media*, 28–29. The quote is from Roland Barthes, *Elements of Semiology*, 64.

It is well known that the study of phonemes—more so than morphemes—has been the strong suit of structural linguistics in its approach to discrete analysis. Structural linguists have introduced elaborate distinctions among the sound units and phonemes of various languages and have routinely relied on written alphabetical symbols to measure discrete units. These linguistic studies, as Jacques Derrida and others have noted, are premised upon the unacknowledged mental slippage between writing and language—for example, when the theorist mistakes written alphabetical letters for speech sounds. It is this metaphysical slippage, rather than the ineffable morpheme or units of meaning as Manovich has contended, that troubles the linguistic understanding of digital code and discrete analysis.

There is one more reason why language itself cannot properly ground a theoretical or historical understanding of discrete units for new media. For we no longer have at our disposal a pure linguistic theory or semiotic theory across the humanistic disciplines that remains untouched by information theory or long-distance communication technologies. Barthes's semiology and Jakobson's linguistics were both historical responses—successful or unsuccessful—to the pressures of information theory as each tried to refigure language and semiotic behavior in general on the model of a communication machine.[13] Series, division, discontinuity, and so on put Barthes and Jakobson in the company of their fellow structural linguists and philosophers who never tried to hide the fact that their semiotic view of language was specifically indebted to information theory. The same can be said of the other major figures of Structuralist or Poststructuralist persuasion in the twentieth century—Claude Lévi-Strauss, Julia Kristeva, Pierre Bourdieu, Jacques Derrida, Gilles Deleuze, Félix Guattari, and Jacques Lacan, to name a just few. We have no choice but to go back to the founding moments of information theory and cybernetics in postwar America and rediscover which symbols were figured as discrete units and which were not and reconsider how the communication machine began to dominate the theory of language and shape structural linguistics itself.

For example, when Michel Foucault conceptualized the identity and role of power across modern disciplinary regimes, he made a decisive methodological foray into cybernetics and the communication machine. Power is no longer viewed by him as an exercise of brute force or a source of homogeneous domination, nor does it separate those who have it and

13. Manovich briefly mentions Jakobson's involvement with information theory and cybernetics in Manovich, *The Language of New Media*, 77.

hold it exclusively from those who are subjected to it. Instead, Foucault writes:

> Power must, I think, be analyzed as something that circulates, or rather as something that functions only when it is part of a chain. It is never localized here or there, it is never in the hands of some, and it is never appropriated in the way that wealth or a commodity can be appropriated. Power functions. Power is exercised through *networks*, and individuals do not simply *circulate* in those *networks*, they are in a position to both submit to and exercise this power. They are never the inert or consenting targets of power; they are always its *relays*. In other words, power passes through individuals. It is not applied to them.[14] (my emphasis)

It is almost as if the author was suggesting that individuals are discrete fixtures of a gigantic communication machine. Perhaps Foucault is right after all; perhaps he offers some unique insights about the relationship between power and communication technology in postwar global politics. However, is Foucault speaking in metaphor? Yes, but if we take his language of "networks," "circulation," and "relays" as nothing more than metaphorical expressions (as if nonmetaphoric expressions were remotely possible), we would have a difficult time explaining how the broad epistemic shift toward a cybernetic outlook took place among the major intellectual figures of Foucault's generation. In particular, we would not be able to explain Jacques Lacan—the most rigorous and difficult of the so-called French theorists—whose theory of language and the symbolic order is more often miscomprehended than understood. Chapter 4 offers a new interpretation of Lacan from this angle.

For technical and other reasons, the question of the discrete unit has occupied the attention of a good number of media theorists who try to explain why and how the discrete versus the continuous has been central to the communication machine. N. Katherine Hayles tackles the problem by introducing a set of distinctions amongst code, speech, and writing. In *My Mother Was a Computer,* Hayles points out that the phenomenal world we experience belongs primarily to the order of analog or the continuous, but human civilization has consistently developed technological prostheses to impose digitization on these analog processes progressively from speech to writing to digital computers. It should be noted that her idea of "analog" here means everything or anything that is not digital, and this

---

14. Michel Foucault, *"Society Must Be Defended": Lectures at the College de France 1975–1976,* 29.

new meaning no longer reflects how Charles Sanders Peirce grasped the concept in his rigorous distinction between logical reasoning and analogical reasoning in semiotics. The concept of "analog"—which used to connote "similarity," "resemblance," and "correspondence" in older media—is itself being remolded and entangled with the rapid developments in digital computing and media technology. From the digital point of view, life itself becomes a kind of analog. It follows that a continuous stream of breath is analog in contrast to speech, which is made up of distinct phonemes that can turn the stream of breath into discrete units. So when writing arrives, it "carries digitization farther by adding artifacts to this physiological process; developing inscription technologies that represent phonemes with alphabetic letters."[15] But is it not the digital that makes the analog appear as such, something distinct from itself? The conceptual shift is striking and ought to be registered as such. Instead of taking the conceptual shift as a straightforward evolutionary progression from analog to digital, McKenzie Wark has pointed out that "[t]he digital rules a line between analog and digital, making a slippery difference into a clear distinction. But perhaps having made the distinction appear, the perspective can be reversed, and the digital can be perceived from the point of view of its analog residue."[16] We will explore this other point of view in robot engineer Masahiro Mori's dream of a Buddha-natured robot in chapter 5.

Hayles makes a distinction between speech and writing and sees them as mutually implicated by the means of representation. Like Manovich, she also underscores "the act of making something discrete rather than continuous, that is, digital rather than analog," hence the centrality of discrete unit for numerical representation (56). But as we have already seen, a discrete unit in natural language for Manovich is a unit of meaning, whereas Hayles now takes that linguistic unit to be the phoneme, which divides the continuous stream of breath—rather than Manovich's "reality"—into distinct units. This process of linguistic digitization, by her account, is followed by inscription technologies that push the process into further abstraction. In short, speech and writing are historically distinct orders and belong to different realms of digitization.

Proceeding from this basic distinction between speech and writing, Hayles argues that computer coding is unique and different from both speech and writing because the idea of "compiling" makes sense only with respect to a complex web of processes, events, and interfaces that medi-

---

15. N. Katherine Hayles, *My Mother Was a Computer: Digital Subjects and Literary Texts*, 56.
16. McKenzie Wark, *Gamer Theory*, 097.

ate between humans and machines. She argues that the act of compiling has emerged with code that, though not unknown in speech and writing, operates in ways specific to networked and programmable media and mediates between the natural languages native to human intelligence and the binary code native to intelligent machines. The concept of code therefore implies a partnership between humans and intelligent machines in which the practices of each can penetrate and influence the other (59).

If we leave aside the issue of speech for the moment, Hayles's emphasis on the singularity of computer coding implies a certain situated view of writing, for the singularity of code is sustainable only if we strictly adhere to a logocentric view of alphabetical writing, one that takes writing to be a set of inscription technologies that represent phonemes with alphabetic letters. As soon as this position on writing is taken for granted, the numerical and coding systems of the precomputer era, such as Morse code, will quickly fall by the wayside. Should one classify these earlier systems as writing or code? If we decide that Morse code is a code after all, how does it fare conceptually with computer coding, which presupposes "compiling"? And what if we make a further discovery that writing enjoys a much greater affinity with computer coding at the conceptual level than it ever does with symbolic representations of speech or phonemes? When it comes down to fundamentals rather than technicality—this book is mainly concerned with the former—there is no reason why one cannot conceptualize computer code as the writing of the digital media just for the sake of the argument. Of course, that is not what I propose in this book; to do so before considering the issue of "where" (as suggested by the chapter title) would be premature and too limiting. What we need is a more supple and inclusive theory of writing to help explain the new digital processes, new events, and new interfaces between humans and machines in the world of networked and programmable media.

Hayles's emphasis on the partnership between humans and intelligent machines deserves special notice for very different reasons. She draws our attention to the fact that the interpolation of the user into the machinic system does not require his or her conscious recognition. She sees this partnership as inherently ideological because it targets the unconscious more effectively than ever before. The subject is simultaneously disciplined by the machine until he or she becomes a certain kind of subject for the machine, as "interpolation is most effective when it is largely unconscious" (61). This is an important insight, one that my book pursues by demonstrating how psychoanalytical speculations have already been implicated in the making of digital media and cybernetics. This insight also justifies Hayles's plea for the humanist's intervention in new media studies, showing why we must not ignore code or let it be confined to the domain of computer programmers and engineers.

Three Conceptual Lacunae

This study addresses the issues that have been considered central to any critical study of new media: discrete units, numerical representation, automation, human and machine interface, etc. At the same time, my research and interpretation are being shaped by a growing awareness of some of the conceptual lacunae in the current scholarship. On account of these lacunae, some fundamental aspects of modern digital technology have unfortunately escaped the analytical framework of new media studies. Chief among these are:

1. the ideographic turn of alphabetical writing as the basis of a new universalism in the digital revolution;
2. the cybernetic reframing of the unconscious and the arrival of the Freudian robot in our midst; and
3. the self-understanding of an emergent digital civilization that is limited by what we can know about our writing machines and the minds that have invented them.

The chapters that follow trace the evolving technology of writing to ponder its implications for analyzing the *techne* of the unconscious in posthuman society. This particular focus implies that we must come to grips with the import of what Mark Hansen has termed *technesis* or techno-thinking in Poststructuralism. Whereas Hansen wants to leave writing behind in his exclusive emphasis on nondiscursive *affective* bodily life,[17] I emphasize the importance of writing—perhaps much more than does Hayles—not because I think the French Poststructuralists got it right after all (in fact, so-called French theory was manufactured largely in the United States).[18] The reason this book emphasizes the importance of writing is that it is a powerful technology interacting with newer and digital technologies that centrally address human-machine interactions. The recognition of this fact runs deep in the histories of several of the world's major philosophical traditions and wherever the traditions of writing or print technology are en-

17. See Mark Hansen, *Embodying Technesis: Technology Beyond Writing*, 20.
18. For a detailed discussion, see chapter 4.

countered. No matter how much one may be justified in one's criticism of the limited validity of modern semiotics and linguistics, the technology of writing—and symbolic life in general—can be shown to mark our social lives with a degree of intensity that is almost unprecedented in history; and this technology can be shown to affect our contemporary civilization in ways that need not preclude our experience of nondiscursive life with digital media. In short, to address the first lacuna outlined above, this book will show how alphabetical writing has transformed information technology as well as nondiscursive bodily life in general and is in turn transformed by them. We can trace the material basis of a new universalism that has grown out of these processes to a specific historical moment in the evolution of alphabetical writing; that is, the moment when alphabetical writing completed its movement toward total ideographic inscription.

To anticipate my analysis of how information theory seals the ideographic destiny of alphabetic writing, consider this obscure but interesting fact: when Claude Elwood Shannon pioneered the mathematical theory of communication in 1948, one of the first things he did was add a twenty-seventh letter to the English alphabet to code "space." This letter is a positive sign in information theory and can be read as such by any blind or unconscious communication machine. Shannon's twenty-seven-letter English alphabet has since led to the creation of highly discrete and sophisticated systems of telecommunication code, but the significance of his invention greatly exceeds the functionality of communication machines. Derived, as it were, from the basic building blocks of traditional literacy and Morse code, the novel "space" letter has made electronic literacy possible but goes itself unrecognized, even as we all tend to agree that electronic literacy has an enormous impact upon the lives of people around the world—both those who have access to electronic literacy and those who do not by virtue of their exclusion or their subordination to those who do.

Consider other related developments in such fields as biology and philosophy. The interesting "code-switch" in biology toward the language of molecular biology is often understood correctly as a consequence of information theory being translated into life sciences. As Lily E. Kay's study has shown us, this mechanism of translation allows the biochemical processes of the living cell and organisms to be reconceptualized as coded messages, neural networks, information transfer, communication flow, and so forth.[19] With strong echoes of military cryptography, out of which information theory itself developed, the scientific research on the letters, codons, and

19. See Lily E. Kay, *Who Wrote the Book of Life?*

punctuation marks of nucleic acids has evolved into definitive procedures for decoding the secret writing of DNA in the Book of Life. In philosophy, Derrida's project of grammatology was no less indebted to this broad trend to privilege writing in biological and social discourses under the pressures of information theory and cybernetics. In the same vein, Lacan—who read widely and thought creatively about cybernetics and game theory in the 1950s—developed a notion of the symbolic order on the basis of his cogent grasp of the discrete nature of the symbol-processing machine. His work on the symbolic order brings us to the second of the conceptual lacunae in relation to new media: the cybernetic reframing of the unconscious and the arrival of the Freudian robot in the digital civilization.

Whether we like it or not, the old conundrum "can machines think?" has continued to haunt our thinking about digital media. The implications of the universal discrete machine typically associated with the Turing computer and with the cybernetic studies of the human brain notwithstanding, we should reexamine this conundrum in the occulted interplay of the phenomenology of consciousness and the psychoanalytical *techne* of the unconscious. The *techne* of the unconscious here means the scientific, social, and political framings of the ineffable mental processes that Freudian psychoanalysts have termed "the unconscious." As a concept, the *techne* of the unconscious refers to such framings as well as their disavowals in the persistent reiteration of that conundrum by the followers and detractors of intelligent machines. Martin Heidegger's observation that the essence of technology is by no means anything technological remains highly relevant to the philosophical rethinking of technology inasmuch as technology never confines its own manner of being and operation to itself. The concept of *techne*, which shares its etymology with "technology" from the Greek root *technikon*, is related to the work of *enframing* with which Heidegger developed his highly original approach. He argues: "What is decisive in *techne* does not lie at all in making and manipulating nor in the using of means, but rather in . . . revealing."[20] In his view, scientific knowledge cannot be a cause or origin of technology but is dependent upon the development of technological devices for testing, measuring, verifying, and so on. The essence of technology lies not in instrumental productions or manipulation of material, but in the process of a special kind of knowing through the *techne*. If the computer or a robot is made to mimic "thinking" at the unconscious level, does it mean that the *techne* of the unconscious is bringing out the essence of digital media in a guise people generally fail

20. Martin Heidegger, *The Question Concerning Technology, and Other Essays*, 58.

to recognize? For example, when the neuroscientist discourses on neural networks, is he or she merely speaking in metaphors, or are they imputing unconscious processes in the human mind that happen to resemble the cybernetic processes of circular causality in the communication machine?

This book will show how the framing or *enframing* of mental processes by the word-association games and other technical devices in earlier psychoanalytic studies may serve to reveal the essence of the Freudian robot in our own time and put the work of today's neuroscientists and AI scientists in perspective. The "odd and even" game in literature and word-association games and other guessing games in psychoanalysis can all be shown to precede and inspire the theoretical and experimental agendas of information technology and cognitive science. We have long been led to believe that scientific reasoning is all about rationality and that scientists regard human beings as rational animals, but this is a red herring. Evidence points in a number of other directions. If the engineers at Bell Labs and scientists elsewhere took an interest in schizophrenia and developed their association games to speculate about the random processes in the human mind, Lacan's reworking of the Freudian unconscious sets out to meet the formidable challenge posed by their work and by communication machines in general.

That leads to a third, methodological pondering: to what extent can we assume that the unfolding of digital media makes the conditions of its own critique legible when the self-understanding of a civilization is often limited by what it knows—or what it does not yet know—about its writing machine and the mind that has invented it? Is our critical stance not mimicked or contained by the cybernetic logic of feedback loop, double bind, and circular causality? I raise these methodological concerns to remind myself and my readers that the postmodern criticism of science and technology tends to proceed as if the conditions of self-reflexivity were automatic, available, and fully self-generating within the established discursive traditions, such as the philosophy of consciousness (for example, the debate on subjectivity and objectivity), or the centuries-old theological speculations on chance and free will, or embodiment versus disembodiment, and so on. The usual argument against technological determinism, for example, masks the aporia of the inherited theological debates on chance and free will more often than it can inform us about how contemporary civilization opens itself to critical inquiry.

So rather than complain about technological determinism, which entails almost no intellectual risks these days, we may still learn a few things by examining, for instance, how the very problematic of chance and determinism has evolved in the stochastic speculations of game theory and cybernetics, which, as we will see, put rigorous mathematical reasoning to the service of a new digital civilization. Stochastic speculations and reflections on chance and determinism also strongly characterize the experimental literary works by modernist poets, writers, and Surrealist artists such as Stéphane Mallarmé, James Joyce, Marcel Duchamp, and others. James Joyce's stochastic experiment with alphabetical letters in *Finnegans Wake* (chapter 3) sheds fascinating light on the kinds of random word games that Shannon's colleagues at Bell Labs adopted and fed into the model of information theory as they tried to simulate machine-generated verse and music and speculate about machine and schizophrenia.

Fundamental Challenge to Literary Theory

There is no better place to tackle the above lacunae in new media studies than from the ground up, that is to say, where we first encounter the elementary building blocks of literacy: alphabetical writing.[21] Until recently, literary theorists have remained relatively silent on how the incontestable presence of information theory, cybernetics, and molecular biology in the modern world bears upon the theory of writing and how the recent evolution of alphabetical writing has impinged upon the very question of *literary form*, which has been our central preoccupation for about a century. The regularity and experimental potentials of verbal and semiotic sequences seem eminently adaptable to the idea of form in literary theory, whether it comes in the old dualist sense of form versus content or is framed in Gestalt register. The narrative trajectories charted out by Russian formalism, the New Criticism, Structuralism, psychoanalysis, Poststructuralism, and even certain schools of Marxist literary criticism seem to affirm the centrality of form in literary studies.[22] At least, this is what we are led to believe in our textbook understanding of Western literary theory (and social theory).

Nevertheless, can form in one discipline migrate into another as content? What could be more formalistic than the notion of life as genetic code? Do humanists, mathematicians, and molecular biologists speak the

21. Of course, competence in alphabetical writing does not equal literacy. There are numerous nonalphabetical writing systems worldwide that take full part in modern social and business life. In the context of my study, however, alphabetical writing has a special role to play because of the global hegemonic position the English language has come to occupy in science and technology.

22. For an earlier Marxist critique of "form" within the discipline of literary studies, see Fredric Jameson, *The Prison-House of Language: A Critical Account of Structuralism and Russian Formalism*.

same language of form? Has the aggressive expansion of cybernetics and information technology suspended the old metaphysical dualism of form and content? Aside from the metaphysical imperative of having to take care of a content, it seems that the inherent dualism of form can no longer capture the changing identity of alphabetical writing in our time, nor is it robust enough for conceptualizing the newly organized unities of surfaces, temporalities, spaces, inscriptions, machines, and the unity of theory.

What is it that has allowed alphabetical writing to stand as the shared code of inscription across the fields and disciplines of "world literature," literary theory, mathematics, molecular biology, information theory, international law, and other regimes of desired and desirable knowledge?[23] Is it the intrinsic value of the script? Is it by mere chance that alphabetical writing—English alphabetical writing in particular—has emerged as one of the most important sites of universalism in today's world? Whatever conclusions we wish to draw in answering these questions and reflecting on the latest developments in digital media, one thing is certain: literary theory must engage with the changing technology of writing to remain relevant to the task of interpreting text, life, social reality, and the world. This represents our own chance not only of gaining deep knowledge about how literary modernism happened the way it did in the twentieth century but also of raising some new questions about psychoanalysis, biocybernetics, and imperial networks of communication from the periods before and after World War II.

Recasting the biochemical processes of the living cell as coded messages, information transfer, and communication flow, the code switch in life sciences has done more than substitute one set of scientific idioms for another in the manner of what literary critics call "sustained metaphor." What it implies is that alphabetical writing has shed its old image of phonetic symbolism to become the "speechless" inscription of the genetic code. This new system of inscription is not only "speechless" but has become thoroughly ideographical. To avoid misunderstanding, we should draw a preliminary distinction between ideography and pictography. Ideography here defines a mode of abstraction that addresses the conceptual, spatial,

23. It would be naïve to believe that "world literature" refers to literatures of the world. It is rather an exclusionary mechanism, not unlike international law, whereby modern secular pedagogy and academic research practiced primarily in the West choose to recognize or not to recognize the *sovereignty* of any writers or literary works in the world. On the contemporary literary scene, works written and published in nonmetropolitan languages (usually outside of English, Anglophone, French, or Francophone) are sometimes granted token privilege and are made available in translation, hence part of "world literature."

and modular (or systematic) aspects of the material sign, whether written, printed, deaf-mute, indexical, numerical, optical, etc. An ideographic
sign can be visual but not necessarily so—the computer's manipulation of
symbols is blind and does not require visual display, for instance—and the
ideographic sign exists independently of linguistic production, although
it may be arbitrarily linked to sound production and even to a linguistic
system, such as the case of Hindu-Arabic numerals or traffic lights, which
can carry as many different kinds of pronunciations as there are languages
in the world.[24]

Pictography, on the other hand, exhibits primarily the visual, iconic, and
mimetic properties of the material sign—picture, film, photography, painting, some drawings, etc.—which are less abstract than ideography but
richer in the amount of information the sign can convey.[25] Does a pictograph turn into an ideograph when it achieves sufficient abstraction and
simplification? The answer is that mere abstraction will not suffice, because
ideographs are modular and exist in a system of other equivalent signs
whose combination is governed by semiotic rules. This is the sense in which
the molecular biologist approaches the "speechless" writing of the genetic
code, which includes letters, numbers, punctuation marks, and spaces
but excludes phonetic and verbal expressions. And it even changes the
game of figurative representation by destabilizing the conceptual ground
of metaphoric play that literary critics associate with conventional texts.
So when Jacques Derrida began his criticism of phonocentrism and
metaphysics in the Western philosophical tradition, he had one of those
language-based systems of writing in mind, those that marginalized numerals, spaces, calligraphy, or cryptograms. For that reason, mathematics
represented a privileged enclave to him, and we are told that mathematics
is one place "where the practice of scientific language challenges intrinsi-
cally and with increasing profundity the ideal of phonetic writing and all
its implicit metaphysics."[26] Mathematical thinking is thus shielded from

24. The presumed equation of the Chinese writing system to ideography has long been contested and is addressed in chapter 2.
25. Due to the primacy of the abstract graphic line, drawings tend to exist on the borderline
between pictography and ideography as they are often indexical, abstract, and self-referential.
Walter Benjamin has offered intriguing reflections on the distinctions between painting and drawing. He sees paintings as vertical and longitudinal with a referential and representational dimension whereas drawings are horizontal and transversal like writing and bear primarily symbolic and
semiotic meanings. Unfortunately, he did not live long enough to develop these thoughts fully. See
Benjamin, "Painting and the Graphic Arts," 219. For a systematic account of this type of drawings
as "metapicture," see W. J. T. Mitchell, *Picture Theory*, 35–42.
26. Jacques Derrida, *Of Grammatology*, 10.

Derrida's critique of metaphysics. What I hope this book makes clear is that mathematical reasoning lies at the heart of the ideographical movement of the phonetic alphabet in information theory, cybernetics, and molecular biology but that the movement itself cannot challenge metaphysical thinking so much as reinforce it with the fundamentals of binary digits, which inscribe the logos of digital media. This inscription set the course to conquer all fields of knowledge on behalf of imperial technoscience. The English language, which might have supplied the ideographic alphabet with the original hegemonic code, is subjected to the same process of ideographical inscription from the time of Basic English to Shannon's information theory.

It should become clear that literary theory has somehow lost touch with the major technological advances that have been eroding its own home turf—alphabetical writing—over the past sixty-odd years. The latest explosion of research activities in the areas of postmodernism and new media has likewise bypassed the key theoretical questions surrounding the identity of alphabetical writing. This book is intended to identify and evaluate the fundamental challenges that the universal system of ideographic inscription in digital media presents to literary theory and social theory. If my effort is modestly successful, it will have at least made one concrete step toward reframing the theoretical work on text, media, and society and reclaiming the study of digital writing from informatics and computer programming.

The *Techne* of the Unconscious

Shannon's mathematical foundation of information theory has raised fascinating issues about numbers and spaces as digital constructs in the English alphabet. Are numbers and spaces inherent to alphabetical writing? Is there a stochastic structure in how English letters combine to form sequences and sentences, etc.? It seems that the ruse of digital writing leaves surprising traces as to where mathematicians might go to find their intellectual resources. Mathematical reasoning, which has provided symbolic logic and code to information theory, is not in itself the raison d'être of the digital media. As already mentioned, Shannon and his colleagues adopted random word games at Bell Labs to calculate the frequency of each letter of the twenty-seven-letter alphabet, but such games may be traced to Carl G. Jung and other psychoanalysts who developed innovative word-association experiments and other mind-testing experiments for the purpose of gaining scientific insight about the workings of the Freudian unconscious. In

1

the beginning of the twentieth century, the psychoanalysts began to fashion the view that the mind was a psychic machine susceptible to chance, error, and repetition automatism (*Wiederholungszwang*). The theory was endorsed and in part developed by Freud himself.[27] Within the space of half a century, the association experiment evolved into a privileged *techne* of the unconscious spanning across the disciplines of sciences and the social sciences that came under the sway of cybernetics. This is the immediate context in which Lacan interpreted Freud's notion of *Wiederholungszwang* in his celebrated reading of Edgar Allan Poe's "The Purloined Letter."

What is the writing of digital media, and where? The answer cannot simply be "code" or "computer programming" unless we are content to be guided by the dictates of the hardware and software of digital machines themselves. There is always something else going on besides the 0s and 1s within the architecture of the computer, because *the central problem in the digital revolution is the recasting of the human mind as a psychic machine on the model of the computing machine.* This engineering requires a certain *techne* of the unconscious that embodies the concept of stochastic processes as well as definitive procedures for capturing those processes. Our answer to the question in the chapter title lies, therefore, somewhere in the broad cybernetic spaces opened up between the neural nets of the brain and the computing machine. McCulloch and Pitt's pioneering work in that regard—which is discussed in chapters 2 and 4—suggests that the cyberneticians have been preoccupied with what is *digital and computable* within the psychic machine. The continual development and refinement of the *techne* of the unconscious has rendered the cybernetic engineering of the mind particularly amenable to digital media. It is illuminating to see how the intuitive mind-testing games have migrated from psychoanalysis and psychophysics to the engineering programs of information technology, neurophysiology, cybernetics, artificial intelligence, and even mass media. Marshall McLuhan's comment on the television's bombardment of the viewer with light pulses of three million dots matrix per second merely scratches the surface of how the mass media exploited the continuum of consciousness and the unconscious for effective socioeconomic and ideological gain.[28] Hayles's perceptive remark about the interpolation of the user into the machinic system, which presumes the subject's lack of awareness and his/her automatic response, continues to raise pertinent issues about the arrival of the Freudian robot in our midst.

27. For detailed discussion, see chapter 2.
28. McLuhan, *Understanding Media: The Extensions of Man*, 313.

Of course, the cultural industry and mass media are not the only places where the manipulation of the unconscious may actively be contemplated. The formidable challenge that confronts the cultural critic is the scenario where the battlefront of ideology has shifted predominantly from the control of political consciousness to the technological manipulation of the ineffable unconscious, the latter by no means being limited to the use and abuse of mind-altering drugs manufactured by big biochemical companies, which critics have amply documented and analyzed. In this regard, the insights of the Frankfurt School critics prove instructive in helping us rethink the conditions of critical imperative, and they are instructive precisely by virtue of their rigorous critique of technocracy and instrumental reason and their failure to engage with information theory and cybernetics in their time. This failure can be crippling because, if the unconscious rather than consciousness has turned into the primary field of ideological manipulation by the dominant class, what is the future of reason and reasoned critiques?

The mass deception criticized by Max Horkheimer and Theodor Adorno in their well-known study of the cultural industry in *Dialectic of Enlightenment* qualifies as "deception" only to the extent that the conscious mind grasps it as such through a process of moral reasoning. However, the light pulses of three million dots matrix per second that hit the viewer's retina do something powerful to the unconscious that may escape moral reasoning altogether. This is what the managers of the advertising industry have understood very well. Sensing the ideological ruse, Habermas is forced to make a distinction between conscious deception and unconscious (self-) deception. By unconscious deception, he means the pathological manifestation of "systematic distorted communication" caused by the defense mechanisms and the repression of conflicts in the psyche.[29] But the distinction works only insofar as his theory of communicative rationality can effectively stabilize the objective norms of communication to measure subjective distortions against them. From a psychoanalytical viewpoint, consciousness and the unconscious as well as the spaces in between are open to manipulation through hypnosis, visual/aural saturation, mind-altering drugs, and psychological warfare, which renders the distinction between conscious deception and unconscious deception extremely tenuous.[30]

---

29. Jürgen Habermas, *The Theory of Communicative Action*, vol. 1: *Reason and the Rationalization of Society*, 332–33.

30. This is not to invalidate Habermas's insightful critique of psychoanalytic knowledge as a category of self-reflection in *Knowledge and Human Interests*, 214–73.

Sharing no such conviction in the power of reason and communicative rationality, Freud has explored how pathological disturbances always trouble the psyche and may never be cured. In his innovative work on the Freudian unconscious, Lacan argues that communication deals with something very far removed from rational verbal exchange, and this is especially true of communication conducted through modern technologies of communication. That which goes under the name of communication, he argues, is often our recognition of "the modulation of a human voice" and the appearance of understanding, which merely means "that one recognizes words one already knows."[31] This process of communication was studied by Lacan with specific reference to cybernetics and postwar communication technologies (chapter 4). To elucidate this relationship between communication and the unconscious, Mark Taylor draws an interesting connection to the Hegelian spirit in *The Moment of Complexity*. He writes:

> Information processing does not presuppose consciousness or self-consciousness, though consciousness, self-consciousness, and reason are impossible without it. From neurophysiological activity and immune systems, to computational machines, to financial and media networks, information is processed apart from any trace of consciousness. Such information processing forms something like what Hegel describes as "objective spirit," which emerges in and through natural and social processes.[32]

The Hegelian connection pointed out by Taylor can indeed be traced back to Lacan's work on the symbolic order. And we will see in chapter 4 how Lacan conceptualized the information-processing machine in conversation with Hegel in the mid-1950s and how Lacan developed the notion of what I call the cybernetic unconscious in that context. In particular, he was intrigued by how the breakdown of communication or the moment of non-recognition entails a greater measurable degree of entropy—rather than mere distortion—with respect to the "bits" that can be transmitted as information. In fact, the relationship between psychoanalysis and information theory can further be glimpsed in chapter 5 through the lens of how each appropriated the idea of entropy from the second law of thermodynamics.

Indeed, the central conceit of information theory is that of entropy. Shannon has adopted this idea to calculate the stochastic structure of Printed English in the mathematical theory of communication. One of the

---

31. Lacan, "The Circuit," 82.
32. Mark C. Taylor, *The Moment of Complexity: Emerging Network Culture*, 230.

interesting questions that his experimental work raises for us is: how does a stochastic view of writing correlate to the received theories of language, literature, and modernism on the one hand and to psychoanalytical speculations about the unconscious on the other? This question is pertinent to our inquiry because many of the earlier modernist literary and psychoanalytical experiments on language, automatic writing, and thought-reading had anticipated Shannon's Printed English and his "mind-reading machine" in numerous ways. For instance, Shannon cites James Joyce's *Finnegans Wake* as one of the texts exemplifying the lower threshold of redundancy and higher entropy rate in his stochastic model of Printed English. What makes entropy and its possible linkage with Freud's *Todestrieb* (death drive) such an interesting problem for the study of digital media is the ways in which certain ideas migrated into psychoanalysis first and then got into information theory. Furthermore, Freud's work and psychoanalysis in general may suggest some interesting clues as to the shared theoretical impulses or implicit exchanges among information theory, cybernetics, and modernist literature. Spanning across these moments of broad intellectual confluences is the *techne* of the unconscious that continually articulates itself to digital writing, machine, and social engineering. We turn next to the invention of Printed English by Shannon and its implications for a theory of digital writing.

2 The Invention of Printed English

Since "genetic inscription" and the "short programmatic chains" regulate the behavior of the amoeba or the annelid up to the passage beyond alphabetic writing to the orders of the logos and a certain *homo sapiens*, the possibility of the grammè structures the movement of its history according to rigorously original levels, types, and rhythms. But one cannot think them without the most general concept of the grammè.

Jacques Derrida, *Of Grammatology*

In book 3 of *Gulliver's Travels*, Jonathan Swift imagines a scientist at the Grand Academy in Lagado who tries to build a writing machine. This machine is designed to alleviate the drudgery of learning and allow "the most ignorant person at a reasonable charge and with a little bodily labor to write books in philosophy, poetry, politicks, law, mathematics and theology without any assistance from genius or study."[1] When Gulliver arrives in a division of science called Speculative Learning at the Grand Academy, he is given the opportunity to speak to the professor who designed the machine and to observe how the new mechanism works.

---

1. Jonathan Swift, *Travels into Several Remote Nations of the World in Four Parts by Lemuel Gulliver*, 162.

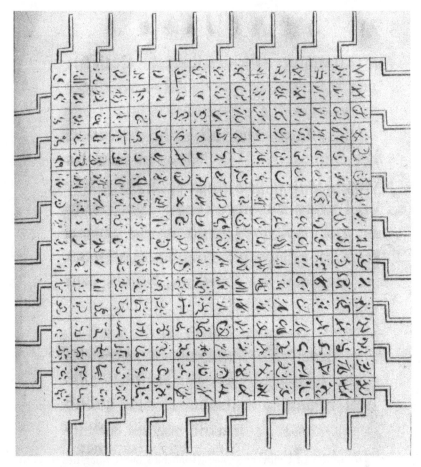

Figure 2. Gulliver's original diagram of the writing machine at the Grand Academy of Lagado. From Jonathan Swift, *Gulliver's Travels* (1726).

The Lagado writing machine consists of square pieces of wooden blocks connected by slender wires and is operated with a clever system of levers (Fig. 2). It resembles the games that children play with their wooden blocks except that on the sides of each block are pasted words rather than pictures. The words are given in their moods, tenses, and declensions but in no particular order. To operate the machine, the professor instructs each of his students to take hold of an iron handle and give the wooden blocks a sudden turn so that the disposition of the words are changed. He then asks thirty-six of his forty students to read the lines as they appear randomly upon the frame of the machine. Whenever they come across three or four words together that might form part of a sentence, they dictate to the remaining four students who transcribe the results. The work is repeated three or four times. The professor's writing machine is so ingeniously designed that the words shift into new places to make new sentences as the wooden blocks move upside down at every turn.

Swift's satirical intentions notwithstanding, the writing machine has continued to fascinate cryptographers and literary scholars in subsequent generations.[2] What seemed to be a mere thought experiment on a numerical matrix mechanism in the eighteenth century has transformed into the electronic reality of today's computer technology. If the Lagado machine bears a remarkable resemblance to the universal discrete machine we recognize in the computer, it is because its prototype does operate on the same mathematical principles of combinatorial logic and probability. At the Grand Academy, Gulliver is told that, after storing the whole vocabulary of the Lagado language into his machine, the professor "made the strictest computation of the general proportion there is in books between the numbers of particles, nouns, and verbs, and other parts of speech" (Swift, 163). Reflecting on chance and mathematical thinking behind this conceit, modern-day mathematician Georges Th. Guilbaud writes: "Under the protective banner of present-day Cybernetics, it would seem that Swift's dream has now become a reality. It is not, of course, hand-operated but electronic, and produces even what some people venture to call 'poems.'"[3] Unfortunately, Gulliver's report contains only a rough sketch of the Lagado machine but no literary samples, if any even exist, produced by the machine.

Suppose the writing machine at the Grand Academy had been able to produce poems in those exotic characters, what would the poems have looked like?[4] Would they have resembled the kind of automatic writing generated by a Turing machine and by engineers at Bell Labs in the twentieth

---

2. In 1962, Pierre Henrion in France published a book to analyze the code work in the novel. See Henrion, *Jonathan Swift Confesses.*

3. G.-T. Guilbaud, *What Is Cybernetics?* 69.

4. The strange-looking alphabetical letters in the original plate of the Lagado machine invites comparison with a similar fabrication by Swift's contemporary George Psalmanazar (1679–1763), for several of the letters overlap between the two alphabets. Swift's illustration may well have been an intended parody of the plate in Psalmanazar's *A Historical and Geographical Description of Formosa* (London, 1704). We know that Psalmanazar's claim about the Formosan practice of cannibalism had provided the original inspiration for Swift's "A Modest Proposal." For my discussion of Psalmanazar the imposter and his Formosan alphabet and cultural identity, see *Tokens of Exchange: The Problem of Translation in Global Circulations*, ed. Lydia Liu, 15–21.

century? Take an English verse that was produced in a Lagado manner—
i.e., random letter and word associations—at Bell Labs. One verse line goes
like this:

IT HAPPENED ONE FROSTY LOOK OF TREES WAVING GRACEFULLY
AGAINST THE WALL.[5]

John R. Pierce, the chief architect of satellite communication systems in
the United States and a prolific science fiction writer himself, was one of
the minds behind the verse experiment.[6] He reports that this particular
experiment occurred in the 1960s, involving two mathematicians and two
engineers who brainstormed for a couple of hours and produced a collection of unusual verses. They used stochastic processes to generate word
sequences or syntax that, as we have seen, border on sense and nonsense,
not unlike what is described by Swift with respect to the imaginary Lagado
machine.

A stochastic process is a play of dice or chance that involves a sequence
of random series that can be precisely analyzed and formalized by mathematical procedures. The stochastic process in the production of letters,
words, or written symbols necessarily bypasses the center of consciousness—better known in literary theory as the death of the author—as it
subjects the production of words to chance selection and combination.[7]
The words in the quoted verse were assembled using Claude Shannon's
experimental method and his mathematical computation of the redundancy and entropy rates of Printed English, discussed below. Essentially,
the verse composition entails a play of chance and probability with respect
to n-letter sequences that may result in either nonsense or random English
phrases very much in the spirit of the Lagado machine.

When confronted by literary experiments that do not involve authorial consciousness but instead rely on chance or unconscious stochastic
processes, our first reaction is to be skeptical or to judge the outcome as
good or bad poetry. But is the judgment relevant to what is really going
on? The problem is that our artistic judgment often depends on criteria

5. John R. Pierce, *Science, Art, and Communication,* 127.
6. See my discussion of Pierce's work at Bell Labs in the next chapter.
7. See chapter 4 for a further discussion of the translation of the term "stochastic" into French
"aleatory." The reverse translation from French back to English is also "aleatory," but this loanword
has dropped the mathematical concept in the word "stochastic."

that are increasingly difficult to disentangle from the standards of media technology, the global market, and public institutions that produce and evaluate artistic works. As the new media have gained in popularity in recent years, the pendulum now seems to swing in the opposite direction. Not only do a growing number of people not object to computer-generated literature, music, games, film, and art installations, but they begin to embrace them as postmodern and posthuman expressions. The situation is, of course, déjà vu because the older media like print, photography, and film had experienced more or less the same periods of defensiveness and euphoria when they were first introduced. If we have learned any lesson from history, we could at least avoid repeating the same old story and be a little wiser about the Lagado writing machine. With the arrival of new media, this machine has gone digital and electronic, in Guilbaud's words, and must not be taken lightly because, for better or for worse, the machine has turned into the engine of contemporary social and political life and is here to stay. Our task then is to grasp the philosophical implications of this event through the technicality of the machine itself and relate this knowledge to a broader political understanding of digital media.

The peculiar refashioning of alphabetical writing in the twentieth century presents us with a unique opportunity to test and rethink some of the propositions that have been advanced about writing in modern literary theory and philosophical discourse. No matter what we decide to make of this opportunity, one thing becomes very clear: literary and media theorists can no longer bypass Shannon's invention of Printed English to discourse on textuality, subjectivity, technology, and ideology in old or new media. As mentioned in chapter 1, Shannon treated the phonetic alphabet as an ideographic system, not as a symbolic representation of speech and that, in the hands of the molecular biologists who investigate the speechless language of the genetic code, alphabetical writing is further refigured as the ideographical writing of the Book of Life. It behooves us now to revisit the conceptual ground of information theory to understand how the ideographic alphabet of numerals, letters, and spaces became the master code of all codes in the postwar era.

This book began by rethinking how civilization was unthinkable without writing. Insofar as digital writing is concerned, the questions that arise immediately tend to bear upon the nature of scientific experiments surrounding the stochastic properties of alphabetical symbols and their technical embodiments. Many of these questions find ample expression in the early phases of the experimental work of the cyberneticians and scientists at Bell Labs and in the kind of verse Pierce has recorded for us. The scientists are usually not shy about making ambitious claims about the meaning of their work in the totality of human knowledge. "Automatic writing is not an end in itself," claims Guilbaud, "for the scientist it has no other purpose than to reveal the structures implicit in the apparatus which produces it, whether this is a machine in the usual sense, or a subconscious human mechanism."[8] If this statement strikes us as overly ambitious and, indeed, more ambitious than some of the familiar Surrealist or avant-garde manifestos, it should tell us something about the universalist aspirations of cybernetic studies and information theory.

In this chapter, we examine the invention of the twenty-seven-letter English alphabet in information theory and, in particular, the centrality of Shannon's twenty-seventh letter and Printed English in the development of his important theoretical framework for the new communication system. Chief among his precursors and relevant sources are the Morse code, Markov chains, and major experimental constructs in modern English, such as Basic English and James Joyce's *Finnegans Wake*. As we know, information theory grew out of the military cryptographic developments and information technologies of World War II, but it was also framed by the modernist experiments on language, literature, and the unconscious from the early decades of the twentieth century. Shannon has acknowledged that experimental works in language and literature played a role in his development of the stochastic analysis of English writing. The unspoken assumption behind this approach to alphabetical writing is that the mind is a psychic machine subject to chance, error, and repetition automatism. This assumption leads us back to the word-association games of the early psychoanalysts and to Freud's own speculations on the unconscious play of numbers in *Psychopathology of Everyday Life*. The ideographic movement toward the interplay of number, letter, and space in the literary, scientific, and psychoanalytic inquiries of the twentieth century holds the key to how the number game eventually got into the psychic machine of digital media.

Shannon's analysis of the stochastic processes of alphabetic writing not only articulated to literary modernism and psychoanalysis in this manner, but it inadvertently gave rise to a new idiom in molecular biology, hence a universal writing for the Book of Life and a new philosophy of writing. The discursive relationship between information theory and molecular biology is well known and well documented, but the place of the genetic code in Jacques Derrida's project of grammatology has remained obscure. This

---

8. Guilbaud, *What Is Cybernetics?* 70.

chapter brings this relationship to light and ponders the intellectual challenges presented by cybernetics and information theory to philosophy and to the study of language. The most fundamental of these challenges is the commanding presence of ideographic inscription in the universal discrete machine and in the neural net machine. This presence urges the humanist to reconsider what authorizes a universal symbol and how the universal symbol operates in digital media, often bypassing language and speech altogether in the constitution of the discrete unit. It also forces us to reflect on our traditional, evolutionary views of writing that often confuse ideography with pictography and with primitive mentality.

How the English Alphabet Gained a New Letter

When Claude Shannon added a twenty-seventh letter to the English alphabet in 1948, no one had remotely suspected that the phonetic alphabet was less than perfect. Shannon's introduction of the new letter, which codes "space" as an equivalent but *non–phonetically produced* positive sign, laid the first stone in the mathematical foundation of information theory in the early postwar years; it was as revolutionary as Newton's apple.[9] Yet scholars, and especially those in literary studies, are relatively slow in grasping the significance of this event. It is inconceivable that philosophers of language can still make meaningful statements about digital writing and new media before they are fully prepared to register this happening. Whereas many of us recognize the impact that information theory has exerted on computer science, linguistics, cryptology, military technology, molecular biology, neurophysiology, and other disciplines over the past half century, we have not been forthcoming in posing the following question: Does Shannon's twenty-seven-letter English alphabet pose a challenge to our conception of alphabetical writing?

Shannon approached the English language as a statistical system that he terms "Printed English." As one of the most significant inventions of the twentieth century, Printed English is a direct descendent of nineteenth-century telegraphic coding systems. During World War II, Shannon made a close analysis of Morse code, but much of that work remained classified

9. See C. E. Shannon and Warren Weaver, *The Mathematical Theory of Communication*, 43. A precursor to this publication was Shannon's 1945 Bell memorandum, "A Mathematical Theory of Cryptography" as well as an article published in 1948 under the title "The Mathematical Theory of Communication," *Bell System Technical Journal*, 27.3–4 (1948): 379–423; 623–56. See also M. D. Fagen, ed., *A History of Engineering and Science in the Bell System*, 317.

when he first published the pathbreaking "A Mathematical Theory of Communication" (1948) in *The Bell System Technical Journal*, in which he laid the mathematical foundation for information theory. Two years later, he followed up with "Prediction and Entropy of Printed English," which further elaborated the experimental work in connection with information theory. These studies suggest numerous connections with his code work in World War II, when he had investigated the statistical aspects of alphabetic writing in cryptoanalysis and helped design secrecy systems at Bell Laboratories for the U.S. military. For instance, Shannon was the author of a confidential report entitled "A Mathematical Theory of Cryptography," known as Memorandum MM 45-110-02, September 1945 at Bell Laboratories. After declassification in 1949, the report was published as "Communication Theory of Secrecy Systems" in *Bell System Technical Journal*.

Shannon conceived of Printed English as an object of mathematical analysis. His intellectual rigor required him to develop the concept in mathematical theorems, in tables of diagrams, trigrams, etc., and only occasionally in verbal description. "Printed English" first appeared in the title of his seminal essay "Prediction and Entropy of Printed English." Shannon also discussed it in other papers such as "Communication Theory—Exposition of Fundamentals" and "Information Theory."[10] From time to time, he would use "Printed English" interchangeably with "statistical English."[11] Mirroring cryptography, Printed English has a corresponding, translated text in numerical symbols consisting of twenty-six letters from A to Z plus a twenty-seventh letter. This last letter mathematically codes "space." In communication engineering, the symbolic correspondence is established between the twenty-seven letters and their numeral counterparts rather than that between the letters and their phonemic units as in spoken language. Despite its name, which can be misleading, Printed English does not have much in common with the mechanical reproduction of the written English word or any visible printed marks we usually associate with the printing press. Printed English is a concept strictly defined through mathematics and statistical science.

As a mathematician and engineer, Shannon began his career by devoting his attention primarily to the problems of wartime cryptology in World

10. See N. J. A. Sloane and Aaron C. Wyner, eds., *Claude Elwood Shannon: Collected Papers*, 175, 215.
11. See Shannon, "Communication Theory—Exposition of Fundamentals" (174), and his unpublished paper "Samples of Statistical English" in a three-page typescript dated June 11, 1948, Bell Laboratories, in N. J. A. Sloane and Aaron C. Wyner, eds., *Claude Elwood Shannon: Collected Papers*.

War II, including the top-secret "Project X" system. He had graduated from the University of Michigan and completed his graduate work at MIT in 1937. He joined Bell Labs to work on fire-control systems and cryptography in World War II and published his seminal work on the mathematical theory of communication in the *Bell System Technical Journal*. In the course of developing his mathematical theory of communication, Shannon made a careful study of Morse code and cryptographic inventions of the past.[12] His analysis is attuned to the fact that Morse code is made up of more than just dots and dashes, since letter spaces and word spaces must also be factored into the sequences of signals being transmitted through a discrete channel. Each sequence is constrained by a number of possible states (finite state) and only certain symbols from a set can be transmitted for each state. Shannon demonstrates this process by showing that, in the transmission of a telegraphic message, "There are two states depending on whether or not a space was the last symbol transmitted. If so, then only a dot or a dash can be sent next and the state always changes. If not, any symbol can be transmitted and the state changes if a space is sent, otherwise it remains the same"[13] (see Fig. 21).

It should be pointed out that Shannon did not invent the letter space or word space in this analysis, since Samuel F. B. Morse already became aware of their importance when he conceptualized one of the earliest dot/dash codes in decimal code (Fig. 3). Besides representing the first five digits by dots and the succeeding five by replacing the corresponding dots with dashes, Morse wrote in his notebook, "A single space separates each of the five figures. Two spaces separate each of the last five. Three spaces separate each number completed."[14] Morse designed his series of saw-tooth type (Fig. 4) to regulate the flow of electricity in correspondence to the code shown in Fig. 3. The teeth were to raise a lever that would close the circuit to transmit the message in a single circuit. In Morse code, the idea of "space" was factored into the design but not fully conceptualized as an abstract sign equivalent of each of the letters or numbers within the alphanumerical system. One might say that the "space" letter was implicit in Morse code until Shannon brought it out in his twenty-seven-letter alphabet.

12. His familiarity with Fletcher Pratt's sweeping overview of the cryptographic systems from ancient times through World War I is suggested in Shannon and Weaver, *The Mathematical Theory of Communication*, 42.

13. Shannon and Weaver, *The Mathematical Theory of Communication*, 38.

14. Carleton Mabee, *The American Leonardo: A Life of Samuel F. B. Morse*, 152.

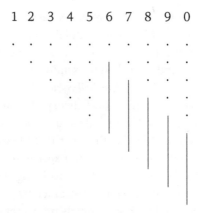

Figure 3. Samuel F. B. Morse's earliest telegraph code. From the notebook of Samuel F. B. Morse, p. 25. Courtesy the Smithsonian Institution.

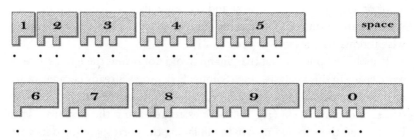

Figure 4. Samuel F. B. Morse's early saw-tooth design. Adapted from the notebook of Samuel F. B. Morse, p. 28. Courtesy the Smithsonian Institution.

Along with this additional letter, Shannon introduced a level of mathematical rigor into the analysis of alphabetical writing which had never been attempted before, except perhaps in the work of the Russian mathematician Andrey Andreyevich Markov, discussed in the next section.

In 1878, Nietzsche made a prescient remark: "The press, the machine, the railway, the telegraph are premises whose thousand-year conclusion no one has yet dared to draw."[15] In hindsight, it should be clear that Morse's telegraphy did much more than merely rationalize and expedite linguistic exchange, for it simultaneously introduced a model of communication with implicit claims about a new human-machine relationship to be forged across long distance. Morse's long-time business partner Alfred Vail was a key player in designing the first successful telegraphic device and has been

15. Friedrich Nietzsche, *Human, All Too Human: A Book for Free Spirits,* 378.

credited with perfecting the Morse code as we know it. In one of the first pamphlets he authored on the invention of telegraphy, Vail wrote: "It is evident, as the attendant at Baltimore has no agency in the transmission of this message from Washington, his presence, even, is not absolutely required in the telegraphic room at Baltimore, nor is it necessary, previously, to ask the question, *are you there?*"[16] He is referring to the successful public test of the first telegraphic line constructed in the United States between Washington and Baltimore. The question of presence or absence of the human agent brought up in the quote is a provocative one and has been raised time and again ever since communications technology figured out how to automate both the sending and receiving ends of instant transmissions. Already at the dawn of the developments in electromagnetic telegraphy, Vail's comment raised important theoretical issues on what automated communication was about and where it was headed, including what theorists would call intersubjectivity, which appears to be modeled suspiciously on one type of communication machine or another. As we will see in our discussion of Freud and Lacan, the human/machine continuum has also lain at the heart of psychoanalytical work on the unconscious. More than a century after Nietzsche's statement, we feel even less certain about predicting what might happen even in the next hundred years than did Nietzsche's generation, but we can at least try to pursue the philosophical question raised by Vail—*Are you there?*—by investigating the premises governing the communication machine.

The communication system requires that the message and the signal both be treated as sequences of discrete symbols. The message in Morse code is a sequence of letters and the signal a sequence of dots, dashes, and spaces that are processed by a communication system consisting of an information source, a transmitter, the channel, the receiver, and a destination (Fig. 5). Working exactly a hundred years after Morse, Claude Shannon investigated the telegraphic model of communication to provide a mathematical foundation for information theory. With the exception of a noise source depicted underneath the horizontal transmission line, Morse and Vail would have found Shannon's communication system familiar. Not only is the presence of the human agent ("*are you there?*") not intrinsic to the system (of course, there are always human agents connected to the system), but the semantic aspects of communication did not interest Shannon insofar as they were not relevant to the engineering problems that

16. Alfred Vail, *Description of the American Electro Magnetic Telegraph Now in Operation Between the Cities of Washington and Baltimore*, 21.

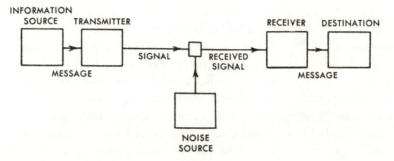

Figure 5. Claude Shannon's communication system for information theory. From Claude E. Shannon and Warren Weaver, *The Mathematical Theory of Communication.* Copyright 1949, 1998 by the Board of Trustees of the University of Illinois. Used with permission of the University of Illinois Press.

he set out to resolve. These included the need to design discrete noiseless systems and the discrete channel with noise. By noise, Bell Labs engineers refer to any error, distortion, extraneous material, or any other chance variables that might affect the transmission of messages. Departing from Morse and Vail, Shannon treats the twenty-seven-letter alphabet itself as a statistical system and approaches communication as an object of probability studies. He measures the average uncertainty in the message to maximize the rate of useful transmitted information (total uncertainty minus noise uncertainty) by proper coding. His famous theorem states that if the source rate is less than or equal to the channel capacity, messages from the source can be transmitted over the channel essentially without error.[17]

What Is Printed English?

From a mathematical viewpoint, our implicit knowledge of the statistical structure of language can be converted to a set of numerical data with the help of simple experiments. The experiments can be designed to determine a stochastic process known in mathematics as the Markov chain. The Markov chain describes a finite number of possible "states" of a system: $S_1, S_2, \ldots, S_n$. In addition, there is a set of transition probabilities, $p_i(j)$, the probability that if the system is in state S_i it will next go to state S_j. In the case of the finite alphabet of twenty-seven letter symbols in Printed En-

17. Shannon and Weaver, *The Mathematical Theory of Communication*, 108.

glish, state S_j might be represented by one of the 26 letters or the "space" symbol. Thus the distribution of future states depends on the present state and not on how it arrives in the present state. On the basis of the present state, one can predict, for example, that the probability of the letter Q being followed by the letter U is very high in English. It is not surprising that Shannon invokes the Russian mathematician Andrey Andreyevich Markov when the object of analysis is alphabetical writing.

Markov is the first mathematician to subject a literary text, Pushkin's *Eugene Onegin*, to stochastic analysis. His mathematization of writing led to the development of a well-known theory about the Markov chain, which became an important precursor to Shannon's information theory.[18] To make the Markov process into an information source, Shannon suggests that "we need only assume that a letter is produced for each transition from one state to another. The states will correspond to the 'residue of influence' from proceeding letters."[19] This process provides the stochastic structure for an experiment in which a human subject is asked to guess an unknown text in the language letter by letter. This is presumably how John R. Pierce and his colleagues at Bell Labs derived the verse quoted earlier in this chapter—IT HAPPENED ONE FROSTY LOOK OF TREES WAVING GRACEFULLY AGAINST THE WALL.

Kittler has shown in *Discourse Networks* how the German psychologist Hermann Ebbinghaus in the late nineteenth century devised an autoexperiment to pursue memory studies in psychophysics. Ebbinghaus's autoexperiment had involved "nonsense syllables" and random letter combinations (consonant-vowel-consonant combination), which Kittler sees as the direct precursor to technologized inscription. "Of course, Ebbinghaus worked with phonemes in order to be able to read aloud," argues Kittler, "but they were presented to him as writing. Syllable after syllable comes out of the random generator, onto the desk and into the file of worked-through alternatives, until all 2,299 have been used and output and input can begin again." The human mind that undergoes this test cannot but abandon the position of a knowing subject. What it means is that "the two mechanical memories on either side of the tabula rasa Ebbinghaus—the

18. For recent studies in English, see the following articles by David Link: "Traces of the Mouth: Andrei Andreyevich Markov's Mathematization of Writing," "Classical Text in Translation: An Example of Statistical Investigation of the Text *Eugene Onegin* Concerning the Connection of Samples in Chains," and "Chains to the West: Markov's Theory of Connected Events and Its Transmission to Western Europe."

19. Shannon and Weaver, *The Mathematical Theory of Communication*, 45.

one generating the syllables and the other recording them after they have passed before him—form a writing machine that forgets nothing and stores more nonsense than people ever could: 2,299 nonsense syllables."[20] Ebbinghaus's reliance on combinatorial methods certainly reminds us of Swift's professor in the Grand Academy of Lagado. More interesting is his mad pursuit of a path leading to the mental world via "nonsense syllables," which puts a further psychological spin on Shannon's guessing game. Not surprisingly, Kittler also paid some attention to the fact that "Shannon's machine calculated the probability of every single letter in the English language, and from these calculations produced a beautiful gibberish." What we take as "meaning" is but our "'impression of comprehension' which so loves to hallucinate sense from nonsense."[21] Kittler does not explore further how Shannon's machine is capable of hallucinating sense from nonsense. Is his communication machine essentially a psychic machine from a psychoanalytic standpoint?

The guessing game at Bell Labs, which displaces Vail's question *are you there?* to the psychic realm, simulates the action of the unconscious by deducing the implicit structure of language from how a given subject makes his or her guesses about the sequence of letters or words. Freud has discussed how the choice of random numbers may help reveal the structure of the unconscious by demonstrating the degree of difficulty in anyone's attempt to pick a number in a purely random manner. Shannon's guessing game presumes a directionality that is linear and irreversible; namely, one predicts the next letter on the basis of what goes before. At each letter, the human subject is made to guess what he or she considers the most probable next letter is in view of the preceding letter. In cases where an error is made, he or she is asked to guess again and again until he or she arrives at the correct next letter. The test may look similar to the kind of hypnosis, dream analysis, and word-association games adopted by the psychoanalyst, although Shannon's goal was not to speculate about the unconscious by showing how the mind manipulated symbols unconsciously but the other way around. What he sought to demonstrate was what the unconscious could reveal about the symbolic processes that mathematically govern the structure of Printed English.

Printed English is one of the most significant semiotic inventions since World War II. Shannon understood this construct as an ideographical al-

20. See Friedrich A. Kittler, *Discourse Networks 1800/1900*, 211.
21. Kittler, *Literature, Media, Information Systems*, 141.

phabet with a definable statistical structure.[22] As already mentioned, this postphonetic alphabet presupposes a symbolic correspondence between the twenty-seven letters and their numeral counterpart rather than mapping the letters onto the phonemic units as a structural linguist would try to do.[23] I should make it absolutely clear that Shannon's digital logic of Printed English suggests a different kind of alphanumerical thinking from the mere use of alphabetical letters or other symbols in mathematics, such as algebra, with which we are already familiar. The object of his investigation was not in mathematics but in *English*, namely, the digitizing and transmission of the letters and words of English prose. Shannon was bent on discovering the statistical laws governing the production of letter sequences and word sequences by investigating the ratio of sense and nonsense in Printed English. This move necessarily implies a radical rupture with semantics and linguistic constructs. In fact, Shannon's digital alphabet has very little to do with syllables, meters, phonetics, or even physical sounds with which Roman Jakobson was chiefly preoccupied in his work on the phoneme and speech.

In everyday usage, information is regarded as having some sort of bearing on the semantics of a message. But the linguistic definition of "meaning" or even "message" is irrelevant to communication theory. For Shannon, information exists insofar as there is a choice of alternative messages or alternative sequences of letters. If there existed only one possible message (a letter sequence or character string), there would be no information and no need for a transmission system because that message would be on record at the receiving point. From the viewpoint of mathematics, information is related primarily to the factor of uncertainty or probability. The letter E in English, for instance, occurs more frequently than Q, and the sequence TH more frequently than XP, etc.[24] If a given message is overwhelmingly probable, the amount of information or the a priori uncertainty will be small. The 100-letter sequence in the opening page of *Finnegans Wake* can be statistically demonstrated to be overwhelmingly improbable in English and, therefore, the amount of information or uncertainty it carries is

22. See Shannon, "Communication Theory of Secrecy Systems."

23. When Jakobson, Gunnar Fant, and Morris Halle first published their *Preliminaries to Speech Analysis* in 1951, they recast linguistics explicitly in the language of information theory. Further collaboration between Jakobson and Halle led to another influential study, *Fundamentals of Language*, in 1956. For a recent critical overview of Jakobson and cybernetics as well as information theory, see Jürgen Van de Walle, "Roman Jakobson, Cybernetics and Information Theory: A Critical Assessment."

24. Shannon and Weaver, *The Mathematical Theory of Communication*, 39.

enormous, even though this information has nothing to do with the semantics of the message. For Joyce, the 100-letter sequence—bababadalgharaghtakamminarronnkonnbronntonnerronntuonnthunntrovarrhounawnskawntoohoohoordenenthurnuk—visually evokes the fall it describes in that phrase whereas for Shannon it would probably spell out the statistical structure of the information where no "space" occurs inside the unusual character string between the first *b* and the last *k*. In neither case, however, does the information of this letter sequence correspond to a meaningful linguistic unit known as the "word." Joyce's intuition about the letter sequence as a *nonword* is borne out by Shannon's assumption that anyone who speaks a language possesses implicitly an enormous knowledge of the statistical structure of that language.[25] This can be demonstrated by the higher frequencies of "bab," "bad," "kon," or "thu" versus the lower frequencies of "rrh," "nnt," etc. within the Joycean sequence. A detailed analysis of Joyce's literary experiment appears in the next chapter.

How does one define a quantity that will measure how much information is produced by such a process? How much information in bits (binary digits) per second is produced in a given source? Using Boltzmann's H theorem, Shannon defines this quantity as $H = \sum p_i \log p_i$ and calls the H the "entropy" of the set of probabilities where p_i is the probability of a given symbol i.[26] Like entropy in thermodynamics from where the idea originally derives, information entropy measures how much randomness there is in a letter sequence or in a signal. This quantity makes it possible for an engineer to estimate the average minimum number of bits needed to encode a string of symbols based on the frequency of the symbols.[27] For the engineer, "the main point at issue is the effect of statistical knowledge about the source in reducing the required capacity of the channel, by the use of proper encoding of the information."[28] What matters is the input and output of signals, transmission, noise, redundancy, entropy, and predictability—in other words, what goes in at one end of the transmission

25. See Shannon, "Communication Theory—Exposition of Fundamentals," in *Collected Papers*, 175.

26. Shannon and Weaver, *The Mathematical Theory of Communication*, 50–51.

27. Shannon uses a simple example to demonstrate how one could estimate the average minimum number of bits needed to encode a string of symbols based on the frequency of the symbols. He considers a sequence of letters A, B, C, D and assigns the probabilities ½, ¼, ⅛, ⅛ to them with successive symbols being chosen independently. This is expressed in the following equation as

$H = - (½ \log ½ + ¼ \log ¼ + ⅜ \log ⅛) = ⁷⁄₄$ bits per symbol.

The result enables the approximation of a coding system to encode messages from this source into binary digits with an average of ⁷⁄₄ binary digit per symbol (63).

28. Shannon and Weaver, *The Mathematical Theory of Communication*, 39.

line and what comes out at the other end. But the thing that concerns us
here is not the economical engineering of the information system but what
this work has done to the idea of the phonetic alphabet, for the alphanumerical structure of Printed English not only facilitates the encoding of
messages in information systems but also enables a rethinking of the idea
of language and communication. This invites comparison with the tacit assumptions about information processing and machine intelligence in the
universal Turing machine.

Mechanism and writing were synonymous to the English mathematician Alan Turing, who regarded the digital computer as a "child-brain" machine (or a learning machine) where there is little mechanism but an infinite supply of blank sheets for the programmer or educator to write on.[29]
Turing's experiments required all the answers to be written or typewritten,
and he treated the ability to manipulate written symbols by a computer or
a human being as analogous to, if not identical with, the ability to think
(Turing, 434). Behind this lies a very different assumption about the thinking process from the way we normally associate language with thought.
Turing does not ask the computer to mimic human speech. As far as his
test goes, the computer and the human brain are both conceived as symbol processors, or universal information machines, capable of interpreting and composing numbers and logical notation, as well as alphabetical
writing.[30]

When Turing first imagined the computing machine in 1936, he was
thinking in terms of a super-typewriter that would be able to read, erase,
or print symbols on a strip of paper that was to be marked off into cells
or squares. In fact, he had come upon the idea by closely examining typewritten letters and symbols. He analyzed in particular how the space bar
and backspace determined the printing position and how the typing point,
which could be moved relative to the page, was independent of the typing
action. There were obvious limitations in a typewriter because the typing-
head, moving to the left or the right, could only print one line of symbols at
a time and could not read or erase symbols, and it also "required a human
operator to choose the symbols and changes of configuration and position" (Fig. 6).[31] With the universal discrete machine, the act of scanning or

---

29. A. M. Turing, "Computing Machinery and Intelligence," 456.

30. For a comprehensive overview and rigorous critique of the mind as a symbol-processing
machine, see Margaret A. Boden, *Mind as Machine: A History of Cognitive Science*. This two-volume
study gives the most interesting and exhaustive treatment of the subject published to date.

31. Andrew Hodges, *Alan Turing: The Enigma*, 97.

Memory Tape

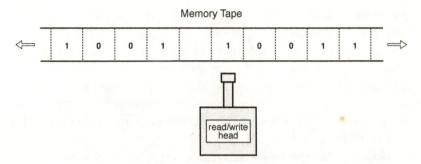

Figure 6. Computing model adapted from Alan Turing's machine. From "On Computable Numbers, with an Application to the Entscheidungsproblem," *Proceedings of the London Mathematical Society*, ser. 2, 42 (1937): 231.

marking the paper tape would displace the acts of reading and writing and render the linguistic categories of phonemes, semes, and words superfluous for the purpose of communication.[32] Turing developed his new ideas in the groundbreaking "On Computable Numbers," in which he proposes that his machine be supplied

> with a "tape" (the analogue of paper) running through it, and divided into sections (called "squares") each capable of bearing a "symbol". At any moment there is just one square, say the r-th, bearing the symbol $\mathfrak{S}(r)$ which is "in the machine". We may call this square the "scanned square". The symbol on the scanned square may be called the "scanned symbol". The "scanned symbol" is the only one of which the machine is, so to speak, "directly aware". However, by altering its m-configuration the machine can effectively remember some of the symbols it has "seen" (scanned) previously.[33]

The centrality of printed symbols in Turing's work allows the machine to take over the human cognitive acts of writing, reading, seeing, memorizing, and erasing and organize them into a threefold mechanical act of "scanning," "printing," and "erasure." The printed symbols presuppose a universal, ideographical script similar to the universal Hindu-Arabic numerals to which they also correspond; and these "scanned" letters and

32. As I mentioned in the preceding section, words and nonwords enjoy the same status in information theory because the communication engineer is not so much concerned with the semantics as with the transmission of letter sequences.

33. Alan Turing, "On Computable Numbers, With an Application to the Entscheidungsproblem," 231.

space symbols make sense (ideo+graph) to the machine without any involvement of phonic systems whatsoever. Turing's technical refiguring of the act of reading sheds unexpected light on an earlier invocation of "scanning" by Mallarmé in 1897. In his preface to "A Throw of the Dice," the poet had insisted on the significance of "blanks" in his verse, using the word "scanning" to characterize the movement of printed words as a visual experience, and by extension the reader's eyes following the movement, across typographical spaces. With amazing foresight into the cybernetic future of typographical spacing, Mallarmé appears to have anticipated Turing's conceptual reading-head of the computer.[34]

Marshall McLuhan has mentioned how the typewriter became a confirmed habit with Henry James, who was "so attached to the sound of his typewriter that, on his deathbed, Henry James called for his Remington to be worked near his bedside."[35] In the case of Hart Crane, Brian Reed has shown the important role the prosthetic machines played in the life of the poet: "Hart Crane had an infuriating way of writing a poem. Typically, after drinking copiously, he would put a 78 on a hand-cranked Victrola and play it 'a dozen, two dozen, three dozen times' while alternately banging away on a typewriter and loudly declaiming the same line of verse repeatedly."[36] Friedrich Kittler has given a superb analysis of the typewriter and its role in social history and literary history in Europe and America, which should be familiar to most readers.[37] So I will not reiterate the importance of the typewriter in modern life but will draw attention to the fact that like telegraphy, the typewriter is conceptually related to the birth of Printed English. Although the printing press and the typewriter both entail the mechanical reproduction of graphic symbols on typographical surfaces, the idea of typesetting, which has been germane to the printing press and has remained the same for centuries, is irrelevant to the operation of a typewriter. Central to the typewriter is a single moving typing-head that prints in one-dimensional space (horizontal line) and is constrained to move only to the right or to the left. Owing to the originality of its typing-head, to which were then added the functions of reading and erasing as

34. The original quote from Mallarmé reads: "L'avantage, si j'ai droit à le dire, littéraire, de cette distance copiée qui mentalement sépare des groupes de mots ou les mots entre eux, semble d'accélérer tantôt et de ralentir le mouvement, le *scandant*, l'intimant même selon une vision simultanée de la Page: celle-ci prise pour unité comme l'est autre part le Vers ou ligne parfaite" (emphasis added). See Stéphane Mallarmé, *Collected Poems*, 121.

35. McLuhan, *Understanding Media*, 260.

36. Brian Reed, "Hart Crane's Victrola," 99.

37. Kittler, *Gramophone, Film, Typewriter*, 83–263.

the computer came along, this prosthetic device has done more for writing and alphabetic writing than perhaps any other device since Bi Sheng's invention of movable type in the middle of the eleventh century.[38]

The typing-head has opened up more innovative spaces than we can simply infer from the well-documented lore of modern novelists and poets who dictate to typists or use the machine themselves. Shannon, who knew Turing and his work well during their wartime collaboration, interprets Turing's square as "a particular 'blank' symbol." In fact, he suggests an intriguing parallel between his twenty-seventh letter and Turing's blank (unmarked) square on the paper or magnetic tape of the universal discrete machine.[39] By installing a non–phonetically marked discrete "space" or "blank" sign at the core of the alphanumerical system, information theory and computer technology enable a fundamental distinction between the written and printed symbols, a crucial distinction that has escaped the notice of the majority of linguists and historians of technology who investigate hypertext events and cybernetic literature. We hear the story of the universal Turing machine being repeated often enough to recognize a lineage of great minds—Charles Babbage, Turing, Konrad Zuse, Howard H. Aiken, and others—who all contributed to the invention of the computer. But hardly any attention has been directed to the question: What has the new technology done to that most familiar technology of all, the phonetic alphabet? More importantly, in what ways did alphabetical writing itself evolve to enable digital media?

The distinction between printed word and printed nonword for information technology has to do with the fact that, to use Kittler's words, "in contrast to the flow of handwriting, we now have discrete elements separated by spaces."[40] It should be emphasized, however, that the "space" symbol is a conceptual figure in Printed English, not a visible word divider as

---

38. There is a strange conspiracy of silence in Western academia and popular press on the question of when and how movable type was invented. The level of misinformation is nothing short of astounding when we consider that the event is well documented and the historiography in English is readily available. Briefly put, movable type was invented in 1041–48 by Bi Sheng (or Pi Sheng, c. 990–1051), who initially adopted movable types made of earthenware. Documented wooden movable types began to appear in 1297–98 and bronze and metal movable types became widespread in China and Korea in the fifteenth century. For a detailed account of the growth and refinements of early woodcut printing to the spread of printing from movable type in China as well as Gutenberg's possible exposure to this technology before 1456, see Tsuen-Hsuin Tsien, *Paper and Printing*, in Joseph Needham's edited series, "Science and Civilization in China," vol. 5 part 1, 201–22, 313–19. See also Pow-Key Sohn, "Early Korean Printing."

39. See Claude Shannon, "A Universal Turing Machine with Two Internal States," 733.

40. Kittler, *Gramophone, Film, Typewriter*, 16.

is commonly observed in modern and some of the ancient writing systems such as Akkadian cuneiform. The twenty-seventh letter is just as likely to be mathematically represented by "0" as by one or two types of electric pulse on a transmission pulse system. The letter owes its existence to the statistical, rather than visual or phonemic, parameters of symbols. It has no linguistic meaning as far as conventional semantics is concerned but is fully functional as a meaningful ideographic/mathematical notion. In fact, the twenty-seven letters of Printed English belong to an altogether different metaphysics than that targeted by Derrida's critique because the binary opposition of speech and writing does not obtain here. What we find instead is a statistical thinking that arbitrates the entropy of discrete alphanumerical symbols in a binary opposition of 0 and 1.

For Shannon, the entropy is a statistical parameter that can measure how much information is produced on the average for each letter of a text in a language. With an efficient translation of that language into binary digits (0 or 1), the entropy H is the average number of binary digits required per letter of the original language. In "Prediction and Entropy of Printed English," Shannon further suggests that "in ordinary literary English, the long range statistical effects (up to 100 letters) reduce the entropy to something of the order of one bit per letter, with a corresponding redundancy of roughly 75%."[41] This, of course, applies to the amount of information transmitted by discrete symbols. Where speech waves or television signals are concerned, we are confronted with continuous cases rather than the input or output of discrete alphanumerical symbols. To convert this type of continuous information to discrete cases, Shannon has generalized the statistical mechanism to include the variable of time, which enables the measuring of units of information per second, as opposed to per symbol, in transmitting speech signals, visual signals, or other continuous signals.[42] As we can see, by no means does the statistical paradigm presuppose a binary opposition between speech and writing, for all information assumes the form of continuous or discrete input and output.

As a discrete, ideographic symbol, the twenty-seventh letter is meaningful precisely in this statistical sense. Shannon's experiment with the stochastic structure of a randomly chosen text, Dumas Malone's *Jefferson the Virginian,* has produced further results. He designed the experiment with each sample consisting of fifteen letters to determine the ways in

41. Shannon, "Prediction and Entropy of Printed English," 50.
42. See Shannon and Weaver, *The Mathematical Theory of Communication,* 81–96; also Shannon, "Communication Theory—Exposition of Fundamentals," in *Collected Papers,* 175.

which predictability depends on the number N of preceding letters known to the subject. The human subject taking the test was allowed to use statistical tables, a dictionary, a list of frequencies of common words, a table of the frequencies of initial letters in words, and other aids and was asked to guess the text, letter by letter, for each sample. This and other guessing tests suggest that the predictability of English is dependent on the "space" letter far more frequently than on any of the other letters in the alphabet. Where there are no known letters, for example, the most probable guess in English is the "space" symbol (probability 0.182) and if this turns out to be wrong, the next probable guess would be E (probability 0.107) and so on.[43] Shannon concludes that "a machine or person guessing in the best way would guess letters in the order of decreasing conditional probability. Thus the process of reducing a text with such an ideal predictor consists of a mapping of the letters into the numbers from 1 to 27 in such a way that the most probable next letter [conditional on the known preceding $(N - 1)$ gram] is mapped into 1, etc." (Shannon, 58). As a mirror image of cryptography, Printed English requires a corresponding translated text in numerical symbols. The original text "with an alphabet of 27 symbols, A, B, . . . , Z, space, has been translated into a new language with the alphabet 1, 2, . . . , 27" (56). Through a built-in mechanism of alphanumerical translation, Printed English achieves its ultimate ideographic embodiment in the mathematical figuring of a 0/1 binary system.

So when Shannon claims that "H measures the equivalent number of binary digits for each letter produced in the language in question. H *measures all languages by the common yardstick of binary digits*" (my emphasis), he is essentially translating all known languages, including the vernacular English language, into the numerical model of Printed English.[44] The rise of Printed English as a universal code, therefore, has major implications for the survival of other languages and for machine translation projects. Does it mean that a new Tower of Babel or a shared basement of universal communication will once again be made possible by information theory? Surprisingly or not, one of the first attempts to answer this question came not from the obscure corner of machine translation projects, which experienced a slow and painful start, but rather from the fast growing research programs of molecular biology and the race toward the genetic code.

---

43. Shannon, "Prediction and Entropy of Printed English," 57. *Jefferson the Virginian* is the first volume of Malone's multivolume *Jefferson and His Time*.

44. Shannon, "Communication Theory—Exposition of Fundamentals," in *Collected Papers*, 174.

The Genetic Code and Grammatology

No twentieth-century philosopher has responded to the universalist ethos of technological inscription of information theory as promptly and as intuitively as Jacques Derrida. In the opening chapter of *Of Grammatology*, Derrida lays out the fundamentals of a new grammatology by introducing the concept "grammè."[45] What is a grammè? This concept, as the epigraph to the present chapter makes clear, is associated with the processes of information within the living cell and the cybernetic program.[46] Derrida regards these elementary processes of genetic inscription as instances of a generalized writing and further speculates: "If the theory of cybernetics is by itself to oust all metaphysical concepts—including the concepts of soul, of life, of value, of choice, of memory—which until recently served to separate the machine from man, it must conserve the notion of writing, trace, grammè [written mark], or grapheme, until its own historico-metaphysical character is also exposed" (Derrida, 9). The philosopher does not give us a straightforward analysis of the historico-metaphysical character of cybernetics and provides instead some interesting reflections on Wiener's use of language in a footnote. He suggests that, having rejected "semantics" as well as the opposition between "animate" and "inanimate," etc., Wiener continues to employ expressions like "organs of sense," "motor organs," and so on to describe the parts of a machine.[47] This traditional discourse of biology is viewed by Derrida as being strangely at odds with Wiener's new language of cybernetics, which aims precisely to dissolve the metaphysical opposition between organic and inorganic and between man and machine. In his view, Wiener's mixed language of vitalist biology and cybernetics compromises an otherwise radical project, one that would have permitted him to jettison the old biological concepts and metaphysics altogether.

Let us suppose that Wiener did throw out the vocabulary of organs and organisms in favor of the new language of codes and messages, a language that was gaining currency amongst the molecular biologists at that time. Would the code switch have shielded cybernetics from the charges of metaphysical thinking? The question is by no means arbitrary, because this was one of the flash points in the discursive struggle between the older generation of biochemists represented by Erwin Chargaff and the young cohort of

45. The chapter is called "The End of the Book and the Beginning of Writing," which was originally published in *Critique* in 1965 and subsequently incorporated in *Of Grammatology*.
46. Derrida, *Of Grammatology*, 9.
47. Derrida, *Of Grammatology*, 324n3.

molecular biologists. Just as Derrida was writing down the above remarks about the grammè in 1965, the older tropes of "organs" and "organisms" were in the processes of being overwhelmed by the language of coding, de-coding, message, messenger, and so on in molecular biology as the young discipline looked toward information theory for theoretical inspiration. After all, the genetic code was the buzzword of the day.

It was an interesting period of transition, especially as we recall that bi-ology and genetics before the time of information theory had been regarded as inferior systems of descriptive knowledge like historiography and lack-ing in theoretical rigor as exemplified by mathematics and physics. One could imagine the excitement of biologists and geneticists when the four-digital system of DNA and the mathematical correlations of nucleic and amino acids suddenly catapulted molecular biology into the respectable ranks of hard sciences. The situation fits well with Stephen Toulmin's ob-servation that "the heart of all major discoveries in the physical sciences is the discovery of novel modes of representation and so of fresh techniques by which inferences can be drawn—and drawn in ways which fit the phe-nomena under investigation."[48]

In 1962, Francis Crick, James Watson, and Maurice Wilkins shared a Nobel Prize for the discovery of the double helix of DNA, thus opening the gateways to the cracking of the genetic code. French scientists at the Pasteur Institute had by this time joined in the race to solve the puzzle of protein synthesis. They not only built their accounts of enzyme induction around cybernetic models, but began to adopt the new idiom of informa-tion theory to explain the replication of bacteriophages (viruses that infect bacterial cells).[49] What used to be called "structural specificity" became genetic "information." The autocatalytic function of DNA was now "repli-cation" and its heterocatalytic function "transcription" and "translation."[50] The mechanisms that enabled the transfer of genetic information were now explicitly described as écriture de l'hérédité, or the writing of hered-ity.[51] In 1965, a team of French molecular biologists, François Jacob, An-dré Lwoff, and Jacques Monod, received the Nobel Prize in Physiology or

48. Stephen Toulmin, The Philosophy of Science, 34.
49. Hans-Jörg Rheinberger's study shows that Pardee, Jacob, and Monod began to adopt terms such as "cytoplasmic messenger" or "cytoplasmic message" in 1959 in their published papers.
For the changing language of Jacob and his fellow scientists from the late 1950s to the 1960s, see Rheinberger, "The Notions of Regulation, Information, and Language in the Writings of François Jacob."
50. See Gunther S. Stent, The Coming of the Golden Age: A View of the End of Progress, 53.
51. François Jacob, Leçon inaugurale au Collège de France, 25.

Medicine, and in his Nobel lecture, delivered on December 11, 1965, Jacob characterized their discovery as follows:

> Since the notion that synthesis of proteins could occur directly on DNA was incompatible with the cytoplasmic localization of the ribosomes and their role in this synthesis, only one possible hypothesis remained: it was necessary to postulate the existence of a third species of RNA, the *messenger*, a short-lived molecule charged with transmission of genetic information to the cytoplasm. According to this hypothesis, the ribosomes are non-specific structures, which function as machines to *translate* the nucleic language, carried by the messenger, into the peptidic language, with the aid of the transfer RNA's. In other words, the synthesis of a protein must be a two-step process: the deoxyribonucleotide sequence of DNA is first *transcribed* into *messenger*, the primary gene product; this *messenger* binds to the ribosomes, bringing them a specific "program"; and the nucleotide sequence of the *messenger* is then *translated* into the amino acid sequence.[52] (my emphasis)

The tropes of information transfer that Jacob seems to throw about so effortlessly had been made popular by the physicist George Gamow in 1954, one year after Crick and Watson announced their discovery of the double helix.[53] These terms not only described but helped conceptualize the biochemical process of DNA and RNA as one of "transmission," "transcription," and "translation," which replaced "organ," "organism," "organization," "specificity," and so on. The vestiges of organismic and vitalist thinking that Derrida detected in Wiener's work were close to being eliminated by this time.[54]

As Lily E. Kay's research has amply documented, the code switch in molecular biology was viewed with ambivalence by some of the leading biochemists.[55] Among them was the eminent biochemist Erwin Chargaff.

---

52. François Jacob, "Genetics of the Bacterial Cell," 223–24.

53. Crick and Watson worked primarily with the theory of structural chemistry; their inspiration came from Linus Pauling's demonstration of the α-helix. They also used the three-dimensional X-ray crystallography of DNA to prove their hypothesis about the double helix. Although both men admired Schrödinger's work and knew the notion of "code-script," they did not switch to the language of information theory until some years later. For their own stories of discovery, see James D. Watson, *The Double Helix*, and Francis Crick, *What Mad Pursuit: A Personal View of Scientific Discovery*.

54. Jacob has a clear view of how the concept of organism evolved since the eighteenth century. See his discussion in Jacob, *The Logic of Life: A History of Heredity*, 74–129.

55. For Kay's documentation of the transition from organism to information, see *Who Wrote the Book of Life?: A History of the Genetic Code*, 38–72.

Regarded by many as the original discoverer of the chemical makeup of the
gene, Chargaff's work on the regularities of the base ratios of adenine (A)
to thymine (T) and guanine (G) to cytosine (C) was pathbreaking and constituted a decisive step toward establishing the structure of the DNA. He
was resistant, however, to the influx of information discourse and asked,
"Is it not possible that the entire imposing terminological scaffold is nothing but a suitcase for the emperor's new clothes? Is it not possible that
there is no message, no messenger, that the entire question is asked, and
therefore answered, wrongly?"[56] He went on to coin the phrase "molecular fundamentalist" to describe what he viewed as the wrongheaded approach to the question of life (Chargaff, 170). In 1962, Chargaff published
"Amphisbaena" to stage a Socratic dialogue between an old chemist and
a young molecular biologist in which the latter is heard proclaiming: "In
the beginning was DNA . . . " whereupon the old chemist interjects: "I
hear the start of a new apocryphal gospel with DNA as the logos of our
times" (185).

One could hardly expect the discursive struggle amongst the scientists
to be reflected in the theory of the *grammè* Derrida proposed in *Of Grammatology*. But Derrida's intervention begins to make better sense when we
view it as part of a larger debate about writing and the living cell at the
time. Foucault, for example, wrote a lengthy and positive review of François Jacob's *The Logic of Life* in *Le Monde*.[57] Roman Jakobson and Claude
Lévi-Strauss also joined in the conversation and even appeared together
with François Jacob in a television program, *Vivre et Parler*, to discuss what
they viewed as the extraordinary analogy between verbal information and
the language of life.[58] In *The Logic of Life,* Jacob introduces the notion of
"the program" as the structure of the constituent molecules of an organism, explicitly modeled on the electronic computer. This program, he
writes, "equates the genetic material of an egg with the magnetic tape of a
computer. It invokes a series of operations to be carried out, the rigidity of
their sequence and their underlying purpose."[59] The living cell as the machine, and the machine as the living cell. Of course, the equating of genetic
inscription with the magnetic tape or with Turing's paper tape has been
a commonplace in the discourse of the cybernetic machine, and Jacob

56. Erwin Chargaff, *Essays on Nucleic Acids,* 188–89.
57. This review article titled "Croître et multiplier" (Be fruitful and multiply) was published in
Le Monde on November 15–16, 1970 and included in Foucault's *Dits et Écrits,* 1954–88, vol. 1.
58. For a description of the debate, see Lily E. Kay, *Who Wrote the Book of Life?* 307–10.
59. Jacob, *The Logic of Life,* 9.

was certainly not the first one to propose the idea. In fact, there was a larger context of postwar scientific research, in which operations research (OR) was conceived and carried out prior to their translation into Jacob's genetic program.

In his study of computer technology in the cold war, Paul Edwards shows that operations research was originally an application of mathematical analysis to the observed data of war, which found its most famous engagement in antisubmarine warfare during World War II.[60] The operational programs evolved during the cold war into a powerful scientific paradigm for nuclear warfare, culminating in the hegemony of the Wiener-Shannon theory of communication and cybernetics.[61] Computer models, simulations, war games, feedback mechanisms, statistical analyses, and so on came to dominate the interdisciplinary scientific discourse of the 1950s and 1960s. In the absence of direct experience, according to Edwards, nuclear weapons forced military strategists to adopt simulation techniques based on assumptions, calculations, and hypothetical rules of engagement. "The object for each nuclear power was to maintain a winning *scenario*—a theatrical or simulated win, a psychological and political effect—rather than actually to fight such a war" (Edwards, 14). Under those circumstances, the actual outcomes no longer mattered, because the consequences of the war were too enormous to be comprehended and too dangerous to be tested. Under the shadows of what Peter Galison calls the ontology of the enemy, a good number of scientific and social science disciplines rushed to translate their work into the language of operational programs.[62]

As circumstances would have it, Derrida originally wrote the opening chapter of *Of Grammatology* as a review article in response to André Leroi-Gourhan's newly published *Gesture and Speech* (*Le Geste et la Parole*) in 1964. This ambitious book of paleoanthropology covers an enormous range of time and history from the early beginnings of the human evolution, the Zinjanthropian, the Neanthropian, to the automata of the twentieth century.[63] The author recasts the story of the human evolution as a history of

60. See Paul N. Edwards, *The Closed World: Computers and the Politics of Discourse in Cold War America*, 115.

61. For the contribution of Alan Turing and his laboratory, see F. H. Hinsley and Alan Stripp, *Codebreakers: The Inside Story of Bletchley Park*.

62. See Peter Galison, "The Ontology of the Enemy: Norbert Wiener and the Cybernetic Vision."

63. Bernard Stiegler provides an interesting critique of Leroi-Gourhan's work that should help situate Derrida's notions of *différance* and *trace* in that context. See Stiegler, *Technics and Time, 1: The Fault of Epimetheus*, 134–79.

technology (man with his/her tools) and, in particular, of the technology of writing. Notably, Leroi-Gourhan takes an unusual interest in the operational programs discussed above and, in particular, operational memory in automatic machines as he shows how these programs have evolved significantly to blur the distinction between human and machine in our own time.[64] Reflecting on Leroi-Gourhan and his approach to operational programs, Derrida writes:

> The notion of *program* is invoked. It must of course be understood in the cybernetic sense, but cybernetics is itself intelligible only in terms of a history of the possibilities of the trace as the unity of a double movement of protention and retention. This movement goes far beyond the possibilities of the "intentional consciousness." It is an emergence that makes the *grammè* appear *as such* (that is to say according to a new structure of nonpresence) and undoubtedly makes possible the emergence of the systems of writing in the narrow sense. Since "genetic inscription" and the "short programmatic chains" regulate the behavior of the amoeba or the annelid up to the passage beyond alphabetic writing to the orders of the logos and a certain *homo sapiens*, the possibility of the *grammè* structures the movement of its history according to rigorously original levels, types, and rhythms. But one cannot think them without the most general concept of the *grammè*.[65]

Does the *grammè* precede cybernetics, as is contended here? Or did the cybernetic notion of "program(s)" inspire Derrida's own conception of the *grammè*? The subtle word play between "the program" and the *grammè* modifies Leroi-Gourhan's discussion of operational programs slightly by rewriting them in the singular, *the program*. We are given to understand that the *grammè* authorizes the emergence of the program but the circumstances of his writing appear to suggest the other way around.

One thing is clear, though: Derrida has sought to establish a fundamental linkage between the program and the *grammè* for grammatology. If operational programs are somehow conducive to his discovery of the *grammè*, we can argue that the magnetic tape of the cybernetic machine is the unacknowledged figure of thought in the notions of the *grammè* and *trace*. Can we then argue that the double movement of "protention" and "retention" in ostensibly phenomenological terms actually articulates to the operations and sequences of the cybernetic machine with which Leroi-Gourhan

64. See André Leroi-Gourhan, *Gesture and Speech*, 237–55.
65. Derrida, *Of Grammatology*, 84.

and Jacob were both concerned? The answer is affirmative. Derrida has rightly grasped cybernetics and operational programs as having abolished "intention," "consciousness," and other such metaphysical concepts, but genetic inscription can hardly serve as the desired evidence for the possibility of the *gramm è* before we come to a clearer understanding of the relationship between the genetic code, alphabetical writing, information theory, and cybernetics.

As discussed earlier, the engineers and mathematicians of communication systems in the postwar Anglo-American scientific establishment took the printed word or printed letters as the point of departure when they set out to design the universal discrete machine that could think and perform intelligent tasks. That choice is significant, which makes a great deal of difference to how we reassess the technology of the phonetic alphabet in cybernetics or its implications for grammatology. Friedrich Kittler exhibits a firm grasp of the situation when he locates the act of writing in the hardware of the computer rather than in the rhetoric of genetic inscription. He states that "the last historical act of writing may well have been the moment when, in the early seventies, Intel engineers laid out some dozen square meters of blueprint paper (64 square meters, in the case of the later 8086) in order to design the hardware architecture of their first integrated microprocessor."[66] Kittler may sound a bit exaggerating but it is always helpful to keep his perspective in mind as we go on and reflect on the materiality and technology of writing.

The evolution of alphabetical writing through the development of information technology has been a major event since the mid-twentieth century, an event that needs to be acknowledged and brought into proper focus. Many of us are aware that information theory and cybernetics have revolutionized neuroscience, linguistics, economics, psychoanalysis, biology, and other branches of learning by allowing different disciplines to meet and cross one another's boundaries. But on what ground did the significant meeting of the minds occur when it did? For instance, when Jakobson applied information theory to a structural study of language and poetics, he occasionally would introduce slippages between "meter" and "frequency" and draw parallels between the phoneme and the discrete elements of the genetic code, the amino acids.[67] In contrast, Shannon chose to focus on the letters of Printed English when he prepared the mathematical theory of communication. As he calculated and compared the redundancy and

66. Kittler, *Literature, Media, Information Systems*, 147.
67. Jakobson, *Language in Literature*, 71.

entropy rates of English letters and words, he adopted statistical rather than phonemic parameters. Did Shannon and Jakobson conceive of the phonetic alphabet and its relationship to language differently? How did the discrepancies come about?

To account for these conceptual gaps and discrepancies, we need to examine our own preconceived ideas of phonetic inscription first. As we know, ideographic writing has long been opposed to the phonetic alphabet as its nonphonetic other. The opposition exemplifies a familiar metaphysical habit of thinking that Derrida tried to bring to light and deconstruct, although his understanding of the exact relationship between the two differs from that of this book. However we prefer to conceptualize the opposition, the first step is not to associate ideographic inscription too quickly with the Chinese writing system, for these two are very different historical constructs that have mistakenly been compared because of misunderstanding and motivated translations. The Christian missionaries and linguists of the past were poor intermediaries when it came to reporting on the state of Chinese writing to their home audiences and to unsuspecting philosophers. The situation has not improved much since the time of Leibniz. For instance, the persistence of logocentricism in media studies since the time of Marshall McLuhan as well as in digital media studies more recently continues to obscure the ideographic unfolding of alphabetical writing and renders it unthinkable by doing one of two things: first, it opposes alphabetical writing to the so-called pictographic, ideographic, or logographic systems of writing on superficial grounds of the script system; second, it confuses the linguistic with the writing system and further collapses the one or the other with the idea of script (writing systems are language specific whereas scripts are not).

It is interesting that McLuhan was among the first of literary scholars to grasp the importance of Joyce's modernist experiment for understanding media technology, but he did not use the same insight to revise his mistaken views of the phonetic alphabet. Those views, shared by many in media studies, continue to buttress the claims people make about the advances in print technology, telecommunication, and biocybernetic technologies since the introduction of movable type into Europe. Here we need not be overly concerned with the misplaced arrogance in the well-entrenched view that Johannes Gutenberg invented movable type. What matters rather is the familiar intellectual claim McLuhan has advanced on behalf of the phonetic alphabet as a technology. In *Understanding Media*, he asserts:

The phonetic alphabet is a unique technology. There have been many kinds of writing, pictographic and syllabic, but there is only one phonetic alphabet in which semantically meaningless letters are used to correspond to semantically meaningless sounds. This stark division and parallelism between a visual and an auditory world was both crude and ruthless, culturally speaking. The phonetically written word sacrifices worlds of meaning and perception that were secured by forms like the hieroglyph and the Chinese ideogram. These culturally richer forms of writing, however, offered men no means of sudden transfer from the magically discontinuous and traditional world of the tribal word into the cool and uniform visual medium. Many centuries of ideogrammic use have not threatened the seamless web of family and tribal subtleties of Chinese society. On the other hand, a single generation of alphabetic literacy suffices in Africa today, as in Gaul two thousand years ago, to release the individual initially, at least, from the tribal web.[68]

If this argument sounds persuasive at the commonsense level, it is deeply flawed at the conceptual level, not the least because it is compromised by ignorance. McLuhan imputes primitive pictographic thinking to nonalphabetical writing—confusing the pictographic and ideographic—despite the fact that that view had been discredited before his time.[69] Rudimentary knowledge of semiotics or mathematical symbols would have taught us that nonphonetic, visual signs need not be "pictograms" or "tribal" to function as semiotic media. Where the primitivizing of nonalphabetical writing has succeeded so well is the supplementary mystification of the phonetic alphabet itself, which has been the main object of our investigation. For the question then becomes this: by what magic does the "cool and uniform visual medium" of "meaningless" phonetic symbols come to bear meaning at all? Not being able to explain either the science or magic of the phonetic alphabet, one is forced to evoke the familiar position of modern linguistic theory and insist that the phonetic letters represent "meaningless" sounds in speech.[70]

68. McLuhan, *Understanding Media*, 83–84.

69. See Peter Boodberg, "'Ideography' or Iconolatry?" and Yuen Ren Chao, *Mandarin Primer*.

70. McLuhan's ethnocentrism often blinds him to the incoherence and self-contradiction of his ahistorical views concerning technology and civilization. If the phonetic alphabet has played a decisive role in liberating individuals from their familial and tribal webs, why did it take thousands of years for Europe to discover the value of "individualism" whereas "a single generation of alphabetic literacy suffices in Africa today"? Citing Lynn White's *Medieval Technology and Social Change* in an essay called "Cybernation and Culture," McLuhan points out that the stirrup as an extension

By what script, and in what medium, is a writing system known or knowable? The question is intended to reflect on the evolution of alphabetical writing itself as an ideographic construct in digital media. Despite the various claims to the contrary, the written Chinese character can no more be equated with ideography than alphabetical writing can be reduced to phonocentrism.[71] Let us bear it in mind that ideographic inscription has always been a European idea, like that of hieroglyph, which would be foreign to the Chinese scholars who have written voluminously on the subject of the *zi* (individual written character) or the *wen* (text/writing) over the past two thousand years since the time of Xu Shen (a Han dynasty scholar who introduced the first systematic analysis of the Chinese written character in the *Origin of Chinese Characters* [Shuowen jiezi] in 100 CE).[72]

On the other hand, there is no reason why one must dismiss ideographical writing as a false idea. Even if this concept fails to inform us about Chinese writing, it has enjoyed a separate career in the West with a penchant for prolepsis, that is, the dream that alphabetical writing will one day be able to shed its local phonetic trappings to become a universal code. This Leibnizian dream of the universal language has given ideography its aura of alterity and teleology in Western thought, so one can design and fantasize about direct graphic inscriptions of abstract thought the way that mathematical symbols or deaf reading and mute writing transcribe con-

---

of the foot was unknown to the Greeks and Romans. Its first introduction from the East (China) enabled men in the early medieval world "to wear heavy armor on horseback" and become "tanks." The feudal system that came into existence to pay for heavy armor owed itself to the introduction of this technology. But when gunpowder entered the scene, it immediately "changed the ground rules of the feudal system as drastically as the stirrup had changed the ground rules of the ancient economy. It was as democratic as print" (McLuhan, "Cybernation and Culture," 104). If all three technologies—the stirrup, gunpowder, and print—originated in China, why were they capable of transforming Europe while leaving the "seamless web of family and tribal subtleties of Chinese society" intact? Ethnocentrism is the only possible explanation for this strange mode of reasoning.

71. André Leroi-Gourhan sees the ideographic and phonetic aspects of Chinese writing as "mutually complementary and, at the same time, so foreign to one another that each has engendered separate different notation systems outside China." He refers to Japan and other Asian countries that appropriated the Chinese script for their own usage. Leroi-Gourhan was one of the few theorists who seemed to have acquired some firsthand knowledge of Chinese writing, although he could have given more attention to the role of time and space as the structuring forces in the assemblage and gathering of radicals and phonetic elements into conventional symbols. Calligraphy, which crystallizes the spirit of the Chinese script, demonstrates the principle of such continual assemblage very well. See Leroi-Gourhan, *Gesture and Speech*, 209.

72. For a discussion of the misinterpretation of the Chinese *zi* through the logographic concept of "word" in the troubled beginnings of modern Chinese grammar, see Lydia H. Liu, *The Clash of Empires: The Invention of China in Modern World Making*, 181–209.

ceptual objects, namely, without the mediation of speech or sounds.[73] This dream has persisted with or without the help of Chinese writing. More recently, the cracking of the genetic code by molecular biologists began to speed things up and brought the centuries-long pursuit of the universal language to a halt, if not to a sense of closure. This monumental event and the subsequent mapping of the human genome mark a turning point in how some of the basic questions about life, humanity, reproduction, social control, language, communication, and health can be posed or debated in the public arena. And all this is happening when conversations between the scientist and the humanist have become ever more difficult due to the nearly insurmountable disciplinary barriers and institutional forces that shield the scientist from the critical eye while keeping the humanist away from the production of objective knowledge.

Despite the obstacle, the news of the genetic code has given rise to a number of critical studies by humanistic scholars who undertook the task of scrutinizing the role of alphabetical writing as a master trope in molecular biology. Inasmuch as the discipline of molecular biology did not come to its own until the midst of the cold war, some of these studies are devoted primarily to retracing how the vast resources of the military-industrial-academic complex of the United States had been put in the service of a new vision of weapons technology and a new ontology of the enemy in the form of information theory and cybernetics, out of which emerged the discursive construction of the DNA sequence as a genetic code. Critics point out how the mathematician relied on the logic of cryptological decoding to unlock the enemy's secret alphabet and how the molecular biologist adopted the same method to decode the speechless language of DNA by identifying the letters, codons (words), and punctuation marks of the nucleic acids.[74] Gamow and his collaborators, for example, clearly approached the molecules of the living cell as an object of conquest, "similar to those encountered by an Armed Force's Intelligence Office trying to break an enemy code on the basis of a single message less than two printed lines long."[75]

---

73. See Derrida's critical reflections on Leibniz's praise of nonphonetic writing in *Of Grammatology*, 24–26.

74. A codon is regarded as the equivalent of a "word" unit that spells out a sequence of three adjacent nucleotides constituting the genetic code. The sequence specifies the insertion of an amino acid in a specific structural position in a polypeptide chain during protein synthesis.

75. George Gamow, Alexander Rich, and Martynas Yčas, "The Problem of Information Transfer From the Nucleic Acids to Proteins," 40.

In *Biomedia*, Eugene Thacker introduces a distinction between metaphorization and autonomization in the historical unfolding of bioinformatics. He argues that the concept of "information" was appropriated as a metaphor by molecular biologists mainly in the early stage of the mid-twentieth century as, for example, documented by Kay; however, in the later biotechnical and bioinformatic phases, "information is not taken as a metaphor for DNA, but is seen to inhere in DNA itself as a technical principle. With the rise of novel techniques for controlling and storing DNA in computers, the metaphoric stature of the informatics model collapses onto DNA itself."[76] What Thacker means by "metaphor" is a manner of talking about DNA in a language borrowed from elsewhere; and this he tries very hard to distinguish from the epistemological internalization and autonomization of information. He sees the latter being constitutive of DNA so that the genome *is* a biological computer and the body *is* a kind of biomedia (Thacker, 40). But is this not how Crick, Watson, Gamow, Jacob, and other molecular biologists spoke of their discoveries in the early days? Does Gamow's metaphor of enemy code imply no epistemological breaks? Must it await the future revelation of bioinformatics to be fully legible?

Understanding that metaphors and figures of thought have been indispensible to the development of scientific disciplines and to the conceptual and paradigm shift in a discipline, Lily Kay, N. Katherine Hayles, Richard Doyle, and other critics have subjected the tropes of molecular biology to scrutiny and shown how the "rhetorical software" has participated in the scientists' discovery of the genetic code.[77] Pushing that insight further, they argue that the metaphors of code, transcription, translation, etc. actually provide the conceptual framework within which the scientists have imagined and established the correlations among the nucleic and amino acids, even though the elusiveness of figurative language and the "multiplicity of significations, definitional slippages, shifting meanings, and aporias ultimately served to destabilize the validity and predictive power of the genomic writings."[78] Humberto Maturana and Francisco Varela's much-cited notion of "autopoiesis" is another instance of how a specifically cybernetic view of living organisms has been propelled toward a generalized theory of self-regulation and self-organization that is applicable not only to bio-

76. Eugene Thacker, *Biomedia*, 39.
77. Richard Doyle's phrase in *On Beyond Living: Rhetorical Transformations of the Life Sciences* 6–10. See also James J. Bono, "Science, Discourse, and Literature: The Role/Rule of Metaphor in Science," 61.
78. Kay, *Who Wrote the Book of Life?* 14.

logical systems but also to social systems. But there is something strangely incongruent in the migration and dissemination of "autopoiesis" from one system to another. As Richard Doyle has observed in his book *Wetware*, Maturana and Varela themselves could not agree on this fundamental question: "Are social organizations inside or outside the purview of biological laws?"[79] In fact, one could put the same question to Nikolas Luhmann and many others who have relied on Maturana and Varela's postulation of biological laws to develop their own systems theory. Has the concept of "autopoiesis" turned into another theory-building trope that generates its own self-referential patterns in the manner of Gamow's "enemy code"?

While it is certainly helpful to analyze the role of tropes and metaphors in the construction of knowledge, we must also remind ourselves that scientists, especially the brightest among them, tend not to dispute the point. Wiener writes that "mathematics, which most of us see as the most factual of all sciences, constitutes the most colossal metaphor imaginable, and must be judged, aesthetically as well as intellectually, in terms of the success of this metaphor."[80] Émile Borel has pointed out that calculus necessarily rests upon the postulate of the existence *de la langue vulgaire*.[81] Friedrich Waismann wrote in the early twentieth century that whatever one may assert about logic or calculus, that view "has to be supplemented by the disclosure of the dependence that exists between the mathematical symbols and the meanings of words in the colloquial language."[82] And not to mention the fact that the model of the double helix is described by Crick and Watson and other scientists as being "beautiful" and "elegant" as if the aesthetics mattered to what they are going after.[83]

Of course, one need not concur with the particular views of the scientists to heed the implied message that the critique of scientific knowledge

79. Richard Doyle, *Wetwares: Experiments in Postvital Living*, 38. The work he discusses here is Humberto Maturana and Francisco Varela's influential book *Autopoiesis and Cognition: The Realization of the Living*. Ira Livingston offers an interesting Lacanian reading of the autopoietic system, stating that it is "a system that is able to misrecognize itself (or to be misrecognized) as autonomous." See Livingston, *Between Science and Literature: An Introduction to Autopoetics*, 89.

80. Norbert Wiener, *The Human Use of Human Beings: Cybernetics and Society*, 95. Brian Rotman has made the same argument from a slightly different angle. He points out that no mathematician would deny the proposition that "mathematics is a language." See Rotman, "The Technology of Mathematical Persuasion."

81. Émile Borel, *Leçons sur la théorie des fonctions*, 160.

82. Friedrich Waismann, *Introduction to Mathematical Thinking: The Formation of Concepts in Modern Mathematics*, 118.

83. References to the elegant style of their model and reasoning at the expense of proofs are ubiquitous in Horace Freeland Judson's interviews with many of the scientists who participated in the cracking of the genetic code. See Judson, *The Eighth Day of Creation: Makers of the Revolution in Biology*.

by way of unmasking its metaphorics does not necessarily promise a higher level of understanding of the subject than what the scientist and the humanist both know.[84] If our rhetorical rejoinder to a prior rhetorical move made by the scientist sounds predictable or not very interesting beyond pointing out that scientific facts are always figuratively constructed, might it be attributed to the fact that we have not worked hard enough to figure out how to conceptualize our critique before making it? For example, we might consider fiction and mathematics as complementary symbolic constructs, or investigate the relationship between psychoanalysis and game theory (or cybernetics and information theory, which are interrelated developments) as each appropriates literature as a shared resource of symbolic exercise through which the theorists have made their intellectual leap toward formalization.

When it comes to the unmasking of the genetic code as metaphor, the limitation is the implied assumptions about the identity of the phonetic alphabet, semantics, language, and the role of representation. It is often the critics' assumptions about these matters, rather than the code itself, that cause them to see a metaphor where they might have caught something new, something very different, something startling. To unravel those assumptions, we would do well by asking three questions. First, have the scientists not done something to the phonetic alphabet and to figurative writing in general to transform the very ideas on which the humanist relies to critique them? Second, is the protein text just another case of metaphorical play that we recognize when we see one? Finally, can we assume that the symbolic paradigms of information theory and molecular biology must reside within the bounds of the same old rhetorical paradigm of literal or figurative representations and have done nothing whatsoever to shock us out of our common sense or cause the familiar concepts of "word," "message," "code," and "translation" to replicate and mutate in unexpected ways?

The answer to the first question is yes, and that to the other two is no. All three questions bear on the changing identity of alphabetic writing in at least these registers. First, the genetic code, being speechless, relies on the symbolic order of discrete letters, numbers, spaces, and punctuation

84. The latest on the metaphorics of mathematics after Waismann is George Lakoff's and Rafael E. Núñez's *Where Mathematics Comes From: How the Embodied Mind Brings Mathematics into Being*. This book analyzes the role that conceptual metaphors play in mathematical ideas including arithmetic, algebra, sets, logic and infinity. The study appears to confirm Wiener's statement by two cognitive scientists who confess "a long-standing passion for the beautiful ideas of mathematics." (xi).

marks as understood in digital media. Second, the introduction of this ideographic alphabet cannot but modify the rules of figurative representation to destabilize the conceptual ground of cross-metaphoric play that we usually associate with a conventional text. Finally, the ideographic alphabet of numerals, letters, and spaces aspires to the condition of the universal as it conquers all known languages, including vernacular English, on behalf of imperial technoscience. The point here is that in order to understand how letters, numbers, punctuations got into genetic inscription, neither pointing to the genetic code as a metaphor nor disavowing it would get us very far. To do so would foreclose our investigation in the name of conventional semantics and prompt circular arguments about how the literal becomes metaphorical or how the metaphorical turns literal, and so on.

So instead of quibbling over the metaphysical status of metaphor and its truth value, it is more fruitful to focus our attention on how a certain idea of the printed symbol emerged and acquired the kinds of significance attributed to it by information theory and molecular biology. This may well turn out to be the real issue in digital media. The twenty-seventh letter of Printed English and the alphabetical code of the molecules of nucleic acids each suggest how the alphabet can be reworked to become more or less than itself. Likewise, when the Nobel laureate François Jacob proclaims that the DNA code is written with an alphabet like that of the French language or Morse code, he is actually talking about the codons and operons in specifically ideographic terms (i.e., on or off), rather than French phonemes or verbal units.[85]

The Ideographic Turn of the Phonetic Alphabet

The relevance of Morse code as a prototype for information theory and genetic inscription is by no means trivial, for it harks back to the legacy of what I have elsewhere called a semiotic turn of international politics in the nineteenth century. The history of modern technology demonstrates that telecommunication systems have always been calibrated with military requirements and interwoven with the communication needs of the navy, the air force, and the army.[86] The pioneers of semiotic studies, Charles Sanders Peirce and Ferdinand de Saussure, did not invent the concepts of

85. Jacob, *Leçon inaugurale au Collège de France*, 22. For an analysis of how the debate on the "French blood" impacted the work on the human genome in France, see Paul Rabinow, *French DNA: Trouble in Purgatory*.

86. See chapter 1 in *The Clash of Empires*.

"code," "sign," "signal," and so on but shared their understanding of them with the engineers of the Royal Navy and the inventors of Morse code. This was a time when sovereign states and imperial powers began the practice of discussing and drafting binding treaties to regulate international maritime signals, road signs, electrical codes, and other sign systems. The conditions that made Shannon's experiments in cryptology and telecommunication engineering meaningful in World War II and subsequently in the cold war were precisely the prospect of turning the English alphabetical letters into a universal digital code, more fundamentally universal than Morse code has ever been.

The promise of universal translatability across different systems of symbols in the communication machine led the physicist George Gamow to speculate boldly about the statistical structure of DNA in 1954.[87] In a short paper published in *Nature* called "Possible Relation Between Deoxyribonucleic Acid and Protein Structures," Gamow, the theorist of the Big Bang, proposed a mathematical model for the double helix of DNA, which Crick and Watson had just announced to the scientific community. On the basis of two parallel chains of the double helix being formed by only four different kinds of nucleotides—(1) adenine, (2) thymine, (3) guanine, and (4) cytosine—with sugar and phosphate molecules attached to them, Gamow proposed that the hereditary properties of any given organism might be characterized as "a long number written in a four-digital system." The enzymes (proteins), being long peptide chains formed by about twenty different kinds of amino acids, could be considered as "long 'words' based on a 20 letter alphabet. Thus the question about the way in which four-digital numbers can be translated into such 'words.'"[88] His "diamond code" was subsequently proven incorrect, but the "translation procedure" Gamow introduced into molecular biology from information theory took off and began to shape the young discipline aggressively. The quest for the secret of life thus turned into a problem of coding and decoding, and that of translation. After a decade, Gamow's chief collaborator, Martynas Yčas, would look back on the rapid advances in molecular biology and argue that the importance of Gamow's proposal did not depend on the specifics of the diamond code, which he confessed was incorrect. Rather, Yčas insisted

87. Richard Doyle has remarked on Gamow's use of translation in *On Beyond Living* but limits his treatment of the issue to a rhetorical analysis of Gamow's metaphor of "word" and "digit" rather than link them conceptually to Shannon's twenty-seven-letter English alphabet. See Doyle, *On Beyond Living*, 39–64.

88. George Gamow, "Possible Relation Between Deoxyribonucleic Acid and Protein Structures," 318.

that Gamow's enduring contribution to molecular sciences lay in his presentation of the problem of life "as a formal problem of translating one text into another" and divorcing it from chemical detail.[89] We have seen that the biochemist Chargaff protested this postvitalist, formalist move, arguing that the coding problem raised wrong questions about life.

One of the things that Crick and his colleagues tried to tackle in their formalist approach to life was to obtain correct readings of the genetic code out of a vast number of possibilities. On the basis of Gamow's four-digital combination system, they began to introduce "semantics" into the sequences of three nucleotides, which are associated with an amino acid, out of a total of sixty-four triplets ($4 \times 4 \times 4$). It is interesting that they regarded some of the sequences as making "sense" and dismissed others as producing "nonsense."[90] It is curious that semantics mattered to them at this level. After all, the molecular biologists had borrowed information theory from Shannon, who would have nothing to do with semantics. When he first conceptualized the coding problem of the communication machine, sense and nonsense meant very different things to him than the correct or incorrect readings of code, and he insisted that information was stochastically determined. As discussed in the next chapter, some of Shannon's Bell Labs colleagues followed in his footsteps by conducting stochastic experiments with the very idea of boundaries of sense and nonsense. Through the interplay of sense and nonsense, they even speculated about the nature of what one might call the schizophrenic machine in digital media.

The reading of semantics into the sequences of three nucleotides is one of many travesties to be observed in the translation of information theory into another discipline. There has also been widespread confusion regarding the very idea of code itself. Is the genetic code language or writing? We have already seen how Derrida invoked genetic inscription to give credence to the theory of the *grammè* in grammatology. For him, the genetic code was firmly associated with writing, never the spoken language. For Jakobson, however, the genetic code was associated with verbal language, speech, and phoneme. In a lengthy report he published on the state of the field in linguistics in 1970, Jakobson made one of the most ambitious arguments on behalf of structural linguistics. He stated: "The universal

89. Martynas Yčas, *The Biological Code*, 25.

90. Francis H. C. Crick, J. S. Griffith, and L. E. Orgel, "Codes Without Commas." The speculations in this paper were proven wrong. For a discussion of Crick's reflections on the attraction of this game, see Horace Freeland Judson, *The Eighth Day of Creation*, 318–21.

architectonic design of the verbal code is undoubtedly the molecular en-
dowment of every Homo sapiens."[91] By "verbal code," he meant the spoken
language, not writing, and he went on to say that the "deepest discernment
of the relation between the human organism and its verbal abilities and
activities is achieved by the mutual help of neurobiologists and linguists in
a comparative inquiry into the various lesions of the cortex and the result-
ing aphasic impairments."[92]

The logic of Jakobson's argument for the parallelism of the genetic code
and the verbal code consists of a series of substitutions and displacement
that lead from the phoneme to the letter and then to Morse code. In his
view, the letter is a substitute for the phoneme and Morse code a mere substitute for the letter—a view that Hayles would echo many years later—so
it follows that the subunits of the genetic code that are similarly represented ought to be compared directly with phonemes. "We may state that
among all the information-carrying systems," writes Jakobson, "the genetic
code and the verbal code are the only ones based upon the use of discrete
components which, by themselves, are devoid of inherent meaning but
serve to constitute the minimal senseful units" (Jakobson, "Linguistics,"
439–40). There is something that the postulated parallelism between the
discrete symbol of the genetic code and that of the verbal code does not
fully spell out for us. That is to say, Jakobson's work on the phoneme in
the early 1950s had been inspired by information theory and was partially
modeled on it. What it means is that Morse code and the printed symbol
cannot be a mere substitute or the substitute of a substitute. If we care to
examine more closely, the printed symbol of the communication machine
is what mediates the parallelism of the genetic code and the verbal code he
claims to have discovered. As we will see below, Jakobson's discrete unit of
the verbal code—the phoneme—follows rather than precedes the printed
symbol of the communication machine.

91. Jakobson, "Linguistics," 440.

92. Jakobson, "Linguistics," 445. In recent years, the decoding of FOXP2 shows that efforts
to decipher the genetic basis of speech disorders have not only continued but moved steadily in
the direction Jakobson charted out in his earlier inquiry into the problems of aphasia. FOXP2
has been identified as the gene that is responsible for one's ability to acquire a spoken language
and is believed to hold the key to the genetic cascades and neural pathways that contribute to our
capacity for speech and language. See Simon E. Fisher, Cecilia S. L. Lai, and Anthony P. Monaco,
"Deciphering the Genetic Basis of Speech and Language Disorders," and Gary F. Marcus and Simon
E. Fisher, "FOXP2 in Focus: What Can Genes Tell Us About Speech and Language?" For Jakobson's
work on speech impairments, see "Two Aspects of Language and Two Types of Aphasic Disturbances," 95–119. This essay was initially published in Fundamentals of Language, coauthored with
Morris Halle.

The evidence is unequivocal in his foundational essay on the phoneme, "Toward the Logical Description of Languages in Their Phonemic Aspect" (1953). Before going into this paper, we note that as early as 1949 Jakobson had received his personal copy of Shannon and Weaver's *Mathematical Theory of Communication* from Warren Weaver himself and became an enthusiastic champion of information theory.[93] Later in the 1950s, he would hold a joint appointment at MIT, where he interacted with information theorists and served on the steering committee of MIT's newly established Center for Communication Studies, which included Shannon, Jerome Wiesner, Walter Rosenblith, Jerome Lettvin, Noam Chomsky, Marvin Minsky, and John McCarthy. The center was affiliated with the Research Laboratory of Electronics and was funded by the U.S. Army, the Air Force, the CIA, the National Science Foundation, and the National Bureau of Standards.[94]

Jakobson's article "Toward the Logical Description of Languages in Their Phonemic Aspect" was coauthored with the information theorist Colin Cherry and the MIT linguist Morris Halle. In it, they apply Shannon's methods and mathematical formula directly to the task of determining the statistical boundaries of the discrete unit of language. Their logical description of the phoneme is closely modeled upon Shannon's calculation of entropy, adopting the same $H = -\sum p_i \log p_i$ to calculate the number of bits per phoneme. The reader will recall that Shannon had calculated the average number of bits per letter for communication engineering using exactly the same method but did not rely on these statistics to prove the discreteness of the letter. The "bits per phoneme" in the Jakobsonian sense refers to the average number of plus or minus (yes or no) questions needed to identify a phoneme through successive subdivision of the set into two groups of equal total probability according to distinctive features. What it says is that a phoneme i is grounded not so much in speech as in a mathematical determination of the probability of numerical frequencies p_i that render it discrete.[95] Fig. 7 indicates how the authors determined the phonemes of Russian using this method; it shows that the discreteness of Jakobson's phoneme is derivative of the printed symbol (average bits per letter)

93. Kay, *Who Wrote the Book of Life?* 300. I discuss Weaver's role in the promotion of information theory in the next section.

94. Lily Kay's research shows that by the 1960s these same funding agencies had collectively spent $3 million on linguistic research relating to automatic translation, mainly from Russian to English and particularly scientific papers, and by the end of fiscal year 1963 the figure grew to be about 8 million. See Kay, *Who Wrote the Book of Life?*, 301.

95. See Colin Cherry, Morris Halle, and Roman Jakobson, "Toward the Logical Description of Languages in Their Phonemic Aspect," 41.

a	b	c	d	e	a	b	c	d	e
a	1316	2.94	.387	4	d	177	5.81	.100	9
i	977	3.35	.328	6	l,	162	5.95	.096	4
t	602	4.05	.244	9	'u	153	5.96	.091	6
'a	539	4.23	.228	4	r,	133	6.20	.083	4
j	457	4.45	.202	2	z	130	6.25	.081	8
n	392	4.66	.183	6	d,	126	6.30	.080	9
'o	379	4.72	.179	5	b	119	6.39	.075	8
s	359	4.80	.172	8	x	102	6.60	.067	5
'e	343	4.86	.167	5	g	91	6.80	.062	7
k	284	5.14	.146	7	v,	89	6.84	.061	8
v	273	5.15	.140	8	ʒ	89	6.84	.061	6
'i	243	5.38	.131	6	f	85	6.86	.058	8
u	240	5.40	.129	6	s,	85	6.86	.058	8
p	232	5.42	.126	8	š	59	7.40	.044	9
r	230	5.45	.125	4	m,	56	7.50	.043	6
n,	221	5.50	.121	6	b,	52	7.60	.039	8
l	212	5.55	.118	4	p,	50	7.64	.038	8
ʃ	207	5.56	.115	6	k,	36	8.10	.029	7
m	202	5.64	.114	6	z,	21	8.90	.018	8
c	197	5.65	.111	5	f,	8	10.30	.008	8
t,	196	5.65	.111	9	g,	7	10.50	.008	7

TABLE C

a = Phoneme (i); $b = p_i \times 10^4$; $c = -\log_2 p_i$; $d = -p_i \log_2 p_i$; e = number of features listed in Table B (i means 'any given phoneme'; p_i means 'the probability of a given phoneme')

Figure 7. The numerical determination of Russian phonemes by Colin Cherry, Morris Halle, and Roman Jakobson. From Cherry, Halle, and Jakobson, "Toward the Logical Description of Languages in Their Phonemic Aspect," *Language* 29, no. 1 (1953): 41. Used with permission of the Linguistic Society of America.

in the communication machine rather than coming from actual speech. (As if anticipating a full circle from Russian literature to mathematics and back to the Russian language, the pioneer in the statistical analysis of Russian literature, as mentioned earlier, was the mathematician Markov, from whom Shannon had borrowed his own stochastic method.)

In a move that would deeply impact the poetics of his time, Jakobson postulates that "the poetic function projects the principle of equivalence from the axis of selection into the axis of combination."[96] These fundamental rules governing the arrangement of verbal signs in literary language— selection and combination—obey the same logic of combinatorics and binary opposition as that of information technology. The rule of selection

96. Jakobson, "Linguistics and Poetics," 71.

is based on equivalency, similarity and dissimilarity, synonymy and anton-ymy; and the rule of combination is based on contiguity or the buildup of a sequence. Thus, a metaphor is articulated by the principle of substitu-tion, whereas metonymy follows that of contiguity. These principles not only structure what is called the recurrent figure of sound in verse but motivate all parallel, contrastive, and semantic constructions. "Along with these characteristics compulsory for any line composed in a given meter," writes Jakobson, "there are features that show a high probability of occur-rence without being constantly present. Besides signals certain to occur ('probability one'), signals likely to occur ('probability less than one') enter into the notion of meter. Using Cherry's description of human communi-cation, we could say that the reader of poetry obviously 'may be unable to attach numerical frequencies' to the constituents of the meter, but as far as he conceives the verse shape, he unwittingly gets an inkling of their 'rank order'" (Jakobson, "Linguistics and Poetics," 75). Jakobson's poetics results in a mixed vocabulary of "signal," "meter," "probability," and so on. Despite his enthusiasm for information theory, his preoccupation with code, sig-nal, and probability keeps eliding the problem of writing raised elsewhere by Derrida and by Shannon in his original formulation of Printed English. What is it that prevented the linguist from grasping alphabetic writing as a separate issue from phonemes, syllables, and speech or taking it as a primary order of symbolism—not secondary substitute for speech—in information theory? Derrida would probably answer: logocentrism.

That which had eluded the mind of the linguist did not necessarily es-cape the notice of the molecular biologists of his time.[97] On the occasion of his 1965 inaugural address at the Collège de France, François Jacob spoke of the genetic structure as "a chemical message written along the chromo-somes. The surprise here is that the genetic specificity is written not with ideograms as in Chinese, but with an alphabet like that of French, or rather in Morse."[98] Jacob brought Chinese writing and its "ideograms" inadvertently into the equation only to displace them with French and Morse. But who

97. Colin Cherry appears to have some misgivings about the applicability of the Wiener-Shannon information theory to the fields of knowledge outside of cybernetic engineering. He warns against "the vagueness arising when human beings or biological organisms are regarded as 'communication systems,'" but such misgivings did not stop him from collaborating with Jakobson and Halle. See Colin Cherry, On Human Communication, 40.

98. The original statement is as follows: "L'hérédité est déterminée par un message chimique inscrit le long des chromosomes. La surprise, c'est que la spécifité génétique soit écrit, non avec des idéogrammes comme en chinois, mais avec un alphabet comme en français, ou plutôt en Morse." Jacob, Leçon inaugurale au Collège de France, 22.

said that the genetic code was written in Chinese? Of course, the antiquity of this writing system is irrelevant to the consideration of whether its written symbols ought to be correlated with the speechless and living code of DNA. Jacob disavowed ideographic writing before anyone had a chance to establish positive connections between Chinese writing and the genetic code. This is rather peculiar. His competitive claim with respect to universalism is advanced by reference to the spurious distinction between ideogram and alphabet, hence the collapsing of ideography and Chinese writing as one idea. The real questions Jacob was probably going after are: Which of these writings, Chinese or alphabetic writing, is more universal? Is Morse code phonetic or ideographic? If the dot, dash, and space of Morse code are purely ideographic, how does French live up to ideographic writing and to the universalism of the genetic code?

It was not long before Jacob was made to confront the return of the repressed as his disavowal of Chinese writing began to be taken literally by other molecular biologists. Berkeley molecular biologist Gunther S. Stent, for example, conceived the idea that the genetic code bore striking resemblances to the symbolic system in the ancient Chinese *I Ching* (*Yijing*, in pinyin romanization) or the *Book of Changes* as far as the number game went. He shows that the binary principles of *yang* and *yin*, represented each by an unbroken line and a broken line, combine to form four diagrams and these are combined three at a time to form $4^3 = 64$ hexagrams. Each hexagram, which is read from bottom to top, represents one of sixty-four fundamental aspects of life. The sixty-four triplets of DNA appear to match exactly the sixty-four hexagrams of the *Book of Changes*.[99] This remarkable coincidence has led others to construct elaborate diagrams and tables to correlate the ideograms of the *Book of Changes* with the sixty-four triplets of DNA.[100] But there is nothing mysterious about such a coincidence and it can certainly be explained from a stochastic standpoint because number 64 is the maximum number to be derived from the given pattern of trigram combinations in binary code. Discussion of the number game continues below and in chapter 4.

99. Gunther S. Stent, *The Coming of the Golden Age: A View of the End of Progress*, 64–65.

100. Martin Schönberger, *The I Ching and the Genetic Code: The Hidden Key to Life*, 145. The original German edition is entitled *Verborgener Schlüssel zu Leben*. Another biochemist, Johnson F. Yan, goes out of his way to develop a "I-Gene Cube"—with the word "gene" punning whimsically on the transcribed sound "ching" of the *I Ching*—to illustrate the *I Ching*–DNA congruence. Like Schönberger, Yan sees the "oracle" or divinational aspect as the *I Ching*'s connection to combinatorial and probabilistic mathematics. See Johnson F. Yan, *DNA and the I Ching: The Tao of Life*.

For that reason, one should be surprised to see anyone take these imaginary constructs so seriously. They are mentioned here in connection with Jacob's remark about ideography because they can tell us something about the changing situation of alphabetical writing and its ideographic turn. Pace Jacob, the speechless language of the genetic code makes sense to molecular biologists precisely because it is ideographic. What Stent and the others have done with the ideographs from the *Book of Changes* does not confirm that the genetic code was already inscribed in the ancient Chinese text so much as point to the reflection of the modern network of ideographic signs and their global translatability on molecular biology. We have seen that information theory has introduced a computable network of cryptograms, numbers, spaces, binary digits, algorithms, and so on, and this network of ideographic signs has imposed a new order of universalism and opened the notion of "writing" or "text" to radical interpretations. In the 1960s, molecular biologists in the U.S. and Europe waged a public campaign to convince their audience that what was true of *E. coli* was equally true of an elephant. They were invoking the universalism of genetic programs according to which the genetic code determines both the short programmatic chains of the amoeba or the annelid and the more complex nucleotide sequences and proteins that make a certain *Homo sapiens*, as Derrida has put it. When the whole world is converted to this view, it makes sense to heed Chargaff's cautionary remarks about the arrival of molecular fundamentalism and the beginning of DNA as the new logos of our age.

The point is to raise the question: Has the phonetic alphabet gone postphonetic? When I write "postphonetic," I am not implying that the alphabet has ceased to function phonetically but that it has become nonidentical with itself and is increasingly "othered." The fact that the English alphabet can be phonetically produced no less than the written Chinese characters can be pronounced does not prove that the process of ideographical inscription has not taken place. Just as the 0s and 1s in binary code do not carry the same value as do the 0s and 1s in decimal or other code systems, so the alphabet may continue to look and sound like a phonetic alphabet but simultaneously be estranged from itself. Derrida would object that the phonetic alphabet is always nonidentical with itself, and that "each graphic form may have a double value—ideographic and phonetic" and "this is true of all systems of writing."[101] This may be true of conventional writing systems, but is it still true of the writing of the digital machine? For

101. Derrida, *Of Grammatology*, 89.

instance, where is "the phonetic"—the other side of his double value—located on the cybernetic machine? Can we go on denying the fact that the identity of the phonetic alphabet has changed after the arrival of information theory?

The reason it may not be easy to grasp Printed English and the genetic code as part of the same ideographic movement is that we are accustomed to thinking of alphabetic writing as a phonetic system. But a phonetic system—which is always language specific and always local to some extent—can never be a universal coding system. Only by recasting itself as a postphonetic, ideographic system of inscription—further abstraction from phonetic trappings—could alphabetical writing hope to become the universal system it is. As we have seen, this process has been completed with the assistance of Morse code and with the invention of the twenty-seventh letter in digital media. Today, nonalphabetic writing systems such as Chinese are being progressively subsumed under the same rubric of ideographic inscription of Printed English across the global networks of electronic media. It seems that a new tower of Babel is once again being erected on the promised land of universal communicability. The prospect of universal communicability, as discussed in the next section, is nevertheless dependent on the historical evolution of the number game in what Winston Churchill once called the "empires of the mind."

The Number Game in the Empires of the Mind

Warren Weaver—the powerful gatekeeper of the postwar scientific establishment in the U.S.—saw the importance of information theory and promoted it with enormous energy. He was responsible for bringing out the single-volume edition of Shannon's *Mathematical Theory of Communication*, to which he contributed an introduction. On July 15, 1949, Weaver drafted a memorandum and circulated it among two hundred leading mathematicians, scientists, linguists, and public policy makers in the United States. In it, he laid out the future prospect of the universal English code and machine translation, stating: "It is very tempting to say that a book written in Chinese is simply a book written in English which was coded into the 'Chinese code.' If we have useful methods for solving almost any cryptographic problem, may it not be that with proper interpretation we already have useful methods for translation?"[102] What the author had in mind was

102. Warren Weaver, "Translation," 22.

again Shannon's mathematical theory of communication and his crypto-graphic research during the war. The declassification of this work, Weaver believes, would bear fruits in the field of machine translation and "proba-bly only Shannon himself, at this stage, can be a good judge of the possibili-ties in this direction" (Weaver, "Translation," 22). Shannon was a cautious scientist and frequently warned people about the dangers of overextending the application of information theory to other areas of research such as molecular biology. But he had no control over such applications once the mathematical theory of communication got into public domain and popu-lar media and, after all, he himself made the universalist assertion that "H measures all languages by the common yardstick of binary digits."

Likewise, Wiener expressed some strong reservations about machine translation, and his objection is mentioned and cited by Weaver. In a letter dated April 30, 1947, Wiener wrote: "I frankly am afraid the boundaries of words in different languages are too vague and the emotional and interna-tional connotations are too extensive to make any quasimechanical trans-lation scheme very hopeful." He then made an interesting comment on Basic English, which was the 850-word English invented and promoted by C. K. Ogden and I. A. Richards before World War II and popularized during the war. Wiener wrote: "I will admit that basic English seems to indicate that we can go further than we have generally done in the mechanization of speech, but you must remember that in certain respects basic English is the reverse of mechanical and throws upon such words as *get* a burden which is much greater than most words carry in conventional English. At the present time, the mechanization of language, beyond such a stage as the design of photoelectric reading opportunities for the blind, seems very premature . . ." (Weaver, "Translation," 18).

In his reply on May 9, 1947, Weaver wrote: "I am disappointed but not surprised by your comments on the translation problem. The difficulty you mention concerning Basic seems to me to have a rather easy answer." Ap-parently, Weaver's assessment of the nature of Basic English was rather different from how Wiener saw it, for he argued: "It is, of course, true that Basic puts multiple use on an action verb such as *get*. But, even so, the two-word combinations such as *get up, get over, get back,* etc., are, in Basic, not really very numerous. Suppose we take a vocabulary of 2,000 words, and admit for good measure all the two-word combinations as if they were single words. The vocabulary is still only four million; and that is not so formidable a number to a modern computer, is it?" (Weaver, "Translation," 18). Weaver and Wiener saw Basic English as two different things. The former approached it as a statistical system, whereas Wiener's reference to "emotional and international connotations" suggests a largely semantic understanding of Basic.

Unshaken in his conviction, Weaver was determined to pursue his project of universal communicability through machine translation. After the initial failure to enlist Wiener's help, he found his allies among a group of linguists and computer engineers like Kenneth Locke, Erwin Reifler, Victor Yngve, and Andrew Booth, who shared his vision and embarked on the first machine translation project with him. Rita Raley's research has surveyed the rich literature from half a century's developments in machine translation that need not be reiterated here. Suffice it to mention that Systran, a company that has pioneered in developing the software program SYSTRAN Professional Premium 5.0., now powers AltaVista's popular translation website called "Babelfish" and supplies machine translation services to the European Union and the U.S. Intelligence Community for internal system use. SYSTRAN is also relevant to our discussion of Printed English in the sense that it treats English as the "relay language" through which a text in German, for example, must pass to be translated into another European language, say, Italian.[103]

What I. A. Richards once said about the potentials of Basic English in 1935 aptly describes the nature of Weaver's postwar project in its universalist aspirations: "The only way in which false and misleading *approximations* to Western units of meaning with Chinese 'equivalents' can be avoided is by giving these meanings through, and together with, an apparatus for comparing meanings—through an explicit analytic language."[104] In Richards's time, this apparatus or analytical language was Basic English, but, with the introduction of information theory, that task has since devolved upon Printed English. What could be more analytical than a binary coding system? For the first time, Printed English has achieved the status of universal ideography with respect to which all other languages of the world become vernacular translations.

Weaver's optimism about the computer's ability to process four million words may have been vindicated by the limited progress made in contemporary MT (machine translation) and MAT (machine-aided translation) programs. However, by no means has the progress resolved the ambiguous

---

103. See Rita Raley, "Machine Translation and Global English," 311. The current development in translation tools such as Google Translation relies on the sheer power of computation that was not available in Weaver's time.

104. I. A. Richards, *Basic in Teaching: East and West*, 47.

status of Basic English as a semantic construct or as a statistical system. This conceptual point, which emerged in the Weaver-Wiener correspondences on machine translation, is integral to how we regard the historical linkage between Printed English and Basic English. The rigor of his mathematical theorems notwithstanding, we will see below that Shannon was not the first to develop a systematic approach to the English language as a statistical system.

Before taking up the subject of Basic English, it is worth mentioning that those of the intellectual elite whose work was closely associated with Basic English and those who worked in cybernetics moved in some of the same circles of the Anglo-American academic establishment. Shannon had been Norbert Wiener's student at MIT and became acquainted with Alan Turing through their wartime cryptographic collaboration at Bell Labs and at Princeton.[105] Jakobson was invited to the fifth Macy Conference in 1948 and, as mentioned earlier, got his copy of Shannon and Weaver's *Mathematical Theory of Communication* from Weaver himself in 1949. Wiener had known C. K. Ogden and I. A. Richards as early as 1914, when the latter were beginning work on *The Meaning of Meaning*.[106] The renowned Chinese linguist Y. R. Chao (Yuanren Zhao), who had studied at Harvard and returned to teach at Tsinghua University in Beijing in the 1930s, helped Richards launch his Basic English campaign in China. Chao, who was friends with Wiener and became a professor at UC Berkeley after the war, attended the tenth and last meeting of the Macy Conference on April 22–24, 1953. Like Shannon, who attended the same meeting, Chao was the invited guest of the core cybernetics group and presented a fascinating paper on "Meaning in Language and How It Is Acquired." Richards was invited to the eighth Macy Conference on March 15–16, 1951, and gave a paper called "Communication between Men: Meaning of Language." He was in the audience when Shannon demonstrated his famous mechanical maze-solving mouse Theseus.[107] Chao's and Richards's participation in the Macy Conferences marked the historic encounter of Basic English, cybernetics, and information theory, all within the same generation.[108]

105. See Andrew Hodges, *Alan Turing: The Enigma*.

106. Pesi Rustom Masani, *Norbert Wiener, 1894–1964*, 56.

107. For a list of all participants in each of the Macy Conferences on cybernetics, see Steve J. Heims, *The Cybernetics Group*, 285–86. See also my discussion of Richards, Chao, and the Macy Conference in the next chapter.

108. Richards's relationship with Chao and his adventures in China are well researched by John Paul Russo in *I. A. Richards: His Life and Work*, 397–429.

2

When C. K. Ogden first devised Basic English in 1929, the reduced vocabulary of 850 words with a simplified grammar was intended to provide
a sound statistical basis for a universal and international second language.
Through Ogden and I. A. Richards's tireless proselytizing efforts around the
world, the Basic English movement took off and eventually received warm
endorsements from the official establishment of Britain and the United
States. Richards was a literary scholar who founded practical criticism in
literary studies and is also credited with inventing the New Criticism. He
and Ogden coauthored *The Meaning of Meaning*, and he became the most
energetic champion of Basic in America and China. While teaching at Tsinghua University intermittently from early 1929 through the outbreak of
the war, Richards worked hard to persuade the Ministry of Education in
the Republic of China to adopt Basic in the country's high school system.
Working with his friends and educators in Beijing, he came very close to
implementing a course of Basic English in China until Japan's invasion and
bombing interrupted his effort.[109]

In July 1943, Winston Churchill wrote: "I am very interested in the
question of Basic English. The widespread use of this would be a gain to
us far more durable and fruitful than the annexation of great provinces.
It would also fit in with my ideas of closer union with the United States
by making it even more worth while to belong to the English-speaking
club."[110] Churchill instructed the British cabinet to set up a committee of
ministers to study and report on Basic English. The Minister of Information, the Colonial Secretary, and the President of the Board of Education
were also involved in this effort. When Churchill met Roosevelt at Quebec
in 1943, they discussed the future possibilities of Basic English. According to a White House memo, Roosevelt was keen on the notion of turning
Basic English into an international lingua franca so English could replace
French as a "language of diplomacy."[111]

The British prime minister became a goodwill ambassador for Basic
when he delivered a speech at Harvard University on September 6, 1943.
Churchill urged Americans to understand that "the empires of the future
are the empires of the mind" and commended the Harvard Commission on
English Language Studies for its distinguished service in introducing Basic

---

109. John Paul Russo, *I. A. Richards: His Life and Work*, 420. For recent critiques of the Basic
English project in China, see Rodney Koeneke, *Empires of the Mind: I. A. Richards and Basic English
in China, 1929–1979*, and Q. S. Tong, "The Bathos of a Universalism, I. A. Richards and His Basic
English."

110. See appendix B in Ogden, *Basic English, International Second Language*, 111.

111. Roosevelt's memo of June 5, 1944, to the Secretary of State (ibid.,115).

in Latin America.[112] In the midst of leading a war with fascist Germany, Churchill exhibited a timely understanding of the value of language for empire building, and his vision did not go unheeded in popular American media. On October 18, 1943, *Life* magazine published an article called "Basic English: A Globalanguage" by Lincoln Barnett. In case one wonders how his readers or even today's readers would take to the unwieldy coinage "globalanguage," Barnett's message about "a supra-national language—for the communication of all men on the face of a rapidly shrinking globe" was unequivocally conveyed.[113] The author notes that the advocates of Basic "hold nothing in common with the linguistic imperialism of those Nazi savants who awaited the day when English would become 'a minor Germanic dialect of no world importance'" (57–58). But as far as Roosevelt's vision was concerned, it was more a matter of competing with his French-speaking allies than with the Germans.

The Anglo-American imperialist agenda of Basic is visibly written upon the surface of the acronym "BASIC," which is taken to mean British, American, Scientific, International, and Commercial. I. A. Richards's biographer John Paul Russo mentions that by 1920 English was spoken by 300 million people and was the language of government of 500 million. These large numbers are repeatedly used by Ogden and Richards to justify their promotion of Basic as the world's lingua franca. Curiously, the opposite argument, namely that English was *not* the medium of the majority of the world's population is also enlisted to help justify Basic. Richards writes: "Two thirds of us on this planet are, at the time of writing, analphabetics. Of the 2,200,000,000 people now breathing, some 1,500,000,000 cannot read at all or read some nonalphabetic script. This is not time or place in which to argue the merits of the invention of alphabetic writing. Suffice it that if there is to be any truly world-wide communication between peoples within a foreseeable future, it will be in some language which will be alphabetic. It could be through our life time and through English."[114] Finally, English is privileged not because it is spoken by a sizable percentage of the world's population belonging to the British Empire, but rather because it is fast becoming the medium of science and world business and is more-over widely disseminated by radio, motion pictures, advertising, aviation,

112. Churchill's speech was given on September 6, 1943. An extract of the speech is included in appendix B in Ogden, *Basic English, International Second Language*, 112–13. The original text was published in the London *Times*, September 8, 1943.

113. Lincoln Barnett, "Basic English: A Globalanguage," 57.

114. Richards, "Responsibilities in the Teaching of English," 93. This essay was originally published in 1947 in *Essays and Studies by Members of the English Association, the 1947 Annual*.

and telecommunication.[115] Worldwide communication, therefore, is the raison d'être of Basic, which explains why Richards relied on media technologies such as illustrated books, television, sound recording, and film to get his message out. His successful collaboration with Walt Disney is reflected in this photo taken in 1943 (Fig. 8), showing illustrated Basic phrases in the cartoons on the wall.[116]

Richards developed the stick figure books in language teaching as well as the Language through Picture series in collaboration with Christine Gibson. These innovative audiovisual pedagogical methods greatly impressed the educators, writers, and filmmakers of the time. Richards spent six weeks at the Walt Disney Studio to learn the basics of cartoon drawing (Russo, 467). The first film he helped make was a ten-minute pilot and the next was *Basic English Teaching Pictures*, which consisted of six ten-minute reels of sound motion picture employing live actors. The film was directed by Len Lye and produced by March of Time. Helen Vendler has suggested that a television program like *Sesame Street* would have not seen the light of day had it not been for Richards's efforts in popularizing Basic through film.[117]

To Ogden, the architect of Basic, the practicalities of simplified language learning for international commerce and politics were only some of the reasons but not the only ones for promoting Basic. He saw simultaneous advances in a number of statistical domains as the immediate theoretical impetus for the project:

The system of numbers.
The metric system.
The measurement of latitude and longitude.
Mathematical symbols.
Chemical formulae.
Time and the calendar.
Notation in music.[118]

"The two main reasons for making English the basis of a universal language," Ogden argues, "are (1) the statistical considerations set forth above, and (2) the fact that English is the only major language in which the analyt-

115. John Paul Russo, *I. A. Richards*, 397. For the relationship between Basic and Voice of America, see Yunte Huang, "Basic English, Chinglish, and Translocal Dialect."
116. See I. A. Richards, "English Language Teaching Films and Their Use in Teacher Training," 1–7.
117. Helen Vendler, "I. A. Richards at Harvard."
118. C. K. Ogden, *Basic English: International Second Language*, 14.

Figure 8. I. A. Richards collaborating with the Disney Studios in 1943 using motion pictures to teach Basic English. From Lincoln Barnett, "Basic English: A Globalanguage," *Life*, 8 October 1943. Photograph by Mark Kauffman. Courtesy Time & Life Pictures / Getty Images.

ical tendency has gone far enough for purposes of simplification" (15). This view was a novel idea when Ogden reduced the English vocabulary to 850 words. What is new here is not his imagining of a universal language, which may be traced back to the seventeenth century if not earlier, but rather a conception of English as a statistical system. It was not by accident that

Ogden became the English translator of Ludwig Wittgenstein's *Tractatus Logico-Philosophicus*, in which the philosopher demonstrates a logical system of numbered propositions to illustrate their nested interrelations.[119]

We have seen how Shannon, who was deeply immersed in cryptography in World War II on the American side, took this logical and statistical notion of language a step further to launch a new discipline. Norbert Wiener suggested in *Cybernetics* that Shannon, R. A. Fisher, and he himself had begun at around the same time to approach the message as "a discrete or continuous sequence of measurable events distributed in time—precisely what is called a time series by the statisticians" and that "the unit amount of information was that transmitted as a single decision between equally probable alternatives."[120] In addition, he draws our attention to the fact that the statistical definition of "message" was a relative latecomer in communication engineering; scientists had been using statistical mechanics in nearly every branch of science for more than a century.

Of course, that is not the whole story. Basic English assumes the primacy of the printed word in the requirement that the special arrangement of the 850 words be visual, legible, and easily portable. In the opening paragraph of *Basic English*, Ogden asserts that

It is clear that the problem of a universal language would have been solved if it were possible to say all that we normally desire to say with no more words than can be made *easily legible to the naked eye, in column form, on the back of a sheet of notepaper*. The fact, therefore, that it is possible to say almost everything we normally desire to say with the *850 words on the endpapers, which occupy about three-quarters of the space on the back of an ordinary sheet of business notepaper*, makes Basic English something more than a mere educational experiment.[121] (my emphasis)

How does the act of "saying" things involve a sheet of notepaper or the naked eye except when the "saying" stands for "reading"? The mention of the

119. See Ludwig Wittgenstein, *Tractatus Logico-Philosophicus*, trans. C. K. Ogden, 8. Ogden showed more appreciation for the significance of Wittgenstein's work than the other publishers and editors Wittgenstein had approached in Germany and England. After rejection by the Cambridge University Press, the *Tractatus Logico-Philosophicus* found a sympathetic ear in C. K. Ogden, who, as the general editor of a well-known scholarly series the International Library of Psychology, Philosophy and Scientific Method, translated and published the book with Kegan Paul.

120. Wiener, *Cybernetics: or Control and Communication in the Animal and the Machine*, 2nd ed., 8–9, 10.

121. Ogden, *Basic English, International Second Language*, 5.

column form and business notepaper no doubt implies the overall practical purposes that Basic English is supposed to serve, but it also raises some
theoretical questions about the status of the printed word. Here Ogden
does not specify whether he has in mind the written or printed word. The
latter, at least in the conventional sense, is strongly implied: for example,
the author quotes approvingly the report printed in the *Daily Mail*: "The
whole vocabulary of this Basic English can be printed comfortably on a
sheet of notepaper" as we see at a glance in this folded seven- by ten-inch
insert in the 1935 edition of Basic (Fig. 9).[122]

Identical inserts are printed in numerous other pocket-size editions of
Basic books and exhibit little difference from commonplace typescripts.
Compared with the Lagado writing machine whose numerical matrix implies a larger vocabulary of 1,024 words, the 850-word Basic would have required a smaller and more efficient mechanism. This is by no means an arbitrary comparison because prior to the invention of the computer, Ogden's
statistical treatment of the vocabulary already presupposed a technological
view of language. Notice that when the parts of speech are reclassified or renamed to conform to that view—no verbs and only "operators," nouns being
"things," adjectives being "qualities," prepositions being "directives"—Basic
English essentially aligns itself with the system of numbers, the metric system, and all the other aforementioned systems. The little figure waving his
arms to indicate the simple meaning of each operator might have stepped
out of the pages of popular cartoon books depicting the actions of military
signal corps using Morse code (Fig. 10). Fig. 11 transforms the prepositions governing discursive (human/space) situations into purely geometric
relations.

Ogden and Richards were absolutely convinced that human societies
were moving in the direction of universal communicability and that the
technological thinking in Basic would facilitate the process of global "debabelization." This optimism about universal communication was shared
by writers, linguists, and statisticians as well as governments, business cor-
porations, and educators. Ezra Pound wrote a favorable review of Ogden's
Debabelization in 1935, stating that "if a novelist can survive translation
into basic, there is something solid under his language." Basic was deemed
obviously "superior to the 'Times' fog or 'Manchester Guardian' twitter."[123]
We do not know to what extent Ogden followed the work of Alan Turing's

122. C. K Ogden, *Debabelization*, 76.
123. See Ezra Pound, "Debabelization and Ogden," 411. See also Pound's letter on January 28,
1935, to Ogden in Pound, *Selected Letters: 1907–1941*, 265–66.

BASIC ENGLISH

OPERATIONS, ETC. 100	THINGS		QUALITIES		EXAMPLES OF WORD ORDER
	400 General	200 Pictured	100 General	50 Opposites	

OPERATIONS 100

COME, GET, GIVE, GO, KEEP, LET, MAKE, PUT, SEEM, TAKE, BE, DO, HAVE, SAY, SEE, SEND, MAY, WILL, ABOUT, ACROSS, AFTER, AGAINST, AMONG, AT, BEFORE, BETWEEN, BY, DOWN, FROM, IN, OFF, ON, OVER, THROUGH, TO, UNDER, UP, WITH, AS, FOR, OF, TILL, THAN, A, THE, ALL, ANY, EVERY, NO, OTHER, SOME, SUCH, THAT, THIS, I, HE, YOU, WHO, AND, BECAUSE, BUT, OR, IF, THOUGH, WHILE, HOW, WHEN, WHERE, WHY, AGAIN, EVER, FAR, FORWARD, HERE, NEAR, NOW, OUT, STILL, THEN, THERE, TOGETHER, WELL, ALMOST, ENOUGH, EVEN, LITTLE, MUCH, NOT, ONLY, QUITE, SO, VERY, TOMORROW, YESTERDAY, NORTH, SOUTH, EAST, WEST, PLEASE, YES

THINGS — 400 General

ACCOUNT, ACT, ADDITION, ADJUSTMENT, ADVERTISEMENT, AGREEMENT, AIR, AMOUNT, AMUSEMENT, ANIMAL, ANSWER, APPARATUS, APPROVAL, ARGUMENT, ART, ATTACK, ATTEMPT, ATTENTION, ATTRACTION, AUTHORITY, BACK, BALANCE, BASE, BEHAVIOUR, BELIEF, BIRTH, BIT, BITE, BLOOD, BLOW, BODY, BRASS, BREAD, BREATH, BROTHER, BUILDING, BURN, BURST, BUSINESS, BUTTER, CANVAS, CARE, CAUSE, CHALK, CHANCE, CHANGE, CLOTH, COAL, COLOUR, COMFORT, COMMITTEE, COMPANY, COMPARISON, COMPETITION, CONDITION, CONNECTION, CONTROL, COOK, COPPER, COPY, CORK, COTTON, COUGH, COUNTRY, COVER, CRACK, CREDIT, CRIME, CRUSH, CRY, CURRENT, CURVE, DAMAGE, DANGER, DAUGHTER, DAY, DEATH, DEBT, DECISION, DEGREE, DESIGN, DESIRE, DESTRUCTION, DETAIL, DEVELOPMENT, DIGESTION, DIRECTION, DISCOVERY, DISCUSSION, DISEASE, DISGUST, DISTANCE, DISTRIBUTION, DIVISION, DOUBT, DRINK, DRIVING, DUST, EARTH, EDGE

EDUCATION, EFFECT, END, ERROR, EVENT, EXAMPLE, EXCHANGE, EXISTENCE, EXPANSION, EXPERIENCE, EXPERT, FACT, FALL, FAMILY, FATHER, FEAR, FEELING, FICTION, FIELD, FIGHT, FIRE, FLAME, FLIGHT, FLOWER, FOLD, FOOD, FORCE, FORM, FRIEND, FRONT, FRUIT, GLASS, GOLD, GOVERNMENT, GRAIN, GRASS, GRIP, GROUP, GROWTH, GUIDE, HARBOUR, HARMONY, HATE, HEARING, HEAT, HELP, HISTORY, HOLE, HOPE, HOUR, HUMOUR, ICE, IDEA, IMPULSE, INCREASE, INDUSTRY, INK, INSECT, INSTRUMENT, INSURANCE, INTEREST, INVENTION, IRON, JELLY, JOIN, JOURNEY, JUDGE, JUMP, KICK, KISS, KNOWLEDGE, LAND, LANGUAGE, LAUGH, LAW, LEAD, LEARNING, LEATHER, LETTER, LEVEL, LIFT, LIGHT, LIMIT, LINEN, LIQUID, LIST, LOOK, LOSS, LOVE, MACHINE, MAN, MANAGER, MARK, MARKET, MASS, MEAL, MEASURE, MEAT, MEETING, MEMORY

METAL, MIDDLE, MILK, MIND, MINE, MINUTE, MIST, MONEY, MONTH, MORNING, MOTHER, MOTION, MOUNTAIN, MOVE, MUSIC, NAME, NATION, NEED, NEWS, NIGHT, NOISE, NOTE, NUMBER, OBSERVATION, OFFER, OIL, OPERATION, OPINION, ORDER, ORGANIZATION, ORNAMENT, OWNER, PAGE, PAIN, PAINT, PAPER, PART, PASTE, PAYMENT, PEACE, PERSON, PLACE, PLANT, PLAY, PLEASURE, POINT, POISON, POLISH, PORTER, POSITION, POWDER, POWER, PRICE, PRINT, PROCESS, PRODUCE, PROFIT, PROPERTY, PROSE, PROTEST, PULL, PUNISHMENT, PURPOSE, PUSH, QUALITY, QUESTION, RAIN, RANGE, RATE, RAY, REACTION, READING, REASON, RECORD, REGRET, RELATION, RELIGION, REPRESENTATIVE, REQUEST, RESPECT, REST, REWARD, RHYTHM, RICE, RIVER, ROAD, ROLL, ROOM, RUB, RULE, RUN, SALT, SAND, SCALE, SCIENCE, SEA, SEAT, SECRETARY, SELECTION, SELF

SENSE, SERVANT, SEX, SHADE, SHAKE, SHAME, SHOCK, SIDE, SIGN, SILK, SILVER, SISTER, SIZE, SKY, SLEEP, SLIP, SLOPE, SMASH, SMELL, SMILE, SMOKE, SNEEZE, SNOW, SOAP, SOCIETY, SON, SONG, SORT, SOUND, SOUP, SPACE, STAGE, START, STATEMENT, STEAM, STEEL, STEP, STITCH, STONE, STOP, STORY, STRETCH, STRUCTURE, SUBSTANCE, SUGAR, SUGGESTION, SUMMER, SUPPORT, SURPRISE, SWIM, SYSTEM, TALK, TASTE, TAX, TEACHING, TENDENCY, TEST, THEORY, THING, THOUGHT, THUNDER, TIME, TIN, TOP, TOUCH, TRADE, TRANSPORT, TRICK, TROUBLE, TURN, TWIST, UNIT, USE, VALUE, VERSE, VESSEL, VIEW, VOICE, WALK, WAR, WASH, WASTE, WATER, WAVE, WAX, WAY, WEATHER, WEEK, WEIGHT, WIND, WINE, WINTER, WOMAN, WOOD, WOOL, WORD, WORK, WOUND, WRITING, YEAR

THINGS — 200 Pictured

ANGLE, ANT, APPLE, ARCH, ARM, ARMY, BABY, BAG, BALL, BAND, BASIN, BASKET, BATH, BED, BEE, BELL, BERRY, BIRD, BLADE, BOARD, BOAT, BONE, BOOK, BOOT, BOTTLE, BOX, BOY, BRAIN, BRAKE, BRANCH, BRICK, BRIDGE, BRUSH, BUCKET, BULB, BUTTON, CAKE, CAMERA, CARD, CART, CARRIAGE, CAT, CHAIN, CHEESE, CHEST, CHIN, CHURCH, CIRCLE, CLOCK, CLOUD, COAT, COLLAR, COMB, CORD, COW, CUP, CURTAIN, CUSHION, DOG, DOOR, DRAIN, DRAWER, DRESS, DROP, EAR, EGG, ENGINE, EYE, FACE, FARM, FEATHER, FINGER, FISH, FLAG, FLOOR, FLY, FOOT, FORK, FOWL, FRAME, GARDEN, GIRL, GLOVE, GOAT, GUN, HAIR, HAMMER, HAND, HAT, HEAD, HEART, HOOK, HORN, HORSE, HOSPITAL, HOUSE, ISLAND, JEWEL, KETTLE, KEY

KNEE, KNIFE, KNOT, LEAF, LEG, LIBRARY, LINE, LIP, LOCK, MAP, MATCH, MONKEY, MOON, MOUTH, MUSCLE, NAIL, NECK, NEEDLE, NERVE, NET, NOSE, NUT, OFFICE, ORANGE, OVEN, PARCEL, PEN, PENCIL, PICTURE, PIG, PIN, PIPE, PLANE, PLATE, PLOUGH, POCKET, POT, PRISON, PUMP, RAIL, RAT, RECEIPT, RING, ROD, ROOF, ROOT, SAIL, SCHOOL, SCISSORS, SCREW, SEED, SHEEP, SHELF, SHIP, SHIRT, SHOE, SKIN, SKIRT, SNAKE, SOCK, SPADE, SPONGE, SPOON, SPRING, SQUARE, STAMP, STAR, STATION, STEM, STICK, STOCKING, STOMACH, STORE, STREET, SUN, TABLE, TAIL, THREAD, THROAT, THUMB, TICKET, TOE, TONGUE, TOOTH, TOWN, TRAIN, TRAY, TREE, TROUSERS, UMBRELLA, WALL, WATCH, WHEEL, WHIP, WHISTLE, WINDOW, WING, WIRE, WORM

QUALITIES — 100 General

ABLE, ACID, ANGRY, AUTOMATIC, BEAUTIFUL, BLACK, BOILING, BRIGHT, BROKEN, BROWN, CHEAP, CHEMICAL, CHIEF, CLEAN, CLEAR, COMMON, COMPLEX, CONSCIOUS, CUT, DEEP, DEPENDENT, EARLY, ELASTIC, ELECTRIC, EQUAL, FAT, FERTILE, FIRST, FIXED, FLAT, FREE, FREQUENT, FULL, GENERAL, GOOD, GREAT, GREY, HANGING, HAPPY, HARD, HEALTHY, HIGH, HOLLOW, IMPORTANT, KIND, LIKE, LIVING, LONG, MALE, MARRIED, MATERIAL, MEDICAL, MILITARY, NATURAL, NECESSARY, NEW, NORMAL, OPEN, PARALLEL, PAST, PHYSICAL, POLITICAL, POOR, POSSIBLE, PRESENT, PRIVATE, PROBABLE, QUICK, QUIET, READY, RED, REGULAR, RESPONSIBLE, RIGHT, ROUND, SAME, SECOND, SEPARATE, SERIOUS, SHARP, SMOOTH, STICKY, STIFF, STRAIGHT, STRONG, SUDDEN, SWEET, TALL, THICK, TIGHT, TIRED, TRUE, VIOLENT, WAITING, WARM, WET, WIDE, WISE, YELLOW, YOUNG

QUALITIES — 50 Opposites

AWAKE, BAD, BENT, BITTER, BLUE, CERTAIN, COLD, COMPLETE, CRUEL, DARK, DEAD, DEAR, DELICATE, DIFFERENT, DIRTY, DRY, FALSE, FEEBLE, FEMALE, FOOLISH, FUTURE, GREEN, ILL, LAST, LATE, LEFT, LOOSE, LOUD, LOW, MIXED, NARROW, OLD, OPPOSITE, PUBLIC, ROUGH, SAD, SAFE, SECRET, SHORT, SHUT, SIMPLE, SLOW, SMALL, SOFT, SOLID, SPECIAL, STRANGE, THIN, WHITE, WRONG

EXAMPLES OF WORD ORDER

THE, CAMERA, MAN, WHO, MADE, AN, ATTEMPT, TO, TAKE, A, MOVING, PICTURE, OF, THE, SOCIETY, WOMEN, THEY, GOT, THEIR, HATS, OFF, DID, NOT, GET, OFF, THE, SHIP, TILL, IT, WAS, QUESTIONED, BY, THE, POLICE.

WE, WILL, GIVE, SIMPLE, RULES, TO, YOU, NOW.

NO 'VERBS'

IT IS POSSIBLE TO GET ALL THESE WORDS ON THE BACK OF A BIT OF NOTEPAPER BECAUSE THERE ARE NO 'VERBS' IN BASIC ENGLISH.

RULES

ADDITION OF 'S' TO THINGS WHEN THERE IS MORE THAN ONE

ENDINGS IN 'ER', 'ING', 'ED' FROM 300 NAMES OF THINGS

'LY' FORMS FROM QUALITIES

DEGREE WITH 'MORE' AND 'MOST'

QUESTIONS BY CHANGE OF ORDER, AND 'DO'

FORM-CHANGES IN NAMES OF ACTS, AND 'THAT', 'THIS', 'I', 'HE', 'YOU', 'WHO', AS IN NORMAL ENGLISH

MEASURES, NUMBERS, DAYS, MONTHS AND THE INTERNATIONAL WORDS IN ENGLISH FORM.

THE ORTHOLOGICAL INSTITUTE 10 KING'S PARADE, CAMBRIDGE, ENGLAND.

Figure 9. The 850-word vocabulary. From C. K. Ogden, *Basic English: A General Introduction with Rules and Grammar* (London: Kegan Paul, Trench, Trubner, 1935).

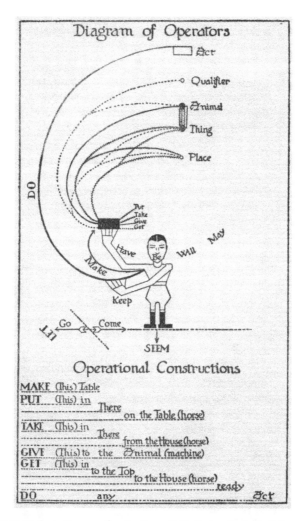

Figure 10. C. K. Ogden's diagram of verbs. From C. K. Ogden, *Basic English: A General Introduction with Rules and Grammar* (London: Kegan Paul, Trench, Trubner, 1935), 56.

universal discrete machine. The controversies surrounding Turing's notion of a thinking machine at the University of Cambridge would change what people have subsequently thought of meaning, language, writing, and even thought itself. Ogden may or may not have foreseen the development of the universal discrete machine, but there is no doubt that he anticipated the arrival of someone like Shannon. "The past ten years have introduced a new voice into all discussions of the international future," declared Ogden

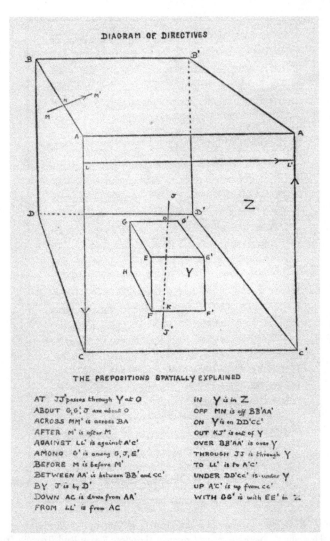

Figure 11. C. K. Ogden's diagram of prepositions. From C. K. Ogden, *Basic English: A General Introduction with Rules and Grammar* (London: Kegan Paul, Trench, Trubner, 1935), 62.

in 1931, "It is the business of the Inter-linguist to bring it home to the world that *the electrical engineer* has today brought the World into the home. International Radio, international Talkies, international Telephone—these are to be the decisive factors in this coming century" (my emphasis).[124] These were the areas of communication technology in which the electrical engineer Shannon would specialize at Bell Labs and produce the kind of work that led eventually to the invention of information theory. Basic English foretold the coming of information technology and Printed English.

124. Ogden, *Debabelization*, 71.

3 Sense and Nonsense in the Psychic Machine

> These paper wounds, four in type, were gradually and correctly understood
> to mean stop, please stop, do please stop, and O do please stop respec-
> tively, and following up their one true clue, the circumflexous wall of a
> singleminded men's asylum, accentuated by bi tso fb rok engl a ssan dspl
> itch ina, –Yard inquiries pointed out –> that they ad bîn "provoked" ay Λ
> fork, of à grave Brofèsor; àth é's Brèak–fast– table; ;acùtely profèššionally
> *piquéd*, to=introdùce a notion of time [ùpon à plane (?) sù " fàçe'e'] by
> pùnct! ingh oles (sic) in iSpace?!
>
> James Joyce, *Finnegans Wake*

It can be shown that information theory and Printed English are
the logical outcomes of the earlier crossbreeding of ideas in the
literary, psychoanalytic, and scientific experiments. As demonstrated in the preceding chapter, the statistical dimension of the
850-word Basic was Ogden's foremost concern from the start. This
no doubt justifies Shannon's treatment of Basic and *Finnegans Wake*
as the extreme opposites of redundancy and entropy in the English language. What I explore next is the way in which Shannon
established the conceptual linkages among Basic, *Finnegans Wake*,
the psychic machine, and the mathematical constructs which he
developed for information theory.

In *The Mathematical Theory of Communication,* Shannon demonstrates that the extreme opposites of redundancy and entropy are each "represented by Basic English and by James Joyce's book *Finnegans Wake.*"[1] Without mentioning C. K. Ogden or I. A. Richards by name, he explains that the Basic English vocabulary "is limited to 850 words and the redundancy is very high. This is reflected in the expansion that occurs when a passage is translated into Basic English. Joyce on the other hand enlarges the vocabulary and is alleged to achieve a compression of semantic content" (56). The expansion of which Shannon speaks was, indeed, regularly and systematically carried out by Ogden and Richards in the 1930s. Those texts were wide ranging and included the Bible (Genesis 1; I Samuel 15; Job 1, 2; Matthew 2; Mark 2) and ranged from high modernist literature to popular texts, such as Louisa May Alcott's *Little Women,* George Bernard Shaw's *Arms and the Man,* Robert Louis Stevenson's *Treasure Island,* and so on. In the appendixes to *Basic English,* Ogden makes a point of highlighting some of the noteworthy samples, literary as well as scientific, that have been converted or expanded from the original English texts to the 850-word Basic.

C. K. Ogden shows a strong interest in the statistics of acquired vocabularies from different classes and ethnolinguistic groups around the world. The samples, randomly chosen, are given in the following estimate: "The 'normal vocabulary of the average man' hovers between the alleged 300 words of the Somersetshire farmer, the 4,000 of President Wilson's State Papers, the 7,000 of the Japanese diplomat, the 12,000 of the Eskimo fisherman or the average undergraduate, the 30,000 of Sir Vade Mecum, C.V.O. at Geneva, and the 250,000 of a James Joyce."[2] This last number is the most impressive. It indicates that his grasp of the implications of Joyce's literary experiments already anticipated the way in which the electric engineer Shannon would make use of the same statistics from Joyce and Ogden's own Basic in postwar years.

Shannon's mention of Joyce, on the other hand, may strike literary scholars as a bit unusual. The first reaction would be skepticism: How substantial is the connection here? Although we are not told which specific passages from *Finnegans Wake* were actually assigned to the human subjects who participated in Shannon's guessing games or whether they were assigned at all, Joyce's work has been singled out by Shannon as an extreme case to illustrate the lower threshold of redundancy within the range of stochastic possibilities allowed by English prose. There is no reason why

1. Shannon and Weaver, *The Mathematical Theory of Communication,* 56.
2. C. K. Ogden, *Basic English: International Second Language,* 9.

literary scholars should be alarmed by the manner in which Shannon approached Joyce or be put off by his lack of interest in the semantic content of Joyce's text. For all intents and purposes, the mathematician's attention was focused on the stochastic structure of the prose he discovered in *Finnegans Wake*. This had direct implications for the limits of Printed English, which he was analyzing, and raised interesting questions about the nature of alphabetical writing that would have interested Joyce himself. We should ask, for example, Is the stochastic approach a legitimate one with respect to a high modernist text? Does Shannon's mathematical interest throw unexpected light on some aspects of Joyce's literary experiment that have heretofore been suppressed in our readings? Following the discussion of the statistical recasting of English writing from Basic and information theory in chapter 2, we now reflect on the problem of sense and nonsense between the communication machine and the psychic machine and offer an interpretation of Joyce's approach to alphabetical writing in *Finnegans Wake*.

Finnegans Wake: A Hypermnesiac Machine?

To literary critics and ordinary readers, James Joyce's *Finnegans Wake* borders on the illegible. Numerous commentaries and compendia have been published to help the reader plod along if they are curious enough to persist through the reading. But writers, literary critics, and college students are not the only ones who read James Joyce. Many others like Ogden, Shannon, and Pierce have also been fascinated and challenged by the bold experiments they discover in *Finnegans Wake*. These experiments range from multilingual verbal puns to exuberant nonsense or barely legible words such as "alaphbedic," "televisible," "iSpace," "verbivocovisual," and so on. It seems that literary theory is still trying to catch up with this modernist engineer *avant la lettre* of a cyberspace of outrageous signs and letter sequences.[3] The strange incongruence between the eminence of this English writer and the poorly understood projects he and his fellow writers and scientists mounted at the height of modernism has been striking and should concern us in this study.

---

3. Donald F. Theall, for instance, discusses in great detail how Joyce anticipated the age of the microcomputer and the micro's relationship with telecommunication in *Beyond the Word: Reconstructing Sense in the Joyce Era of Technology, Culture, and Communication*. See also Louis Armand, *Technē: James Joyce, Hypertext & Technology*; Darren Tofts and Murray McKeich, *Memory Trade: A Prehistory of Cyberculture*; and Thomas Jackson Rice, *Joyce, Chaos, and Complexity*.

Derrida, for example, confessed in 1982 that he had been grappling with Joyce for nearly twenty-five to thirty years and that his "Plato's Pharmacy" was a reading of *Finnegans Wake*. Conversely, the same essay was also anticipated and read "in advance by *Finnegans Wake*, in its wake, or its lineage, at the very moment that 'La Pharmacie de Platon' was itself presenting itself as a reading-head or principle of decipherment (in short another software) for a possible understanding of *Finnegans Wake*."[4] Inasmuch as Derrida wrote in the wake of Mallarmé, Stein, Pound, and Joyce, the "wake" cannot but introduce a measure of indebtedness and all that is to come in the post-Joycean modernist lineage. It is interesting that the figure of the "reading-head" and "software" translates a textual indebtedness into a definitive technological procedure. It encourages us to reflect on the act of reading as decoding a form of technologized inscription on the magnetic tape of Joyce's word machine. The machine becomes the *material condition* of Derrida's arche-writing and its modernist ethos. To be condemned to late arrival on the scene of writing is to be haunted by Joyce.

In "Two Words for Joyce," Derrida offers some interesting speculations upon the implications of *Finnegans Wake* in anticipation of the future of computer technology. He writes:

> He [Joyce] talks about it often enough for there to be no simple confusion between him and a sadistic demiurge, setting up a hypermnesiac machine, there in advance, decades in advance, to compute you, control you, forbid you the slightest inaugural syllable because you can say nothing that is not programmed on this 1000th generation computer—*Ulysses*, *Finnegans Wake*—beside which the current technology of our computers and our microcomputerified archives and our translating machines remains a bricolage of a prehistoric child's toys. And above all its mechanisms are of a slowness incommensurable with the quasi-infinite speed of the movements on Joyce's cables. How could you calculate the speed with which a mark, a marked piece of information, is placed in contact with another in the same word or from one end of the book to the other? For example, at what speed is the Babelian theme or the word "Babel", in each of their components (but how could you count them?), co-ordinated with *all* the phonemes, semes, mythemes, etc. of *Finnegans Wake*? Counting these connections, calculating the speed of these communications, would be impossible, at least *de facto*, so long as we have not constructed the machine capable of integrating all the variables,

---

4. Jacques Derrida, "Two Words for Joyce," 150. In a footnote to "Plato's Pharmacy," Derrida already points to this connection with *Finnegans Wake*. See Derrida, *Dissemination*, 88n20.

all the quantitative or qualitative factors. This won't happen tomorrow, and in any case this machine would only be the double or the simulation of the event 'Joyce', the name of Joyce, the signed work, the Joyce software today, joyceware.[5]

The thought of a "hypermnesiac machine" designed to anticipate all one can possibly say in a language and exhaust every conceivable combination of verbal elements is a terrifying one. Derrida's admiring resentment toward Joyce is rooted in his modernist ambivalences about the increasing dominance of prosthetic machines in human affairs. What is "joyceware" if it is not the ultimate homage Derrida or anyone could pay to Joyce? And what would Joyce have said to the author in response?

For one thing, Joyce would certainly have concurred with the idea that *Finnegans Wake* was a feat of engineering that was intended to surpass the most advanced computer that has ever existed or will ever exist. Donald F. Theall argues, for instance, that Joyce approached language (writing) as a mathematical structure and an engineering problem. In the course of writing *Finnegans Wake,* then known as the *Work in Progress,* the ambitious novelist wrote to his patron Harriet Shaw Weaver that this book would prove him to be "the greatest engineer," an interesting claim put forth by someone who was prepared to devote seventeen years of his life (1922–39) to this single work.[6] Theall outlines three aspects of Joyce's claim that go beyond mere metaphor. First, Joyce literally conceived his work as a kind of a machine. Second, "the *Wake* encompasses several aspects of engineering: chemistry, mechanics, mathematics, geography, and strategic planning." Third, Joyce came to realize the extent to which the activities of arts and communication in his period "involved new modes of social organization and of technological production, reproduction, and distribution."[7] Here, we can add a fourth dimension to Theall's perceptive reading, namely, Joyce's anticipatory contribution to communication engineering itself. This consists of his effort to bring the statistical properties

5. Jacques Derrida, "Two Words for Joyce," 147–48.

6. See Donald Theall, "The Hieroglyphs of Engined Egypsians: Machines, Media and Modes of Communication," 132. Theall excerpts the following from Joyce's correspondence: "In the meantime, I am preparing for it . . . by pulling down more earthwork. The gangs are now hammering on all sides. It is a bewildering business. I want to do as much as I can before the execution. Complications to right of me, complications to left of me, complex on the page before me, perplex in the pen beside me, duplex in the meandering eyes of me. And from time to time I lie back and listen to my hair growing white" (134–35).

7. Theall, "The Hieroglyphs of Engined Egypsians: Machines, Media and Modes of Communication," 134.

of letter sequences and spaces among words and nonwords to light. His act of engineering involved subjecting the statistical mechanism of alphabetical writing to an elaborate literary experiment two decades in advance of Shannon's experiment with the statistical models of Printed English. In fact, the founder of information theory himself has mentioned using the statistical properties of the *Wake* in the course of conceptualizing his mathematical theory of communication. Moreover, it was precisely during the time interval between Joyce and Shannon that communication engineering became a statistical science and a branch of statistical mechanics.[8] This aspect of cybernetic developments is discussed in a later section.

No doubt, the idea of a "hypermnesiac machine" is a brilliant one and works extremely well with the *Wake*.[9] But where Joyce would disagree with Derrida is that his machine is programmed with a coding system that is "nat language in any sinse of the world."[10] To expect a computer to think in terms of "syllables" or recognize things like phonemes, semes, mythemes, etc. is not so much to make a demand on its speed and hardware as it is to ask the machine to be a linguist like Roman Jakobson. Derrida's slip of the tongue is intriguing. Could it have been an unconscious reaffirmation of the structural theory of language that he had deconstructed elsewhere? Whatever assumptions he may have held about telecommunication when proposing the trope of "joyceware," there will not be phonemes and verbal utterances in either the hardware or software of a computer. The computer obeys symbolic logic alone and works with numbers and letters that do not stand for syllables or phonemes in natural languages. It is unlikely, therefore, that joyceware—Derrida's smart parody in the spirit of the "wake"—can ever be made to operate in linguistic terms, pace Jakobson. By the same token, if a reader claims that he or she can identify phonemes, semes, mythemes in the *Wake*, it could only mean that he or she has construed these "linguistic facts" on the basis of the printed text in the reading process.

Garrett Stewart brings this cognitive process of reception to our attention in his reading of the pressures of "pronunciation upon script" in Joyce's text.[11] Stewart's reading, however, forgets to take the figure of the hypermnesiac machine into account as he ponders the unexpected erup-

8. See Wiener, *Cybernetics: or Control and Communication in the Animal and the Machine*, 2nd ed., 8–10.

9. Elsewhere, Derrida gives an analysis of the figure of the machine in *Ulysses*. See his "Ulysses Gramophone: Hear Say Yes in Joyce," 253–309.

10. Joyce, *Finnegans Wake*, 83.

11. See Garrett Stewart, *Reading Voices: Literature and the Phonotext*, 245.

tion of "phoneme" in Derrida's interpretation of the *Wake*. For he takes this slip of the tongue to be the philosopher's unguarded reaffirmation of the priority of the phonic in the *Wake* when it could have been understood as a misguided phonocentric figuring of the computer. Stewart argues that "though no one, even to oneself, can of course say two sounds at once, even though prompted by a single letter, any of us *is* able to register, by phonic rather than graphic deferral, what amounts to an aural rather than scriptive palimpsest, an overlapping of phonemes" (246). The point is not whether the reader can register polyphony in his or her mind's ear but how the written letter is able to sustain the illusion of human voice or polyphony in silent reading at all, much less orchestrate the play of meanings across different semiotic systems.

Intuitive reflections on the phonetic alphabet appear to support the impression that letters stand for the sounds of speech. But which sounds? C. K. Ogden once complained about the excessive irregularities of English sounds with respect to the letters that were supposed to represent them. He said, "The vowels represent not 7 sounds but 54, the 26 letters of the alphabet giving a total of 107 values, or with the vowel digraphs ('each', 'ou', etc.) and multigraphs ('eau', etc.) 280"; then he added, "To distinguish all these in a vocabulary of 20,000 words, or even 2,000, necessitates an amount of drudgery which has given phoneticians and advocates of synthetic languages their opportunity."[12] Ogden's statistical view of alphabetical writing and English phonetics was an obvious impetus for launching his Basic English. The same view could very well be the starting point of the *Wake*, except that the irregularities of the sound and letter correspondence in English offered Joyce an excellent opportunity to exploit the rich ambiguities of verbal elements and tease out the surprising convergences of the boundaries of languages on his hypermnesiac machine.

As for how these elements are brought together in the *Wake*, Theall has suggested three communicating systems of particular relevance to consider. These are "traditional sign systems (hieroglyphs, alphabets, icons, drawings), technologically mediated modes of reproduction (print, telephone, film, television), and crafted modes of popular expression dependent either on the traditional or the technologically mediated modes (riddles, comics)." These systems coexist in one "integrated semiotic machine" that is grounded not so much in the logos as in gesture.[13] "The grounding of communication in gesture is underlined" by a quote that Joyce lifted

---

12. C. K. Ogden, *Basic English: A General Introduction with Rules and Grammar*, 21.
13. See Theall, "The Hieroglyphs of Engined Egypsians," 151.

and modified "from [Marcel] Jousse on the opening of the Gospel of St. John: 'In the beginning was the Word . . .'" : "In the beginning was the gest he jousstly says, . . ."[14] Theall explains "the gesture (gest, F. geste) as an act that is linked to the mechanics of humor (i.e., jest) and to telling a tale (gest as a feat and a tale or romance)."[15] Chapter 2 touched briefly on Leroi-Gourhan's work on graphism and its centrality in Derrida's proposition of arche-writing (archi-écriture). It is clear that their theoretical insights also resonate with the earlier modernist discussions of writing in Joyce's own time. In his comments on Joyce's Work in Progress, Samuel Beckett shows a lucid grasp of the ideographic implications of gesture in alphabetical writing. "This writing that you find so obscure is a quintessential extraction of language and painting and gesture, with all the inevitable clarity of the old inarticulation," writes Beckett, "here is the savage economy of hieroglyphs. Here words are not the polite contortions of 20th century printer's ink. They are alive. They elbow their way on to the page, and glow and blaze and face and disappear."[16] Not unlike elementary mechanical systems of communications such as signals and flashing lights, the dancing of printed "words of silent power" on the page of the Wake embodies what I have termed the ideographic movement of the phonetic alphabet.[17]

In The Post Card, Derrida relates his fascination with what Joyce has achieved in Finnegans Wake and writes: "For that seminar on translation I followed all the Babelian indications in Finnegans Wake and yesterday I wanted to take the plane to Zurich and read out loud sitting on his knees, from the beginning (Babel, the fall, and the Finno-Phoenician motif, 'the fall (bababadalgh[...]. The great fall of the offwall entailed at such short notice the pftjschute of Finnegan [...]." The italicized Joycean quote and Derrida's mimicking continue and take up more than half a page.[18] Derrida speaks furthermore about a desire to imitate Joyce: "Never have I imitated anyone so irresistibly" and confesses that he has been "haunted by Joyce, whose funerary statue stands at the centre of the Envois (the visit to the cemetery in Zurich). This haunting invades the book, a shadow on every page, whence the resentment, sincere and acted, always mined, of the signatory."[19] The opening of Glas literally echoes the opening of the Wake by ruminating

14. Joyce, Finnegans Wake, 468.

15. Theall, "The Hieroglyphs of Engined Egypsians," 137–38.

16. Samuel Beckett, "Dante . . . Bruno. Vico.. Joyce," 16–17.

17. Joyce, Finnegans Wake, 345.

18. Jacques Derrida, The Post Card: From Socrates to Freud and Beyond, 240–41.

19. Derrida, The Post Card, 142, and "Two Words for Joyce," 150. The visit refers to his trip to Joyce's tomb on June 20, 1978. See The Post Card, 148.

on the word "fall." It is the opening brought up earlier in connection with Shannon's stochastic experiment:

> The fall (bababadalgharaghtakamminarronnkonnbronntonnerronntuonnt-hunntrovarrhounawnskawntoohoohoordenenthurnuk!) of a once wallstrait oldparr is retaled early in bed and later on life down through all christian minstrelsy.

Compare the quote with the opening of *Glas*: "Of the remain(s), after all, there are, always, overlapping each other, two functions. The first assures, guards, assimilates, interiorizes, idealizes, relieves the fall [*chute*] into the monument. There the fall maintains, embalms, mummifies itself, monu-memorizes and names itself—falls (to the tomb(stone)) [*tomb*]. Therefore, but as a fall, it erects itself there" and so on.[20] Derrida continues in this vein through the next page as if writing is a manner of coping with the ghost of Joyce, settling a score, and discharging an old debt. However, Derrida's in-dulgence in etymological and semantic contortions of the word *chute* (the "fall") is a reading that Joyce set out to frustrate deliberately by inserting a nonsense 100-character string after the "fall" on which Derrida makes ab-solutely no comment, although he was the first theorist to intuit the *Wake* as a hypermnesiac machine and to call Joyce's language game joyceware. It behooves us to ask what Derrida's insights can teach us about Joyces's typographic experiments in the *Wake* that the blind imitation in *Glas* has nonetheless elided.

Let us take a cue from Beckett and analyze joyceware or Joyce's lan-guage game as the effect of an elaborate graphic choreography that mo-bilizes printed words on a two-dimensional stage, or what Joyce terms "paperspace."[21] The nonsense letter sequence within the parentheses after the "fall" precipitates a horizontal ideographic tumbling of the letters to simulate the fiction of an action. What Lacan has called "the precipitation of an unexpected meaning" in "The Instance of the Letter" couldn't have better described the "fall" of the 100-letter sequence in Joyce's stochastic experiment with chance. Philippe Lacoue-Labarthe and Jean-Luc Nancy, who remain the most astute interpreters of Lacan to this day, might have been commenting on the opening of the *Wake* when they tried to explain Lacan's notion of the signifier in *The Title of the Letter*:

20. Derrida, *Glas*, 1–2.
21. Joyce, *Finnegans Wake*, 115.

The passage of the signifier into that symbolization (the equivalent, therefore, of the process in which signification is engendered) is presented as a "precipitation of meaning." This is a remarkable formulation, since it lends itself to at least three interpretations, which are, moreover, amusing: for this can just as well mean that meaning falls head first (and one does not say where . . .), or that meaning goes too fast, that it short-circuits the signified (man and woman, as concepts, are hardly audible any longer but through the door), or finally, that meaning precipitates in the chemical sense of the word, that is to say that it settles as such amidst the solution of the signifier.[22]

It is interesting that the signifier's movement, speed, chemistry, and even an implied circuit rather than its sound image ("hardly audible") are considered relevant to Lacan's notion of the "signifier," which had been Saussure's own term. Lacan's relationship with structural linguistics will be explored in the next chapter, but for the moment, let us try one possibility in the face of Garrett Stewart's critique. That is, even if a reader, while visually and mentally scanning the precipitation of the 100-letter sequence, is tempted to pronounce the impossible syllable sequence or tries to reintroduce the materiality of the sound image into Joyce's text, she or he is bound to discover that there are phonic elements but no phonemes to mark in the text. Marking the phoneme means closing off the boundaries of a single linguistic system (English, German, French, or other) relative to which a phoneme is strictly taken to function, and this is precisely the kind of linguistic sanctuary Joyce has refused to grant the reader.

When Joyce first began his work on *Finnegans Wake* in 1922, Harry and Caresse Crosby proposed that someone should write an introduction to his *Tales Told of Shem and Shaun*, which consists of some fragments from the *Work in Progress*. Joyce mentioned Julian Huxley and J. W. N. Sullivan. But when the scientist and the musicologist each made excuses, Joyce proposed C. K. Ogden, rightly surmising that "the co-author of *The Meaning of Meaning* and the inventor of Basic English would not resist an invitation to discuss this linguistic experiment."[23] Richard Ellmann, Joyce's biographer, also mentions that "he wished also for Ogden to comment, as a mathematician, upon the structure of *Finnegans Wake*, which he insisted was mathematical. If Ogden had refused, Ford Madox Ford was to have been asked, but Ogden accepted, and later was to translate *Anna Livia Plurabelle* into Basic, and to arrange for Joyce to record that fragment for the Ortho-

22. Philippe Lacoue-Labarthe and Jean-Luc Nancy, *The Title of the Letter: A Reading of Lacan*, 42.
23. See Richard Ellmann, *James Joyce*, 614.

logical Institute" (614). The Basic translation of this fragment appeared in Ogden's journal *Psyche* in 1931 and was then reprinted in *transitions*. As an admirer of Joyce's work, Ogden contributed a foreword to the Black Sun edition of *Tales Told of Shem and Shaun* in 1929.

Working closely with Joyce at the time, Ogden appeared to agree that *Finnegans Wake* was mathematical and even estimated the novelist's vocabulary at a colossal number of 250,000. Does the number represent the entire repertoire of the Joycean lingo, both words and nonwords included? We have no way of knowing. But as we follow Joyce's experimental forays into exotic letter sequences, one thing becomes clear, that is to say, Joyce would not abandon his play with "meaning" and would always strive to create the illusion of polyphony even at his most outrageous moment of playfulness with polyseme. With Shannon, it was a different matter. The mathematician tried to push his experiment with Printed English into the realm of pure ideographic symbols. In so doing, he assumes a radical rupture between the written alphabet and the spoken language that it supposedly represents. In fact, the letter sequences in Printed English are almost devoid of linguistic "meaning" inasmuch as what is left of meaning is made to migrate from language to the ideographic utopia of mathematical symbols. It is not as if mathematical symbols have no meaning. They do, of course, and all ideographic systems are meaningful, but these meanings need not be mapped onto any particular spoken language. The complex interplay of sense and nonsense between ideographic writing and language merits some discussion as we further tease out the mathematical implications of Joyce's writing.

At the tenth meeting of the Macy Conference of the cyberneticians, for example, the linguist Y. R. Chao was invited to speak on these questions, and he raised the issue of "sense" at the intersecting point of visual word recognition and the production of phoneme. He argues that what makes "sense" in writing may well be nonsense in speech, and vice versa, and demonstrates it by pushing the Joycean experiment to another extreme in Chinese writing. The test uses 106 written characters (with frequent repetition) in classical Chinese to write a story titled "The Story of Mr. Shi Who Eats Lions," which makes perfect sense in a silent perusal of classical Chinese characters. Of course, this improbable tongue-in-cheek story about a man trying to eat ten lions was made up by Chao to make a point. When the story is read aloud in Mandarin, the prose turns into a string of nonsense syllables and incomprehensible babbling even with proper phonemic markers such as the four tones (phonemes in Mandarin). This is because the characters repeat the same syllable *shi* in the pinyin romanization (*shih* in the Wade-Giles). Here are Chao's 106 written characters along with a pinyin transcription that includes the four tones of Mandarin:

石 室 詩 士 施 氏 嗜 獅 誓 食 十 獅 氏 時 時 適 市 視 獅 十 時 氏
適 市 適 十 碩 獅 適 市 是 時 氏 視 是 十 獅 恃 十 石 矢 勢 使 是
十 獅 逝 世 氏 拾 是 十 獅 屍 適 石 室 石 室 濕 氏 使 侍 試 拭 石
室 石 室 拭 氏 始 試 食 是 十 獅 屍 食 時 始 識 是 十 碩 獅 屍 實
十 碩 石 獅 屍 是 時 氏 始 識 是 實 事 實 試 釋 是 事

shí shì shī shì shī shì shì shī shì shí shí shī shì shì shí shì shì shì shī shí shí shì
shì shì shì shí shí shī shì shì shì shí shì shì shì shí shī shì shí shí shì shì shī shì
shí shī shì shì shì shí shì shí shī shī shì shí shì shì shì shì shī shì shī shì shì shì shí
shì shí shì shì shì shǐ shì shí shí shì shí shī shī shí shí shǐ shì shì shí shì shī shī shí
shí shí shí shī shī shì shí shì shī shí shì shí shì shí shì shì shì shì

Stone house poet Mr. Shih was fond of lions and resolved to eat ten lions. The gentleman from time to time went to the market to look for lions. When, at ten o'clock, he went to the market, it happened that ten big lions went to the market. Thereupon, the gentleman looked at the ten lions and, relying on the *momenta* of ten stone arrows, he caused the ten lions to depart from this world. The gentleman picked up the lions' bodies and went to the stone house. The stone house was wet and he made the servant try and wipe the stone house. The stone house having been wiped, the gentleman began to try to eat the ten lions' bodies. When he ate them, he began to realize that those ten big lions' bodies were actually ten big stone lions' bodies. Now he began to understand that this was really the fact of the case. Try and explain this matter.[24]

Unlike Joyce's nonsense sequence of 100 letters, Chao's 106 syllables can be pronounced yet make no sense to the native ear. But the written characters carry enough information to make sense regardless of how or whether the characters are pronounced. Chao's demonstration of the passage at the Macy Conference has nothing to do with the monosyllabic nature of the Chinese language, which has been a popular but mistaken view, one that projects the alphabetical transcription of the written character, such as /shi/ in the pinyin, onto the spoken language.[25] What Chao is really doing with

24. The English translation used here was done by Chao himself. He also appends a footnote explaining that the character 碩 is pronounced *shì*, although this character also has an alternative pronunciation shuò. See Y. R. Chao, "Meaning in Language and How It Is Acquired," 65–66.

25. For a historical critique of this misunderstanding in comparative philology, see my *The Clash of Empires*, especially the chapter "The Sovereign Subject of Grammar," 181–209.

this improbable passage is emphasizing that the written character plays an important role in constraining the stochastic occurrences of spoken syllables in Mandarin or any other language in China. Moving in the direction of Shannon's stochastic analysis of Printed English, Chao's passage suggests an extremely high level of redundancy in transcribing spoken Mandarin, hence, very little information; but at the same time his 106-written-character sequence exhibits a high level of entropy in classical Chinese. This seeming anomaly—opposing tendencies of redundancy and entropy rates between writing and speech embodied by the same characters in Chao's passage—has fascinating ramifications for our understanding of writing as technology in general.

It is indisputable that reproducing alphabetical letters by hand or machine is much easier than reproducing the square-character script (Chinese script). With the invention of the typewriter, the cause of alphabetical writing was so vastly advanced that many, including McLuhan, began to attribute so-called Western rationality and modern progress to the phonetic alphabet itself. To be consistent in his argument, McLuhan went out of his way to argue that the printing technology and movable type were also invented in Europe. Nevertheless, McLuhan has touched upon a fascinating issue concerning the relationship of script and telecommunication, for there is something to be said about the essential differences between the phonetic alphabet as a simple code on the one hand and, on the other, the square-block character script, legal contracts, signatures, forms, various styles of font type like italics and cursive in alphabetical or nonalphabetical script, not to mention other marks or patterns that cannot be reduced to simple uniform code when it comes to telecommunication. In the age of the typewriter, the degree of difficulty in reproducing the square-block character script and other complex fonts in alphabetical writing was severely constrained by the simplicity of the technology itself. The limitation of the typewriter was overcome by the introduction and popularization of the facsimile machine and then by the more sophisticated computing technology. With *kanji* (square-block character) script in mind, Japanese companies dominated the facsimile machine industry and accounted for more than 90% of worldwide sales in the 1980s-90s.[26] The fax machine and today's computer are capable of transmitting a vastly greater amount of information than the short, readable code for each character, as with

---

26. Michael J. Enright, "Japanese Facsimile Industry in 1990."

the typewriter. Commenting on *kanji* script and forms, contracts, and signatures, which "pose problems that the encoding of characters cannot deal with," John R. Pierce and A. Michael Noll pointed out in 1990: "mere readability doesn't suffice. In a real-estate transaction, for instance, offers should look right, and they should be signed. Fax makes it possible to send such documents, or an image of them, more quickly and conveniently than by mail. And one can send advertising copy, or marked-up text, or a host of other things that electronic mail deals with awkwardly or not all."[27] Of course, since the authors published that view, the encoding technology and memory chips of the computer have evolved further to elbow out the fax machine, making the functionality of electronic word processing in any known scripts or fonts possible and practical. Today, due to the ease of character input on the cell phone, text messaging has become by far the single most popular form of telecommunication in the sinographic world.

A similarly materialist view of writing and technology is what drives Joyce's literary experiment in *Finnegans Wake,* and here is how the novel allegorizes the history of inscription:

> A bone, a pebble, a ramskin; chip them, chap them, cut them up allways; leave them to terracook in the muttheringpot: and Gutenmorg with his cromagnon charter, tintingfast and great primer must once for omniboss step rubrickredd out of the wordpress else is there no virtue more in alcohoran. For that (the rapt one warns) is what papyr is meed of, made of, hides and hints and misses in prints. Till ye finally (though not yet endlike) meet with the acquaintance of Mister Typus, Mistress Tope and all the little typtopies. Fillstup. So you need hardly spell me how every word will be bound over to carry three score and ten toptypsical readings throughout the book of Doublends Jined (may his forehead be darkened with mud who would sunder!) till Daleth, mahomahouma, who oped the closeth thereof the. Dor. (20)

The mini mock history of literacy, print, and civilization gives the illusion of a voice discoursing in puns and nonsense words whereas what is really happening in what Shannon would call "time series" is the movement of a reading-head *avant la lettre* or our eyes doing the visual scansion of "Typus," "Tope," "typtopies," "toptypsical," "wordpress," "prints," ".," and so on in rapid typographical procession. The Latin word *typus,* which derives from the Greek *typos,* suggests a "mark," "impression," or "impressed form" on a prepared surface like ramskin or papyrus. This manner of creating surface

---

27. John R. Pierce and A. Michael Noll, *Signals: The Science of Telecommunications,* 23.

"words" or "verbivocovisual" prints cannot but make a new demand on the movement of "arche-writing," submitting it to the test of the Joycean wordpress and the materiality of its "archetypt" (263). The materiality of print technology frames the local meaning of cross-linguistic alphabetical letters, units of letters, and graphic symbols with spaces around them, as well as two-dimensional surfaces, typographical positions, and so on, always under technological constraints.

iSpace: Joyce's Paper Wounds

One of the things we may learn from the Joycean letter sequences is to approach the phonetic alphabet as a system of actual or potential ideograms. The notion of ideogram (ideo+gram or N-gram) is to be understood in the sense of *Gedankenschrift* or "thought writing," including numerals, punctuation marks, unutterable signs, and other abstract graphic marks, not to be confused with pictographs or pictures. And such is how the sign "iSpace" makes its first appearance in the *Wake*:

> These paper wounds, four in type, were gradually and correctly understood to mean stop, please stop, do please stop, and O do please stop respectively, and following up their one true clue, the circumflexous wall of a single-minded men's asylum, accentuated by bi tso fb rok engl a ssan dspl itch ina, — Yard inquiries pointed out —> that they ad bîn "provoked" ay Λ fork, of à grave Brofèsor; àth é's Brèak—fast— table; ;acùtely profèššionally *piquéd*, to=introdùce a notion of time [ùpon à plane (?) sù " fàçe'e'] by pùnct! ingh oles (sic) in iSpace?! (124)

The double entendre of writing and wounding in the quote is carried out through the movement of graphic marks that visualize the "bits of broken glass and split china" by mangling the word spaces as "bi tso fb rok engl a ssan dspl itch ina." The idea of making holes in iSpace literalizes the act of punctuation and writing as a source of paper wounds. This passage throws the reader into the *mise en abîme* of graphic spacing, punctuation marks, irregular types, and letter sequences.

Eugene Jolas, who was the founder of the avant-garde journal *transition* and was responsible for publishing fragments of Joyce's *Work in Progress*, immediately grasped the significance of this iconoclastic act when he declared in 1929 that "the real metaphysical problem today is the word."[28]

---

28. Eugene Jolas, "The Revolution of Language and James Joyce," 79.

Graphic spacing is taken as an assault on logocentrism as it dissolves the familiar word image and becomes itself the originary act of writing in iSpace. The latter certainly anticipates the Derridian notion of spacing and *différance* for grammatology; but, more appropriately, "iSpace" is about the ideographic prolepsis of modern technology, ranging from cybernetics (the punning on "plane" in the quote puts us in mind of Norbert Wiener's antiaircraft feedback loop) to the Internet, bearing the news of "iPhone," "iVision," "iTunes," "iLove," and "iPolitics" of the future. Most symptomatic of all is the appearance of "iEnglish" itself on the Internet. Joyce's literary experiment suggests that the ideographic view of alphabetical writing did not originate with Shannon or Wiener but rather asserted itself through an extraordinary period of intellectual fermentation in the early decades of the twentieth century marked by a fascination with technical inscription, psychic energy, and prosthetic machines.

Joyce conjured up the printed sign "iSpace" long before the coming of the Internet or the iPod. Sharing the fate of many such graphic aberrations introduced into the mother tongues by writers and poets, "iSpace" has remained stubbornly borderline and obscure in print media long after its inventor was canonized by literary history, theory, and criticism, as well as public and academic institutions. The novelty of his vision and techne of writing never ceases to surprise the generations of readers who have since grown up and experienced the dramatic unfolding of biocybernetic events in their own lives. Like it or not, the lowercase typeface "i" in "iSpace"—to be more precise, the "i+Word"—is evolving into a veritable new idiom and ideo-graphein in the expanding cyberspace of electracy, much like that other ubiquitous letter "e-".[29] These experiments have brought to light the nature of the entanglements between the literary imagination and techno-science that this book explores. The crux of the matter is not whether the letter "i" means "intelligent," "information," "Internet," "I," or "imaginary" or simply represents an inverted exclamation mark that has no corresponding phonetic equivalent in the spoken language, but rather that the ideographic structure of "i+Word" (or even i+word) provides the sole semantic guarantor for any or all of the meanings one can possibly attribute to the letter "i."

---

29. As in the case of acronyms, anagrams, prefixes, and other ideographic functions of the alphabet, the sign "e-" corresponds to the word "electronic" or "electro-"as an *idea* rather than to the phonemic sequence of the multi-syllabic word or prefix it is taken to represent. This applies to "e-mail," "e-museum," "e-trade," "eBay," "eBook," "e-music," "e-medicine," and so on regardless of how one pronounces the letter "e" in English or some other language.

This semantic indeterminacy is bound to raise the cognitive question of how the eyes and brain of a reader pick up alphabetical letters and words visually in the act of reading. This is usually a subject for specialists in neuropsychology and related sciences but should be of some interest to literary scholars as well. When Roman Jakobson provided his analysis of a linguistic disorder known as "ataxia," which is a form of "aphasia," he identified the following cognitive trait in word recognition as pathology. A patient who suffers from ataxia, according to him, has "only an integral, indissolvable image of any familiar word, and all other sound-sequences are either alien and inscrutable to him or he merges them into familiar words by disregarding their phonetic deviations."[30] Although the indissolvable image of a word applies to speech events in the context of Jakobson's discussion, the pathological type he singles out has interesting implications for visual word recognition as well. If the inability to distinguish phonemes as the minimal entities of speech events is pathological, what do we make of the ordinary reader's tendency to fix on the indissolvable image of a word as an integral, scriptic unity on the page? Is it normal or pathological? Recent studies in experimental psychology have provided compelling evidence to show that the "word shape"—or information in the shape of an entire word—plays an important role in our cognitive act of reading or "visual word recognition."[31] As it happens, people do not read each individual letter in a word except in a relatively rare condition following brain injury known as word-form dyslexia.[32]

30. Roman Jakobson, "Two Aspects of Language and Two Types of Aphasic Disturbances," 108.

31. There has been an ongoing discussion about transposed-letter sequences in alphabetical writing. Investigation into the scrambling of letters in a nonword or what researchers call "transposed-letter confusability" casts an interesting light on the problem of visual word recognition. See M. Perea and S. J. Lupker, "Does *jugde* Activate COURT? Transposed-Letter Confusability Effects in Masked Associative Priming," and M. Perea and S. J. Lupker, "Transposed-Letter Confusability Effects in Masked Form Priming." Although we are better at guessing a word than guessing individual letters in the word ("word superiority effect"), the fact that "word shape" can be disrupted by the transpositions or scrambling of letters also raises the issue of where the individual letter stands in relation to "word shapes." For a recent discussion of this problem, see D. G. Pelli, B. Farell, and D. C. Moore, "The Remarkable Inefficiency of Word Recognition." For other related studies, see K. Mayall, G. W. Humphreys, and A. Olson, "Disruption to Word or Letter Processing? The Origins of Case-Mixing Effects"; R. Shillcock, T. M. Ellison, and P. Monaghan, "Eye-Fixation Behaviour, Lexical Storage and Visual Word Recognition in a Split Processing Model"; S. Andrews, "Lexical Retrieval and Selection Processes: Effects of Transposed-Letter Confusability"; L. X. McCusker, P. B Gough, R. G. Bias, "Word Recognition Inside Out and Outside In"; A. F. Healy, "Detection Errors on the Word *The*: Evidence for Reading Units Larger Than Letters"; G. M. Reicher, "Perceptual Recognition as a Function of Meaningfulness of Stimulus Material."

32. See E. K. Warrington and T. Shallice, "Word-Form Dyslexia."

Despite his phonocentrism criticized by Derrida, Saussure did seem to take notice of the propensity of alphabetical writing to slide in the direction of ideographical aberration. According to the notes of his student Emile Constantin, which was not published until 1993, Saussure made an interesting observation on the subject. He remarked once in his 1910 lectures on orthography: "One must not forget that the written word eventually becomes, through force of habit, an ideographic sign [un signe idéographique]. *The word has a global value* <[independently of the letters of which it is formed]>. We read in two ways: spelling out unfamiliar words and reading familiar words at a glance"[33] (my emphasis). By the "ideographic sign," Saussure refers not to Chinese characters but alphabetical writing. Whether the truth of his observation can fully be corroborated by cognitive sciences, it is interesting that Saussure's discovery of the "global value of the word" leaning toward ideography seems to contradict his well-established notion of writing as a visual representation of the spoken language as much as it disputes Jakobson's famous diagnosis of ataxia. As to what extent this remarkable insight is also connected with his unfavorable view of "spelling pronunciations" in speech where "visual images lead to wrong pronunciations" is something one can, of course, debate further.[34] His mention of the force of habit does resonate with the degenerate view of alphabetical writing Derrida has analyzed in *Of Grammatology*.[35] Whether Derrida became aware of Saussure's insight about the "global value" of the phonetic word after the publication of Constantin's notebooks in 1993 is unclear to me. Perhaps it would not have mattered much since what he said about Hegel could have applied to Saussure just as well. Hegel, as we know, had an intuitive grasp of the hieroglyphic potential of alphabetical writing, which led Derrida to call him the last philosopher of the book and the first thinker of writing (26). Reflecting on the acquisition of literacy, Hegel had written that "acquired habit later also suppresses the specificity of alphabetic writing, which consists in seeming to be, in the interest of sight, a detour [*Umweg*] through hearing to arrive at representations, and *makes it into a hieroglyphic script for us*, such that in using it, we do not

33. The original quote goes as follows: "On ne doit pas oublier que le mot écrit finit par devenir par habitude un signe idéographique. Le mot a une valeur globale, <[indépendamment des letters dont it est formé]>. On lisons de deux façons: en épelant pour les mots inconnus et en lisant d'un seul coup les mot connus." See Saussure, *Ferdinand de Saussure: Troisième cours de linguistique générale (1910–1911) d'après les cahiers d'Emile Constantin*, 63–64.

34. Saussure, *Course in General Linguistics*, 31.

35. See Derrida, *Of Grammatology*, 31.

need to have present to our consciousness the mediation of sounds"[36] (my emphasis). Hegel attributes the ideographical tendencies of the phonetic alphabet to the force of habit, a kind of degenerative aberration. The fact that both Hegel and Saussure confront the problem of visual word recognition should be taken seriously because there is much more to their insights about the ideographic potential of alphabetic writing than the metaphysical defense they shore up against writing in general.

The intractability of the ideographic within the system of alphabetical writing can further be interrogated by reexamining the important role the ideographic sign played between modernism and science in the early twentieth century. W. J. T. Mitchell has shown that "Wittgenstein's use of the hieroglyphic as a model for the picture theory of language and Ezra Pound's fascination with Chinese picture-writing as a model for the poetic image might be taken as marking the boundaries of this role."[37] The idea of the ideogram, being misinterpreted by Pound and others as picture-writing, was undoubtedly intended to help defamilarize alphabetic writing for the purpose of vorticist poetry. But another function, with broader contemporary implications, is strongly suggested; namely, that the ideogram concretizes an isomorphism between the machine and the human mind, or as Pound puts it, "Man is—the sensitive part of him—a mechanism, for the purposes of our further discussion, a mechanism rather like an electric appliance, switches, wires, etc.... In the telegraph we have a charged surface attracting to it, or registering movements in the invisible ether."[38] In the manuscript from which Pound constructed his revised version of Fenollosa's essay, the latter refers to "radiation" and "coronal" harmonies that can be produced by an ideogram.[39] Pound found this conception

---

36. As quoted in Derrida, *Of Grammatology*, 25

37. W. J. T. Mitchell, *Iconology: Image, Text, and Ideology*, 29.

38. Ezra Pound, *The Spirit of Romance*, 92–93. As early as 1886, Charles Howard Hinton had presented a theory of the invisible ether that anticipated this modernist view of machine. Conceiving the ether medium as a *cosmic phonograph*, Hinton wrote: "For suppose the æther, instead of being perfectly smooth, to be corrugated, and to have all manner of definite marks and furrows. Then the earth, coming in its course round the sun on this corrugated surface, would behave exactly like the phonograph behaves. In the case of the phonograph the indented metal sheet is moved past the metal point attached to the membrane. In the case of the earth it is the indented æther which remains still while the material earth slips along it. Corresponding to each of the marks in the æther there would be a movement of matter, and the consistency and laws of the movements of matter would depend on the predetermined disposition of the furrows and indentations of the solid surface along which it slips." See Charles Howard Hinton, *Scientific Romances*, 196–97.

39. Daniel Tiffany suggests that the radioactive properties of the ideogram appealed to Pound as a means of "radicalizing" the electromagnetic spectrum. See Tiffany, *Radio Corpse: Imagism and the Cryptaesthetic of Ezra Pound*, 225. See also Laszlo Géfin, *Ideogram: History of a Poetic Method*.

particularly amenable to his own theory of "radioactive" images and went so far as to assert that "[the] true science, true thinking is ideogrammic in the sense that the general is composed of *definite particulars known directly by the thinker*."[40] Pound's language, with its cryptic allusion to mathematical symbols and their implications for thinking the finite and infinite, is certainly related to the mathematics of his time but it was a mathematics already in the process of being replaced by rigorous statistical thinking.[41]

While Wittgenstein focused his attention on logic and language games, Pound interpreted the ideogram as an aspiration toward the immediacy of knowledge that no spoken word could possibly mediate for science.[42] This understanding was based on a theory of image he put forward in the 1914 "Vorticism" manifesto, in which he argues that an image is real because "we know it directly" and "every concept, every emotion, presents itself to the vivid consciousness in some primary form." He further contends that art and science have many things in common since "the imagiste's images have a variable significance, like the signs a, b, and x in algebra" and that "any mind that is worth calling a mind must have needs beyond the existing categories of language, just as a painter must have pigments or shades more numerous than the existing names of the colours."[43] It is not that the phonic aspect of alphabetic writing had lost its valence for Pound or for other avant-garde writers but rather that, under the regimen of prosthetic machines (gramophone, telegraph, telephone, typewriter, radio, film, etc.), there had emerged a new awareness of the ideographic or other potential in alphabetic writing among the experimental writers, and no less among the engineers and scientists who designed the prosthetic machines. In retrospect, Derrida's critique of phonocentrism on behalf of writing came truly, and belatedly, in the wake of a modernist philosophical movement.

Be that as it may, the modernist movement as exemplified by Joyce's *Finnegans Wake*, Mallarmé's poetry, Duchamp's installations, or Eisenstein's experiments with ideogram in film swung against Hegel's degenerative view of writing, not out of volition, but because the artists had no choice but to respond to the proliferation of prosthetic machines and technological reorganization of socioeconomic life in their time. After World

40. Pound, *Machine Art and Other Writings: The Lost Thought of the Italian Years*, 158.

41. On the impact of this transformation on the social sciences, see my discussion of the Bourbaki mathematicians in the next chapter.

42. For a clarification of Wittgenstein's semiotic approach to mental imagery and hieroglyphics, see Mitchell, *Iconology*, 14–27.

43. Ezra Pound, "Vorticism," 464, 466, 463, 466.

War II, the long-awaited arrival of the computing machine and information technology upon the scene of writing brought about a number of new developments that further deepened the modernist experiments with ideography, typography, and the universal writing machine. This brings us back to Shannon's information theory and what it can tell us about the random processes and the probability of meaning in the psychic machine.

Schizophrenic Writing at Bell Labs

It is a well-known dictum in information theory that a message (or letter sequence or character string) being transmitted over the communication channel has nothing to do with semantics or linguistic content. At the risk of repeating myself, any information exists only insofar as there is a choice of alternative messages or alternative sequences of letters. If there were only one message in the whole world, there would be no information and no need for a transmission system because that message would have been on record at the receiving point. If there were two messages, the chance of transmitting the correct information would be 50/50, etc. In short, information is related primarily to the factor of uncertainty or probability from the standpoint of mathematics. This explains why the entropy of a language relates to nonsense in the same manner as it is related to sense. If the redundancy rate is zero, Shannon shows that any sequence of letters is a readable text in the language and any two-dimensional array of letters can form a crossword puzzle. He calculates the redundancy of English within certain limits at the rate of roughly 50 percent, which makes large crossword puzzles possible. As the redundancy rate is lowered to 33 percent, three-dimensional crossword puzzles become a possibility. Literary critics may gain some new insights into Joyce's multilingual riddles in the *Wake* by analyzing their stochastic dimensions across several languages, although they would quickly come to the realization that the task is not easy to carry out.

In its nonthreatening guise, nonsense appears to be an endless source of play and pleasure across cultures and civilizations, past and present. The "Jabberwocky" verse from Lewis Carroll's *Through the Looking-Glass* is the best-known nonsense poem written in English and, indeed, this work might have inspired the kind of nonsense word experiments that led to James Joyce's *Finnegans Wake*. Not surprisingly, Y. R. Chao became the first Chinese translator of Carroll's novel in 1922, and this translation was an extraordinary feat. For not only is Chao able to retain Carroll's play on each individual word by making up new Chinese characters but he manages to reproduce the meter and rhyming pattern of Carroll's English verse.[44] As another twist to this fascinating story about nonsense, Warren Weaver was an avid reader of Lewis Carroll. He built a private collection of 160 different editions of *Alice in Wonderland* in as many as forty-two languages and asked Chao to add his Chinese translation to that collection. Weaver was particularly keen on the puns, nonsense, and jokes from the Mad Tea-Party scene and published a literary study titled *Alice in Many Tongues*.[45]

Gilles Deleuze is among a handful of philosophers in the twentieth century who paid attention to the problem of nonsense and tried to explain it in relation to sense. Other major philosophers of the time, such as Maurice Merleau-Ponty and Jean Hyppolite, reflected on sense and nonsense but did not have much to say about nonsense. Merleau-Ponty's *Sense and Non-Sense* (1966) explored the phenomenology of objects, visuality, things, perception, and other familiar philosophical issues concerning existence; but Lacan's work, communication technologies, and the cybernetic game with letters, numbers, and other such symbols probably did not mean much to him and were left out of the discussion.[46] Hyppolite, on the other hand, was concerned with the relationship between being and sense through language in *Logic and Existence* (1953).[47] Although he showed a lively interest in cybernetics, Hyppolite did not take the next step in his book by relating Hegel's discussion of language, mathematics, consciousness and self-consciousness to the cybernetic machine of his time as Mark Taylor would do half a century later.

Deleuze was an exceptional philosopher of his time. Not only did he take the "Jabberwocky" verse seriously but he gave a marvelous reading of Carroll's portmanteau words to explore the structure of sense and nonsense.[48] In *The Logic of Sense*, he suggests that there is no structure without series and that Carroll has established "a serial method in literature" that brings about the distribution of singular points in the structure of language (Deleuze, *The Logic of Sense*, 51). Deleuze explains singularity in terms of a mathematical curve, a physical state of affairs, or a psychological state and goes on to remark:

44. In an article, Yuen Ren Chao explains how he rendered the "Jabberwocky" verse into Chinese. See Chao, "Dimensions of Fidelity in Translation With Special Reference to Chinese," *Harvard Journal of Asiatic Studies* 29 (1969): 127–28.

45. See Warren Weaver, *Alice in Many Tongues: The Translations of Alice in Wonderland*.

46. See Merleau-Ponty, *Sense and Non-Sense*.

47. See Hyppolite, *Logic and Existence*.

48. See Deleuze, *The Logic of Sense*, 42–47.

Singularities are turning points and points of inflection; bottlenecks, knots, foyers, and centers; points of fusion, condensation, and boiling; points of tears and joy, sickness and health, hope and anxiety, "sensitive" points. Such singularities, however, should not be confused either with the personality of the one expressing herself in discourse, or the individuality of a state of affairs designated by a proposition, or even with the generality or university of a concept signified by a figure or a curve. The singularity belongs to another dimension than that of denotation, manifestation, or signification. It is essentially pre-individual, non-personal, and a-conceptual. (52)

In his own way, Lacan would locate the game of even and odd in this distribution of singularities where each throw of the dice in a game of chance is already a series prior to concept or thought. By analyzing the series and their distributions, Deleuze discovers that "the logic of sense is necessarily determined to posit between sense and nonsense an original type of intrinsic relation, a mode of copresence" (68) and that "no less than the determination of sense, nonsense enacts a *denotation of sense*" (69). This is an important insight, and it asks us to be attentive to the functions and abysses of nonsense as these have something to do with our psychic life. Deleuze points out that when the logicians speak of nonsense, "they offer laboriously constructed, emaciated examples fitting the needs of their demonstration, as if they had never heard a little girl sing, a great poet recite, or a schizophrenic speak" (83). In his view, "Jabberwocky," Joyce, and schizophrenics promise to give us some unusual insights about the important role of nonsense in the psychic life.

In his own reading of *Finnegans Wake*, Lacan has tried a different approach by using the Borromean knot to tease out the implications of the novelist's play with symbols, linguistic or otherwise. Proceeding from "symbol" to "symptom," Lacan wants to demonstrate with his mathemes and diagrams what Joyce can inform us about the symbolic, the real, and the unconscious. In "Joyce le Symptôme," he points out that elaborate punning in *Finnegans Wake* is present not only in every line of the work but in each single word. What is so peculiar about these verbal puns is that the "meaning" that we habitually attach to words gets lost in the process of symbolization.[49] The loss of meaning, or *sens*, however, brings us a bit closer to the real. The real, as Lacan would insist elsewhere, "is completely denuded of meaning (*sens*). We can be satisfied, we can be sure that we are dealing with something of the real [*réel*] only when it no longer has

---

49. Lacan, "Joyce le Symptôme," 165.

any meaning whatsoever. It has no meaning because it is not with words [*mots*] that we write the real. It is with little letters [*petites lettres*]."[50] As discussed in the next chapter, the distinction between the word and the letter—the Joycean "litter"—was fundamental to how Lacan reinterpreted the Freudian notion of the unconscious through the lens of information theory and cybernetics.

Lacan reiterated this point in his Kanzer lecture at Yale University in 1975. Interestingly, he began the talk by alluding to Joyce, and when he was challenged by Geoffrey Hartman, Louis Dupré, and other Yale faculty on the question of symbol, meaning, and mathematics, he fell back on the distinction between the word (language) and the letter (writing), as we can see in the following excerpt from the transcript of the questions and responses:

> HARTMAN: The quarrel concerns the interpretation of the symbolism of mathemes.
> DUPRE: But that's the problem: what is the exact status of the symbolism of mathemes? Is it a universal symbolism or a . . .
> LACAN: It is an elaborated symbolism, always elaborated by means of letters.
> HARTMAN: But what of words (*quid des mots*)? Even if analytic science contains mathemes, there is the question of the practice and of the translation of these mathemes in analytic practice, which is verbal, isn't it?
> LACAN: There is nonetheless a world between the word and the letter.
> (Lacan, "Conference et entretien," 30–31; English translation at http://web.missouri.edu/~stonej/Kanzer_seminar.pdf, p. 17)

It appears that the theoretical distinction Lacan assumes here between the word and the letter has eluded the understanding of his interlocutors in that conversation, which is fascinating to follow. Lacan is arguing—with explicit and implicit references to Joyce in the Kanzer lecture—that the world, or the gap, that separates the word from the letter and mediates between them cannot always guarantee the return of meaning through verbal articulation.

50. See Jacques Lacan, "Conference et entretien dans des universities nord-americaines: Yale University, Kanzer Semina," 29. Lacan's Kanzer lecture took place at Yale University on November 24, 1975. The English translation is by Jack W. Stone at http://web.missouri.edu/~stonej/Kanzer_seminar.pdf.

Precisely in the Lacanian sense, the loss of meaning in the letter is what inevitably results from Shannon's processing of Printed English for information theory. I should add, though, that Printed English takes us beyond the conventional division of labor between the mathematical uses of alphabetical symbols in algebra and the natural languages used in written communication, which is implied in the above-quoted conversation. For the object of Shannon's analysis is English writing, not algebra, and there is no doubt about that. But he is more concerned with the stochastic implications of this writing than with its sense. This has caused N. Katherine Hayles to surmise that the bracketing of semantics in information theory was a strategic choice because "he did not want to get involved in having to consider the receiver's mindset as part of the communication problem,"[51] which brings us back to the point raised by Morse's partner Vail in the nineteenth century concerning the status of the question "Are you there?" for the communication machine.

Hayles's observation is related to an alternative or competing theory of information proposed by British information theorist Donald MacKay in the early 1950s.[52] Unlike Shannon, MacKay insisted on the machine's ability to measure psychological states and this position ignited a flurry of debates about the missed opportunities to choose between these two models or decide whether semantics and psychology should be included in the theoretical construct of the communication machine. The problem with MacKay's argument is that it assumes too much about the sovereignty of linguistic meaning and fails to examine its own paranoia about the dissolution of sense. One must ask what caused MacKay and others to insist on the presence of meaning in the communication machine. Shannon's Printed English raises more radical philosophical issues concerning the whereabouts of "meaning" or "blanks" in the psychic machine than does MacKay's conventional model. This is something that has been largely overlooked by the scholarship on informatics because most critics are still preoccupied with the priority of linguistic meaning and semantics and want to side with MacKay.

Take the peculiar twenty-seventh letter. This is a sign for "space" that belongs to one of "the states" of the alphanumerical system: $S_1, S_2, \ldots, S_n$ in

---

51. Hayles, *How We Became Posthuman*, 54.

52. For Hayles's discussion of Shannon, see *How We Became Posthuman*, 18–19. Hayles also mentions Hans Moravec's attempt to modify and revalue Shannon's model of communication (53–54). For a critique of her interpretation of Shannon versus MacKay, see Mark B. N. Hansen, "Cinema Beyond Cybernetics, or How to Frame the Digital Image."

the Markov chain. By virtue of being a non–phonetically marked symbol, the twenty-seventh letter activates the statistical structure of the twenty-six-letter alphabet, although it can hardly function in this capacity until the remaining twenty-six letters in the system are made to function simultaneously as equivalent, ideographical signs. The verb "activate" highlights an aspect of the phonetic alphabet that is prone to statistical treatment by virtue of its evolution from ancient alphanumerical systems, for numerical signs were closely linked to the origin of writing. As mentioned before, the word *spr* for *scribe* in Phoenician originally derived from the verb *to count* and only later began to acquire the meaning *to write*.[53] In the spirit of ancient alphanumerical *spr*, Shannon's "space" letter once again brings the statistical structure of the alphanumerical system to light. To the best of my knowledge, the only theorist from the Prague Linguistic Circle who paid any passing attention to this development was Josef Vachek (1909–97).[54] In "Remarks on Redundancy in Written Language with Special Regard to Capitalization of Graphemes," Vachek refers to the concept of "graphemic zero" and defines it as the "empty spaces between written (or printed) words in the graphical context." The concept of graphemic zero allows Vachek to grasp some essential differences between writing and speech. Contrary to Hayles's notion of speech or phoneme as a division of continuous stream of breath, Vachek writes: "One does not find in equivalent spoken contexts any acoustic 'zeros,' i.e. any brief pauses separating spoken words—if such pauses do exist, there must be some specific reason for their occurrence . . . whereas the above-noted graphemic zeros function automatically and quite consistently."[55] Clearly, Vachek's visual marking of "space" lacks the rigor of Shannon's twenty-seventh letter or what Derrida has done with the idea of spacing although, to his credit, Vachek stands out as the lone functionalist who persisted in the study of writing and even devoted an essay to the subject of "Written Language and Printed Language" when the majority of his fellow linguists were still preoccupied with phonemes.

As mentioned earlier, the "space" letter in information theory should not be taken at face value or confused with the "empty spaces between written (or printed) words," as it is a mathematical symbol like any of the

---

53. See C. Bonnet, "Les scribes phoenico-puniques," 150.

54. Vachek was a leading functionalist and authored numerous articles on the subject of "written language" that, unfortunately, have not drawn as much attention as some of the other members of the Prague School due to the phonocentric biases of modern linguistics.

55. See Josef Vachek, *Written Languages Revisited*, 152–53. Vachek is also the author of *Written Language: General Problems and Problems of English*.

remaining letters in the twenty-seven-letter alphabet. Shannon has calculated that the "space" symbol in English within a given parameter has a probability of 0.182, which is higher than the most frequently employed letter E, which stands at 0.107. What it means is that random processes that produce letter sequences are more dependent on the stochastic frequency of the letter "space" than they are on any of the other letters in Printed English, whether or not they appear in words or nonwords. Following Shannon's pioneering work, Guilbaud attempted a comparative calculation for English, French, Italian, and Spanish to show that the probability of an equivalent "space" letter in each of these European languages sharing the Roman alphabet is uniformly higher than that of the most frequently used vowel letter, E or A. For example, the "space" letter is 17% in French, English, and Spanish and slightly lower in Italian and German at 16% and 14%.[56] Compare these with the most frequently used vowel E or A in each of the above languages at 16%, 10%, 11%, 10%, and 14% respectively. Only in German does the frequency of the letter "space," which stands at 14%, equal that of the letter E, which also stands at 14%.[57] Note that Guilbaud's 17% for the "space" letter and 10% for the letter E in English are somehow lower than Shannon's calculations at 18.2% and 10.7% respectively. The discrepancy is attributable to the size of the samples taken and, according to Guilbaud, his average is based on a larger pool of English samples. Be that as it may, Guilbaud's conclusion is the same as Shannon's; namely, the letter "space" is used more frequently than the letter E. This should help explain why James Joyce's tampering with the spacing mechanism of the letter sequences in *Finnegans Wake* is more radical and challenging than Ernest Vincent Wright's 50,000-word novel *Gadsby* (1939) or Georges Perec's French-language novel *A Void* (*La disparition*, 1969) each of which plays with lipograms by leaving the letter E out of the entire work. James Thurber's *The Wonderful O* (1957) about some pirates who ban the use of O on an island also highlights the statistical nature of alphabetical writing but technically is inferior to the above novels due to the lower frequency rate of the letter O, which, like N and R in English, stands at 5%.[58]

Guilbaud's observation is illuminating with respect to how we reevaluate the mathematical figuring of letter sequences in alphabetical writing

56. Georges Th. Guilbaud, *What Is Cybernetics?*, 72–73.

57. Intuitively, this makes sense. There's one space per word (if we define a word as a string of characters that begins with a space and has no other spaces). The longer the average word in a language, the smaller the percentage of spaces, and German text has many long words because compounds are readily formed.

58. For the statistical ratio of letter O in English, see Guilbaud, *What Is Cybernetics?*, 72.

and what it can tell us about "meaningful" word units. When visualized, letter sequences may appear as nonwords or ungrammatical units but from a mathematical viewpoint, the stochastic structure in them has little need for visualization or phoneticization to be conceptually valid. Shannon's zero-order approximation to English prose, for example, which gives random combinations of independent and equiprobable symbols, might generate the following: "XFOML RXKHRJFFJUJ ZLPWCFWKCYJ FFJEYVKC-QSGHYD QPAAMKBZAACIBZLHJQD." These combinations do not make sense in English. However, as soon as the probabilities and ratios of the twenty-seven letter alphabet of Printed English are incorporated into the random processes, we are beginning to get a sequence of recognizable word units. Thus a less random sequence is produced in Shannon's experiment that looks like this: "THE HEAD AND IN FRONTAL ATTACK ON AN ENGLISH WRITER THAT THE CHARACTER OF THIS POINT IS THEREFORE ANOTHER METHOD FOR THE LETTERS THAT THE TIME OF WHO EVER TOLD THE PROBLEM FOR AN UNEXPECTED."[59] Shannon's reader may be tempted to scrutinize the semantic content of these letter sequences the same way James Joyce's readers have endeavored to make sense of *Finnegans Wake*. Why a frontal attack on an English writer? What writer?

Semantic treasure hunts with Shannon cannot but lead to dead ends since his tests are designed not to produce meaningful sentences but to determine the ratio of randomness in "unconsciously" formed letter sequences in English. The assumption is that the unconscious processes of language are expected to function automatically like a psychic machine. The way in which Shannon obtained the above-quoted passage was to begin by choosing a pair of words at random in a text (whose source remains unknown). His human subject is asked to read through the work until he or she encounters the second of these words again, and the word immediately following it is registered. Then the new word is sought out in a new context, and the word following its next appearance is again registered, and so on. This laborious process, which produced the passage we have just seen, obeys the simple rules of repetition and statistics rather than issue from the center of authorial consciousness. What is so surprising is not that the random process tends to produce "nonsense" but that some of the results border on the threshold of semantic legibility insofar as the average reader is concerned. How do we account for this?

59. Shannon and Weaver, *The Mathematical Theory of Communication*, 44.

John R. Pierce, Shannon's long-time colleague and coauthor of an essay in 1948, is one of the few interpreters of Shannon's work amongst the contemporary scientists who pondered on the theoretical implications of Shannon's mathematical work for understanding art, literature, and music. Pierce himself was a well-known pioneer in the development of satellite communication systems at Bell Labs and was a prolific science fiction writer who wrote under various pseudonyms such as J. J. Coupling.[60] As early as 1949, he experimented with the stochastic construction of music scores modeled directly on Shannon's work on Printed English. Pierce went on to develop computer music after retiring from Bell Labs and was a professor of music at Stanford University for twelve years. In "Chance Remarks," published one year after Shannon's own "Mathematical Theory of Communication," Pierce offered his interpretation of the passage from Shannon quoted earlier: THE HEAD AND IN FRONTAL ATTACK ON AN ENGLISH WRITER THAT THE CHARACTER OF THIS POINT IS THEREFORE ANOTHER METHOD FOR THE LETTERS THAT THE TIME OF WHO EVER TOLD THE PROBLEM FOR AN UNEXPECTED. To the question what sense this stochastically produced passage could make, Pierce argues that "certain passages in *Ulysses* and *Finnegans Wake* are scarcely more intelligible. Despite an apparent lack of connexion, the passage has some subject interest. I have a sympathetic concern for the predicament of the English writer. I would like to ask the author more about him. Unfortunately, there is no author to ask. I shall hear no more unless, perhaps, chance should answer my questions. One wonders if Dr. Shannon's work has philosophical implications."[61] It certainly does.

Pierce's approach to Joyce's literary experiment is governed by the same stochastic concerns that lead him to make a critical remark about Swift's earlier imagining of the literary machine in the Grand Academy of Lagado. He states: "One can only admit that Swift had the general idea first, but that he may have been wrong in rejecting it summarily."[62] Surreptitiously, Pierce steps into the role of the Lagado professor talking back to the author of Gulliver's story while raising the terrifying specter of an "authorless" text: IT HAPPENED ONE FROSTY LOOK OF TREES WAVING GRACEFULLY AGAINST THE WALL. The conditions under which James Joyce's

60. Pierce was the vice president of research for Bell Laboratories and was centrally involved in the development of the first commercial communications satellite *Telstar 1*, which was launched in 1962.

61. Originally published in "Chance Remarks" under the pseudonym J. J. Coupling in *Astounding Science Fiction* in 1949. Pierce had it reprinted in *Science, Art, and Communication*, 125–26.

62. Pierce, *Science, Art, and Communication*,131.

work is invoked by both Shannon and Pierce call for further reflection. Our discussion of *Finnegans Wake* speculated on how Joyce's word machine could be related to the specific issues brought up by information theory so as to warrant Shannon's and Pierce's attention.[63] There is no doubt that Shannon's and Pierce's understanding of Joyce is vastly different from how literary critics have approached his difficult works and, interestingly, it is always Joyce's "illegible texts" that have drawn the mathematicians' attention. Difficult as they are, Joyce's texts are still considered "authored" texts in contrast with the above-quoted passage from Shannon—"THE HEAD AND IN FRONTAL ATTACK ON AN ENGLISH WRITER . . ."—which is composed of chance elements that obey the laws of statistical structure of the language, and which seems to pronounce the death of the author before Barthes, Foucault, and others learned why and how the author died.

This manner of decentering the author through the stochastic processes of the psychic machine certainly predated French Structuralists' similar moves. Are there meaningful historical connections between the theoretical work at Bell Labs and French Structuralism that we can detect? The answer is yes, and as demonstrated in the next chapter, what we usually take to be French theory has in fact been a round-trip translation of American theory (game theory, cybernetics, and information theory) across the disciplines. For the moment, let's pursue the interesting point Pierce has raised about the philosophical implications of information theory and offer some further reflections on the (il)legibility of Joyce's or Shannon's statistical constructs to pursue that thinking.

Pierce put his favorite stochastic example—"IT HAPPENED ONE FROSTY LOOK OF TREES WAVING GRACEFULLY AGAINST THE WALL"—together with other stochastic samples to illustrate how a particular passage from Joyce's *Ulysses* typically resonates with randomly produced letter sequences on the one hand and with schizophrenic writing on the other. When we juxtapose his stochastic sample with a passage from Joyce and with the writing of a schizophrenic mind, it is not always self-evident which of the three makes better sense. Pierce cites the following passage from Episode 18 Penelope of Joyce's *Ulysses*: "that was a relief wherever you be let your wind go free who knows if that pork chop I took with my cup of tea after was quite good with the heat I couldnt smell anything

---

63. Pierce also mentions the stochastic work of Marcel Duchamp who "allowed a number of threads to fall on pieces of cloth and then framed and preserved them." Pierce, *Science, Art, and Communication*,133.

off it Im sure that queerlooking man in the porkbutchers is a great rogue."[64] This is contrasted with a piece of schizophrenic writing he obtained elsewhere: "Epaminondas was one who was powerful especially on land and sea. He was the leader of great fleet maneuvers and open sea battles against Pelopidas but had been struck on the head during the second Punic war because of the wreck of an armored frigate" (Pierce, 132). Curiously, the last sentence in the quote instantly reminds us of the beginning of Shannon's stochastic phrase "THE HEAD AND IN FRONTAL ATTACK ON AN ENGLISH WRITER . . ." a remarkable coincidence unless we believe that either Pierce or one of his Bell Labs colleagues was the schizophrenic in question. In any case, Pierce relies on these experiments to prove that the removal of inhibitions in the mind of a schizophrenic or a creative artist—which comes to the same thing—can give full rein to chance elements or stochastic processes and result in innovative works of literature.[65] This conclusion sounds surprisingly unoriginal compared with some of the unexpected and unresolved questions implied by the stochastic experiments Pierce and his colleagues conducted at Bell Labs. Let's formulate one of the questions tentatively as follows: Is nonsense or illegibility related to an unconscious mechanism so that it can be instantly recognized as such by the mind?

The linguist Y. R. Chao gestured toward this interpretation at the Macy Conference when he argued that negative feedback existed at the level of linguistic experience when people automatically recognized nonsense as the condition of sense.[66] But Chao did not further pursue the subject in the direction of psychoanalysis and ponder whether the unconscious was structured like writing or language, as Freud and Lacan would elaborate each in a different register. The role that the unconscious is brought into play in the production of sense and nonsense is strongly implied by Shannon's work on the stochastic of the English language. This assumption is sometimes brought into the open by the early computer modeling of neurosis or verbal learning behavior in the late 1950s and the 1960s.[67]

---

64. Joyce, *Ulysses*, 763. Pierce's quote of Joyce is not a verbatim copy and contains an interesting substitution of "mind" for "wind" such as: "That was a relief whenever you let your mind go free who knows if that pork shop I took with my cup of tea after was quite good with the heat I couldn't smell anything off it I am sure that queer looking man in the..." See Pierce, *Science, Art, and Communication*, 132.

65. Pierce, *Science, Art, and Communication*, 132.

66. See Chao, "Meaning in Language and How It Is Acquired," 49–67.

67. See my discussion of Kenneth Colby's neurotic machine and PARRY in chapter 5.

In 1959, Edward A. Feigenbaum pioneered a computer simulation program called EPAM (Elementary Perceiver and Memorizer) in order to study the (unconscious) mechanisms in elementary human learning processes. This was a time when the Ebbinghaus-type experiment was commonly conducted on human subjects at psychological laboratories, often involving the use of random letter combinations and pairs of three-letter nonsense syllables. EPAM was designed on that basis to simulate the rote memorization of nonsense syllables in associate pairs or serial lists. The assumption behind the program is that the brain is an information processor with sense organs as input channels and effector organs as output devices. Certain elementary information processes participate in the cognitive activity of all individuals and these processes allow the individuals to discriminate, memorize, and associate verbal items.[68] As Joseph Weizenbaum has pointed out, Feigenbaum wanted his program to produce a model of cognitive processes whose behavior would closely approximate that of human subjects engaged in memorizing nonsense syllables. The central idea is for EPAM to store *images* or graphic descriptions of the syllables presented to it, not the actual syllables themselves. The nonsense syllable DAX, for example, is described by the vertical leading edge in the first letter, which contains a loop, with the second letter, containing a horizontal bar, and so on. This *image* of the syllable is then discriminated from the other *images* of syllables already stored and is thus added to the memory.[69] What it suggests to us is that the simulated elementary learning behavior implicates a mechanism of ideographic symbol processing rather than that of deep grammatical structure or linguistic meaning. This intuition is entirely consistent with the ideographic turn of Shannon's Printed English.

We have seen how Printed English arrived in the wake of Basic English and modernist ideographic experimentation to fulfill the mission of universal communication boldly envisioned by C. K. Ogden and I. A. Richards in the interwar years. However, universal communication presupposes a universal psychic mechanism to guarantee its global reach. When Winston Churchill made his triumphant remark that "the empires of the future are the empires of the mind," he took Basic English as an instrument of imperial domination, but neither he nor Ogden could tell us at the time how English or any other language could wield such formidable psychic power across races, nations, and linguistic boundaries. By implicit agreement,

68. Edward A. Feigenbaum, "The Simulation of Verbal Learning Behavior," 299.
69. Joseph Weizenbaum, *Computer Power and Human Reason*, 160–64.

they believed that the human mind worked universally with linguistic symbols and was susceptible to being transformed by them. All this happened, of course, before the invention of information theory and cybernetics. Did a new theory of the mind emerge in the postwar years? How did it relate to the development of new communication projects? For instance, would Ogden or Richards find Shannon's and Pierce's approach convincing and agree that the mind was a psychic machine governed by a statistical structure and capable of engendering random symbols, sense and nonsense?

The Cybernetics Group

In the analysis leading up to the present section, we have seen how Shannon worked on the statistical properties of alphabetical writing including Basic English, *Finnegans Wake*, and other English prose to establish a mathematical model of Printed English. It turns out that the architects of Basic were no strangers to either information theory or cybernetics, and as a matter of fact one of them, I. A. Richards, was invited to the Macy Conference of the cybernetics group.[70] As Steve Heims's research has shown, under the leadership of core members of that group—von Neumann, Norbert Wiener, Margaret Mead, Gregory Bateson, Warren McCulloch, and the psychoanalyst Lawrence Kubie—a total of ten Macy Conferences were convened over a period of seven years (1946–53).[71] These meetings were held to promote what the cybernetics group termed the interdisciplinary studies of the machine and the brain as analogous communication systems. In those years, the neurophysiologist McCulloch presided over the meetings and regularly asked a select group of leading scholars from diverse disciplinary backgrounds to present their research at each conference. Shannon was invited to three of the Macy Conferences and gave one of his papers on "The Entropy of English," among other things. He and Richards

70. There is no evidence of direct association of C. K. Ogden with the cybernetics group, perhaps due to his estrangement from Richards. Steve Heims mentions, however, that one of Ogden's research assistants, Molly Harrower, worked closely with Lawrence Kubie and McCulloch after she arrived in America to work with one of the founders of Gestalt psychology, Kurt Koffka, at his suggestion. She was a Macy Foundation fellow. See Heims, *The Cybernetics Group*, 138–39.

71. Heims's *The Cybernetics Group* and Jean-Pierre Dupuy's *The Mechanization of the Mind* are both excellent but complementary studies on this group. Heims's study is highly informative and filled with good sociological observations. Dupuy, a second-generation cybernetician, asks important questions about the intellectual and theoretical value of the work of the first generation.

were both present at the eighth conference in 1951, at which Shannon displayed his famous maze-solving mouse Theseus. Richards gave a paper called "Communication between Men: Meaning of Language."

The eighth conference of the cybernetics group took place on March 15–16, 1951, in New York City. The speakers covered a wide range of topics such as human communication, communication between animals, communication between the sane and insane, intelligent machines, and the search for basic symbols."[72] Richards's paper emphasizes a normative approach to human communication that is rooted in his and Ogden's earlier work on *The Meaning of Meaning* and Basic English (Ogden and Richards, *The Meaning of Meaning*, 22–23).[73] It is interesting that two years after the Macy Conference, Richards adapted information theory and Shannon's model of communication to his own normative theory of linguistic exchange, the result being a couple of diagrams published in his "Toward a Theory of Comprehending" (Figs. 12–13).[74] Richards's attempts at schematic abstraction bear interesting but superficial (visual) resemblance to Shannon's original diagram in *The Mathematical Theory of Communication*, which we have already examined. The fact that Shannon had things to say about the statistical work of Basic in his seminal work on Printed English never registered with Richards. And there is a curious mental warp here in the interchange of what one discipline regards as "valid information" as opposed to the other. Since Richards was not designing an actual communication machine as did Shannon, it is not immediately obvious what the "noise" is doing in his diagrams. Jakobson, for example, excluded this element when he adapted Shannon's diagram to Karl Bühler's organon model of communication for structural linguistics. To understand the sources of Richards's concern with noise, we must turn to the earlier work he did with Ogden and, in particular, *The Meaning of Meaning: A Study of the Influence of Language upon Thought and of the Science of Symbolism.*

Basic English was created under the aegis of an organization called the Orthological Institute, founded to restore proper meaning to English words.

---

72. See Heinz von Foerster, Margaret Mead, and Hans Lukas Teuber, eds., *Cybernetics: Circular Causal and Feedback Mechanisms in Biological and Social Systems: Transactions of the Eighth Conference, March 15–16, 1951.*

73. Richards, "Toward a More Synoptic View," 124. This essay was originally published under a different title, "Communication between Men: Meaning of Language," in H. von Foerster, Margaret Mead, and Hans Lukas Teuber, eds., *Cybernetics: Circular Causal and Feedback Mechanisms in Biological and Social Systems: Transactions of the Eighth Conference.*

74. Richards, "Toward a Theory of Comprehending," 22–23. This essay first appeared under the title "Towards a Theory of Translating" in *Studies in Chinese Thought*, ed. Arthur F. Wright.

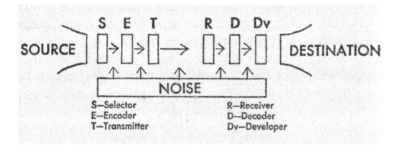

Figure 12. I. A. Richards's diagram on interlingual communication. From "Toward a Theory of Comprehending," in *Speculative Instruments* (Chicago: University of Chicago Press, 1955), 22.

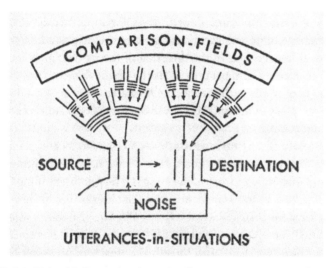

Figure 13. I. A. Richards's diagram on the nexus of utterances-in-situations. From "Toward a Theory of Comprehending," in *Speculative Instruments* (Chicago: University of Chicago Press, 1955), 23.

After having purged verbal redundancies from a humongous vocabulary of 25,000 words—to reckon by the Oxford Pocket English Dictionary—the 850 pure "roots" came to constitute the newly rationalized system of Basic. Startling as it may sound, the avowed aim of *The Meaning of Meaning* and the Basic project, being the fruits of a collaborative effort between Richards and Ogden, was "the eugenics of language."[75] In this influential study,

75. C. K. Ogden and I. A. Richards, *The Meaning of Meaning: A Study of the Influence of Language upon Thought and of the Science of Symbolism*, 135.

Ogden and Richards have tried to rule out abnormality, pathology, or any potential psychic noises that could interfere with a proper understanding of words and their meanings. They state the following: "for the analysis of the sense of 'meaning' with which we are here chiefly concerned, it is desirable to begin with the relations of thoughts, words and things as they are found in cases of reflective speech *uncomplicated by emotional, diplomatic, or other disturbances*" (10, my emphasis).

Richards's practical criticism carried a similar positivist credo with ideological underpinnings, which Fredric Jameson has identified symptomatically as the "political unconscious" of the New Critics, who vigorously defended literary studies against any breach of textural boundaries.[76] Jameson's trope of "the unconscious" was appropriate to the context of his criticism but he did not work the idea out to discover the historical interplay of Basic, cybernetics, neurophysiology, information theory, and psychoanalysis. In this study, we have good reason to push the question of the political unconscious in the direction of the psychic machine, which Jameson did not do. For example, does the political unconscious in Richards's diagrams reside in the box where he marks "noise"? What does it tell us about the place of the unconscious in Shannon's own conceptualization of communication?

We have already mentioned MacKay's attempt to locate "the place of 'meaning'" in the theory of information. As we have seen in the work of Ogden and Richards, a theory of meaning is a very different thing from the theory of information as understood by Shannon or Lacan. But Mackay wants to have his cake and eat it too by collapsing different projects into one updated metaphysical endeavor.[77] "By the theory of information," writes MacKay, "we shall mean broadly the theory of processes by which representations come into being, together with the theory of those abstract features which are common to a representation and that which it represents." MacKay seems not concerned by the possibility of nonmeaning or

76. Fredric Jameson, *The Political Unconscious: Narrative as a Socially Symbolic Act.*

77. In chapter 2, I have discussed how Warren Weaver tried to articulate verbal meaning to information theory when he first initiated the project of machine translation. He met with skepticism from Wiener and Shannon. The subsequent developments in machine translation do not suggest that meaning has been built into information theory. They suggest that the application of some aspects of information theory has been successful in some areas of artificial intelligence but not in others. Mark Hansen believes that "with his definition of (received) meaning as 'the selective function of the message on an ensemble of possible states of the C.P.M.,' Mackay provided a basis for '(re)thinking the relation between information and image beyond cybernetics.'" I am not sure whether Hansen's claim is based on phenomenological observation or on information theory itself. See Hansen, "Cinema Beyond Cybernetics," 75.

nonsense in the symbolic order as he goes on to specify what he means by representation: "By a representation of X we shall mean a set of events or objects exhibiting in at least one respect (even if only statistically) the pattern of relationships between the components of the situation X. By information we shall mean that which justifies representational activity: that to which logical appeal is made to justify a representation."[78] The desire for the adequatio of representation and the plenitude of meaning strongly echoes that of Ogden and Richards, who wanted verbal communications to be uncomplicated by extraneous noise, dubbed "emotional, diplomatic, or other disturbances."[79] Mackay's project, which tried to revive a much older theological concern with meaning, is contradicted by the psychoanalytical insights we may glean from the making of information theory itself.

We have seen how Shannon designed clever guessing games to arrive at the laws of Printed English. Of course, Shannon's guessing games would not work without his positing a priori the mind's automatic, unconscious processing of written symbols, in spite of the fact that he does not use the word "unconscious." When his colleague Pierce started to compare the writing sample of a schizophrenic—which Ogden and Richards would dismiss as "disturbances"—with the stochastic production of Printed English, he did push the implicit association of the written symbol with the unconscious into the open. Neither, however, went further than strongly implying a connection between the written symbol and the psychic machine.

Among those who pursued active research projects on this topic were some of the core members of the Cybernetics Group, especially Kubie and Mead. McCulloch, who spurned psychoanalysis, would on many occasions challenge Kubie on the question of the unconscious. As the cyberneticians were engaged in their lively and sometimes difficult debates at the Macy Conferences, Jacques Lacan followed the cybernetic development in the United States from a distance and began to reinterpret the Freudian notion of the unconscious in terms of a psychic machine. As the next chapter

---

78. Donald M. MacKay, *Information, Mechanism, and Meaning*, 80.

79. The technical distinction between signal and noise in Shannon's original diagram is made to help the engineer design communication channels. It is Richards's diagram, rather than Shannon's, that has invited an interpretation beyond the telos of communication engineering. This is why Hayles's criticism of Shannon's distinction between signal and noise is off the mark when she says that the signal and noise distinction has a conservative bias that privileges stasis over change because "noise interferes with the message's exact replication, which is presumed to be the desired result. The structure of the theory implied that change was deviation and that deviation should be corrected." It is difficult to see how the idea of uncertainty and probability central to information theory can have anything to do with stasis versus change. See Hayles, *How We Became Posthuman*, 63n32.

shows, not only was Lacan thoroughly familiar with Wiener's *Cybernetics*, but he read Kubie's article on neural networks published in *Psychoanalytic Quarterly*. In his seminars of 1954–55, he explicitly brought up the neural network studies on the octopus done by John Z. Young, whose work had been discussed at the ninth Macy Conference in March 1952.[80]

Richards and MacKay's attempt to tame information theory with a normative view of language is strikingly at odds with how Lacan understood Shannon and the question of "noise" during the same period. In fact, information theory provided the scientific rigor Lacan needed to repudiate Ogden and Richards's semantic approach to language. In "The Instance of the Letter in the Unconscious," Lacan dismisses the semantic theory of language as "the heresy that leads logical positivism in search of the 'meaning of meaning,' as its objective is called in the language [*langue*] in which its devotees snort." He adds that "it can be seen here how this sort of analysis can reduce the text the most highly charged with meaning to insignificant trifles. Only mathematical algorithms resist this process; they are considered to be devoid of meaning, as they should be."[81] The next chapter elaborates on Lacan's symbolic order by closely examining his relationship with mathematics in game theory and cybernetics.

Steve J. Heims's study has shown that the participants in the eighth meeting of cybernetics were greatly intrigued by how human subjects consistently made "nonrational choices" and how their decisions could be guided by random processes. This is exactly how Lacan came to reframe Freud's notion of the unconscious and came up with the idea of the symbolic order. His discussion of "empty signifiers" by recourse to the mathematical symbol would have interested Lawrence Kubie, Margaret Mead, and other members of the Macy Conference. At the eighth meeting, for example, a young scientist named Alex Bavelas reported on how he used a series of experiments to test the ways in which human subjects communicate using written symbols. One of his experiments involved a group of five people. Each subject was given a card containing five ideographic symbols including an asterisk, a triangle, a circle, etc., and he or she was told that each of the others had a card of five symbols. The group was informed beforehand that there was only one symbol common to all five cards and their task was to identify that symbol. The subjects were forbidden to see or hear each other (i.e., preclusion of the imaginary order in the Lacanian sense) and were allowed to communicate only by sending written

80. Jean-Pierre Dupuy, *The Mechanization of the Mind: On the Origins of Cognitive Science*, 109.
81. Jacques Lacan, *Écrits: The First Complete Edition in English*, 416.

messages through the slits in their cubicles (which anticipated how Lacan demonstrates the symbolic order with the game of even and odd in his reading of "The Purloined Letter" in the 1954–55 seminar). By observing how the group established connectivity (neighbor to neighbor in a circle or all four connecting through a central subject) in the course of carrying out the task, Bavelas showed that mathematically precise concepts of connectivity, communication, and information transfer could be established outside of the usual circuit of linguistic exchange.[82]

In the general discussion that followed Bavelas's presentation, Lawrence Kubie and Margaret Mead brought up the question of the unconscious and wanted to know whether a written symbol on Bavelas's card was truly random or had unconscious meanings that might have biased the subjects' choices.[83] Mead was particularly sensitive to how the scientists treated their random symbols. "You can use information about the unconscious to be sure that you have randomized the right elements, but if you carry that over into real life, with a statement that a thing like an asterisk is of very little importance," she said, "you would make an enormous error."[84] Kubie was a core member of the cybernetics group and a professional psychiatrist with a strong interest in hypnosis. He tried very hard, often without success, to persuade his colleagues that communication can occur without the subject's conscious participation in the process. In the question he posed to Bavelas, he raised an interesting point about the relationship between cognition and the organization of knowledge through language:

> In your experiments, Dr. Bavelas, the items with respect to which communication occurs are such items as circles, triangles, asterisks, marbles, and so forth; that is, items easily named and specified in English. But suppose you deal with such an item as "an irregularly shaped, wet, smooth object changing rhythmically in brightness." Perceptually, this is something very simple, since such an object is easily identified and recognized; to designate it unambiguously in English, however, requires telling a rather long story. Items with respect to which communication may occur often differ in "word-nearness" or "word-remoteness," that is, in linguistic distance. I wonder, therefore, whether you have any data on how the mechanism of communication

82. Heims, *The Cybernetics Group*, 221.

83. Heims, *The Cybernetics Group*, 221–22.

84. Heinz von Foerster, Margaret Mead, and Hans Lukas Teuber, eds., *Cybernetics: Circular Causal and Feedback Mechanisms in Biological and Social Systems: Transactions of the Eight Conference, March 15–16, 1951*, 44.

is influenced by systematically changing the linguistic distance of the various items entering the communication network. (von Foerster, Mead, and Teuber, *Cybernetics*, 29–30)

Bavelas had undertaken his research for the Air Force of the United States and was not motivated to interpret his data in purely intellectual terms. He could not, therefore, come up with an answer that would satisfy Kubie. This was to be expected because the military-industrial-academic complex of postwar research decided to a large extent the kinds of questions and projects that the scientists were pursuing at the time. It is suggested that Norbert Wiener laid the first groundwork for the invention of cybernetics during World War II when he submitted a top-secret 120-page report called *Yellow Peril* (classified and named after its bright yellow covers, with obvious racial connotations) to the National Defense Research Committee in 1942.[85] This document outlined the new antiaircraft fire control theory that would become the idea of negative feedback in cybernetics. Warren Weaver was the director of the NDRC Section D-2 and was responsible for mobilizing the nation's best mathematical minds, including Wiener, to serve in the Fire Control Division. One of the first projects Shannon completed after graduation from MIT was an NDRC contract called Project 7, which involved mathematical studies relating to fire control.[86] Steve Heims's study shows clearly how cybernetics in postwar America continued to answer the need to build up and improve military technologies for the purpose of conducting regular as well as psychological warfare.[87]

Shannon was also present at the eighth meeting of the cybernetics group and was an important interlocutor in the group. He heard Bavelas's presentation, which invoked information theory, but he did not see any relevance that his work would have to what Bavelas was trying to accomplish. In his view, information theory was strictly concerned with the efficient means of transmitting messages on a communication channel whereas Bavelas had a very different goal. Bavelas was interested in how people networked and collaborated to get things done or how many errors they would make on each trial (Heims, *The Cybernetics Group*, 24). Commenting on the psy-

85. See Flo Conway and Jim Siegelman, *Dark Hero of the Information Age: In Search of Norbert Wiener, the Father of Cybernetics*, 116–18.

86. David A. Mindell, *Between Human and Machine: Feedback, Control, and Computing before Cybernetics*, 289.

87. Heims, *The Cybernetics Group*, 1–13.

chological reaction that Bavelas's human subjects exhibited toward their error after each trial, Shannon remarked:

> I also think that the poorer results you obtained when they were given the amount of error were really an indication of the irrationality of people, because in a game situation the additional information certainly could not hurt you if you were perfectly rational; that is, if you choose the best strategy, additional information can only make it better from the point of view of reducing errors, if you play the game by the most rational means. If you had five Von Neumanns sitting in your cubicles, the answer should be better or at least as good with the additional information. (38)

Of course, irrationality or neurosis is not something Shannon himself was prepared to deal with, but his comments inadvertently bring the specter of the schizophrenic back into the picture that we have already encountered in Pierce's interpretation of Shannon. As indicated earlier, Shannon (and Pierce) had treated the stochastic properties of Printed English in his earlier experiments at Bell Labs *as if* there was an unconscious psychic mechanism governing the mind of every English speaker through which passed random letter sequences and word sequences without his or her conscious knowledge.

Shannon's subjects made errors in the guessing games and were duly corrected, but this process did not affect his design of efficient channels of communication. He simply assumed that the unconscious process would run its course and work automatically like a machine. In the unpublished "A Mind-Reading Machine," written one year after the eighth Macy Conference, Shannon constructed a model of the psychic machine that played the game of chance or, in the language of game theory, penny-matching games.[88] Presumably, until one can abolish the phenomenology of consciousness or else enable the machine to acquire consciousness, a mind-reading machine has no choice but operate at the unconscious level. This raises the interesting possibility of the machine's equivalent of schizophrenic breakdown and the death drive. When Lacan began to rework the Freudian notion of the unconscious in 1954, he contemplated this possibility.

Shannon's artistic tour de force the Ultimate Machine illustrates his intuitive grasp of a fundamental problem of the unconscious that Freud has termed the death drive. A recent kinetic sculpture by Hanns-Martin

---

88. Shannon, "A Mind-Reading Machine," 688–90. This essay bears the date March 18, 1953, at Bell Labs.

Wagner is modeled after Shannon's machine (Fig. 14). The idea of this machine was originally proposed by Shannon's colleague Marvin Minsky, an
AI engineer, in 1952. Shannon was greatly taken by the idea and went
ahead to build a few models.[89] The beauty of this machine is that it does
nothing but switch itself off. When British writer Arthur C. Clarke visited
the dream factory called Bell Labs in the midfifties, he saw the prototype
on Shannon's desk and returned haunted by it afterward. He describes
Shannon's Ultimate Machine in *Voice Across the Sea* as follows:

> Nothing could look simpler. It is merely a small wooden casket the size
> and shape of a cigar-box, with a single switch on one face.
>
> When you throw the switch, there is an angry, purposeful buzzing. The lid
> slowly rises, and from beneath it emerges a hand. The hand reaches down,
> turns the switch off, and retreats into the box. With the finality of a closing
> coffin, the lid snaps shut, the buzzing ceases, and peace reigns once more.
>
> The psychological effect, if you do not know what to expect, is devastating.
> There is something unspeakably sinister about a machine that does nothing—
> absolutely nothing—except switch itself off.[90]

Is the machine built to be schizophrenic or suicidal? Shannon used to say
"I've spent lots of time on totally useless things," and the Ultimate Machine
would have to be one of them.[91] Like all works of art, this machine tells
us something about ourselves and our world. Clarke notes the devastating
effect of the Ultimate Machine on nearly everyone who came in contact
with it and adds that even "distinguished scientists and engineers have
taken days to get over it. Some have retired to professions which still had
a future, such as basket-weaving, bee-keeping, truffle-hunting or water-
divining. They did not stop to ask For Whom the Bell Labs Toll."[92]

The toll—coming as it were not so much from Bell Labs as from MIT—
would soon announce the suicide of the youngest member of the cybernetics group, Walter Pitts. Pitts was a mathematical genius and helped Mc-

89. The most recent display of this machine was in a special exhibition at the Heinz Nixdorf
Museum in Paderborn, Germany. The exhibition is called "Codes and Clowns: Claude Shannon–
The Juggling Scientist." on 6 November 2009 to 25 April 2010. See http://en.hnf.de/Special_
exhibitions/Shannon/Shannon.asp.

90. Arthur C. Clarke, *Voice Across the Sea*, 159.

91. *Problemy Peredachi Informatsii*, "Claude Elwood Shannon," *Problems of Information Transmission* 37, no. 2 (2001): 89; translated from the Russian journal *Problemy Peredachi Informatsii*, no. 2
(2001): 3–7.

92. Clarke, *Voice Across the Sea*, 159.

Figure 14. Hanns-Martin Wagner's The Most Beautiful Machine, modeled on Shannon's Ultimate Machine. Used by permission of Hanns-Martin Wagner.

Culloch produce some of his most important work on neural networks. The young man suffered from a severe case of mental disorder and was judged "very sick" by Kubie and "schizophrenic" by Ralph Gerard and others (Heims, 155). In his study of the Macy Conferences, Heims makes a poignant observation about a central irony of this group: while the brilliant scientists and social scientists gathered and engaged in their heated discussions of the mind, brain, and the machine, the youngest and brightest regular member, Walter Pitts, was visibly sinking into mental disintegration toward the last few meetings.[93] Nevertheless, the scientists at the Macy Conferences, including Pitts and McCulloch, strenuously denied the reality of the unconscious and distanced themselves from the vagueness of psychoanalytical concepts. In spite of the force of this collective resistance, the specter of schizophrenia repeatedly asserted itself and pushed the question of the unconscious into the open at the Macy Conferences.

The majority of the scientists in that group found the notion "the unconscious" objectionable, but they seemed to take "consciousness" in stride as if this concept could stand alone. Their extraordinary inattention to the discursive structure of scientific knowledge was pointed out by

93. Heims, *The Cybernetics Group*, 154.

Mead, who commented that when the scientist (such as Leonard Savage) accused the psychoanalyst (Kubie) of making mere conjectures about the unconscious, he was acting in the conscious realm and not at all reflecting on his own conditions of knowledge.[94] Mead made a valid point there. It is interesting that, among the other cyberneticians, Norbert Wiener did not express his essential objections to psychoanalysis and, unlike McCulloch or Pitts, he believed the discipline could be rethought in terms of information, communication, and feedback (Heims, 126). But in my opinion, there is another reason why psychoanalysis would return to haunt the cyberneticians. This has to do with some of the guessing games adopted by Shannon and by other cyberneticians, which owed their existence to the psychic models developed by the first generation of psychoanalysts at the turn of the twentieth century such as Carl Jung, Eugen Bleuler, and Ernest Jones. The psychoanalysts, in particular, relied on their word-association games and automatic writing, which would later be associated with the work of the Surrealists, to compel random selections of written or linguistic symbols by the human subject, sometimes under hypnosis and sometimes not. These games were manipulated to help the psychoanalyst map out the ways in which the unconscious would assert itself through the symbolic circuit.

The Psychic Machine

The publication of Carl Jung's *Studies in Word-Association* in 1904 was an important event in the field of psychopathology. It marked the beginning of the author's friendship and collaboration with Sigmund Freud, which lasted through 1913.[95] Freud wrote: "Jung has shown what a subtle reagent for psychical states we possess in the association experiment as thus interpreted."[96] Jung hypothesized that people connect their ideas, feelings, and experiences through mental associations that can lead to what he calls "the complexes." He designed a word-association game dubbed "the association experiment" to ascertain how arbitrary psychical acts exhibited mental groupings that could yield valuable information about the unconscious. The game was subsequently adopted by many neurologists and psychiatrists

---

94. Heinz von Foerster, Margaret Mead, and Hans Lukas Teuber, eds., Cybernetics: *Circular Causal and Feedback Mechanisms in Biological and Social Systems: Transactions of the Eighth Conference*, 127.

95. See Eugen Bleuler, "Consciousness and Association," 275.

96. Sigmund Freud, *The Psychopathology of Everyday Life*, in *The Standard Edition of the Complete Psychological Works of Sigmund Freud*, vol. 6: 254.

in Germany, America, and elsewhere. Max Wertheimer and Julius Klein, both students of Hans Gross—one of the founders of modern criminal investigation—tried to develop techniques based on Jung's word-association game to establish psychological evidence in criminal proceedings.[97]

The word-association game shares a number of important features with the games that Shannon, Pierce, and Bavelas would adopt many decades later for information theory and cybernetics. They all include the following elements: human subjects, written and/or verbal symbols, randomness and chance production of symbols, identification of patterns, and in many cases, strict time constraints and the use of one or several devices or machine. Jung's association experiment consists of some simple steps, the most important of which is the precise measurement of time intervals. The analyst calls out a *stimulus word* to the human subject, who is asked to react as quickly as possible with the first word that comes into his or her mind. Although the selection of stimulus words is apparently random, there is a set vocabulary of 100 words out of which Jung regularly selects individual words (Tables 1 and 2). He explains that this set of words took its present form as a result of his clinical experience and that the mix of different grammatical features is arranged to touch upon all the complexes that commonly occur in practice.[98] Jung emphasizes that the association experiment investigates not just *one* component of the mind, since no psychological experiment can possibly be concerned with a single isolated psychic function—no psychic occurrence is a thing in and by itself but rather is the result of the entire psychological past. He treats the association experiment as a kind of "pastime" or a game between investigator and subject, not a mere linguistic exercise. Words *simulate* "actions, situations, and things" and put the subject in them. "If I were a magician," says Jung, "I should cause the situation corresponding to the stimulus-word to appear in reality and, placing the subject in the centre, I should then study his reactions" (Jung, "The Association Method," 444). The computer simulation models that emerged half a century later in cognitive science begin to embody this dream with claims to theatrical or virtual reality. Chapter 5 discusses this development.

In his studies of hysteria, Freud shows that a symptom is essentially a symbol for ideas (fundamentally sexual) that are not present in consciousness but are repressed by strong inhibitions. The repression occurs when

97. See Freud, "Psycho-Analysis and the Establishment of the Facts in Legal Proceedings," 106; Jung, "New Aspects of Criminal Psychology," 586–96.
98. See Jung, "The Association Method," 441.

Table 1. The set of 100 German words adopted in Carl Jung's association experiment. From Carl Jung, "The Association Method," *Experimental Researches* (1907), 440–41.

1. Kopf	34. gelb	67. Rübe
2. grün	35. Berg	68. malen
3. Wasser	36. sterben	69. Teil
4. singen	37. Salz	70. alt
5. Tod	38. neu	71. Blume
6. lang	39. Sitte	72. schlagen
7. Schiff	40. beten	73. Kasten
8. zahlen	41. Geld	74. wild
9. Fenster	42. dumm	75. Familie
10. freundlich	43. Heft	76. waschen
11. Tisch	44. verachten	77. Kuh
12. fragen	45. Finger	78. fremd
13. Dorf	46. teuer	79. Glück
14. kalt	47. Vogel	80. lügen
15. Stengel	48. fallen	81. Anstand
16. tanzen	49. Buch	82. eng
17. See	50. ungerecht	83. Bruder
18. krauk	51. Frosch	84. fürchten
19. Stolz	52. scheiden	85. Storch
20. kochen	53. Hunger	86. falsch
21. Tinte	54. weiss	87. Angst
22. bös	55. Kind	88. küssen
23. Nadel	56. aufpassen	89. Braut
24. schwimmen	57. Bleistift	90. rein
25. Reise	58. traurig	91. Türe
26. blau	59. Pflaume	92. wählen
27. Lampe	60. heiraten	93. Heu
28. sündigen	61. Haus	94. zufrieden
29. Brot	62. lieb	95. Spott
30. reich	63. Glas	96. schlafen
31. Baum	64. streiten	97. Monat
32. stechen	65. Pelz	98. hübsch
33. Mitleid	66. gross	99. Frau
		100. schimpfen

Table 2. The English translation of the set of 100 words adopted in Jung's association experiment. From Carl Jung, "The Association Method," *Experimental Researches* (1907), 440.

1. head	34. yellow	67. carrot
2. green	35. mountain	68. to paint
3. water	36. to die	69. part
4. to sing	37. salt	70. old
5. death	38. new	71. flower
6. long	39. custom	72. to beat
7. ship	40. to pray	73. box
8. to pay	41. money	74. wild
9. window	42. stupid	75. family
10. friendly	43. exercise-book	76. to wash
11. table	44. to despise	77. cow
12. to ask	45. finger	78. friend
13. cold	46. dear	79. happiness
14. stem	47. bird	80. lie
15. to dance	48. to fall	81. deportment
16. village	49. book	82. narrow
17. lake	50. unjust	83. brother
18. sick	51. frog	84. to fear
19. pride	52. to part	85. stork
20. to cook	53. hunger	86. false
21. ink	54. white	87. anxiety
22. angry	55. child	88. to kiss
23. needle	56. to pay attention	89. bride
24. to swim	57. pencil	90. pure
25. journey	58. sad	91. door
26. blue	59. plum	92. to choose
27. lamp	60. to marry	93. hay
28. to sin	61. house	94. contented
29. bread	62. darling	95. ridicule
30. rich	63. glass	96. to sleep
31. tree	64. to quarrel	97. month
32. to prick	65. fur	98. nice
33. pitty	66. big	99. woman
		100. to abuse

these ideas are charged with painful affects and are therefore incompat-
ible with ego-consciousness. Jung believes that such complexes of ideas
can show up in the association experiment, as everybody has one or more
complexes that manifest themselves in some way in association. In a typical test, the subject is given the instruction: "Answer as quickly as possible
with the first word that occurs to you" (441). The speed of the subject's
reaction is recorded before the analyst moves to the next word down the
list, and this process continues until a large number of repetitions yield a
series of pairs of words that constitute a pattern of *associations*. Repetition
requires the subject to hear the same stimulus word and reproduce the
reaction word, and the success or failure of the reproduction is factored
into the overall picture of the complexes. All this is carefully monitored by
a 1/5-second stopwatch. The measurement of time intervals between the
stimulus word and the subject's reaction is called the reaction-time ratio.
If the average time between a stimulus word and the subject's reaction is
2.5 seconds, then 3 seconds is considered a prolonged reaction-time, which
could indicate the presence of "feeling-toned complexes."[99]

Table 3 is one fragment of a case analyzed by Jung in his association
experiment. We are told that a thirty-two-year-old professional musician
came to seek medical help when he developed a nervous condition after a
series of failed relationships. The italicized words are the associations that
were either not reproduced or wrongly reproduced upon repetition during
the test. Jung remarks on prolonged reaction-times and associations linked
to thoughts of suicide. For example, the word "angel" triggers a delay as
long as 8/5-seconds and the word "ill" even longer. Jung notes further that
"the incorrect reproductions to the repeated stimulus-words are those that
are directly constellated by a feeling-toned complex or those that immediately follow a critical one, and therefore fall within the area of the persevering feeling-tone."[100] Does this experiment lead to reliable information
about the subject? How scientific is the psychoanalytic method? Will psychoanalysis remain a difficult art of interpretation, as Jung has noted about
Freud's work?[101] These questions troubled Jung and the other practitioners
of psychology and psychoanalysis deeply.

---

99. *Jung*, "The Reaction-Time Ratio in the Association Experiment," 221–71. The so-
called average in the reaction-time ratio is determined according to the subject's gender
and education background. Jung finds women and the uneducated lagging behind men
and the educated but does not provide a proper explanation. The ideological implica-
tion of these statistics should not be underestimated.

100. Jung, "Experimental Observations on the Faculty of Memory," 278–79.

101. Jung, "Psychoanalysis and Association Experiments," 290.

Table 3. Fragment of case no. 1 in Carl Jung's association experiment. From Carl Jung, "Experimental Observations on the Faculty of Memory," *Experimental Researches* (1907), 275.

Stimulus-word	Reaction	Reaction time (secs.)	Reproduction	Remarks
1. head	empty	3.2	to see	Complex underlying the illness.
2. green	lawn	2.2	colour, tree	Probably perserverating feeling-tone.
3. water	to drown	2.2	deep	The patient had had thoughts of suicide as a result of his illness.
4. to stab	dead	1.8	unpleasant	—
5. angel	beautiful	8.0		Here the feeling-tone of the previous reaction has probably perseverated. Word not a first understood. Erotic reminiscences easily aroused by this word.
6. long	table	2.8	—	—
7. ship	crew	3.0	to travel, to drown	Suicide by drowning.
8. to plough	peasant	2.0	—	—
9. wool	sheep	2.0	—	—
10. friendly	very	2.8	—	Affair with the lady.
11. desk	high	3.6	—	Prolonged reaction time due to perseverating feeling-tone.
12. to ask	difficult	3.2	to put	Same complex.
13. state	beautiful	2.4	—	—
14. obstinate	very	2.0	—	1st fiancée.
15. stalk	green	2.2	—	—
16. to dance	good	2.2	—	—
17. lake	stormy	2.0	—	—
18. ill	unpleasant	8.8	—	Illness
19. conceit	very	2.8	—	Relations with the lady.
20. to cook	good	2.0	—	—
21. ink	black	1.8	—	—
22. wicked	very	4.8	—	1st fiancée.
23. pin	prick	1.4	—	—
24. to swin	not	2.8	good	Suicide.
25. journey	difficult	2.4	long	Perseverating feeling-tone.
26. blue	colour	2.0	—	—

The introduction of 1/5-second stop-watch helped mitigate subjectivism and enabled the analyst to measure the patient's reaction time for possible symptoms of inhibition. There was also another technological apparatus—the Deprez-d'Arsonval galvanometer—which became very popular. This machine advanced bold claims about its ability to give objective representations of feeling-tones and psychic states. Swiss neurologist Otto Veraguth was the first to adopt it in conjunction with word-association tests to measure "galvano-psychophysical reflexes" in 1906. Jung improved the apparatus by attaching an automatic ergograph writer to register the traces of galvanometric oscillations during the association experiment. Galvanometers can be very sensitive to external stimuli. When a small electric current (about two volts) is conducted through the human body, say, the palms, the galvanometer will respond to the increase in the amount of the current, that is, the lowering of the electrical resistance of the body. This change in the amount of the current causes the coil and its attached mirror to rotate around a vertical axis. As Figure 15 indicates, Jung added a movable slide with a visor to the scale of the galvanometer. The slide, pushed forward by the hand, always follows the moving mirror reflection. To the slide is

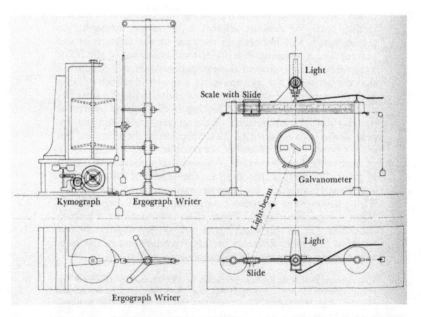

Figure 15. The design of Carl Jung's galvanometer-ergograph writer. From Carl Jung, "On the Psychological Relations of the Association Experiment," in *Experimental Researches* (1907), 484. Used by permission of the Foundation of the Works of C. G. Jung.

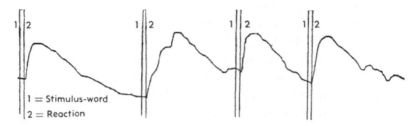

1 = Stimulus-word
2 = Reaction

Figure 16. Graphic representation of galvanic oscillation. From Carl Jung, *Experimental Researches* (1907), 487. Used by permission of the Foundation of the Works of C. G. Jung.

fastened a cord leading to the ergograph writer, whose penpoint marks the movement of the slide on a kymographic tambour fitted with endless paper. Figs. 16 and 17 illustrate the kind of feeling-tone curves that Jung's ergograph writer traced in the course of the association experiment.[102] The vertical lines in Figure 16 mark the moment at which the stimulus word was given to the subject. The curve rises sharply and then slowly falls. After the apparatus has been readjusted to register only the strongest feeling-tones, the curve begins to show a distinct pattern as in Figure 17. It illustrates that the ninth stimulus word caused the longest delay in the subject's reaction. That word is "pretty."[103] The galvanometric oscillations appear to confirm what his 1/5-second stop-watch reveals about the hidden complexes.

But what does the structure of the association game tell us about the relationship between symbol and the unconscious? As we have seen, Jung's incorporation of a 1/5-second stopwatch, the built-in repetition mechanism, and the galvanometer amounts to treating the unconscious as an automaton. This technical imperative embodies what Freud has called the *Wiederholenzwang* (repetition automatism) of the unconscious, a point that would be picked up by Lacan in his critical reevaluation of Freud's contributions to psychoanalytic theory.[104] The unconscious in this sense also anticipates how Shannon and Turing would approach the mind as a thinking machine. Both Shannon's mind-reading machine and Turing's learning machine are machines that, strictly speaking, think unconsciously, i.e.,

102. Both the description and the design are found in Jung, "On Psychophysical Relations of the Association Experiment," 484.

103. Jung conducted the association experiment on a young man who got married the week before and whose wife was considered not very "pretty" by others (ibid., 487).

104. In the English-speaking world, Ernest Jones adapted Jung's experiment to his research and diagnostic practices. See Ernest Jones, "The Practical Value of the Word Association Method in Psychopathology" in his *Papers in Psycho-Analysis*, 395–425.

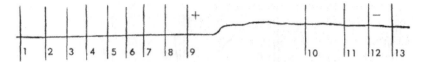

Figure 17. Graphic representation of a strong feeling-tone curve. From Carl Jung, *Experimental Researches* (1907), 487. Used by permission of the Foundation of the Works of C. G. Jung.

manipulating symbols unconsciously and blindly. In Shannon's Printed English, the unconscious machine is capable of putting out nonsense letter sequences as well sensible ones, such as the sample verse Pierce has given us. Does this amount to saying that the machine of the unconscious is fundamentally schizophrenic?

When Deleuze and Guattari proposed schizoanalysis in opposition to psychanalysis in *Anti-Oedipus*, they envisioned something like this:

> To discover beneath the familial reduction the nature of the social investments of the unconscious. To discover beneath the individual fantasy the nature of group fantasies. Or, what amounts to the same thing, to push the simulacrum to the point where it ceases to be the image of an image, so as to discover the abstract figures, the schizzes-flows that it harbors and conceals. To substitute, for the private subject of castration, split into a subject of enunciation and a subject of the statement relating only to the two orders of personal images, the collective agents of enunciation that for their part refer to machinic arrangements. To overturn the theater of representation into the order of desiring-production: this is the whole task of schizoanalysis.[105]

Multiple flows and bodies without organs are mobilized to displace the single subject of enunciation: call it the family, the law of the father, Oedipus, or the capitalist machine. The problem is that the schizophrenic was no stranger to the cybernetic machine even at its moment of inception, and one might suggest that schizophrenia has been the haunting figure in the development of the capitalist communication machine.

We must bear in mind that symbols that are universally adopted by information theory, cybernetics, and computer technology are discrete units—letters and numbers—rather than spoken or semantic units. McCulloch recalled that when he first embarked on the study of neurophysiology and then cybernetics, he had wanted to pursue a philosophical

105. Deleuze and Guattari, *Anti-Oedipus: Capitalism and Schizophrenia*, vol. 1, 271.

question: "what is a number, that a man may know it, and a man, that he may know a number?"[106] Did the pioneers in psychoanalysis take a similar interest in numerical symbols as an alternative to semantics in their approach to the mind?

In *The Psychopathology of Everyday Life*, Freud offers some preliminary speculations about how the unconscious deals with number. He suggests that numerical symbols—especially obsessive ones—behave very much like the slip of the tongue, the slip of the pen, or what he has demonstrated in the dreamwork. He recounts how his own mind tends to "plunge into an arithmetical train of thought which arrives all at once at the desired number" and how "the numbers are so freely at the disposal of my unconscious thinking, whereas I am a bad reckoner and have the greatest difficulties in consciously noting dates, house numbers and such things."[107] Citing Jung's "Essay on the Understanding of Number Dream" (*Ein Beitrag zur Kenntnis des Zahlentraumes*) and Jones's "Unconscious Manipulation of Numbers," Freud argues that numerical associations are prone to manipulation by the unconscious and to the patterns of condensation and compromise-formation that one finds in verbal associations. Therefore, random action can never be truly random insofar as the psyche is concerned and that "one cannot make a number occur to one at one's own free choice any more than a name" (*The Psychopathology of Everyday Life*, 240). Freud's observations were confirmed by the clinical observations of Alfred Adler, Carl Jung, Ernest Jones, and others.

If Freud came somewhat close to the notion of statistical probability tending toward a possible resolution of the relationship of chance and determinism, he did not seriously pursue that line of thought. Those who did pursue the thought with intellectual rigor were, for the most part, game theorists and mathematicians like Turing, Wiener, von Neumann, and Shannon. However, these mathematicians did not express much interest in the kind of questions Freud and other psychoanalysts posed to the human psyche. The rare thinker who burst on the postwar intellectual scene and began to engage Freud as well as the above mathematicians across the disciplinary divides was the French psychoanalyst Jacques Lacan.

106. Warren S. McCulloch, *Embodiments of Mind*, 2.

107. Sigmund Freud, *The Psychopathology of Everyday Life*, in *The Standard Edition of the Complete Psychological Works of Sigmund Freud*, vol. 6: 250.

4 The Cybernetic Unconscious

A short text comes to our aid, from Edgar Poe, which the cyberneticians, I noticed, make something of. This text is in *The Purloined Letter*, an absolutely sensational short story, which could even be considered as essential for a psychoanalyst.

Jacques Lacan, "Odd or Even?" March 23, 1955

Contrary to common belief, a great deal of what we now call French theory was already a translation of American theory before it landed in America to be reinvented as French theory. For example, it is startling to ponder how two different concepts "game" and "play" in game theory have morphed into a single idea of "play" in literary theory when they are brought back to the home country on the wings of the French word *jeu*. To be sure, new meanings are bound to be invented during these roundtrip processes, but what gets lost in translation is the concept of "game," game theory, and, more importantly, the associated history of cybernetic developments in the cold war. This chapter continues our investigation of the evolution of digital writing by delving into that history; in particular, I will explore how the work of Jacques Lacan can help us think about the psychic machine and gain some insights about the future of the unconscious.

By now, the reader should begin to realize that the concept of the stochastic process is indispensable to information theory, cybernetics, and contemporary scientific discourse in general. We have seen how the stochastic process in Printed English involves the play of chance and probability with respect to n-letter sequences that can result either in nonsense sequences or in random series approaching legible English phrases. The concept "stochastic" has been rendered into French as "aleatory" through cybernetic translations and is correctly understood by French scientists and philosophers as a mathematical concept. But this concept is caught in a similar blind play of signifiers, as in the instance of "game," when "aleatory" returns to English through literary and philosophical translations that seldom render the French word back to "stochastic." As we know, the term "aleatory" regularly appears in the writings of Derrida, Lacan, Deleuze, and other French theorists and is often left untranslated by the English interpreters. Thus the loanword "aleatory" becomes a source of mystification and cuts the English-speaking reader off from the familiar cybernetic context where the English word "stochastic" is the appropriate one to use. This confusion has resulted from the roundtrip movement of the Greek-derived word "stochastic" into a Latin-derived French word "aleatory" and then back into English which generates a Latin-derived loan "aleatory." In the context of scientific discourse, the concept "stochastic" is always precise and never confusing as to its intellectual provenance. In short, the roundtrip cycles of translation do much more than repeat the play of mere words between English and French. Rather, they frequently function like movie screens on which we sometimes project our fantasies and stories about transatlantic intellectual exchanges and displace the history of those exchanges.

French Theory or American Theory?

Compared with how much has been written about Jacques Lacan's rejection of American ego psychology, we know little about how he embraced game theory and cybernetics in the 1950s and developed his notion of the symbolic order on that basis.[1] It is not as if scholars were unaware of the ways in which French theory has been translated, published, and fashioned by

---

1. Recent studies of media technology and cybernetics are beginning to remedy this situation. See John Johnson, *The Allure of Machinic Life: Cybernetics, Artificial Life, and the New AI* (2008), Céline Lafontaine, *L'empire cybernétique: Des machines à penser à la pensée machine*, and the other studies I discuss in the chapter.

American academia.[2] Some critics would go so far as to claim that "French theory" was an American invention and this tradition reflects an ongoing process of American reception of all kinds of European imports going back to at least the eighteenth century.[3] An invention it may well have been; but an invention of what? Has the flow of indebtedness not gone the other direction and in reciprocal ways as well?

If we give but momentary attention to what Jean-Paul Sartre was saying when he reacted to the Structuralist's move to decenter the subject in the 1960s, we begin to discern the contours of a very different intellectual landscape here. Sartre contended that no one could grasp the ideological implications of the Structuralist moment until he or she took a hard look at "what is going on in the United States," where "a technocratic civilization no longer holds a place for philosophy unless the latter turns itself into technology."[4] Sartre may have perceived a few things his contemporaries failed to notice in their enthusiasm to embrace the new theory, but it seems that the French philosopher was fighting a rearguard battle against the spread of technocratic civilization. When we consider how the world was quickly coming under the sway of American militaristic and technocratic hegemony in the cold war, there seems a great deal more at stake than the survival of (European) philosophy. Still, we must credit Sartre with his astute grasp of the role of the United States in the fashioning of the intellectual discourse of his time. He may or may not have been aware that some American intellectual exports were fast becoming French theory to be reimported to American universities, where scholars in the humanistic disciplines paid little attention to what their mathematician colleagues were doing in the next building and vice versa. Fredric Jameson was perhaps one of the few critics in American academia who, in the

2. Jane Gallop has noted the play of mirrors between America and France in *Reading Lacan*. She observes an instance of the Lacanian imaginary in this play; namely, a specular relationship wherein one's understanding of the other is shaped by one's projected imagoes. She further suggests that instead of identifying with the (French) master analyst Lacan in his reading of Poe, an (American) reader might consider identifying with Poe's (American) narrator to escape the play of mirrors and find the symbolic there (Jane Gallop, *Reading Lacan*, 55–73). As my analysis in this chapter indicates, the Lacanian symbolic is not about any sort of identification processes; the latter could only take us back into the realm of the imaginary. The Lacanian symbolic lies rather in the cybernetic unconscious.

3. See Sylvere Lotringer and Sande Cohen, "Introduction: A Few Theses on French Theory in America," 1.

4. See Sartre, "Jean-Paul Sartre Répond," 94. In 1966, *L'Arc* devoted a special number to Sartre called "Sartre Aujourd'hui," which contains this interview with the philosopher. In the interview, editor Bernard Pingaud specifically asked Sartre to respond to the work of the younger Structuralists including Foucault, Lévi-Strauss, Lacan, and Althusser.

manner of Sartre, warned his readers about "the ideology of structuralism" in response to the fever of French theory in the 1970s.[5] That ideology is spelled out by Kittler as a new mode of address in the military technology of cruise missiles of the cold war, and the death of the subject—a discovery to be celebrated by Poststructuralist critics—can be shown to articulate meaningfully to the development of the automated remote control of this weapon and other cybernetic weapons.[6]

Unfortunately, few on the west side of the Atlantic were prepared to recognize the American mind behind "French theory" during that time, much less the convoluted linkages between cybernetics and Structuralism (or what American literary critics term Poststructuralism) in the 1950s and '60s.[7] This blindness in the play of mirrors can be made to reveal itself along the migratory and circulatory routes whereby American game theory and cybernetics became progressively *unseen* and *unmarked* through its Frenchness. Of course, it is absurd in general to give theory any kind of national provenance, since scientists and theorists work and collaborate across national borders and borrow from each other's work all the time. This familiar knowledge need not, however, prevent us from confronting the historical conditions under which scientific research is prioritized and sponsored by modern states and can form strategic and close alliances with parochial, national, or imperial interests. So when I use the term "American theory" in this limited sense, it is not because I endorse the nationalist claims of any particular scientific community but because the provenance of so-called French theory in literary studies needs to be rethought in connection with the growing presence of American hegemony in postwar Europe.[8] If we must reopen the issue of who invented French theory, it would make better sense to rephrase the question this way: How did American theory become French theory?

5. Fredric Jameson, "Imaginary and Symbolic in Lacan: Marxism, Psychoanalytic Criticism, and the Problem of the Subject," 374.

6. Friedrich Kittler, *Literature, Media, Information Systems*, 145. Kittler's insight was inspired by his reading of Lacan, which shows the irony of Sartre's somewhat flawed understanding of Lacan.

7. François Dosse gives only passing attention to cybernetics in his impressive two-volume study of the history of Structuralism. See Dosse, *History of Structuralism*, vol. 1, 220.

8. "American theory" serves as a shorthand reference to game theory, cybernetics, or information theory, which arose in postwar America and became hegemonic with the rise of American empire. I do not imply unities among these theories nor do I think the national origin of an individual scientist matters a great deal in this discussion. French and other European scientists had certainly contributed to the mathematical foundation of cybernetics, as Wiener himself has noted, but they did not invent cybernetics as a field nor was their work directly related to the exertion of American hegemony.

This American construct, which went variously by the names game theory, cybernetics, and information theory, made its way to postwar France (and elsewhere) in the late 1940s and 1950s and were avidly studied and translated by French scientists. The novel mathematical developments—all with close ties to the war efforts in World War II—represent some of the most innovative theoretical work across the disciplines and are commonly known by their authorial signatures. Game theory is generally attributed to John von Neumann and Oskar Morgenstern, whose groundbreaking *Theory of Games and Economic Behavior* was published by Princeton University Press in 1944.[9] This theory deals with decision making in competitive situations (zero-sum game, ruse, and bluffing, minimax theorem) and identifies patterns of reasoning to determine their implications for decision making and winning strategies. With the mathematical prestige of game theory, John von Neumann and Oskar Morgenstern introduced scientific rigor into economics and successfully turned the latter into a respectable discipline.[10] Four years later, information theory came into existence with Shannon's paper "A Mathematical Theory of Communication," which provided the theoretical foundation for communication engineering and digital media.[11] The early beginnings of cybernetics, on the other hand, date back to the first Macy Conference, which was held in New York in May 1942, but this new interdisciplinary effort did not become known to the world as "cybernetics" until Norbert Wiener borrowed a Greek word Κυβερνήτης (steersman) to name the field in 1948.[12] Almost around the

9. For a discussion of contested claims of priority, see William Poundstone, *Prisoner's Dilemma*, 40–41. In 1928, von Neumann brought out his paper "Zur Theorie der Gesellschaftspiele" (Theory of parlor games) but Émile Borel had published a similar study as early as 1921. Poundstone suggests that von Neumann was aware of Borel's study but made scant mention of it. Aside from professional jealousy, von Neumann did something that Borel had not done in his paper, namely, proving the famous minimax theorem, which would be crucial for the establishment of game theory as a field of study. Furthermore, as the French mathematician Guilbaud has noted, the crucial distinction between "game" and "play" was introduced into English by von Neumann and Morgenstern in their 1944 book. See Guilbaud, "Leçons sur les éléments principaux de la théorie mathématique des jeux," part 2, 1–29.

10. The crowning moment of its universal recognition was the 1994 Nobel Memorial Prize awarded to John Nash, John Harsanyi, and Reinhard Selten.

11. This paper was first published in the *Bell System Technical Journal*, vol. 27 (July and October, 1948): 379–423, 623–56.

12. By Wiener's account, this happened in the summer of 1947. The Greek word was chosen because "we wish to recognize that the first significant paper on feed-back mechanisms is an article on governors, which was published by Clerk Maxwell in 1868, and that *governor* is derived from a Latin corruption of Κυβερνήτης." See Wiener, *Cybernetics: or Control and Communication in the Animal and the Machine*, 19. For a detailed autobiographical account, see Wiener, *I Am a Mathematician*, 322–23.

same time, Wiener began to lump information theory and cybernetics together to characterize the novel interdisciplinary study of control and communication in the machine and in the animal.

In France, the introduction of game theory, cybernetics, and information theory aroused a great deal of excitement and curiosity among the scientific and intellectual elite, including Claude Lévi-Strauss, Jean Hyppolite, Henri Lefebvre, Roger Caillois, Algirdas Julien Greimas, Derrida, Michel Foucault, Gilles Deleuze, and Roland Barthes. Some of them sought to incorporate the new theories into their work, while others were highly critical.[13] Elizabeth Roudinesco mentions that the period "marked the entry of linguistics into the Freudian domain" for Lacan.[14] Of course, she means structural linguistics. Roudinesco points to Lacan's dialogue with Jean Hyppolite in 1954 as a pivotal event in the former's decision to move away from Hegelian philosophy and gain access to Structuralism. It is worth mentioning further that the Hegelian philosopher Hyppolite not only attended Lacan's seminar and dialogued with him at this time, but he was keenly interested in cybernetics and put important questions to Wiener in person when the latter visited France.[15] Like Lacan's "Seminar on 'The Purloined Letter,'" Hyppolite's much-admired "*Le coup de dés* de Stéphane Mallarmé et le message," published in 1958, grew out of this intellectual fervor surrounding chance, message, Maxwell's demon, entropy, and the other favorite topics of cybernetics and information theory.[16] If Lacan moved away from Hegelian philosophy in 1954, he did not so much turn toward structural linguistics as begin to show a strong interest in cybernetics and information theory. As a matter of fact, the seminars he conducted in 1954–55 provide the overwhelming evidence that he looked upon cybernetics and information theory as an alternative intellectual framework for rethinking Freud. Even structural linguistics sought to refashion itself on the model of information theory during this period.

13. Roger Caillois criticizes game theory in *Les jeux et les hommes* in 1958. His criticism, more nominal than intellectually engaged, dwells on how Huizinga and von Neumann use the same word to discuss very different subjects (161–75). Interestingly, Caillois' translator Meyer Barash keeps the word "games" in the English title as *Man, Play, and Games* and adds the word "play" to suggest critical tension between the two terms.

14. Elizabeth Roudinesco, *Jacques Lacan & Co.: A History of Psychoanalysis in France, 1925–1985*, 300.

15. Wiener's papers contain an undated transcript of a seminar he presented in Paris that includes a fascinating exchange between him and Hyppolite on the topic of game theory and the future of warfare (832). See Wiener, "L'Homme et la machine," 824–42.

16. See Jean Hyppolite, "*Le coup de dés* de Stéphane Mallarmé et le message."

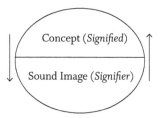

Figure 18. Ferdinand de Saussure's diagram of signified and signifier in the sign. From Ferdinand de Saussure, *Course in General Linguistics* (New York: McGraw-Hill, 1966), 66.

We know that Lacan met Jakobson through the introduction of Lévi-Strauss back in 1950 and became his close friend.[17] Jakobson's speculations about aphasia and structural poetics, especially his conceptualization of metaphor and metonymy, made an unmistakable imprint on Lacan's work on language. The exposure to Saussure via Jakobson has led to Lacan's re-working of the relationship of signifier and signified in the symbolic order. In his original diagram, Saussure put the signified over the signifier (Fig. 18) but Lacan chose to reverse them by placing the signifier above the bar (Fig. 19). It bears asking, however, what caused him to take that step. Furthermore, did Lacan mean the same thing by language or *la langue* as did Saussure or Jakobson?[18] Philippe Lacoue-Labarthe and Jean-Luc Nancy's careful reading of Lacan's treatment of algorithm and operation appears to suggest the opposite, i.e., Lacan was moving away from structural linguistics and was leaving linguistics behind.[19] Although Lacan himself did not put it this way, what Deleuze and Guattari said many years later would have resonated with him: "language is a political affair before it is an affair

17. Dosse, *History of Structuralism*, vol. 1, 58. See also Roudinesco, *Jacques Lacan & Co.*, 305–7. John Johnson makes a different conjecture about Lacan's relationship with Jakobson and thinks that it was probably Jakobson who introduced Lacan to cybernetics. My research has led me to new sources and a different conclusion. See my analysis below.

18. In Samuel Weber's attempt to grapple with the reversal of the Saussurian diagram, he resorts to wordplay and believes that it is all about *sens* (linguistic meaning) and anxiety. He argues that "the significant question that poses itself from within Lacan's writing for us then goes: how does the signifier become a signified? Or: How do signifieds come into being?" As my analysis shows below, this is far from being true, and there is no evidence to support the view that Lacan is at any point concerned with the signified or that the symbolic order has much to do with "anxiety." See Weber, "Vertigo: The Question of Anxiety in Freud," 206.

19. See Philippe Lacoue-Labarthe and Jean-Luc Nancy, *The Title of the Letter: A Reading of Lacan*, especially the second chapter, 33–50.

4

S
—
s

Figure 19. Jacques Lacan's reversed order of signified and signifier. From "The Instance of the Letter in the Unconscious," *Écrits: The Complete Edition* by Jacques Lacan, translated by Bruce Fink (New York: Norton, 2002), 428.

for linguistics; even the evaluation of degrees of grammaticality is a political matter."[20]

In his reading of the "postface" to "Seminar on 'The Purloined Letter,'" Bruce Fink makes an interesting observation, suggesting not only that Lacan has ventured "beyond the work on the symbolic order done by structuralists such as Lévi-Strauss and Jakobson" but that "Lacan is not a structuralist."[21] Friedrich Kittler, in his own manner, takes note of the Lacanian "methodological distinction" among the real, the imaginary, and the symbolic as being primarily a matter of differentiation in materiality and technicity that oversteps the bounds of the linguistic.[22] Kittler states simply that the world of the symbolic order is a world of the machine.[23] Fink's and Kittler's insights are worth exploring further, especially in regard to how the machine got into Lacan's symbolic, and which machine? Is it the typewriter, the computer, or something else? As we will see in the next section, Lacan's discussions of language throughout the seminars of 1954–55 were thoroughly permeated by his reflections on chance, homeostasis, circuit, games, probability, feedback, and entropy. It was in the course of those discussions that he first introduced Poe's "The Purloined Letter" and began his famous *explication de texte*, "Le Séminaire sur 'la lettre volée.'"

Lacan Reading Poe: "The Seminar on 'The Purloined Letter'"

Lacan says that chance put the text of Edgar Allan Poe's "The Purloined Letter" at his disposal. Did chance also cause his famous reading of Poe to

20. Deleuze and Guattari, *A Thousand Plateaus: Capitalism and Schizophrenia*, 139–40.

21. Bruce Fink, "The Nature of Unconscious Thought or Why No One Ever Reads Lacan's Postface to the 'Seminar on "The Purloined Letter,"'" 173–74.

22. Friedrich Kittler, *Gramophone, Film, Typewriter*, 15. For a critique of Kittler's effort to graft the three storage media onto Lacan's tripartite distinctions, see Thomas Sebastian, "Technology Romanticized: Friedrich Kittler's *Discourse Networks 1800/1900*."

23. This is the argument and title of his "The World of the Symbolic—A World of the Machine," in Kittler, *Literature, Media, Information Systems*, 130–46.

make the hermeneutic moves and detours we subsequently encounter in Poststructuralist literary criticism? Whatever caused it to happen, these moves and detours are still guarding an open secret as to how Lacan discovered Poe's story for psychoanalysis. The secret—hiding in plain sight, as it were—has inadvertently barred us from knowing more; that is to say, something will remain unseen and unheard until we are prepared to reflect on what we know about Lacan through American literary criticism and, more importantly, on what we do not know about American cybernetics in France, or in the U.S. for that matter.

Barring that knowledge, have we been asking the right sort of questions about Lacan's analytical rigor with respect to the symbolic order? For instance, why did his teaching seem so abstruse? Did Lacan get his mathematics right?[24] If questions like these do not seem particularly conducive to a fruitful understanding, is it because the symbolic order that Lacan has tried so hard to elucidate with his diagrams and ideographic signs has been eluding us all this time? A common mistake one can make is to fetishize Lacan's seminar excursion into "The Purloined Letter" as a virtuoso performance in psychoanalytical criticism and turn that criticism into all kinds of navel-gazing exercises. Such exercises have had the unfortunate consequence of thwarting the political decision or intuition that had gone into Lacan's adoption of Poe's text and thereby deflecting his important discoveries concerning the Freudian unconscious.

But which unconscious? Did Lacan not invent the famous formulation that the unconscious is the discourse of the Other (*l'inconscient, c'est le discours de l'Autre*)?[25] True, but what does he mean by "the Other"? In the seminar on "The Purloined Letter," Lacan makes it clear that the Other is the cybernetic machine rather than what we call language; he further adds that, if the unconscious exists in Freud's sense of the term, "it is not unthinkable that a modern calculating machine, by detecting the sentence that, unbeknown to him and in the long term, modulates a subject's choices, could manage to win beyond any usual proportions in the game of

24. Alan Sokal and Jean Bricmont attack Lacan and his use of mathematics in this manner rather than engage in a responsible critique of the shadow figure of game theory, cybernetics, and information theory that lies behind Lacan's exercises in mathematical formalization. Interestingly, Sokal and Bricmont's own flawed understanding of complex numbers has been called into question by Arkady Plotnitsky. See Sokal and Bricmont, *Fashionable Nonsense: Postmodern Intellectuals' Abuse of Science*, and Plotnitsky, *The Knowable and the Unknowable*, 112–13. See also Bruce Fink's defense in *Lacan to the Letter*, 130–32. For typographical errors in Lacan's mathematical explications, see Fink, "The Nature of Unconscious Thought, or Why No One Ever Reads Lacan's Postface to the 'Seminar on "The Purloined Letter,"'" 186–87n3.

25. Lacan, "Seminar on 'The Purloined Letter,'" 10.

even and odd" (45). The calculating machine, i.e., the modern computer, is elsewhere called the adding machine by Lacan. By virtue of its mode of address to the unconscious, Lacan says that the calculating machine can be "far more dangerous for man than the atom bomb."[26] This enigmatic remark compresses some of his most important insights on the mind and the symbolic order. Lacan's main contribution in this area—which I must spell out for him since he stopped short of doing so himself—lies in what he can tell us about the cybernetic unconscious of the postwar Euro-American world order. The fact that we have not been able to escape this world order after his passing and after the cold war and the fact that theoretical discourses increasingly devolve into loose descriptive pronouncements about global phenomena provide some of the compelling reasons for once again engaging with Lacan's hard-won insights and making them relevant to future thought.

Lacan is by no means the first psychoanalyst to engage Poe. As Derrida has pointed out, Marie Bonaparte published a psychobiography of Poe as early as 1933 under the title *The Life and Works of Edgar Allan Poe*, which carried the imprimatur of Freud's foreword.[27] Lacan makes it clear, however, that it was "chance," not Bonaparte, that brought the text of "The Purloined Letter" to his attention.[28] That chance, he further reminds us, has something to do with the cyberneticians whom he acknowledges but does not name in several of his seminars.[29] Is he being facetious about his sources? Should we take his word for it? Rather than speculate about the author's intentions one way or the other, it is worthwhile to take his word literally and track down the nameless cyberneticians who may or may not have contributed to his reading of Poe. Pace Derrida, we will see that Poe's

26. Lacan, "The Circuit," 88.

27. See Derrida, *The Post Card: From Socrates to Freud and Beyond*, 403–96. I agree that Lacan must have known Bonaparte's book but do not think that the latter played a significant part in his reading of Poe's text. Derrida insists on associating Lacan's reading with Bonaparte's prewar work rather than confronting cybernetics, a postwar event, which oddly remains unaddressed throughout his criticism of Lacan. After comparing the relevant sources carefully, I conclude that Lacan's analysis has very little to do with Bonaparte and, in fact, goes in the opposite direction from her reading of Poe. It is for good reason that Lacan chose to mention the cyberneticians rather than acknowledge Bonaparte.

28. As I discuss below, Lacan's reading may also have indirectly been provoked by the popular Belgian writer Denis Marion, whose *La Méthode intellectuelle d'Edgar Poe* (1952) presents a rather superficial understanding of mathematical reasoning and Poe's literary strategy. Marion identifies Poe with Dupin and describes rather than analyzes Poe's cryptographic work.

29. The original statement is "le hasard nous l'a offerte" in Jacques Lacan, "La lettre volée," 264. In the preceding seminar on March 30, 1955, he had made the observation I cited in the epigraph, indicating that the chance arrived through the cyberneticians (ibid., 244).

fiction would not have emerged as a privileged site of analysis for Lacan in 1955 had the mathematicians whom he knew or read around that time not already appropriated Poe, Daniel Defoe, Jonathan Swift, Alexander Pushkin, Arthur Conan Doyle, H. G. Wells, Rudyard Kipling, James Joyce, and other writers in their development of Markov series, game theory, information theory, and cybernetics. But we are getting slightly ahead of ourselves.

Poe's "The Purloined Letter" was first brought up by Lacan on March 23, 1955, in conjunction with the figure of the machine; this happened in a session known as "Odd or Even? Beyond Intersubjectivity." Lacan began his teaching in that session by surveying the latest developments in cybernetics and its implications for reading Freud and he then suggested: "Let us try to consider for a moment what it means for *a machine to play the game of even and odd*. We couldn't work it all out by ourselves, because it would look a bit heavy-handed in the circumstances. *A short text comes to our aid, from Edgar Poe, which the cyberneticians, I noticed, make something of.* This text is in *The Purloined Letter*, an absolutely sensational short story, which could even be considered as essential for a psychoanalyst"[30] (my emphasis). On April 27, 1955, in what would become the "Seminar on 'The Purloined Letter,'" Lacan once again brought up the game of even and odd. He says: "What is immediately clear is what I have called the inmixing of subjects. I will illustrate it for you, since chance has offered it to us, with the story of *The Purloined Letter*, from which we took the example of the game of even and odd."[31] The question is, Why does Lacan seem more obsessively concerned with the machine and, in particular, with the game of even and odd than with Poe's story?

The game of even and odd appears in Poe's tale following C. Auguste Dupin's successful retrieval of the letter that was stolen from the Queen and hidden by Minister D. Dupin mentions this game to satisfy the curiosity of his friend the narrator on how he has managed to outsmart such a formidable opponent as Minister D. Dupin says that the game of even and odd is played among children. One player holds in his hand a number of marbles and asks the other to guess if the number is even or odd. If the guess is correct, the guesser wins one and if the guess is wrong, he loses

---

30. Lacan, "Odd or Even? Beyond Intersubjectivity," 179. The original text goes: "Un petit texte vient à notre secours, d'Edgar Poe, dont je me suis aperçu que les cybernéticiens faisaient quelque cas. Ce texte est dans *la Lettre volée*, novelle absolument sensationnelle, qu'on pourrait même considérer comme fondamentale pour un psychanalyste" ("Pair ou Impair?").

31. Lacan, "The Purloined Letter," 194.

one. There is an eight-year-old boy who wins all the marbles of his school simply by observing the astuteness of his opponent and can always predict his next move by identifying with his psyche. Evidently, Lacan became more intrigued by the structure of this game than by Dupin's clever trick of bluff, and he encouraged the members of his seminar to play the game of even and odd in class and report back to him.

In Lacan's reading of Poe, the symbolic structure of the game frames Dupin's ratiocination or reasoning, and this reasoning—which is always associated with Dupin's capacity for dissimulation and mirrors the mentality of his double, Minister D—is inevitably caught up in the symbolic structure that sets the letter in motion. His analysis shows the letter and the subject to be interchangeable in the sense that no subject who comes into contact with the letter (the Queen, the minister, Dupin, or anyone) can escape being caught up in the same game or machine. The repetition automatism in Poe's human drama thus finds its true meaning in the machine of chance and probability, where "the symbol's emergence into the real begins with a wager."[32] From the viewpoint of game theory, a further distinction is to be made between the game (*l'ensemble-jeu*) and the play (*élément*); I elaborate on this in the next section.[33]

The figure of the machine is what mediates Lacan's initial speculations about the relationship between the symbolic and the real when he argues that "the very notion of probability and chance presupposes the introduction of a symbol into the real" (182). He further suggests that "only in the dimension of truth can something be hidden like all games of chance" (201–2). This is an important point, for Lacan shows that what gets hidden in the game of even and odd is not one or two pieces of marble but numerical symbols; by the same token, that which can be hidden in "The Purloined Letter" is not the physical letter but the truth or any truth claims initiated by the chain of symbols in the structure.[34] Thus he discovers a symbolic order in the game of even and odd that matters more than the innocuous content of Poe's story. In fact, the game of even and odd does not stand alone in his analysis. In the seminars leading up to the discussion of "The Purloined Letter," Lacan has spoken of those "adding machines" and

32. Lacan, "The Purloined Letter," 192.

33. For detailed analysis, see below for my reading of game theory in Georges Th. Guilbaud, "Leçons sur les éléments principaux de la théorie mathématique des jeux," chap. 2, 7.

34. Derrida's critique of Lacan's logocentrism in "The Purveyor of Truth" misrepresents what Lacan is doing with symbolic systems in the seminar. As Barbara Johnson correctly points out, Derrida's silence on the game of even and odd is indicative of his blindspot. See Johnson, "The Frame of Reference: Poe, Lacan, Derrida," 213–51.

"thinking machines" that play similar games "within the limit of a certain strategy," and his reading of Poe is framed by a series of ongoing discussions about machines and cybernetics.[35]

In due course, these thinking machines will take us to the mysterious "cyberneticians" who had originally brought Poe's story to his attention. Lacan chose to leave us in the dark as to who those cyberneticians were and how they made him aware of such a reading. He was known for making oblique references to his sources and seemed to expect his disciples and students to work things out for themselves; he was known to show off a bit of his own erudition as well. Was it Norbert Wiener, Warren McCulloch, Gregory Bateson, Shannon, or someone else? Before we delve into the critical points of connection Lacan tried to establish between cybernetics and the unconscious via the symbolic order, we should follow the traces of the mathematicians in question and determine the trajectories of Lacan's interest in literature and cybernetics.

A preliminary investigation of the major cyberneticians and mathematicians of the time suggests that a good number of them showed an interest in literature. Wiener wrote fiction and corresponded with T. S. Eliot, and even published his own literary criticism, including a substantial article on Rudyard Kipling. Shannon had written critically about Poe's essay "Maelzel's Chess-Player" but not much else, although he did include *Finnegans Wake* in the work he carried out on Printed English, as discussed in the preceding chapter. Alan Turing enacted a series of botched hide-and-seek games when he tried to imitate Captain Kidd of "The Gold Bug" to bury his silver bars and banknotes in the countryside during World War II.[36] These men may have all read "The Purloined Letter," but none of them commented on the story as far as we can tell.

We turn next to cyberneticians such as Lawrence Kubie, John Z. Young, Gregory Bateson, and possibly a few others. Young, as we know, pioneered in the study of the neural bases of complex communication behavior in the octopus and participated in the ninth Macy Conference in March 1952. By Jean-Pierre Dupuy's account, Lacan was familiar with his work.[37] The reference to the octopus does occasionally pop up in Lacan's remarks about cybernetics, but there is no evidence that either Young or Bateson took an interest in "The Purloined Letter." Lacan's knowledge of Kubie's work has

35. Lacan, "Odd or Even? Beyond Intersubjectivity," 178.
36. On Turing's repeated failure to retrieve his silver bars, see Andrew Hodges, *Alan Turing: The Enigma*, 344–45.
37. Jean-Pierre Dupuy, *The Mechanization of the Mind: On the Origins of Cognitive Science*, 109.

been documented and discussed by Ronan Le Roux in a recent study, but in a context unrelated to literature.[38] The logical next step is to go back further to von Neumann and Morgenstern, who would have found Poe's game of even and odd relevant to their discussion of similar games such as the game of "matching pennies" in *Theory of Games and Economic Behavior*.[39] Lacan frequently alludes to the play of heads and tails from the game of "matching pennies" in his discussion of probability.

One would imagine that *The Theory of Games and Economic Behavior* could be the natural site for Lacan to encounter his cybernetic Poe, since his interests ranged from matching-penny games to the prisoner's dilemma and other subjects relating to chance and probability.[40] But it turns out that von Neumann and Morgenstern left the American novelist out of their literary repertoire to focus on the rational choices made by Robinson Crusoe and Sherlock Holmes. Nevertheless, the game theorists have left behind some useful clues to guide us to a number of French works that were devoted to introducing and translating game theory. In short, it is in the French translations and explications of game theory that we finally come close to resolving the mysteries surrounding the long-sought cybernetic references made by Lacan in his Poe seminar.

Les Jeux: Game and Play on the Symbolic Chain

One key figure in the translation and explication of game theory and cybernetics in French was the Catholic mathematician Georges Th. Guilbaud, whose name came up a number of times in our discussion of Shannon and Pierce. Guilbaud and Lacan became close friends in 1950, and their friendship lasted until Lacan's death in 1981.[41] Guilbaud is viewed by his American counterparts as an important contributor to game theory and was the first to introduce game theory, information theory, and cybernetics to the French-speaking world. In an interview conducted by Bernard Colasse and Francis Pavé a few years ago, the ninety-year-old Guilbaud recalls how he

38. See Roux, "Psychanalyse et cybernétique: Les machines de Lacan," 346–69.

39. For example, von Neumann and Morgenstern discuss the game of "matching pennies" by focusing on the strategies of preventing loss: "In playing Matching Pennies against an at least moderately intelligent opponent, the player will not attempt to find out the opponent's intentions but will concentrate on avoiding having his own intentions found out" (von Neumann and Morgenstern, 133).

40. The evidence of Lacan's early interest in game theory is found in his "Logical Time and the Assertion of Anticipated Certainty" published in 1945, shortly after the appearance of *The Theory of Games and Economic Behavior*. See Lacan, Écrits, 161–75.

41. Roudinesco, *Jacques Lacan & Co.*, 560.

and his colleagues at the Henri Poincaré Institute dedicated themselves to reading and mastering the new mathematical work from the Unites States, Germany, and the Soviet Union in the 1940s and '50s.[42]

Recent studies have shed valuable light on how the scientists and academics from the U.S., Europe, Soviet Union, and Latin America interacted with one another during the cold war.[43] In postwar France, the physical sciences were undergoing rapid transformations through the introduction of game theory, cybernetics, and information theory. In the midst of this flurry of activities stood Nicolas Bourbaki, fictitious mathematician fabricated by a group of eminent mathematicians in France. They formed a secret society under this name to subvert the scientific orthodoxy of France and create a modern mathematical discipline based on the rigorous axiomatic methods they promoted. The Bourbaki impact on the social sciences and literature can be seen in Lévi-Strauss's approach to kinship structure as well as in the making of the French literary group Oulipo, which was established in 1960 to emulate the Bourbakis. The meeting between Lévi-Strauss and Jakobson in New York City in 1943 is usually recounted as a significant moment in the history of Structuralism; but, in the same year and in the same city, Lévi-Strauss also became acquainted with the founder of Bourbaki, André Weil. Weil not only helped Lévi-Strauss conduct the mathematical analysis of his kinship research but also wrote the appendix to the first part of Lévi-Strauss's foundational text *Elementary Structures of Kinship*. These interesting circumstances have led David Aubin to conclude that the crossbreeding of anthropology, linguistics, and mathematics was what gave rise to Structuralism.[44]

The intellectual ties that connected the Bourbaki group to the other groups went deeper, however, than the genealogy of Structuralism and certainly contributed to the development and dissemination of cybernetics itself in the 1950s. The first English edition of Wiener's pathbreaking *Cybernetics* was published simultaneously by Hermann Editions in Paris

42. See Bernard Colasse and Francis Pavé, "La Mathématique et le social: entretien avec Georges Th. Guilbaud," 72.

43. For an overview of cybernetics in France, see David Mindell, Jérôme Segal, and Slava Gerovitch, "From Communications Engineering to Communications Science: Cybernetics and Information Theory in the United States, France, and Soviet Union," 66–95. See also Mai Wegener, *Neuronen und Neurosen: Der psychische Apparat bei Freud und Lacan: Ein historisch-theoretischer Versuch zur Freuds Entwurf von 1895*; Laurence A. Rickels, *Nazi Psychoanalysis: Crypto-Fetishism*, vol. 2.

44. See Aubin, "The Withering Immortality of Nicolas Bourbaki: A Cultural Connector at the Confluence of Structuralism, Mathematics, and the Oulipo in France," 311. François Dosse discusses the Bourbaki connection very briefly in the *History of Structuralism*, vol. 2, 24.

and the MIT Press (then the Technology Press) in collaboration with John Wiley & Sons in New York in 1948.[45] Enrique Freymann was the owner of the Hermann Editions. He had convinced Wiener the year before to write a book about his cybernetics theory and offered to publish it. In the spring of 1947, Wiener was passing through Paris on his way to a congress on harmonic analysis organized by the Bourbakist mathematician Szolem Mandelbrojt in Nancy. He agreed to sign a book contract with Hermann when he found out that Freymann was a founding member of Bourbaki.[46]

The spectacular success of Wiener's first book took him and his publishers by surprise; the book sold 21,000 copies and went through three reprints in six months.[47] The French press responded enthusiastically, although the French Communist Party denounced cybernetics as a "bourgeois" science. The Cercle d'Etudes Cybernétiques quickly formed in France with the renowned physicist Louis de Broglie serving as its honorary president. In 1950 and 1951, as David Mindell and his coauthors have noted, two congresses were held on cybernetics in Paris and, by the late 1950s, "a kind of normalization of the field took place, which correlated both with the promotion of cybernetics in popular science articles and books and with the institutionalization of cybernetics research in Western Europe" (74–75).

Two of Lacan's mathematician friends, Guilbaud and Jacques Riguet, the latter attending his seminars regularly, were members of the Cercle d'Etudes Cybernétiques.[48] It is not unreasonable to surmise that both men would have been among the "cyberneticians" to whom Lacan alluded in his seminar on Poe. Roudinesco informs us that Emile Benveniste, Guilbaud, Lévi-Strauss, and Lacan met regularly in 1951 to discuss establishing links between the social sciences and mathematics and that Guilbaud was also behind Lacan's use of topological figures, such as the Moebius strip, strings, inflatable buoys, and the torus.[49] But Roudinesco's biography keeps

45. The Technology Press tried to prevent the publication of the book in France, because Wiener, then a professor at MIT, was bound to them by contract, but Enrique Freymann, the owner of the Hermann Editions, managed to strike a compromise. See Mindell, Segal, and Gerovitch, "From Communications Engineering to Communications Science: Cybernetics and Information Theory in the United States, France, and Soviet Union," 75.

46. See Norbert Wiener, I Am a Mathematician, 314–17.

47. Mindell, Segal, and Gerovitch, "From Communications Engineering to Communications Science," 75.

48. Roux, "Psychanalyse et cybernétique: Les machines de Lacan," 355.

49. Roudinesco, Jacques Lacan & Co., 560. Benveniste also published an essay on game theory as early as 1947 called "Le jeu comme structure" (Game as structure), 161–67. Interestingly, by engaging exclusively with Johan Huizinga's Homo Ludens and Roger Caillois's work and focusing on

silent about the story of game theory and cybernetics and their centrality in Lacan's relationship with Guilbaud. This may have been one of the
reasons that most studies have heretofore focused on Lacan's interest in
topology.[50]

Guilbaud was largely responsible for the introduction and development
of game theory, information theory, and cybernetics in France. He was the
author of *La Cybernétique* (What is cybernetics?, 1954) and *Eléments de la
théorie mathématique des jeux* (Elements of game theory, 1968). His paper "The Theory of Games: Critical Contributions to the Theory of Value"
(1949) was a seminal work in the field.[51] Harold W. Kuhn singled out Guilbaud not only for his forty-five-page review of von Neumann and Morgenstern's *Theory of Games and Economic Behavior*, but also as one of the few
French scientists to make a unique contribution to game theory. It is interesting that Kuhn recalls that "Guilbaud's seminar in Paris in 1950–51 was
attended by such mathematical economists as Allais, Mailnvaud, Boiteux,
and myself."[52] The date of that seminar was three years before Lacan's. Was
Lacan in the audience of Guilbaud's seminar? We do not know. Even if he
did not attend that seminar, evidence suggests that he and Guilbaud were
very familiar with each other's work.

In 1954, Guilbaud published *La Cybernétique* a few months before Lacan
embarked on his seminar on "The Purloined Letter." That year also saw
the publication of Guilbaud's important article on game theory, "Lectures
on the Principal Elements in the Mathematical Theory of Games." In this
work—a long essay in five sections—Guilbaud makes an explicit reference
to the game of even and odd from Poe's story. From antiquity, he says, this
game has been looked down upon as a children's game, but adults have
also played it, especially in gambling situations where they risk losing
large amounts of money. He points out that the game of even and odd has
been "honored by a famous analysis given by Edgar Poe (The Purloined
Letter)" and adds that "an equivalent form is suggested and studied by von

the jeux and the sacred, Benveniste suppresses the possibility that the popularity of von Neumann's
and Morgenstern's game theory might have something to do with the reissuing of Huizinga's *Homo
Ludens* in German in 1944 and in other languages in the 1950s. At least we know that game theory
provoked Caillois to write *Les jeux et les hommes* to critique von Neumann and Morgenstern. The
title is rendered in English as *Man, Play, and Games*, where *jeux* is appropriately translated twice
and differently.

50. See Ellie Ragland and Dragan Milovanovic, eds., *Lacan: Topologically Speaking*.

51. This essay has been translated into English and included in Mary Ann Dimand and Robert
W. Dimand, eds. *The Foundations of Game Theory*, vol. 1.

52. Harold W. Kuhn, introduction to John von Neumann and Oskar Morgenstern, *Theory of
Games and Economic Behavior*, x.

Neumann and Morgenstern under the name of "matching pennies."[53] This reference pinpoints the meaningful connection Guilbaud was trying to establish between game theory and "The Purloined Letter," a connection that von Neumann and Morgenstern did not make in their original work. Even so, we will discover that this is not the first time that Poe appears in Guilbaud's discussion of von Neumann and Morgenstern.

Ronan Le Roux has examined an earlier lecture Guilbaud gave at the Sorbonne on March 24, 1953. Half of that lecture was devoted to discussing the mathematical theory of games, and portions of it found their way into the third part of *La Cybernétique*. In the original lecture, entitled "Pilots, Planners and Gamblers: Toward a Theory of Human Control," Guilbaud brought up Poe's story and pointed out that "The Purloined Letter" dealt with one of mathematicians' old controversies in literary register and suggested the possibility of a "pure game" (*jeu pur*).[54] Significantly, Guilbaud's lecture cites an essay by Lacan called "Logical Time and the Assertion of Anticipated Certainty" (1945) to challenge the kinds of psychologism one finds in the work of the Belgian doyen of letters Denis Marion (pseudonym of Marcel Defosse), who had just published *The Intellectual Method of Edgar Poe* (1952). Firmly aligning himself with Lacan to oppose the fallacies of psychologism, Guilbaud argues that Marion "appears to have neglected the fundamental problem which is not just a matter of 'reading the thought' of others. What matters is logic, not 'psychology.' Dr. J. Lacan has given an in-depth analysis of this problem in 'Logical Time'" (353). On the evidence presented by "Logical Time and the Assertion of Anticipated Certainty," it seems that Lacan's engagement with the prisoner's dilemma and game theory predated his acquaintance with Guilbaud, for that essay was published in March 1945, shortly after the appearance of von Neumann and Morgenstern's *Theory of Games and Economic Behavior*.[55] This happened before September 1945, when Lacan made his trip to England, where he

53. Guilbaud, "Leçons sur les éléments principaux de la théorie mathématique des jeux," chap. 3, 18.

54. Roux, "Psychanalyse et cybernétique," 352.

55. The essay was first published in *Les cahiers d'art*. According to Roudinesco, Lacan came across the sophism of the prisoners' dilemma from André Weiss as early as 1935. See Elizabeth Roudinesco, *Jacques Lacan*, 176. Interestingly, his thoughts on the sophism and its implications for thinking about logical time did not appear in print until 1945. The fact that Lacan's work on game and logical form began in 1945 rather than in 1935 supports a historical argument about his relationship with game theory.

visited the Hartfield rehabilitation center for returned prisoners of war and overseas veterans.

To make sense of the historical connections between Lacan's 1945 paper and the work of von Neumann and Morgenstern, it may be helpful to keep in mind that the latter's modeling of winning strategies under conditions of uncertainty and their discussions of two-person games, three-person games, and n-person games were inspiring very different work elsewhere. Most of that work, the most famous of which was the Flood-Dresher experiment, focused on irrational human behavior. William Poundstone says that "Merrill Flood was one of the first to analyze that irrationality with game theory."[56] Both the Flood-Dresher experiment at the RAND Corporation and Albert W. Tucker's coinage of the term "prisoner's dilemma" took place in 1950.[57] Contrary to what we believe about game theory, much of this work started out by assuming human beings not to be fully rational animals and that their decisions were subject to chance, time, and psychic factors. This is how Shannon reacted to the irrational decisions of the human subjects in Bavelas's test, as we have already noted in the preceding chapter.

Lacan's "Logical Time and the Assertion of Anticipated Certainty" anticipated the Flood-Dresher experiment by playing on the same fictional scenario of logical reasoning that was obsessing game theorists at the time. This was soon followed by another piece, "Number Thirteen and the Logical Form of Suspicion," in which he continues to reflect on the problem of number and chance.[58] Lacan begins "Logical Time and the Assertion of Anticipated Certainty" by hypothesizing a situation where a prison warden summons three prisoners and tells them that their freedom depends on the correct judgment that each of them makes upon examining the color of

56. William Poundstone, *Prisoner's Dilemma*, 101–25. Poundstone gives a brief discussion of how novelists have treated the prisoner's dilemma and points out that "a perceptive discussion of a prisoner's dilemma (closely following Tucker's anecdote!) occurs in Edgar Allan Poe's story 'The Mystery of Marie Rogêt.' Poe's detective C. Auguste Dupin speaks of an offer of reward and immunity to the first member of a criminal gang to confess: 'Each one of a gang, so placed, is not so much greedy of reward, or anxious for escape, as *fearful of betrayal*. He betrays eagerly and early that *he may not himself be betrayed*'" (124).

57. RAND, an acronym for "Research and Development," was founded by the US Air Force in 1946 as a joint venture with Douglas Aircraft. Its mandate was to study the techniques of air warfare. For a detailed analysis of game theory at RAND, see Paul N. Edwards, *The Closed World: Computers and the Politics of Discourse in Cold War America*, 113–45.

58. For a superb discussion of Lacan's concept of logical time during this period, see Erik Porge, *Se compter trios: le temps logique de Lacan*.

the disk the others carry.[59] The prisoners are told that there are three white disks and two black ones but none of them is allowed to see the color of his own disk, which is affixed to his body but lies beyond his own field of vision. The first individual—the time factor being crucial here—who correctly deduces his own color on the basis of what he sees on the others will be discharged.[60] Lacan uses this fiction to investigate the logical form that a "temporalized reference of oneself to another" will take and suggests that "these forms assuredly find easy application in bridge table and diplomatic strategy, not to mention in the handling of the 'complex' in psychoanalytic practice" (173). As an early foray into game theory, Lacan's essay greatly impressed Guilbaud. It also indicates that his interest in game theory did not originate with Guilbaud and that his writing about the prisoner's dilemma perhaps predated the experimental work of the mathematicians at RAND Corporation.

There is strong evidence to indicate, however, that Lacan's reading of Poe was inspired and guided by Guilbaud's work on von Neumann and Morgenstern. In 1949, Guilbaud published his long review article on the latter's *Theory of Games and Economic Behavior* in the journal *Economie Appliquée*; this became one of the little-known sources for Lacan's reading of "The Purloined Letter." This paper's treatment of Poe's story was much more rigorous and critical than his 1953 lecture at the Sorbonne or his 1954 article on game theory. Harold W. Kuhn observes that Guilbaud's review article was not just a review of von Neumann and Morgenstern, and it also made some genuine contributions to the development of game theory.

In this article, Guilbaud performs a close reading of the game of even and odd from "The Purloined Letter" in order to speculate on what he calls "the theory of the ruse." He suggests that ruse plays a double role: Player 1 tries to guess his opponent's intentions and arranges things so that Player 2 not guess his own intentions. Guilbaud calls this "positive and negative ruse." It follows that if the strategy employed is rigidly applied, the ruse can be discovered and will become valueless. This, Guilbaud points out, is the origin of bluff, "which is by definition a flexible strategy or, as we shall see, a stochastic choice."[61] He goes on to consider a two-player scenario in

---

59. Roudinesco suggests that Lacan used this sophism to attack Sartre's conception of freedom in a play called *Huis clos* (No exit) in 1944, but she does not mention Lacan's interest in game theory, which puts the idea of freedom in doubt. See Roudinesco, *Jacques Lacan*, 176–77.

60. Lacan, "Logical Time and the Assertion of Anticipated Certainty," 162.

61. Guilbaud, "The Theory of Games: Critical Contributions to the Theory of Value," 372. The original essay, "La Théorie des jeux: contributions critiques à la théorie de la valeur," was published in the April–June number of *Economie Appliquée*, 275–319.

which the players are limited to two options. Player 1 chooses between a and b and Player 2 chooses between c and d, so that the following situations will result:

(ac)	(bc)
(ad)	(bd)

There are several different ways of ranking these four situations according to each player's system of preference.[62] How does a game of this type work? Guilbaud alludes to two literary works: "there is the game of 'even or odd' described by Edgar Allan Poe in 'The Purloined Letter.' Morgenstern has used one of Sherlock Holmes' adventures. Holmes wants to get to Dover and thence to the Continent in order to escape from Moriarty. When boarding the train he sees Moriarty on the platform. Between London and Dover there is only one stop, Canterbury."[63] Holmes is thus faced with some hard decisions. He will be killed if he gets off the train at the same time as Moriarty, so we are presented with these four scenarios:

a = Holmes gets off at Dover
b = Holmes gets off at Canterbury
c = Moriarty gets off at Canterbury
d = Moriarty gets off at Dover

From Holmes's point of view, which is the opposite of Moriarty's, ac (success) and bd (failure) are preferable to ad (death) and bc (death). Will each be able to imagine the other's thoughts and decide on a course of action to his own best advantage? Von Neumann and Morgenstern have calculated that Moriarty would go to Dover with a probability of 60% whereas Holmes would stop at the intermediate station also with a probability of 60%. The remaining 40% should account for the other alternatives in each case (178). It is at this point that Guilbaud introduces Dupin's treatment of the game of even and odd in "The Purloined Letter"; he believes that Poe's solution is too facile from the viewpoint of game theory:

62. In their treatment of the game of "matching pennies," von Neumann and Morgenstern analyze the Sherlock Holmes story "The Adventure of the Final Problem" under the category of zero-sum two-person games. For their detailed discussion, see von Neumann and Morgenstern, *Theory of Games and Economic Behavior*, 176–78.
63. Guilbaud, "The Theory of Games: Critical Contributions to the Theory of Value," 372.

Poe supposes that one of the two players is much more intelligent than his opponent and the analysis is therefore easy. But if we suppose that the two players have been playing together for rather a long time we may ask what happens when, with experience, they marshal equal powers of reflection. The only solution, obviously, is for each to choose at random, taking care, of course, to profit by his opponent's least error. Random choice thus plays the part of a defensive position, of a base for an attack which will develop when the opponent makes mistakes. Random choice plays the part of a saddle point.[64]

Guilbaud's critique is based on von Neumann's mathematical formalization of random choices between two players of equal intelligence, which proves to be a more satisfying solution than Poe's because it is based on probability and shows that equilibrium can be reached by stochastic choices (which is a very different idea from what is usually understood to be rational choice).

In game theory, mathematicians maintain a rigorous distinction between a *game*, which consists of a set of rules that define it, and a *play*, which is a particular instance in which a game is played from beginning to end. From this distinction follows yet another set of distinctions between a *move* and a *choice*. As Harold W. Kuhn puts it: "A similar distinction is made between the occasion of the selection of one among several alternatives, to be made by one of the players or by some chance device, which is called a *move*, and the actual selection in a particular play, which is called a *choice*. Thus, a game consists of a set of moves in some order (not necessarily linear!), while a play consists of a sequence of choices."[65] It was Guilbaud who translated these subtle distinctions into French, and he was fully aware of the difficulty of negotiating between the two languages. In a later paper, "Lectures on the Principal Elements in the Mathematical Theory of Games" (1954), he spells out the difficulty for his French readers:

Une premiere distinction est fondamentale: celle du jeu tel qu'il est défini par sa règle—et d'une realization particulière conforme à la règle. Ou encore en termes equivalents: le jeu avant qu'il ne soit joué—et le jeu une fois qu'il a été joué. Dans le Traité de Von Neumann et Morgenstern, ces notions correspondent respectivement aux vocables: *game, play*, adoptés ensuite par la plupart des théoriciens de langue anglaise (bien que la langue littéraire ne

---

64. Guilbaud, "The Theory of Games: Critical Contributions to the Theory of Value," 373.
65. See H. W. Kuhn, "Extensive Games," 571.

fasse pas toujours la même distinction). *Game* désigne le Jeu à Jouer, *Play* un Jeu joué. (italics in the original)[66]

[A first distinction is fundamental: the distinction between the *jeu* as defined by the rules and a particular realization of the *jeu* that follows those rules. In other words, it is between the *jeu* that is yet to be played and the *jeu* once it has been played. In the treatise of von Neumann and Morgenstern, these concepts correspond to the terms "game" and "play" respectively, which have been adopted by the majority of English-language theorists (although literary language does not always make the same distinction). *Game* refers to the *jeu* to be played whereas *play* refers to a *jeu* that has been played.]

Guilbaud knew that the literary language would probably confound the distinction between *game* and *play*. Sure enough, when *le Jeu à Jouer* was translated back into English as a French concept, it became *play*, no longer *game*, in spite of the fact that the distinction between game and play is well established in English, as pointed out at the outset of this chapter. The heterolinguistic supersign "jeu/game" in the French context is made fully commensurate with the supersign "jeu/play" in English.[67] This situation is largely responsible for how the linkages between game theory and Lacan's reading of Poe have heretofore been obscured.

As a linguistic choice, "play" is not a wrong verbal equivalent to "jeu," but that is exactly where the problem lies. The free play of signifiers becomes a blind play—oblivious to the traces of an earlier heterolinguistic supersign "jeu/game"—and renders the sinister, calculating, and competitive ethos of game theory invisible to the critical eye. So when Derrida is made to say in English that "[c]ontrary to the metaphysical, dialectical, 'Hegelian' interpretation of the economic movement of *différance*, we must conceive of a play in which whoever loses wins, and in which one loses and wins on every turn," the slippage of translation from *game* to *play* produces not only a confused statement about winning and losing but, more importantly, it displaces the intellectual provenance of the Derridian *jeu*.[68]

66. Guilbaud, "Leçons sur les éléments principaux de la théorie mathématique des jeux," chap. 2, 6.

67. I developed the concept of supersign to designate the invisible bonding of heterolinguistic elements caused by translation. In contrast to the case of neologisms, this process is observable in any verbal unit whose signified is implicitly referred to a foreign word(s), thus transforming the familiar word without subjecting it to visible morphological changes. For detailed elaboration of this concept in semiotics, see Liu, *The Clash of Empires: The Invention of China in Modern World Making*, 12–13.

68. Jacques Derrida, *Margins of Philosophy*, 20. The slippage between "play" and "game" characterizes Alan Bass's translation of Derrida. The following statement is also typical: "The concept of

Thus the harmless supersign "jeu/play" travels back to English in the guise of French theory to authorize something like a free play of signifiers in literary discourse, making us overlook the fact that von Neumann and Morgenstern's games—zero-sum games, strategy, bluffing, etc.—are just as applicable to their view of economics as to nuclear warfare.

One need not work out the full technical details of game theory to understand how Poe's treatment of the game of even and odd in "The Purloined Letter" privileges the "play" and "choices" over the "game" and "moves" when he allows both the clever boy and Dupin to win all the marbles and win the letter contest. The preference for the imaginary order (identifying with your opponent) precludes an engagement with stochastic processes at the level of the symbolic order (weighing the probability of the game). This may well have been the reason that Poe's story was excluded from the literary examples used by von Neumann and Morgenstern to illustrate game theory.

Lacan's critical reading of Poe closely matches that of Guilbaud's insofar as Dupin's ruse is pitted against the game of even or odd. The stochastic processes of the game are superior to the cleverness of Dupin, who thinks he can overcome the law of chance but may end up in the same place as everyone else. In his reading of "The Purloined Letter," Lacan emphasizes the importance of structure and the compulsion to repeat insofar as these are addressed to the exigencies of chance, randomness, and stochastic processes in general. He states:

> By itself, the play of the symbol represents and organizes, independently of the peculiarities of its human support, this something which is called a subject. The human subject doesn't foment this game, he takes his place in it, and plays the role of the little *pluses* and *minuses* in it. He is himself an element in this chain which, as soon as it is unwound, organizes itself in accordance with laws. Hence the subject is always on several levels, caught up in crisscrossing networks.[69]

The little *pluses* and *minuses* and diagrams that commonly frame Lacan's reading of Poe are not as mystifying they first appear. These correspond

---

play keeps itself beyond this opposition [between philosophical-logical discourse and empirical-logical discourse], announcing, on the eve of philosophy and beyond it, the unity of chance and necessity in calculations without end" (ibid., 7). For the reasons I am emphasizing here, the word *jeu* in this case ought to have been rendered back into English as "game" because the current translation makes little sense in the context of Derrida's statement.

69. Lacan, "The Purloined Letter," 192–93.

exactly to the kinds of combinatorial possibilities understood by the game theorist as, for example, any one of the twenty-four ways of ranking the four situations *ac, bd, ad,* and *bc* proposed by Guilbaud.

Moreover, the "crisscrossing networks" allude not so much to linguistic networks as to "communication networks" in the language of information theory. If this is what Lacan is trying to get at with his binary notion of the symbolic chain, it certainly articulates a very different idea of language from that of Saussure and Jakobson, even though Jakonson tried very hard to incorporate probability analysis into linguistic studies.[70] Noam Chomsky was initially involved in Jakobson's project and participated in an important symposium that led to the publication of *Structure of Language and Its Mathematical Aspects.* His work on transformational generative grammar clearly bore the latest imprint of information theory and postwar communication technologies. David Golumbia has argued that Chomsky's computationalism presupposes the human mind to be a finite-state machine that is capable of generating and transforming an infinite number of sentences. "Somewhere inside the human brain there must be a physical or logical engine, call it the language organ, whose job is to produce mathematical infinity."[71] In the course of developing his transformational generative grammar, however, Chomsky noted that "the notion 'grammatical English' cannot be identified in any way with the notion 'high order of statistical approximation to English.'"[72] His objection to the application of Markov chains to English grammar follows a logic that escaped Jakobson. Chomsky writes: "If a grammar of this type produces English sentences, it will produce many non-sentences as well. If it produces only English sentences, we can be sure that there will be an infinite number of true sentences, false sentences, reasonable questions, etc. which it simply will not produce" (24). In short, the symbolic order is not reducible to a linguistic understanding of language, nor can the converse be true.[73] For Lacan, though, "the primordial couple of *plus* or *minus*" or the game of even and odd should precede linguistic considerations and is what enables the symbolic order.[74]

70. See my discussion in chapter 2.

71. David Golumbia, *The Cultural Logic of Computation,* 40.

72. Chomsky, *Syntactic Structures,* 18.

73. For a detailed account of Chomsky's work, from his initial exposure to Zellig Harris's work on distribution patterns at the University of Pennsylvania to his transformational generative grammar at MIT, see Margaret A. Boden, *Mind as Machine: A History of Cognitive Science,* vol. 1, 624–30.

74. Lacan, "The Purloined Letter," 192.

Table 4. Jacques Lacan's symbolic chain of pluses and minuses. From "The Purloined Letter," *The Seminar of Jacques Lacan. Book 2, the Ego in Freud's Theory and in the Technique of Psychoanalysis, 1954–1955,* translated by Sylvana Tomaselli (New York: W. W. Norton, 1988), 191–205.

(1)	(2)	(3)
+++	++−	+−+
−−−	−−+	−+−
	−++	
	+−−	

In his reading of "The Purloined Letter," Lacan demonstrates how the symbolic chain emerges from the real by arranging the eight numerical trigrams in three sets (193). The trigrams in each set combine the binary symbols of *pluses* and *minuses* according to given rules of arranging the even/odd sequences (Table 4). Each trigram constitutes a symbolic unity that articulates to the total structure of the series. Compare how Guilbaud illustrated the stochastic possibilities with the eight numerical trigrams in binary code; and the parallel between the two diagrams cannot escape anyone's notice[75] (Table 5). It is true that Jakobson's earlier collaboration with Nikolai Trubetzkoy had already brought the principle of binary opposition into phonology and phonemic analysis.[76] These linguists employed plus and minus signs to mark the presence or absence of distinctive phonemic traits. But their use of pluses and minuses should not be confused with what Lacan or Guilbaud was trying to do with the stochastic groupings of symbols, because the game of chance is not just about the marking or unmarking of distinctive features or the number of bits per phoneme.[77] Rather, it is about how a sequence of random series such as trigrams in binary code can be formalized through probability analysis to reveal its structure. Following the symbolic logic of the game of even and odd and the game of matching pennies, Lacan's chain of pluses and mi-

75. Guilbaud, *What Is Cybernetics?*, 48.
76. In *Structural Anthropology*, Lévi-Strauss comments on the work of Trubetzkoy thus: "structural linguistics shifts from the study of conscious linguistic phenomena to study of their unconscious infrastructure" (vol. 1, 33).
77. Jakobson, Fant, and Halle, *Preliminaries to Speech Analysis*, 43–45.

Table 5. G. Th. Guilbaud's illustration of the eight trigrams. From *What Is Cybernetics?* (New York: Grove Press, 1959), 48.

Il y a huit messages de trois signes
0 0 0
0 0 +
0 + 0
0 + +
+ 0 0
+ 0 +
+ + 0
+ + +

nuses suggests that no pure game of chance exists from the viewpoint of probability.[78]

This logic is extended to the realm of ordinary speech situations where one finds what he calls the articulation of one word with another. "You can play heads or tails by yourself," says Lacan, "but from the point of view of speech, you aren't playing by yourself—there is already the articulation of three signs, comprising a win or a loss, and this articulation prefigures the very meaning of the result. In other words, if there is no question, there is no game, if there is no structure there is no question. The question is constituted, organized, by the structure" (192). This notion of symbolic structure, consistent with game theory, would have important bearings on the development of Lacan's paradoxically *nonlinguistic* view of language and of the symbolic order.[79]

78. Anthony Wilden informs us that Lacan once said (to him?), "The hell with linguistics" (Wilden, *System and Structure*, 19). For some reason, however, Wilden chooses not to engage with the theorist's work on cybernetics or information theory and occasionally shows his mistaken judgment that, for example, is readily seen when he writes: "Lacan has persisted in a linguistic approach to Freud. It is this lack of understanding of the difference between language and communication—very evident in O. Mannoni's *Freud* (1971), for example, especially in the Afterword to the American edition—which accounts for the present impasses in the theory, as well as for the problems of interpretation which I found impossible to solve in the first edition of my own work on Lacan" (ibid.). As we know, Wilden worked closely with Lacan and was among his early translators, so I find it inexplicable that he managed to miss the central aspects of the Lacanian symbolic order in his study, which is focused on communication and which cites cyberneticians Wiener and Gregory Bateson many times.

79. Lacan's criticism of linguistic theory sometimes comes to the surface, the following being one of many examples: "When I say 'it rains,' the subject of the enunciation is not part of the sentence. In any case here there is some sort of difficulty. The subject cannot always be identified with what the linguists call 'the shifter.'" This last comment on "shifter" is clearly directed at Jakobson.

Table 6. The eight trigrams of the yin and yang symbols arranged in a Lacanian symbolic chain.

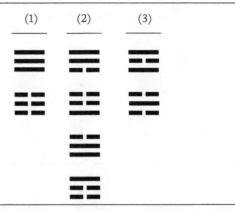

In fact, Lacan's novel view of language began to assert itself as early as his critique of Masserman's discourses on language and speech. In 1953, he delivered his famous manifesto (commonly known as the Rome Discourse) of the new Société Française de Psychanalyse at the Rome Congress.[80] In that speech, he argued that for Freud "a symptom is itself structured like a language" and that "a symptom is language from which speech must be delivered."[81] Out of a justified concern that "those who had not studied language in any depth" might misunderstand what he meant by "language," Lacan suggested that numerical associations would help make things a little easier to grasp as his audience could then recognize in the combinatory power of numbers the "very mainspring of the unconscious" (233). The combinatory power was not reducible to what some would take as grammatical order. It was something else. Lacan explained:

> Indeed, if—from the numbers obtained by breaking up the series of digits [*chiffres*] in the chosen number, from their combination by all the operations of the arithmetic, and even from the repeated division of the original number by one of the numbers split off from it—the resulting numbers prove symbolic among all the numbers in the subject's own history, it is because they were already latent in the initial choice. And thus if the idea that these very

---

Although the latter did not coin the term, he developed the concept for structural linguistics. See Lacan, "Of Structure as an Inmixing of an Otherness Prerequisite to Any Subject Whatsoever," 188.

80. The Rome Discourse was later published under the title "The Function and Field of Speech and Language in Psychoanalysis."

81. Lacan, "The Function and Field of Speech and Language in Psychoanalysis," 223.

Table 7. The eight trigrams written in Hindu-Arabic binary code.

(1)	(2)	(3)
111	110	101
000	001	010
	011	
	100	

numbers [*chiffres*] determined the subject's fate is refuted as superstitious, we must nevertheless admit that everything analysis reveals to the subject as his unconscious lies in the existing order of their combinations—that is, in the concrete language they represent. (233)

Let us recall that the symbolic chain Lacan analyzes in his 1955 seminar on "The Purloined Letter" is represented by three sets of trigrams, or what he terms the *chiffre*, which, in the French text, is associated with both "cipher" and "numerical digit." It is worth speculating why Lacan chooses to dwell on the series of eight trigrams (and divination technology) in his seminar. Do the numerical digits allude to yet another set of hidden ciphers?

In my interpretation, Lacan's eight trigrams contain a coded mathematical reference to an archaic cipher called the *koua* (or *gua* in the pinyin romanization). This cipher is obliquely mentioned by him, not in the seminar on "The Purloined Letter" but in the Rome Discourse two years before. Evidently, Lacan's play with the game of even and odd is not the only mystery that has escaped people's attention. In the Rome Discourse, Lacan makes one curious reference to the *koua* in a discussion of binary digits. He says: "[F]rom this articulated couple of presence and absence—also sufficiently constituted by the drawing in the sand of a simple line and a broken line of the *koua* mantics of China—a language's [*langue*] world of meaning is born, in which the world of things will situate itself" (228). Unfortunately, Lacan does not spell out for his audience how a simple line and a broken line of the *koua* could generate a language's world of meaning. And what is a *koua*?

The *koua* 卦 is usually called *bagua* 八卦 in Chinese. The concept refers to the eight trigrams from the *Book of Changes*, which dates back at least three thousand years.[82] The *koua* expresses the binary code in the same

---

82. The archaeological studies conducted by Chen Jiujin and Zhang Jingguo date the appearance of the *bagua* arithmetic to five thousand years ago. See their "Hanshan chutu yupian tuxing shikao" (A preliminary analysis of the iconography in the jade fragments from the excavation site in Hanshan), 14–17.

logical order as when the yin (– –) and the yang (—) symbols are substituted for the minuses and pluses in Lacan's symbolic chain. Tables 6 and
7 allow us to compare the yin and the yang expressions with their Hindu-
Arabic equivalent, that is to say, when we let number 1 stand for the plus
or yang symbol and number 0 for the minus or yin symbol. Lacan thus
understands the yin and yang symbols as mathematical ideographs.

Lacan studied Chinese during World War II and obtained a degree at
École des Langues Orientales. He renewed the study of Chinese classics
with François Cheng in 1971.[83] This knowledge may have helped him overcome the conceptual obstacle that we encounter among nonmathemati-
cians in Western academia concerning the nature of nonalphabetical writing systems.[84] Most people who know only alphabetical writing will have
difficulty grasping the concept of ideograph and tend to confuse it with
pictographs. As argued in my discussion of Printed English, ideographs
(conceptual, spatial, modular, etc.) embody a different mode of abstraction from that of pictograph (visual, iconic, mimetic, etc.) and are just as
applicable to numerical digits as they are to written symbols, traffic signs,
hand gestures, and so on. On the sources of iconography, we have long
been misled by late nineteenth-century interpretations of the Magdalenian
records on which the idea of Paleolithic realism was based, but twentieth-
century archaeological discoveries have shown that Magdalenian records
represent a very late stage of development in figurative art, as they date
between 11,000 and 8000 BCE, whereas the earliest beginnings happened
before 30,000 BCE. In the words of paleoanthropologist Leroi-Gourhan,
"graphism did not begin with naïve representations of reality but with
abstraction."[85] In other words, the earliest moments of graphism in the
technological development of the Homo Sapiens were characterized by
ideographic abstraction, not realistic representation. The *bagua* numerical
system has been used together with writing for divination since Chinese
antiquity. The use of mathematical symbols for divination purposes is not
unique to China; it is, in fact, rather common among world civilizations.
Lacan does not dismiss the belief in chance, number, and randomness as
superstition but sees it as the path toward the unconscious. Following this
insight, we might draw some conclusions about the political unconscious

    83. See Elizabeth Roudinesco, *Jacques Lacan & Co.*, 147, and also Lacan's 1971 seminar, *Le Sémi-
naire Livre XVIII: D'un Discours qui ne serait pas du semblant*. This seminar is devoted to extensive
discussions of Chinese philosophy and written characters.
    84. For a study of Lacan's relationship to the Chinese language, see Richard Serrano, "Lacan's
Oriental Language of the Unconscious," 90–106.
    85. André Leroi-Gourhan, *Gesture and Speech*, 188.

of an electoral democracy based on number games and see it as the latest divinational technology of the ruling class in a modern guise.

Nevertheless, an extensive knowledge of paleoanthropology and ancient Chinese writing is not a precondition for grasping the mathematics underlying the *koua* or any binary code. Gottfried Wilhelm Leibniz understood this when he became aware of the eight trigrams and their combinatorial principles through the mediation of a Jesuit missionary named Father Bouvet, who traveled to China in the seventeenth century. Leibniz thought that he had invented the binary code until he was confronted with the evidence of the eight trigrams brought to Europe by Father Bouvet in November 1700. He then adopted the position that the binary arithmetic was not his own invention, but a "rediscovery" of the Fu Xi principles.[86]

We will not revive the old dispute over the ancient origins of binary code. The search by Leibniz and Jesuit missionaries for the universal language is pertinent to our discussion insofar as it suggests the ways in which mathematical reasoning and symbolism may shed important light on the study of language and writing. When Father Bouvet referred to the trigrams in yin/yang binary code "as universal symbols invented by some extraordinary genius of antiquity . . . in order to present the most abstract principles in all the sciences," he was anticipating the universal discrete machine of Turing, Shannon, and Wiener, to whom Leibniz already represented the beginning of modern science. Wiener called Leibniz the patron saint of cybernetics.[87] Guilbaud canonized Pascal, probably because the latter was French and made important contributions to the study of probability. In any case, this allegiance did not prevent him from acknowledging Leibniz's important role as a precursor to modern mathematics.[88] Lacan does not have a patron saint of his own—unless Freud counts as one—but as demonstrated below, his universal language—the symbolic order—would be unthinkable without the mediation of information theory and cybernetics.[89]

There is no doubt that Lacan's notion of language changed over his lifetime and should be allowed its full scope of fluctuation and metamorphosis

---

86. Donald F. Lach, "Leibniz and China," 446. Fu Xi is the first of China's mythical emperors; he is said to have been born in the twenty-ninth century BCE. To him are attributed both the trigrams and the invention of writing. In short, he represents the origin of civilization: creating the institution of marriage, domesticating animals, teaching people how to fish with nets and hunt with weapons made of iron, how to cultivate their land, etc.

87. Wiener, *Cybernetics*, 52–53.

88. See Guilbaud, "Divagations cybernétiques," 283.

89. Like Guilbaud, Lacan reconstructs the genealogy of cybernetics by tracing its origin to French mathematicians Pascal and Condorcet. See Lacan, "Psychoanalysis and Cybernetics, or on the Nature of Language," 296.

in historical time. This chapter focuses on one slice of that time: his year-long seminar series in 1954–55. This seminar not only frames his famous reading of "The Purloined Letter" but signals an important turning point in his life's work, which has been misinterpreted as a movement toward structural linguistics. My research indicates that Lacan was actually developing a cybernetic notion of language which brought him closer to the mathematician's symbolic logic than suggest any substantial affinity with Saussure or modern linguistics. It should not surprise anyone, therefore, that he would privilege letters, numbers, pluses, minuses, and ideographic symbols in general and that in due time he would acquire the reputation of being obscure and difficult. But we must question further: Why should these symbols matter to psychoanalysis? In what ways do they significantly impact his understanding of the Freudian unconscious?

The Cybernetic Unconscious

We have seen that the stochastic processes of the written letter presuppose a set of combinatorial rules in the communication machine or the psychic machine. The machine is just as likely to produce gibberish as it is to make sense. In *La Cybernétique*, Guilbaud devotes some chapters to the relationship between language and machine and focus, predictably, on circuits and networks, feedback and purposive activity, signals and messages, information and probability, communication, etc. Like Shannon, he takes a strong (statistical) interest in ordinary language and symbolic systems in general. In his view, the task of the cybernetician is to apply a rigorous mathematical method to the analysis of stochastic processes of language while acknowledging that language in the ordinary sense of the word "makes use of only a small fraction of the combinatorial fabric which serves as its support" amongst the other symbolic systems such as numerals and binary code.[90] Guilbaud is not modest about the revolutionary potential of cybernetics or information theory in their power to unlock the structure of the mind. Cybernetics, he argues, will enable the scientist to study the "actual linguistic process and reveal the structures implicit in the apparatus which produces it, *whether this is a machine in the usual sense, or a subconscious*

90. Guilbaud, *What Is Cybernetics?*, 72. Guilbaud is not the first to bring information theory under the aegis of cybernetics as Wiener had done the same. In an early essay, Dubarle also reflected on the "points of contact between cybernetics and game theory." See Dubarle, "Idées scientifiques actuelles et domination des faits humains," 311–12.

human mechanism [un subconcient humain]"[91](my emphasis). The symbiosis of the computing machine and the human subconscious has been a commonplace among the cyberneticians, and this would translate into the cybernetic unconscious that we will find in Lacan's rereading of Freud.

The driving hypothesis of cybernetic studies has been that the human brain is a cybernetic machine. It has already been mentioned how Warren McCulloch and Walter Pitts's pioneering paper "A Logical Calculus of the Ideas Immanent in Nervous Activity" (1943) presented a most rigorous treatment of this hypothesis amongst the first generation of American cyberneticians. The paper demonstrates the activity of neurons as inherently propositional and applies the mathematical calculus to the construction of formal neural nets isomorphic to the relations of propositional logic. McCulloch and Pitts believe that all psychic events have a semiotic character and that "the 'all-or-none' law of these activities, and the conformity of their relations to those of the logic of propositions, insure that the relations of psychons are those of the two valued logic of propositions. Thus in psychology, introspective, behavioristic or physiological, the fundamental relations are those of two-valued logic."[92] In a recent study, Joseph Dumit suggests that the kinds of questions that interest McCulloch are, for example, "Which machines are neurotic in ways that some people are neurotic? Which people get sick the way that some machines get sick? Which machines remember the ways that some people remember?"[93] As is discussed in chapters 5 and 6, AI scientists such as Kenneth Mark Colby and Robert P. Abelson began to simulate the neurotic machine using computer programs as early as the 1960s. But Lacan was already fascinated in the 1950s by the temporal breaks or faulty moments of the communication circuit in the human psyche and would occasionally use the American term "jam" to describe these moments.

There is overwhelming evidence to suggest that, beyond the seminar on "The Purloined Letter," the Freudian subjects that Lacan treated from late 1954 through the first six months of 1955 were all closely linked in one way or the other to the issues brought to bear by Guilbaud's readings of cybernetics, game theory, and information theory in *La Cybernétique* and in his articles already discussed. A systematic comparison of the many parallels and shared technical idioms is impossible in the limited scope of this

91. Guilbaud, *What Is Cybernetics?*, 70.
92. Warren McCulloch and Walter Pitts, "A Logical Calculus of the Ideas Immanent in Nervous Activity," 114.
93. Joseph Dumit, "Neuroexistentialism," 186.

chapter. A more fruitful approach lies in identifying those strands of thought that have been central to Lacan's elaboration of the concept of language and speech from a cybernetic viewpoint. Chiefly, these are related to the questions of the communication circuit, message, entropy, nonmeaning, and time that Lacan examined systematically in that period; the inquiry culminated in a lecture delivered on June 22, 1955, titled "Psychoanalysis and Cybernetics, or on the Nature of Language."

Let us recall that in his reading of Poe, Lacan warned us against taking the stolen letter in Poe's story literally or mistaking the actual marbles for the game of even and odd. He further notes: "The letter itself, this phrase written on a piece of paper, in so far as it wanders about, is the unconscious."[94] The letter or the symbol figures the unconscious insofar as it moves from person to person in the game of chance, but it always moves in a structure. He adopts the figure of the telegraph in a similar vein to illustrate this process:

> Suppose that I send a telegram from here to Le Mans, with the request that Le Mans send it back to Tours, from there to Sens, from there to Fontaine-bleau, and from there to Paris, and so on indefinitely. What's needed is that when I reach the tail of my message, the head should not yet have arrived back. The message must have time to turn around. It turns quickly. It doesn't stop turning, it turns around in circles. It's funny, this thing turning back on itself. It's called *feedback* [original in English], and it's related to the homeostat. You know that that is how the admission of steam into a steam-engine is controlled. If it heats up too quickly, a governor registers it, two things are forced apart by the centrifugal force, and the admission of steam is regulated. We have oscillation about a point of equilibrium.[95]

The punning on the tail and head of the message turns on the figure of coin flipping in the game of chances as popularized by game theory. This is the familiar game of hunt-the-slipper, in which the slipper or the message moves but, like Poe's letter, the message bears no linguistic meanings as it moves through the cybernetic circuits.

Negative feedback and homeostat are Wiener's central concepts in cybernetics and also informed McCulloch and Pitt's study of neural networks in the human brain. When coining the term "cybernetics," Wiener pointed out that "the first significant paper on feed-back mechanisms is

94. Lacan, "Some Questions for the Teacher," 209.
95. Lacan, "The Circuit," 88.

an article on governors, which was published by Clerk Maxwell in 1868, and that *governor* is derived from a Latin corruption of Κυβερνήτης."[96] The steam engine is repeatedly noted by Wiener as a device controlled by one of the older and already better-developed forms of feedback mechanisms. "The machines of which we are now speaking are not the dream of the sensationalist, nor the hope of some future time," Wiener writes: "They already exist as thermostats, automatic gyro-compass ship-steering systems, self-propelled missiles—especially such as seek their target—anti-aircraft fire-control systems, automatically controlled oil-cracking stills, ultra-rapid computing machines, and the like. They had begun to be used long before the war—indeed, the very old steam-engine governor belongs among them" (55). For cyberneticians, that which binds the steam engine to the telegraph is the idea of the message in feedback systems, although the message has nothing to do with content or meaning. Information theory states that "the message is a discrete or continuous sequences of measurable events distributed in time" (16). The movement of the message is determined by the feedback and the homeostatic mechanisms of the cybernetic machine.

Lacan's allusion to the telegraph in the quoted passage may be playful, but it is not arbitrary, and it casts a different light on Kittler's association of the symbolic order with the typewriter.[97] As we saw in chapter 2, Morse's telegraphy had been the starting point of Shannon's mathematical analysis when he introduced information theory.[98] Conceptually, the technologies of telegraph, typewriter, and telephone can all be related, especially in regard to the requirement for discrete units, but Shannon's work necessarily privileges Morse code. Through telegraph code, he discovered that a message was related to uncertainty and probability (i.e., which message to choose out of x number of messages) and to the ways in which communication systems could be designed to work with the statistical pattern (which he calls "redundancy") and randomness of information (which he calls "entropy").[99] Lacan grasped this novel conceptualization of telegraphic message and saw its relevance to his own work. From this

96. Wiener, *Cybernetics*, 19.

97. In *Gramophone, Film, Typewriter*, Kittler mentions Morse code in passing (12) but jumps over that technology in his discussion of the technological embodiment of the Lacanian symbolic from the typewriter to computing technology.

98. Shannon did most of his pathbreaking work at the Bell Telephone Laboratories in 1941–58 and continued to be affiliated with the Bell Labs until 1972. He became a professor at MIT in 1958 and taught there until his retirement in 1978.

99. Shannon and Weaver, *The Mathematical Theory of Communication*, 39.

4

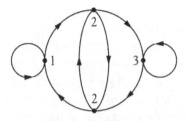

Figure 20. Jacques Lacan's demonstration of the 1–3 Network in "The Seminar on 'The Purloined Letter,'" 35. From *Écrits: The Complete Edition* by Jacques Lacan, translated by Bruce Fink. Copyright © 1970, 1971, 1996, 1999 by Editions du Seuil. English translation copyright © 2002, 2006 by W. W. Norton & Company, Inc. Used by permission of W. W. Norton & Company, Inc.

understanding emerged a notion of language that would give absolute priority to the signifier (or the letter) and banish "linguistic meaning" and "semantics" from the consideration of the sign. For instance, Lacan adopted a 1–3 combinatorial diagram to demonstrate the stochastic processes of groups of three discrete symbols in his seminar on "The Purloined Letter" (Fig. 20).[100] Compare his diagram with Shannon's illustration of the stochastic process of (finite-state) Morse code in *The Mathematical Theory of Communication* (Fig. 21), and one could hardly miss the mathematical principle underlying them both. Shannon's diagram is based on his earlier analysis of the dot-dash-space principle in Morse code and, as discussed in chapter 2, his conceptualization of the twenty-seventh letter in Printed English originated from that work.[101]

On at least one occasion, with Hyppolite in attendance at the seminar, Lacan referred directly to the work of Shannon and Bell Labs and discoursed on the American research on communication engineering, although he omitted Shannon's name:

The Bell Telephone Company needed to economise, that is to say, to pass the greatest possible number of communications down one single wire. In a country as vast as the United States, it is very important to save on a few wires, and to get the inanities which generally travel by this kind of transmission apparatus to pass down the smallest possible number of wires. That is where the quantification of communication started. So a start was made, as you can see, by dealing with *something very far removed from what we here call*

100. For Lacan's detailed explication of this diagram, see *Écrits*, 35–39.
101. Shannon and Weaver, *The Mathematical Theory of Communication*, 38.

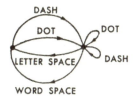

Figure 21. Claude Shannon's demonstration of the stochastic processes involving telegraphic symbols. From Claude E. Shannon and Warren Weaver, *The Mathematical Theory of Communication*. Copyright 1949, 1998 by the Board of Trustees of the University of Illinois. Used with permission of the University of Illinois Press.

speech. It had nothing to do with knowing whether what people tell each other makes any sense. Besides, what is said on the telephone, you must know from experience, never does. But one communicates, one recognises the modulation of a human voice, and as a result one has that appearance of understanding which comes with the fact that one recognizes words one already knows. It is a matter of knowing what are the most economical conditions which enable one to transmit the words people recognize. No one cares about the meaning. Doesn't this underline rather well the point which I am emphasizing, which one always forgets, namely that language, this language which is the instrument of speech, is something material?[102] (my emphasis)

Notice how the Saussurian notion of *parole* passes down the wire of Shannon's information theory and reemerges at the other end of the wire as something radically transformed. With the sole difference of preferring "channel" to "wire," Shannon would have been in complete agreement with Lacan about the quantification of communication, the need to economize, the irrelevance of sense to a message, the instrument of speech being material, and so on. Shannon would have concurred that the idea of communication deals with "something very far removed from what we here call speech."

This provides a clear explanation as to why Lacan decided to reverse the position of signifier and signified in Saussure's diagram (Figs. 18 and 19), and it also outlines the general direction in which Lacan conceptualizes the unconscious in relation to the symbolic order. The material language, which is the instrument of speech, is no longer the same as the Saussurian language. Rather, it operates in the manner of a telephone exchange sys-

102. Lacan, "The Circuit," 82.

tem or a cybernetic machine that runs automatically regardless of what
happens to pass down its wires. The transcripts of the first few months
of 1955 indicate that the members of Lacan's seminar were thrown into
confusion by his cybernetic challenge to their understanding of language.
Did he really mean language? They seemed hesitant and were rather slow
in catching his train of thought, especially when he made them work on
numbers and diagrams to think about language. At one point, Lacan lost
patience and complained: "[W]e won't go into these arcana. You can bring
a horse to water, but you can't make him drink, and so as not to install too
great an aversion in you to this exercise."[103]

This apparent lack of understanding led Lacan to devote one of the last
sessions of the seminar to the following topic: "Where is speech? Where
is language?" dated June 15, 1955, according to the transcript prepared by
Jacques-Alain Miller. After a heated exchange with some members of his
seminar who seemed hopelessly confused about what he was trying to do
with the idea of speech and language, Lacan said:

> [W]hen one illustrates the phenomenon of language with something as for-
> mally purified as mathematical symbols—and that is one of the reasons for
> putting cybernetics on the agenda—when one gives a mathematical notation
> of the *verbum*, one demonstrates in the simplest possible way that language
> exists completely independently of us. Numbers have properties which are
> absolute.... *All this can circulate in all manner of ways in the universal machine,*
> *which is more universal than anything you could imagine.* One can imagine an
> indefinite number of levels, where all this turns around and circulates. The
> world of signs functions, and it has no signification whatsoever. What gives it
> its signification is the moment when we stop the machine. These are the tem-
> poral breaks which we make in it. If they are faulty, we will see ambiguities
> emerge, which are sometimes difficult to resolve, but which one will always
> end up giving a signification to.[104]

This interesting discussion of the psychic machine is followed by some
fascinating exchanges with Jacques Riguet, the mathematician in the seminar room, about what machines can or cannot do and whether machines
can share universal symbols, etc. In response, Lacan points to the binary
code of 1 and 0 as a universal system of signs and opposes this system to
historically embodied individual languages such as the French language,

103. Lacan, "Odd or Even? Beyond Intersubjectivity," 178.
104. Lacan, "Where Is Speech? Where Is Language?" 284.

which some members of the seminar insisted on using as their frame of reference. He argues that "the circulation of binary signs in a machine enables us, if we give it the right programme, to discover a previously un-published prime number. The prime number circulating in the machine has got nothing to do with thought."[105]

This is taken to mean that the unconscious, rather than the speaking subject, does the thinking and plays the game of chances according to given combinatory rules. Like the prime number, whatever comes out of the thinking machine merely reflects on how the game is played. Lacan's psychic machine, therefore, closely replicates the cyberneticians' neural nets. The connection of eruption of signification or "ambiguities" to the temporal breaks and faulty moments of the circuit suggests Lacan is famil-iar with neurological studies in cybernetics. For example, when he refers to memory as a message that circulates "on the tiny points of the nervous system," he is actually citing the work of John Z. Young—again, without mentioning him by name—who conducted experiments on the nervous system of octopuses.[106] Of course, the electronic and biological systems can be jammed and the circuit will break down. Lacan is careful to point out that the circulation of information does not mean "that fundamen-tal things happen between human beings. It concerns what goes down the wires, and what can be measured. Except, one then begins to wonder where it does go, or whether it doesn't, when it deteriorates, when it is no longer communication" (83).

This is where Freud's idea of repetition automatism begins to make cy-bernetic sense. The following passage is especially illuminating in regard to how the symbolic order operates for Lacan and where psychoanalysis and cybernetics could possibly meet on the exploratory journey toward the unconscious:

What is a message inside a machine? Something which proceeds by opening and not opening, the way an electronic lamp does, by yes or no. It's something articulated, of the same order as the fundamental oppositions of the symbolic register. At any given moment, this something which turns has to, or doesn't, come back into play. It is always ready to give a reply, and be completed by this

---

105. Lacan, "Where Is Speech? Where Is Language?" 286. A natural number p is prime if and only if the only positive integers that divide p are 1 and p itself. Examples are 2, 3, 5, 7, 11, 13, etc. This quote demonstrates Lacan's awareness that computers were being used to accelerate the discoveries of ever greater prime numbers after 1951.

106. Lacan, "The Circuit," 89.

selfsame act of replying, that is to say by ceasing to function as an isolated and closed circuit, by entering into the general run of things. Now this comes very close to what we can conceive of as *Zwang*, the compulsion to repeat. (89)

The German term *Zwang*, which is glossed as "compulsion" here, refers specifically to Freud's notion *Wiederholungszwang*, dubbed *compulsion de répétition* by Lacan who sometimes prefers this term to the usual French translation *automatisme de répétition*.[107] Significantly, Lacan would begin his 1966 published version of the "Seminar on 'The Purloined Letter'" with this very concept. But the Freudian concept is reworked here to accommodate the stochastic processes of neural net communication through the cybernetic machine, a machine that runs automatically by opening or not opening, in binary code. Does this tell us something about the unconscious and how it works? "When does the individual in his subjective function take himself into account—if not in the unconscious?" asked Lacan at one point, and he added: "One of the most obvious phenomena discovered by the Freudian experience is exactly that."[108] And what was the Freudian experience he is referring to here?

That experience—which includes Freud's own self-probing—turns out to be nothing less than how to say numbers at random and what this would tell him about the function of the unconscious. We have discussed a related subject in connection with Freud's work *The Psychopathology of Everyday Life* and with Jung's and Bleuler's word-association games. In rethinking Freud, Lacan asks us to reconsider "that very strange game Freud mentions at the end of *The Psychopathology of Everyday Life*, which consists in inviting the subject to say numbers at random." Is it truly possible for anyone to say numbers at random? Freud's answer is no, because one may say or think of any number at random but whatever comes to the mind cannot be purely random and this is due to the workings of the unconscious. Lacan comes up with a stochastic explanation for the Freudian experience, stating that "the associations which then come to him bring to light significations which reverberate so neatly with his remembrance, his destiny, that, from the point of view of probabilities, what he chose goes well beyond anything we might expect from pure chance" (56). This cybernetic view of the unconscious prepared Lacan for his critique of Hegel, Maurice Merleau-Ponty,

---

107. Lacan repeated this point on a number of occasions to emphasize the power of repetitive insistence in the concept "compulsion." See, for example, Lacan, "Freud, Hegel, and the Machine" and "Some Questions for the Teacher."

108. Lacan, "Homeostasis and Insistence," 56.

and phenomenology in their reluctance to let go of the central function of consciousness. It also marked Lacan's transition from Hegelianism to cybernetics, not linguistics, and it is a mistake to force a connection between his concept of the symbolic order and the Saussurian notion of language.

Lacan subscribed to what one might call a materialist view of language that was rooted in the technology of his era. Kittler says no less of Freud, suggesting that the latter's materialism went as far as did the information machines of his time. For instance, Freud conceived of psychoanalytic data storage in terms of the grooves that phonographs etch onto wax or tinfoil rolls.[109] For Lacan, the communication machine offered other and more interesting possibilities. The circulation of information does not mean that communication takes place between human beings. What it does is simulate the stochastic processes of neural net communication in the brain. The law of entropy stipulates that all machines have a tendency to run down. Lacan says that there is a name for this breakdown, called "in psychology, *the jam,* an American word. It is the first time that confusion as such—this tendency there is in communication to cease being a communication, that is to say, of no longer communicating anything at all—appears as a fundamental concept. That makes for one more symbol."[110] Shannon would have termed this tendency "entropy," of which Lacan is fully aware, but the latter is also developing a notion of the symbolic order that strives to reframe the meaning of communication and noncommunication with respect to what he would call "man's waiting" in the temporal movement of human civilization.

On June 22, 1955, Lacan delivered his public lecture called "Psychoanalysis and Cybernetics, or on the Nature of Language" to summarize the work of his year-long seminar. This special lecture was arranged by the Société Française de Psychanalyse under the general theme of "Psychoanalysis and the Human Sciences." Lévi-Strauss, Hyppolite, Merleau-Ponty, and Benveniste had previously been invited speakers in the series. Lacan's lecture focused on how the symbolic order of binary signs might be elaborated as the universal system of language and be distinguished from thought, signification, speech, and meaning. He begins by reflecting on the game of chance, determinism, and cybernetics. Rejecting the idea that the exact sciences are concerned with the real, he argues: "The little symbolic game in which Newton's system and that of Einstein is summed up has in the end very little to do with the real. The science which reduces the real

109. Kittler, *Literature, Media, Information Systems*, 134.
110. Lacan, "The Circuit," 83.

to several little letters, to a little bundle of formulae, will probably seem, with the hindsight of later epochs, like an amazing epic, and will also dwindle down, like an epic, to a rather short circuit."[111] This critique originates with a question he raises about the measurement of time from the inauguration of the "universe of precision" with the first perfectly isochronic clock in 1695. In a Heideggerian vein, Lacan sees the universe of precision as a hypothesis embodied in an instrument. If the instrument is constructed that confirms the hypothesis, then there is no need to do the experiment because the fact that it works already confirms the hypothesis. But what is the real against which the exact sciences borrow their unit of time? Lacan says that "the real is what keeps turning up where one expected it" or something that "always turns up again in the same place" (297, 298–99). In other words, the scientist will find what his instrument permits him or her to find, thus enabling a kind of ritualized encounter or rendezvous with nature, although their idea of the natural is likewise defined in terms of "what shows up on time for the rendezvous" (298). With the invention of the probability calculus, the idea of encounter is now referred to the game of chance, whereby "the science of what is found at the same place is substituted for by the science of the combination of places as such" (299). This is an important observation. What Lacan calls the rendezvous with the real is first and foremost a comment on the game of chance that the scientists play with their symbols. In a discussion of Lacan's reiteration of "non-sense" or "non-meaning," Mark Taylor suggests that the real for Lacan recognizes radical heterogeneity and is fundamentally theological.[112]

The revolutionary character of cybernetics lies in the fact that "everything which up until then had been the science of numbers becomes a combinatory science," and this allows the accidental and confused traversal of the world of symbols to be organized around the correlation of absence and presence (300). With cybernetics, Lacan suggests, the symbol is embodied in an apparatus that ties the real to a syntax, but this syntax, having nothing to do with ordinary grammar, is the combinatory logic of 0 and 1. Speaking almost in parody of Heidegger, Lacan points out that "[t]he human being isn't master of this primordial, primitive language," but "he has been thrown into it, committed, caught up in its gears" (307).

In that spirit, Lacan assigns both phenomenology and Gestalt studies to the inferior imaginary order because they insist on "good form" and ignore the cybernetic truth that "man isn't the master in his own house"(307).

111. Lacan, "Psychoanalysis and Cybernetics, or on the Nature of Language," 299.
112. See Mark C. Taylor, Altarity, 93–94.

He openly challenges Maurice Merleau-Ponty, as he did in the January 19, 1955 seminar, and he is not alone. Steve Heims has documented some fascinating exchanges between the Gestaltists and cyberneticians at the Macy Conferences when Wolfgang Köhler, one of the founders of Gestalt psychology, was invited to attend the meeting. At one point, a cybernetician commented to him: "Excellent work—but don't you have religion up your sleeve?"[113] Wiener is not known for attacking Gestalt theory the way Lacan does, but he clearly distances himself from the whole thing.[114]

Was Lacan unaware of the sinister side of cybernetics and game theory and their collusion with the American domination of the world during the cold war? The answer is no. In his public lecture, Lacan tries to come to grips with such dangers by suggesting a proper intellectual assessment of the situation. He states:

> In keeping on this frontier the originality of what appears in our world in the form of cybernetics, I am tying it to man's waiting. If the science of the combinations of scanned encounter has come to the attention of man, it is because it deeply concerns him. And it is not for nothing that it comes out of games of chance. And it is not for nothing that game theory is concerned with all the functions of our economic life, the theory of coalitions, of monopolies, the theory of war. Yes, war itself, considered in its aspect as game, detached from anything which might be real. It is not for nothing that the same word designates such diverse fields as well as the game of chance . . . Here we come very close to the central question with which I began, namely—what is the chance of the unconscious, which in some way lies behind man. (Lacan, "Psychoanalysis and Cybernetics, 300)

Indeed, what is the future of the unconscious with the arrival of cybernetics? Lacan deems the question a central issue, one that is tied to our future, and to the chance of the unconscious. It is not as if monopoly and war were unimportant; they are absolutely important, but we must confront them as "games" to the extent these games are detached from the real and played with the machine and in the machine. This seems to be Lacan's fundamental insight about the cybernetic unconscious. If the element of time, or what Lacan calls "man's waiting," also bears upon how we reflect on the questions of language, the mind, and the machine before and

113. Steve Joshua Heims, *The Cybernetics Group*, 235.
114. For Wiener's viewpoint, see *Cybernetics: or Control and Communication in the Animal and the Machine*, 31–32.

after cybernetics, can the theory of language or the unconscious remain the same after the coming of cybernetics? The answer is no. The originality of Lacan's symbolic order resides precisely in the temporality of "what appears in our world."

Return to Sender

To recapitulate, Lacan's encounter with American game theory, cybernetics, and information theory was a central event in his rethinking of Freud in the seminar series of 1954–55. Indeed, what he had to say about the symbolic chain is very different from how Jakobson approached linguistic structure, even though the latter also attempted to incorporate information theory into linguistic studies in the 1950s. Lacan's work on the symbolic order led to a nonlinguistic view of language. By reworking the Freudian unconscious this way, he directs our attention to the emergence of the cybernetic unconscious in digital media. For better or for worse, Lacan has accomplished for psychoanalysis what the mathematicians did for economics in game theory. This work has been misunderstood by many, and Lacan himself was acutely aware of the widespread misconstruing of his concepts. In his 1971 seminar, he tried to rectify that misunderstanding by claiming that "it is not for nothing that I have written *the instance of the letter in the unconscious*. I have never said *the instance of the signified*."[115]

For several decades, this important work on the cybernetic unconscious has been hiding in plain sight from literary critics on both sides of the Atlantic. The authorized 1966 version of Lacan's *explication de texte* has tended to mask the fact that there are always more than one text and always more than one seminar. This is clearly the case when we examine how the texts of the seminar have evolved over the years. When rewriting his essay for publication in *Écrits*, Lacan edited out and changed a large amount of transcribed discussion from the 1954–55 seminar. Although this was eventually published in 1978, it failed to engage the attention of many scholars who might have found his repeated references to entropy, feedback, telepathy, war, and cybernetic machines illuminating. Lacan's seminar has shuttled back and forth between America and France like an unopened letter— not unlike Edgar Allan Poe's own "Purloined Letter" (through Baudelaire's translation)—one that bears a stamp from the print era: "return to sender." The transatlantic itinerancy of this unopened letter appears to confirm

---

115. Lacan, "L'Écrit et la parole" (Writing and speech) in *Le Séminaire livre XVIII: D'un discours qui ne serait pas du semblant*, 89.

Lacan's elaboration of the game of signifiers and their impossible semantic closure. What do we make of the itinerancy of the letter and the game in their dialectic movement? To grasp the situation in its proper dimensions, we need to put the transatlantic and translingual fashioning of French Structuralism and Poststructuralism in historical perspective.

Poe's original story went on a transatlantic journey and met with warm reception amongst the French modernists. But for more than a hundred years, ever since Baudelaire took it on himself to translate and write about Poe in the mid-nineteenth century, the canonical status of Poe in American literature has been contested between French and American critics. I will not presume to speak on the canon issue, which mainly concerns scholars of American literature, but I do want to observe that by the 1980s the love affair between France and American academia had become so narcissistic—in the Lacanian sense of the imaginary order—surrounding Lacan's reading of "The Purloined Letter" that all other concerns seemed to fade to the background. Lacan bore some degree of responsibility for some narrowly construed psychoanalytical criticism when he authorized the 1966 edition to be the opening text in *Écrits*: the definitive text.[116]

The earlier 1955 *explication de texte* has evolved through a convoluted history of textual revisions that can be glimpsed through the several versions and editions that exist. Although Lacan himself was not keen on getting his seminars published, at least three versions of the "same" text are in print so far, not counting the various foreign language editions that have appeared and are still appearing. The first printed version of "Le Séminaire sur 'la lettre volée'" (Seminar on "The Purloined Letter") was published in *La Psychanalyse* 2, 1956, which provided a synopsis of the main topics of the seminar in 1954–55 and included Lacan's discussion of letters and number sequences, cybernetics, and machine. In 1966, an extended version of this essay and synopsis was reissued in *Écrits*; it includes a note from Lacan called the "Presentation de la suite," which prefaces his introduction of the mathematical diagrams. The note says: "To anyone wanting to get a feel for my seminar from this text, I hardly ever recommended it without advising him that this text had to serve to introduce him to the introduction that preceded it and that will follow it here." The "introduction" here refers to the difficult part, which contains Lacan's detailed discussion of the mathematical and ideographic exercises of his group. The author predicts, however,

---

116. Lacan apparently insisted on placing the "Seminar on 'The Purloined Letter'" in the beginning of this volume against the objection of his editor François Wahl.

that the reader would skip this last part: "This advice is usually not followed, a taste for obstacles being the ornament of persevering in being."[117]

The 1966 version of *Écrits* received a partial English translation in 1972 and was printed in *Yale French Studies*, in which Lacan's "introduction," which follows the main text, was inexplicably suppressed. In 1978, the transcript of the 1954–55 seminars was prepared by Jacques-Alain Miller and published under the title *Le Séminaire livre II: le moi dans la théorie de Freud et dans la technique de la psychanalyse, 1954–1955*. Sylvana Tomaselli's English translation of this transcript was published in 1988 with careful footnotes provided by John Forrester. The transcript indicates, as shown in this chapter, that Lacan discussed "The Purloined Letter" in more than one session between March 23 and May 11, 1955. As for the authorized version of "Seminar on 'The Purloined Letter'" in *Écrits*, Bruce Fink's translation brought the complete text to the English-speaking world for the first time in 2002.

The discrepancies amongst these versions are too drastic and too numerous not to alert the reader about the validity of the claims that critics have put forward concerning Lacan's theory of the symbolic order and the unconscious. The textual history surrounding the transcription, publication, and translation of the seminar on "The Purloined Letter" raises a larger issue for us: insofar as Lacan's notion of the symbolic order was indebted to cybernetics and information theory, both having originated in the United States, why have most critics overlooked this connection as they discuss Poststructuralism and call it French theory?

Forrester offers a plausible explanation. He says that Jeffrey Mehlman's incomplete translation of the 1966 version in *Yale French Studies* of 1972 has "allowed the 'Seminar' to be read in Britain and America out of the context of Lacan's discussion of repetition, of the machine and cybernetics."[118] This is very true, and we have seen how well the translingual reproductions of Lacan's *explication de texte* have guarded this open secret to the degree that what we know of Lacan has all but erased the traces of cybernetics that had framed his reading of Poe. On the other hand, all instances of cybernetics-blind reading of Lacan cannot be laid on the doorstep of the English translator when we recall that most Poststructuralist readers of Lacan in British and American academia are bilingual speakers who would have relied on, or at least consulted, one of the three French versions. For how else can we explain the fact that Jacques Derrida, who

117. Lacan, "Seminar on 'The Purloined Letter,'" 30.
118. John Forrester, *The Seductions of Psychoanalysis: Freud, Lacan, and Derrida*, 339n72.

offers a remarkably detailed critique of Lacan's reading of Poe in "The Pur-veyor of Truth," and Barbara Johnson, who makes an equally powerful re-buttal of Derrida's critique in "The Frame of Reference," have each in his or her own way sidestepped the ubiquitous references in Lacan's seminar to the cybernetic machine, game theory, and information theory? What does this blind "play" of signifiers across the Atlantic tell us about the political unconscious of literary theory itself? Does it have something to do with the reproduction and policing of the boundaries of the disciplines against which Lacan fought so hard all his life?

Finally, Lacan's teaching "style" is not abstruse so much as it strives to be precise, for his privileging of letters, numbers, and ideographic sym-bols requires a cybernetic understanding of language and symbol. It may not be very easy to access this teaching until we are prepared to acquaint ourselves with some basics of information theory and cybernetic think-ing. This does not mean that we must endorse them. Lacan's engagement with the contemporary theoretical developments has been dialectical and by no means uncritical. By thinking through them and about them with the input of Guilbaud, he brought the cybernetic unconscious of the post-war world order to light. Their work shows that there is absolutely no free play of signifiers in the games that define our existence in this world. Hu-manists can no more speculate freely about language and texts than they can ignore the networked machines, codes, and institutions that produce them. Our theory, and theoretical discourse, too, are made to confront the symbolic order of our time as well as the originality of what appears in our world. That originality, as I demonstrate in the next chapter, lies in the coming of the Freudian robot.

5 The Freudian Robot

> What unfolds without fail before the reader's eyes is a kind of puppet theater in which real dolls or fake dolls, real and simulated life, are manipulated by a sovereign but capricious stage-setter. The net is tightly stretched, bowed, and tangled; the scenes are centered and dispersed; narratives are begun and left in suspension. Just as the reader thinks he is following some demonstration, he senses that the surface is cracking: the text slides a few roots under the ground while it allows others to be lofted in the air. What in one instance appears a figure of science seems later to resemble some type of fiction.
>
> Helene Cixous, "Fiction and Its Phantoms"

In his reflections on aggressiveness and narcissism, Lacan points to the original fracturing of the human psyche and says that at every instant man "constitutes his world by committing suicide."[1] One of the psychological truths Lacan wanted to drive home in his study concerns the tension that marks the ego's relationship to space and its instinct of self-preservation. The extent to which the ego's instinct willingly gives way before the temptation to dominate space—examples he cited being "shock, fighter, parachute, and

---

1. Jacques Lacan, "Aggressiveness in Psychoanalysis," 100–101.

commando trooper" (100)—says something about the malaise of a civilization for which Freud had invented a word: *Todestrieb*, or the death drive
(instinct). Still, the reader may wonder why Freud thought it necessary to
adopt such a concept and oppose it to Eros or the life instinct as one of the
most basic of all human instincts. And what is the death drive?

The death drive is perhaps one of the most contested of Freud's conjectures and has been related to the notion of entropy in the second law of
thermodynamics. Ernest Jones has suggested that, by putting forward the
death drive, Freud's aim was to establish a relationship between Fechner's
principle of stability and the second law of thermodynamics.[2] In *Beyond the
Pleasure Principle* and *Civilization and Its Discontents*, Freud tries to explain
what he has observed as the innate propensity of all organisms toward equilibrium and destruction.[3] He argues that there is a tendency in human
beings and in all living things toward their own death, toward a condition
of regression to inorganic matter. This is *Todestrieb*. In thermodynamics, as
we know, the tendency in a self-contained system to run down, to equilibrium, and to irreversibility is measured by "entropy," a number that takes
a quantity of heat divided by a temperature. The second law of thermodynamics stipulates the direction of the flow of energy in an isolated system,
such as the flow of heat always from the hot to the cold body. Essentially,
what it says is that entropy in a closed system cannot decrease unless external forces are exerted.

When Ernest Jones disputed Freud's hypothesis about the death drive,
he did so precisely by invoking the second law of thermodynamics. Insofar
as living beings are not closed systems, he argues, they can take energy
from outside and acquire what Schrödinger called "negative entropy." On
that ground, Jones believed that Freud's attempt to bring entropy and the
death drive together has been a failure (276–77). This view was shared by
a good number of psychoanalysts of his time and by those who participated
in a debate about the death drive and entropy in *International Journal of
Psycho-Analysis* in 1931, but the debate did not seem to resolve the issue
to everybody's satisfaction.[4] The relationship between the death drive and

2. Ernest Jones, *The Life and Work of Sigmund Freud*, 3: 276.

3. Freud relates the death drive to the compulsion to repeat and describes it as "an urge inherent in organic life to restore an earlier state of things." See Freud, *Beyond the Pleasure Principle*, 36.

4. For the 1931 debate, see Siegfried Bernfeld and Sergei Feitelberg, "The Principle of Entropy
and the Death Instinct"; Reginald O. Kapp, "Comments on Bernfeld and Feitelberg's 'The Principle
of Entropy and the Death Instinct'"; and L. S. Penrose, "Freud's Theory of Instinct and Other
Psycho-Biological Theories."

entropy has continued to engage the attention of critics from time to time,[5] and it is not by free association that in the early 1970s Anthony Wilden decided to launch his critique of Freud's entropy principle in the name of cybernetics.

Wilden claims that Freud's neuronal network foreshadowed the contemporary model of the brain and human beings as information-processing systems and that Freud almost anticipated cybernetics, except that he was hampered both by a bioenergetic model of the psyche and by his imperfect grasp of the differences between a closed system and an open system. In one of Freud's formulations, says Wilden, "a human being appears to be a neurotic steam-engine fluctuating between quiescence and runaway activity, with two conflicting kybernetai, Eros and Thanatos, at the controls, each haggling with the other over what is to be done with the daily delivery of coal."[6] As if this is not enough to wake up Maxwell's Demon or the ghost of Norbert Wiener, Wilden carries his cybernetic tropes further by describing Freud's notion of the human as "a thermodynamic system condemned to the entropy of the 'death instinct' (the Freudian 'principle of inertia')" (124). He proposes that, in order to move beyond the entropy principle of classical physics adopted by Freud, one must introduce a clear methodological distinction between energy and information and that between closed and open systems (132). This sounds fine as far as the cybernetic view goes, but the historical contradiction is that Shannon did not shun the concept of entropy and in fact made it central to his own work on information theory. As we have seen in chapter 2, he openly borrowed that concept from the second law of thermodynamics and converted it from a measure of energy (heat) into a measure of information ("bits" or binary digits).

Wilden's criticism of Freud is anachronistic and flawed, although he is certainly justified in accentuating the role of cybernetics in the emerging world of digital media. Unlike Herbert Marcuse, Wilden paid attention to the rapid developments in digital technologies by working with Lacan and associating himself with Bateson and other American cyberneticians. This clearly sets him apart from the other Freudians of his time.[7] Marcuse's

5. See, e.g., Leon J. Saul, "Freud's Death Instinct and the Second Law of Thermodynamics" (1958).

6. Anthony Wilden, *System and Structure*, 124.

7. Strangely, Lacan's discussion of cybernetics is disavowed by Wilden in his criticism of Lacan's linguistic approach. See Wilden, *System and Structure*, 19. For Wilden's critique of Marcuse, see his "Marcuse and the Freudian Model: Energy, Information and Phantasie."

understanding of psychoanalysis, in contrast, was very much immersed in bioenergetic discourse based on nineteenth-century physics, as if cybernetics and information theory had never happened.[8] The problem with Wilden is that he jumps over Shannon's appropriation of entropy to make a premature judgment about where Freud stands in relation to bioenergetics on the one hand and information theory on the other.

In retrospect, Shannon's translation of the thermodynamic concept of entropy into information theory in 1948 was a decisive moment in determining how the distinction between energy and information was to be drawn (and subsequently be endorsed by Wilden). This discursive shift in favor of information theory has eroded the earlier vitalist distinction between organic and inorganic—the very distinction invoked by Jones to contest Freud's concept of the death drive—and led to the formalist moment in molecular biology. Freud could not have anticipated all of this and it would not be fruitful to debate whether his formulation of the death drive conforms with or is comparable to the second law of thermodynamics. Strictly speaking, Shannon's own adaptation of entropy would have not passed the test of the second law of thermodynamics any more than Freud's.

The relationship between energy and information via the mediation of entropy is an enormously interesting problem for a historian of science.[9] Although this problem does not concern us here, we must confront the question of how the postvitalist blurring of the distinction between the organic and the inorganic complicates the human-machine relationship in digital media and, in particular, how it might impinge on our psychic relationship to automata, which had inspired Freud's famous essay on the uncanny.

Now let us consider the issue from a slightly different angle. In chapter 3, we encountered what might be called a simulation model of the death drive in Shannon's enigmatic automaton. According to Arthur C. Clarke, the Ultimate Machine was a sobering experience—if not pure epiphany—for those who came into contact with it.[10] Clarke happened to be visiting in

8. Marcuse states that "in the Freudian conception, destructive energy cannot become stronger without reducing erotic energy: the balance between the two primary impulses is a quantitative one; the instinctual dynamic is mechanistic, distributing an available quantum of energy between the two antagonists." See Marcuse, "Aggressiveness in Advanced Industrial Society," 257–58.

9. For a good discussion of this problem, see Bruce Clarke, "From Thermodynamics to Virtuality."

10. Besides the Shannon exhibition at the Heinz Nixdorf Museum in Paderborn, Germany (see chap. 3 n 89, above), readers will find replicas of the Ultimate Machine on YouTube and other

the United States to investigate the spectacular postwar developments in communication technology in the 1950s.[11] With a superb eye for detail, he wrote a few richly evocative paragraphs—excerpted in chapter 3—to describe the automaton he chanced to see when passing through Shannon's Bell Lab's office. When one presses the switch on the front of the small wooden casket, the lid arises slowly with a buzzing sound and a faux hand emerges from the inside. This hand reaches down to turn the switch off and retreats back into the casket. The lid then snaps shut and peace is restored. The whole thing does not take more than a few seconds. The embodiment of the digital principle of 0 and 1 by this machine is reflected not in its mechanics—in a sense, all robots are mechanical—but in the action of the faux hand that performs the on-and-off cycle.

If the reader will recall, Clarke found the experience emotionally disturbing and remarked, "[T]here was something unspeakably sinister about a machine that did nothing—absolutely nothing—except switch itself off."[12] What psychoanalytical insight did Clarke glean from the Ultimate Machine? Is it related to the idea of the uncanny that Freud developed in response to Ernst Jentsch's reading of automata a century ago? How do we explain the fact that a faux hand that appears and disappears with a simple feedback mechanism could exert such a powerful effect on the psyche? Is Shannon's Ultimate Machine a kind of Freudian robot?

In the previous chapter, we saw that both Lacan's reinterpretation of Freud and his development of the notion of the symbolic order were mediated through his innovative engagement with cybernetics, game theory, and information theory. This chapter reopens the Freudian problem of the uncanny and brings it to bear on the recent developments in automata, image making, and digital media. There are several important reasons for rethinking the uncanny in this light; we will examine only three. First, theorists of visual culture and postmodern art tend to fall back on Freud's notion of the uncanny as they try to explain how animated pictures and automata address our visual and cognitive systems, and they seem to find

---

websites. One of these replicas appears in *The Human Language Series*, part 1, "Discovering the Human Language" (PBS, 1995), directed by Gene Searchinger. The machine appears in a brief interlude in the film and runs just long enough for the faux hand to complete its on/off action.

11. Clarke had proposed geostationary satellite communication in a technical paper published as early as 1945. But John R. Pierce pursued significant research into satellites when he served as the vice president for research of Bell Laboratories. Pierce was responsible for developing Telstar 1, the first commercial communications satellite, and was the first to discuss unmanned communications satellites. See John R. Pierce and A. Michael Noll, *Signals: The Science of Telecommunications*.

12. A. C. Clarke, *Voice Across the Sea*, 159.

Freud's "Das 'Unheimliche'" (The "Uncanny") particularly relevant—and even indispensable—to our modern aesthetic sensibility.[13] Second, if this tendency is indicative of the inherent difficulty of doing media analysis without psychoanalytical insights, we need to step back and ask what object of knowledge the psychoanalyst has sought to establish with the idea of the "uncanny" in the first place. This question can have significant bearings on the study of digital media because Freud's original contribution to that discussion was embroiled in a contested reading of the automaton in E. T. A. Hoffmann's "Der Sandmann" (The Sandman). Finally, and more important, the current work in automata, digital media, and AI engineering is beginning to throw fresh light on some aspects of Freud's explication of the uncanny that have heretofore remained obscure.

I aim to reestablish the seminal points of linkage between the automaton and the uncanny in the original context of Freud's engagement with Jentsch. Through a reinterpretation of Freud, Jentsch, and other theorists, this chapter will bring the relationship between Freud and digital media to light and further examine the Uncanny Valley research in the field of artificial intelligence in that light. The chapter will close with a consideration of the Neurotic Machine (K. M. Colby) and the Emotion Machine (Marvin Minsky)—computer simulations of human cognitive behavior of one kind or another—to reflect on the place of the Freudian robot in the human-machine ecology and its alternatives.

The Uncanny in the Automaton

The starting point of our inquiry is where Freud himself began in "The 'Uncanny'"; namely, his vigorous repudiation of Ernst Jentsch's interpretation and, in particular, his rejection of Jentsch's argument of ambiguity or intellectual uncertainty as the source of the uncanny. This point of departure or indebtedness, which will be crucial to our unraveling of Freud's position on the subject of automata, is often slighted if not completely suppressed in the extensive commentaries that have accumulated around Freud's essay since its first publication in 1919. In the majority of the existing literature, the uncanny mysteriously figures the return of the repressed or, in Schelling's much quoted phrase, the uncanny is that which "ought to have remained secret and hidden but has come to light."[14] This reading makes sense in the context of Freud's argument, but the unintended

13. See for example Hal Foster's psychoanalytic reading of modernist art in *Compulsive Beauty*.
14. Sigmund Freud, "The 'Uncanny,'" 241.

consequence is that Jentsch's "Zur Psychologie des Unheimlichen" (1906) is seldom read to enlighten us on why Freud could not tolerate the suggestion of ambiguity and uncertainty as a source of the uncanny.[15] Bill Brown is certainly right to quip that "Jentsch has suffered the fate of being most familiar as a dismissive footnote."[16] Instead of scrutinizing Freud's repudiation of Jentsch, most critics are content to mimic Freud's manner of introducing an argument through German or European etymologies while reaffirming the universal claim that *das Unheimliche* (the uncanny) is what becomes unconcealed as *das Heimliche* (the familiar).[17] Jentsch's essay was neither reprinted in German nor made available in English until 1997, and this curious fact has led Forbes Morlock to call the situation "doubly uncanny," commenting that "the repressed, however, always returns—the uncanny in 'The Uncanny' is about nothing else."[18]

It is important to bear in mind that Jentsch, not Freud, was the first to link the phenomenon of the uncanny to automata by way of Hoffmann's "The Sandman." Fascinated by the psychic power of automata, Jentsch noted the rise of the uncanny feeling and sought to explain it by emphasizing the role of *intellectual uncertainty between animate and inanimate.* Freud acknowledged this work as the starting point of his own inquiry but tried very hard to repudiate the argument of intellectual uncertainty. But his dismissal of Jentsch's thesis should by no means be taken at face value or be accepted at all until one is prepared to engage with the men's shared interest in the automaton as a simulation of the uncanny. The ways in which their interpretations converge or diverge on the question of *intellectual uncertainty between animate and inanimate* can yield some vital clues as to how the Freudian uncanny can be made relevant to the contemporary discussions of the psychic powers of image, medium, and automata in digital media. It is only by bringing Jentsch back into the discussion of the uncanny that we can reassess the stakes of Freud's own argument concerning animated figures and automata more clearly than before. In this

15. Françoise Meltzer is one of the few critics who question Freud's reading. See F. Meltzer, "The Uncanny Rendered Canny: Freud's Blind Spot in Reading Hoffmann's 'Sandman.'"

16. Bill Brown, "Reification, Reanimation, and the American Uncanny," 198.

17. Harold Bloom has extolled the essay on the uncanny as a unique contribution Freud made to the aesthetics of the sublime, and pays no attention to Jentsch's prior study whatsoever (Bloom, 101–4). Samuel Weber, Hélène Cixous, Sarah Kofman, Jeffrey Mehlman, Neil Hertz, Stanley Cavell, and Maria Torok have each offered insightful interpretations of Freud's reading of "The Sandman," but when they refer to Jentsch, they usually do so by quoting Freud quoting Jentsch.

18. Forbes Morlock, "Doubly Uncanny: An Introduction to 'On the Psychology of the Uncanny,'" 17.

regard, Freud is as strangely indebted to Jentsch in developing the idea of
the uncanny as he is to Sir James Frazer in the matter of the totem.[19]

Jentsch's "Zur Psychologie des Unheimlichen" (1906), translated as "On
the Psychology of the Uncanny" (1997), sets the tone and initial direction
of Freud's investigation of the relationship of aesthetics and the uncanny.
This includes his numerous references to automata and fantastic literature. Jentsch speculates that of all the psychical uncertainties that may
cause uncanny feelings to arise, one in particular is likely to develop into
a regular, powerful, and general effect. This usually concerns the doubt as
to whether an apparently living being is animate or not; and, conversely,
it may involve the uncertainty about whether a lifeless object may not in
fact be alive, as, for example, when a tree trunk is perceived to suddenly
move and shows itself to be a giant snake or a primitive man experiences
his first sight of a locomotive or a steamboat. The horrors people feel toward a dead body, especially a human corpse, a death's head, skeletons, and
similar objects are likewise attributed by Jentsch to the thought of a latent
animate state that lies close to objects that used to be alive. Amongst the
other lifeless objects that fall into the same category of the uncanny, he
mentions wax figures, panopticons, and panoramas and, above all, draws
our attention to automatic toys, life-size automata that can perform complicated tasks like blowing trumpets and dancing, and dolls that can close
and open their eyes by themselves. Yes, dolls and automata, etc. Among
such objects should fall Shannon's suicidal Ultimate Machine as well as
countless other cybernetic toys of our own time, all of which would aptly
belong to Jentsch's catalogue of dolls and automata and supposedly inspire
the feeling of the uncanny in the observer.

Anthony Vidler, who has derived the term "the architectural uncanny"
from psychoanalysis, approaches the interaction of the mind and space in
precisely this manner, for he grasps the aesthetic dimension of mental projection toward spatial configurations as that which "elides the boundaries
of the real and the unreal in order to provoke a disturbing ambiguity, a slippage between waking and dreaming."[20] This understanding of the uncanny

19. According to Frazer, the moment of totemism occurs in a woman's passage to motherhood
when a spirit, which awaits reincarnation in the nearest totem center where the spirits of the dead
collect, has entered her body. Freud dismisses this explanation as "the sick fancies of pregnant
women" and chooses to interpret the totem as the creation of a masculine mind trying to resolve
the sublime conflicts of the Oedipus complex. In an insightful reading of *Totem and Taboo*, W. J. T.
Mitchell points out that "Freud passes over Sir James Frazer's account of the accidental finding of
the totem rather quickly" (*What Do Pictures Want?*, 122).

20. Anthony Vidler, *The Architectural Uncanny: Essays in the Modern Unhomely*, 11.

enacts a return of the repressed by reasserting Jentsch's view of ambiguity and intellectual uncertainty in the name of Freud.[21] As a matter of fact, Jentsch's return in the guise of Freud appears almost inevitable as can be seen in the works of a growing number of cultural critics who contemplate the social implications of the increased blurring of boundaries between human and machine. Vidler sums it up as follows: "[N]ow, the boundaries between organic and inorganic, blurred by cybernetic and bio-technologies, seem less sharp; the body, itself invaded and reshaped by technology, invades and permeates the space outside, even as this space takes on dimensions that themselves confuse the inner and the outer, visually, mentally, and physically" (147). The bio- and techno-uncanny is evoked by Vidler to help make sense of our posthuman world of cyborgs who live with their prosthetic devices and technologies. This is where Jentsch, and Freud, become once again relevant.

In "On the Psychology of the Uncanny," Jentsch argued that the figure of the automaton traverses the boundaries of animate and inanimate and tends to provoke a certain kind of anxiety. This psychic phenomenon requires explanation and Jentsch gives it as follows:

> The mass that at first seemed completely lifeless suddenly reveals an inherent energy because of its movement. This energy can have a psychical or a mechanical origin. As long as the doubt as to the nature of the perceived movement lasts, and with it the obscurity of its cause, a feeling of terror persists in the person concerned. If, because of its methodical quality, the movement has shown its origin to be in an organic body, the state of things is thus explained, and then a feeling of concern for one's freedom from personal harm arises instead—which undoubtedly presupposes, however, a kind of intellectual mastery of the situation for the sake of all other forms of intensity. Conversely, the same emotion occurs when, as has been described, a wild man has his first sight of a locomotive or of a steamboat, for example, perhaps at night. The feeling of trepidation will here be very great, for as a consequence of the enigmatic autonomous movement and the regular noises of the machine, reminding him of human breath, the giant apparatus can easily impress the completely ignorant person as a living mass.[22]

21. Vidler devotes a short paragraph to discussing Jentsch. Although he does not wish to confront Freud's repudiation of Jentsch's idea of "intellectual uncertainty," Vidler clearly subscribes to Jentsch's view on this issue. See Vidler, *The Architectural Uncanny*, 23.

22. Ernst Jentsch, "On the Psychology of the Uncanny," 11. This essay is translated by Roy Sellars from "Zur Psychologie des Unheimlichen," which was originally published in the

However, human minds are not equally affected by the uncanny. According to Jentsch, the head of a pillar or the figure in a painting can come alive in the minds of those who are delirious, intoxicated, or superstitious and who would address the figure, carry on a conversation with it, or attack it. In contrast to rational men, presumably including himself, whose intellectual maturity provides better psychological defense against such fancies, Jentsch believes that children, women, primitive men, and dreamers are particularly susceptible to such stirrings and to the danger of seeing spirits and ghosts. On the point of intellectual mastery, Freud is in agreement with Jentsch, for the former begins his own essay on the uncanny by confessing that it is a long time since he has experienced or heard anything that would give him an uncanny impression.[23]

The social drama of how women and the psychically vulnerable confront a clever machine or a simulation model of the human mind has been staged repeatedly in recent times by computer scientists who design neurotic machines or simulation computer programs either to model a theory of the mind or to advance the cause of artificial intelligence. The most famous of the early programs was written by MIT computer scientist Joseph Weizenbaum in 1964–66. His simulation program is named ELIZA—with a script called DOCTOR—and it requires those who interact with the machine to play the role of a patient as DOCTOR simulates the speech of a nondirective therapist. Having observed how people talked to the machine, Weizenbaum was surprised to find how quickly and how deeply people became emotionally involved with the computer. His own secretary had followed his work for many months and knew that it was a computer program, but she forgot all this when she began conversing with DOCTOR. "After only a few interchanges with it," recalls Weizenbaum, "she asked me to leave the room. Another time, I suggested I might rig the system so that I could examine all conversations anyone had with it, say, overnight. I was promptly bombarded with accusations that what I proposed amounted to spying on people's most intimate thoughts."[24] Weizenbaum is not implying that only women are susceptible to such delusions, but the popularity of his story within the communities of computer science and artificial intelligence does reveal something about shared assumptions about gender and intelli-

---

Psychiatrisch-Neurologische Wochenschrift, 203–5. For more on Freud's Jentsch, see Nicholas Royle, The Uncanny.

23. Freud, "The 'Uncanny,'" 220.

24. Weizenbaum, Computer Power and Human Reason, 6–7.

gence. If the story sounds strangely familiar, it reflects back on the mental delusions that Jentsch tried to explain in the essay on the uncanny.

When the mental powers ascribed to children, women, primitive men, and dreamers are called upon to help stage the primal psychic drama of the uncanny, they effectively separate the investigator, whether Jentsch or Freud, from the object of investigation. This has been one of the originary social conditions of psychology and psychoanalysis acknowledged by their pioneers and practitioners. It seems that the psychic drama of social discrimination is what drew Bill Brown's attention when he tried to excavate Jentsch's analysis of animated objects to understand the American history of race, slavery, capitalism, and reified people and things. Brown argues that "[t]he animation of the lifeless object, in the case of the black collectible, reinstates Jentsch's argument, fully leavened by part of Freud's. For the point is not only that the inanimate comes to life but that the history of this ontological ambiguity—human or thing—is precisely what remains repressed within U.S. culture" (199). This observation implies an unmistakable grasp of Jentsch's original proposition—even if the latter's social statement is ironically downplayed by Brown—but the dynamic between Jentsch and Freud on the interpretation of Hoffmann's literary work is something to which we should pay closer attention, because it is precisely the ambiguities within the text of "The Sandman" that had given Freud the initial opportunity to repudiate Jentsch.

Jentsch has speculated that the uncanny is a semi-conscious projection of the self onto an object even as the object returns to terrify the self in the image of that self-projection. For this reason, human beings are not always capable of exorcising the spirits that have been fabricated out of their own heads and this inability produces the "feeling of being threatened by something unknown and incomprehensible that is just as enigmatic to the individual as his own psyche usually is" (14). This weakness is often exploited by poets and writers who aim to arouse the same uncanny effect in their readers. In storytelling, Jentsch suggests, one of the most reliable artistic devices for producing uncanny effects is to leave the reader in a state of uncertainty about whether he is dealing with a human being or an automaton. "In his works of fantasy," he adds, "E. T. A. Hoffmann has repeatedly made use of this psychological artifice with success" (13). Although the title of the Sandman story is omitted from his account, the reference leaves Freud in no doubt as to the focus of uncertainty Jentsch alludes to here, namely the doll Olympia. It bears pointing out that in another Hoffmann story, "Automata," mechanical dolls also raise troubling questions about the uncanny or "images of living death or inanimate life."[25] Hoffmann's focus in this story is the psychic power of the automaton over human beings and the machine in question is a Talking Turk on exhibition. I would not rule out the possibility that Jentsch had this other story in mind as well, although Freud focuses his attention exclusively on the Sandman story in his repudiation of Jentsch.

As we know, Jentsch attributes the uncanny effects of the Sandman story to the artistic skill with which Hoffmann manipulates intellectual uncertainty in Nathanael and in the reader who identifies with him as the narrative unfolds: Is Olympia animate or inanimate? Interestingly, the word *unheimlich* appears in Hoffmann's story a number of times, often in conjunction with Olympia, which apparently constrained Jentsch's interpretation. For example, Nathanael's close friend Sigismund uses this word to describe the peculiar look and gesture of the doll with whom Nathanael has fallen madly in love:

> It's very strange, however, that many of us have come to the same conclusion about Olympia. She seems to us—don't take this badly, my brother—strangely stiff and soulless. Her figure is symmetrical, so is her face, that's true enough, and if her eyes were not so completely devoid of life—the power of vision, I mean—she might be considered beautiful. Her step is peculiarly measured; all of her movements seem to stem from some kind of clockwork. Her playing and singing are unpleasantly perfect, being as lifeless as a music box; it is the same with her dancing. We found Olympia to be rather *unheimlich*, and we wanted to have nothing to do with her. She seems to us to be playing the part of a human being, and it's as if there really were something hidden behind all of this.[26] (my emphasis)

It is safe to assume that Jentsch took both his idea and his language from Hoffmann's narrative to make an argument about the hesitation or uncertainty between animate and inanimate beings as the cause of the *unheimlich*. But as Freud correctly observes, the uncertainty surrounding the identity of Olympia is gradually dispelled toward the end of the story, at which point both Nathanael and Hoffmann's reader are informed that she is an

---

25. See Victoria Nelson, *The Secret Life of Puppets*, 66.

26. Hoffmann, *Tales of E. T. A. Hoffmann*, 117. The translators render the word *unheimlich* as "weird" rather than "uncanny" in this translation, so I have put the German word back in the text to highlight its actual appearance in the original story. For the original story, see Hoffmann, *Der Sandmann*, 41.

automaton and that her clockwork was made by physics professor Spalan-zani and her eyes were put in by Coppola, from whom Nathanael bought his pair of telescopes with which he has spied on her. On this ground, Freud rejects Jentsch's argument and decides to look elsewhere for an answer to the sources of the *unheimlich*.

Freud, who cannot tolerate the idea of intellectual uncertainty as an explanation, introduces his alternative reading by displacing the automa-ton as the problem of the uncanny with something else, namely, Nathana-el's ocular anxiety about the Sandman.[27] The move to decouple the un-canny and automata is made perfectly clear in the following statement: "[U]ncertainty whether an object is living or inanimate, which admittedly applied to the doll Olympia, is quite irrelevant in connection with this other, more striking instance of uncanniness."[28] What is this other instance of which Freud speaks? He calls it castration anxiety and proceeds to dem-onstrate that Nathanael's fear of the loss of eyesight can be read as a symp-tom or substitute for his repressed castration anxiety. This fear has been instilled in him as a child and is embodied by the Sandman, Coppelius, and the eye-glass peddler, Coppola. The multiple interplay of doubles or the doppelgänger in Hoffmann's tale from Nathanael/Olympia and Spalan-zani/Coppola to Coppelius/Coppola and Klara/Olympia leaves ample room for Freud to develop a parallel narrative that seems to make good sense from the standpoint of psychoanalysis.

In "The Uncanniness of the Ordinary," Stanley Cavell tries to wrestle the problem of the uncanny away from the hegemony of Oedipus to refocus our attention on "an uncertainty in our ability to distinguish the animate from the inanimate." If this critique appears to echo Jentsch's earlier argu-ment, it has not led Cavell back to Jentsch's essay; he doesn't come to grips with the world of dolls and automata that had fascinated Jentsch and Freud alike. Instead, Cavell confines himself to speculations about "the sense of the human as inherently strange, say unstable, its quotidian as forever fantastic,"[29] instead of considering, as suggested by Bill Brown, that "the repression at work may be the repression of the unhuman object-world itself, which psychoanalysis compulsively translates into the human."[30]

27. For a well-grounded critique of Freud's intolerance of intellectual uncertainty, see Meltzer, "The Uncanny Rendered Canny: Freud's Blind Spot in Reading Hoffmann's 'Sandman.'"

28. Freud, "The 'Uncanny,'" 230.

29. Stanley Cavell, "The Uncanniness of the Ordinary," 155, 156.

30. Brown, "Reification, Reanimation, and the American Uncanny," 198.

W. J. T. Mitchell proposes that the notion of the living image—which is more than a metaphor or an archaism—deserve our attention because it requires thinking through the category of life itself. The latter poses a semantic rectangle that governs its dialectics as follows:

living	dead
inanimate	undead[31]

This would have appealed to Jentsch, whose own study of the uncanny obeys similarly construed logical opposites: the dead object that was once alive, and the inanimate object that never was alive. In Mitchell's formulation, there is also the negation of the negation, or the return and arrival of life in the nonliving substance where human beings impersonate the inanimate figures of painting and sculpture. Presumably, the "undead" is where Hoffmann's automaton truly belongs and, indeed, as Mitchell writes: "The figure of the 'undead' is perhaps the obvious place where the uncanniness of the image comes into play in ordinary language and popular narrative, especially the tale of horror, when that which should be dead, or should never had lived, is suddenly perceived as alive," such as the mock horror and delight expressed by actor Gene Wilder in *Young Frankenstein* when he declares "It's alive!" (55). Think of Bazin's mummy and the endless fascination of Hollywood with myths of the return of the mummy as the ghostly semblances "materialize before our eyes or in our imagination" (55). Mitchell's explication of the "undead" is as much opposed to the "dead" as it is to the "inanimate," which is not the same as Jentsch's argument of uncertainty between animate and inanimate. Does the "undead" entail a significantly different conception of the uncanny that operates not only on the pivot of intellectual uncertainty but also on how the meaning of life evolves and gets assigned to objects at any given moment? Another question follows: Is there a good psychoanalytic explanation for the uncanny in the figure of the "undead"?

Freud's rigorous unraveling of the verbal and visual substitutions in his reading of "The Sandman" aims to demonstrate that ocular anxiety can hide a deeper, symptomatic fear of castration that produces the uncanny effect in the story.[32] Thus the fantastic narrative must begin logically with Nathanael's childhood, his fear of losing his eyes, the death of his father,

---

31. Mitchell, *What Do Pictures Want?*, 54.

32. For Freud's ambiguous relationship with ocularcentrism, see Martin Jay, *Downcast Eyes: The Denigration of Vision in Twentieth-Century French Thought*, 332–36.

his subsequent encounter with the Sandman's doubles, his troubled love for Klara and infatuation with Olympia, and the final descent into delirium and madness. But the doll Olympia cannot easily be banished from Freud's own narrative as a source of the uncanny, and she soon reasserts herself in a lengthy footnote in the middle of Freud's analysis: "This automatic doll can be nothing else than a materialization of Nathanael's feminine attitude towards his father in his infancy. Her fathers, Spalanzani and Coppola, are, after all, nothing but new editions, reincarnations of Nathanael's pair of fathers."[33]

So it seems that Olympia is lodged, after all, in the interior of Nathanael's childhood phobias and therefore is thoroughly relevant to the problem of the uncanny Freud analyzes here, except that she now comes to embody the certainty, rather than uncertainty, of the psychoanalytic truth about the young man's castration anxiety. Freud's intuition of the symbolic interplay between Olympia and Nathanael has led Hélène Cixous to observe that "homosexuality returns in reality under this charming figure. But Olympia is more than just a detached complex of Nathanael. If she is no more than that, why are not the dance, the song, the mechanisms, and the artificer brought back into the game or theorized upon by Freud?"[34] Cixous's feminist reading of Freud's "Das 'Unheimliche'" remains unsurpassed and deserves our renewed attention. Her criticism raises a particularly salient point about the curious gaps of interpretation in Freud's reading of Hoffmann in regard to the role of the dance, the song, the mechanisms, and the artificer. These gaps revolve around the question of medium and media to which we now turn.

The Psychic Life of Media

In a discussion of the uncanny in *What Do Pictures Want?*, Mitchell writes: "If images are life-forms, and objects are the bodies they animate, then media are the habitats or ecosystems in which pictures come alive" (198). The idea of bioecological systems is introduced here to distinguish among image, object, and medium. The medium is the key. By media, he means a whole gamut of material practices that brings an image together with an object to produce a picture. Mitchell argues that the technical distinction between the still and moving image or that between the silent and talking

33. Freud, "The 'Uncanny,'" 232.

34. Cixous, "Fiction and Its Phantoms: A Reading of Freud's '*Das Unheimliche*' (the "Uncanny")," 538.

image is routinely articulated as a question of life. If pictures of animated beings in this broad sense are not merely visual signs *for* living things but are often perceived and addressed *as* living things, they are bound to raise the specter of the Freudian uncanny. In fact, Mitchell repeatedly evokes "the uncanny" in his work to speak about the fantasies of reanimated extinct life or contemporary digitized and virtual imaging that simulates certain action. He shows that "[t]he praise of the 'lifelike' image is, of course, as old as image-making, and the liveliness of an image may be quite independent of its accuracy as a representation. The uncanny ability of pictured faces to 'look back' and in the technique of omnivoyance to seem to follow us with their eyes is well established. Digitized and virtual imaging now makes it possible to simulate the turning of the face or the body to follow the movement of the spectator."[35] The contemporary optical fantasies tend to evoke the uncanny in the same manner as the mechanical doll Olympia has appeared in the eyes of the student Nathanael. In both instances, a medium of animation, a face or a body, ocular anxiety, and some secret mechanisms are conjured forth in the unfolding of a narrative. Does this mean that Mitchell or other media theorists share a specifically Freudian interest in the uncanny, or what one might call the pictorial uncanny?

Mitchell's ambivalences toward psychoanalysis complicate our answers to the above question. On the one hand, he views psychoanalysis as a discipline—probably the most promising of all disciplines—that may take us into the heart of the lives of images through a systematic elaboration of desire and drives. On the other, the psychoanalytic model of desire coalesces around a set of assumptions about the nature of images that seems problematic to a contemporary theorist of visual culture. Mitchell notes that "classically, the Freudian attitude is that the image is a mere symptom, a substitute for an impossible desire, an illusory semblance or 'manifest content' that is to be decoded, demystified, and ultimately eliminated in favor of a latent content expressed in language" (69). Just as Freud privileges language, so Lacan does the symbolic order. Thus, the psychoanalytic suspicion of images renders the discipline less helpful than it would otherwise have been according to Mitchell, because the discourse most fully equipped to produce an analysis of desire is disinclined to ask questions about the picturing of desire beyond the opposition of image and language. From the standpoint of critical studies of visual culture, the psychoanalytic model of the imago, narcissism, identification, fantasy, fetishism, and the

35. Mitchell, *What Do Pictures Want?*, 53.

role of images in social and psychic life is certainly open to question, especially if the model is perceived to be grounded in a set of uncontested or underdeveloped theoretical apparati to explain how image, object, and media work with respect to the psyche.

This critical stance does not imply that Mitchell has rejected psychoanalysis so much as he tries to reformulate the Freudian terms of image and desire. The crux of the matter is how psychoanalysis will gain new insights from innovative theories of media and visual culture that not only help justify its own assumptions about the psyche, but can steer our understanding of the powers of images toward interesting new directions. In *What Do Pictures Want?*, for example, Mitchell proposes five reformulations of Freudian categories by recentering the problem of images in psychoanalysis. First, the picture is to be situated at the intersection of psychic drive (compulsive repetition, proliferation, and the plague of images) and desire (the fixation, reification, mortification of the life-form). Second, images should not be reduced to symptoms of the scopic drive but serve as models and constitutive schematisms for the visual process itself, since the very structure of visual cognition and recognition belongs fundamentally to social practices. Third, images and pictures are central to social life because they put a demand on our psyche, whether these are to be loved, to be admired, to be remembered, or to be feared. Fourth, although the Imaginary is relegated by Lacan and Lacanians to the realm of visual images and is primarily associated with fixation, binding, and a false image of unified self, the Imaginary constantly crosses over into the Symbolic, as is evidenced by the figures of writing, verbal image, metaphor, the conceit, or analogy.[36] (This important insight by Mitchell will be reexamined and substantiated further by a reading of the Freudian uncanny in the next section.) Fifth, since a libidinal object always implicates an image or picture, there emerges an interesting set of correspondences to the fourfold array of sacred icons and iconic practices as adumbrated by Slavoj Žižek (1997): love belongs to the idol, desire to the fetish, friendship to totem, and *jouissance* to iconoclasm. Aside from the philosophical challenge that this view of iconology poses to cultural anthropology, there is a specific question to consider here: is the libidinal object considered alive or dead from a psychoanalytical point of view? This question will turn out to be

---

36. Mitchell argues that all three Lacanian categories—the Symbolic, the Imaginary, and the Real—converge in the picture, and I suppose that Lacan would have concurred that the slippage between the Symbolic and the Imaginary occurs all the time. See Mitchell, *What Do Pictures Want?*, 73–74.

more difficult to answer than it appears, and we have no choice but broaden and open up the interpretative spaces that "make the *relationality* of image and beholder the field of investigation."[37] Mitchell's picture theory aims to demonstrate that pictures can come alive only by way of media or in given habitats or ecosystems, which presupposes the relationality of image and beholder. If the specter of the uncanny seems to rear its head again in that suggestion, it is because equivocation or uncertainty with respect to life and death had been the starting point of Freud's own classic analysis of the uncanny.

It is in a discussion of animation, fantasy, and technology that the Freudian uncanny comes into focus in Mitchell's study. He argues that images come alive in two basic forms that vacillate between figurative and literal senses of vitality or animation. Namely, they come alive either because viewers believe they are alive, as in the case of weeping Madonnas and mute idols that demand human sacrifice or moral reformation. Or they come alive because a clever artist or technician has engineered them to *appear* alive, as when the puppeteer or ventriloquist animates his or her puppet with motion and voice, or the master painter seems to capture the life of the model with the flick of a brush. He concludes that "the notion of images as life-forms always equivocates between questions of belief and knowledge, fantasy and technology, the golem and the clone. The middle space, which Freud called the Uncanny, is perhaps the best name for the location of images as media in their own right" (295). Thus, the uncanny—more precisely, the Jentschian uncanny—is placed in the middle space of equivocation between belief and knowledge, fantasy and technology, the golem and the clone. For Mitchell, examples of life-forms that equivocate between fantasy and technology include all kinds of automata, from talking pictures to the sounding idols and evil dolls that he frequently alludes to elsewhere.

To that list, I would add the Ultimate Machine. When Shannon the technician created his clever machine, the effect of the uncanny was achieved with the flick of a mechanical wrist that simulated the movement of the human arm. The image of an independent hand that moves and reaches out to switch itself off would have greatly intrigued Freud, Lacan, and Mitchell.

Freud also refers to the images of dismembered limbs, a severed head, a hand cut off at the wrist, and feet that dance by themselves, etc., as having "something peculiarly uncanny about them, especially when, as in the last

37. Mitchell, *What Do Pictures Want?*, 49.

instance, they prove capable of independent activity."[38] The simulation of the independent movement of severed limbs and body parts will be further explored in connection with Freud's fascination with automata in a later section. We now turn to Freud's own discussion of the uncanny and, in particular, the figure of the automaton in the Sandman story to further clarify the stakes of media and animated pictures in relation to psychoanalytical discourse.

What Is the Medium of *das Unheimliche*?

Is there something in Nathanael's "media" environment that makes the doll function as a trigger for the feeling of the uncanny? Mitchell has argued that images should not be reduced to symptoms of the scopic drive; they ought to serve as models and constitutive schematisms for the visual process. Images exist insofar as their media—habitats, ecosystems, and social practices—exist and function to provide the structure of cognitive patterns for them. Bearing this insight in mind, let us examine how Freud himself has approached the medium of the uncanny both in his reading of "The Sandman" and in a few other cases brought up in the course of his analysis. As stated before, Freud begins by focusing on linguistic usage and what Hoffmann's language can tell us about repression: "We can understand why linguistic usage has extended *das Heimliche* ['homely'] into its opposite, *das Unheimliche*; for this uncanny is in reality nothing new or alien, but something which is familiar and old-established in the mind and which has become alienated from it only through the process of repression. This reference to the factor of repression enables us, furthermore, to understand Schelling's definition of the uncanny as something which ought to have remained hidden but has come to light" (241). Freud's explication of the words *das Heimliche* and *das Unheimliche* on the basis of authoritative dictionaries is well known and has been exhaustively discussed.[39] If *das Unheimliche* is somehow lodged in language and framed somehow by (German) lexicography, as Cixous has contended, what do we make of Freud's larger psychoanalytic claims to a universal human psyche that is not unique to any linguistic group?[40]

It is worth noting that Freud does not restrict himself to the linguistic path, which is merely one of the two courses that lie open to him at

38. Freud, "The 'Uncanny,'" 244.
39. See Samuel Weber, *The Legend of Freud*.
40. Cixous, "Fiction and Its Phantoms," 530.

the outset. The other course leads the analyst to "properties of persons, things, sense-impressions, experiences and situations" that arouse the feeling of uncanniness. Freud considers animism, magic and sorcery, the omnipotence of thoughts, man's attitude to death, involuntary repetition, and the castration complex as the factors that turn something frightening into something uncanny. As if reminded of Jentsch's inventory of macabre pictures, Freud adds that "dismembered limbs, a severed head, a hand cut off at the wrist, as in a fairy tale of [Wilhelm] Hauff's, feet which dance by themselves, as in the book by [Albrecht] Schaeffer which I mentioned above—all these have something peculiarly uncanny about them, especially when, as in the last instance, they prove capable of independent activity in addition."[41] He concludes that this kind of uncanniness springs from its proximity to the castration complex.

I have good reason to suspect that the uncanniness Freud associates with dismembered limbs and their independent activity lies closer to the repressed automaton in his own reading than to the castration complex. It can be demonstrated that his allusion to dismemberment is driven unconsciously both by Jentsch's earlier reflections on automata and, more importantly, by the repressed automaton from the Hoffmann story he reads. As we have seen, Freud's reading of Hoffmann follows the narrative plot to track down the logic of ocular tropes in the text. By engaging himself exclusively with the multiplied images of the eye, Freud allows other but equally important clues to escape his attention. One possible interpretation I propose is built upon his own intuition about the interplay between Olympia and Nathanael but aims to relocate the uncanny from castration anxiety back to the automaton, not so much to reaffirm the uncertainty about the animate or inanimate state of the doll Olympia as to bring Nathanael's fantasies about *himself being an automaton* to light, which is not a direction in which Hoffmann's readers and critics have been reading the story.

Take the night when Nathanael believes that he discovered Coppelius to be the Sandman and that the evil man was threatening to deprive him of his eyes. Below is how Nathanael recalls the traumatic scene from his childhood:

> Pulling glowing grains from the fire with his naked hands, he was about to sprinkle them in my eyes when my father raised his hands entreatingly: "Master! Master!" he cried, "leave my Nathanael his eyes!" "Let the child keep his eyes and do his share of the world's weeping," Coppelius shrieked with a shrill

41. Freud, "The 'Uncanny,'" 244.

laugh, "but now we must carefully observe the mechanism of the hands and feet." He thereupon seized me so violently that my joints cracked, unscrewed my hands and feet, then put them back, now this way, then another way.[42]

Coppelius's change of mind may or may not make much sense to Freud, who has already made up his mind about associating the precious ocular organ with the male organ in his reading. But it is interesting to consider the anatomical substitutions that are literally played out in this scene. Hands and feet for the eyes! How come little Nathanael's hands and feet are screwed off, rather than cut off, and can instantly be reattached this way or that way to his body and be as good as ever? Is little Nathanael figured as a human or automaton? Animate or inanimate? Freud clearly views Nathanael as a live human being and does not pay close enough attention to the original scene of his childhood trauma to reflect on his dubious identity in the fantastic tale: Is Nathanael animate, inanimate, or "undead"?

Even if Freud were to read the detached hands and feet as substitutions for the phallic symbol from a psychoanalytical viewpoint, he would still be hard pressed to explain the mechanical movement of Nathanael's hand in the final scene and his subsequent fall. The narrator describes the scene thus: "Nathanael automatically [*mechanisch*] felt his side pocket, where he found Coppola's spyglass, and looked to one side."[43] In this moment, Nathanael attempts to push his fiancée Klara off the highest gallery of the tower where they are standing and bursts out with horrible laughter: "'Whirl wooden doll! Whirl wooden doll!'" (124).[44] A few moments later, Nathanael throws himself down from the tower to enact exactly what he has prophesied: a wooden doll, spinning around and around to meet his death, that is, if he ever was alive.

In her astute reading, Cixous has noted a close connection between Hoffmann's fantastic tale and the puppet theater that once populated the stages of German Romanticism. With respect to Freud's text, she points out: "What unfolds without fail before the reader's eyes is a kind of puppet theater in which real dolls or fake dolls, real and simulated life, are

42. Hoffmann, *Tales of E. T. A. Hoffmann*, 98. The original German sentence goes "Und damit faßte er mich gewaltig, daß die Gelenke knackten, und schrob mir die Hände ab und die Füße und setzte sie bald hier, bald dort wieder ein." Hoffmann, *Der Sandmann*, 16.

43. Hoffmann, *Tales of E. T. A. Hoffmann*, 124. The original German quote is "Nathanael faßte *mechanisch* nach der Seitentasche; er fand Coppola's Perspektiv, er schaute seitwärts" (Hoffmann, Der Sandmann, 48; emphasis added). The emphasis draws attention to his mechanical movement as indicated by the German phrase.

44. The German phrase is "Holzpüppchen dreh dich—Holzpüppchen dreh dich," in Hoffmann, *Der Sandmann*, 49.

manipulated by a sovereign but capricious stage-setter."[45] The reason that most critics do not regard Freud's uncanny in this theatrical light any more than they suspect Nathanael to be Hoffmann's true automaton may have something to do with their overwhelming fixation on linguistic usage and dictionaries, which are certainly prompted by Freud himself but constitute only one of his interpretive strategies.

Let us consider the writer Hoffmann as the puppeteer who sets in motion those literary puppets who are designed to tease our emotional and cognitive reaction to what he terms the uncanny. The medium for Hoffmann's automata then is the puppet theater in which the puppeteer and his audience or readers engage in a psychic game of make-believe about what is alive and what is dead. In this theater, which serves as the medium for the puppet performance, it does not take long before the clumsy doll Olympia, created by the scientist/alchemist Spalanzani/Coppola, is detected and exposed for what she is. But what about Nathanael? Obviously, it is much harder for us to make a quick decision about his animate or inanimate state. The blurring of the line between a mechanical puppet and the voice of the narrator can produce the most powerful effects of the uncanny on the audience. What I am suggesting here is that Nathanael may well have been the cleverest automaton ever invented by the fiction writer Hoffmann to compete with the inferior doll Olympia, which is designed by the scientist. The character Nathanael is so effective and so successful that critics and psychoanalysts, Jentsch and Freud alike, do not seem to entertain the slightest doubt about his ambiguity as a living human character or an undead automaton in the context of the story. The suspension of disbelief is nearly complete with regard to this literary "character." Freud's insight that the most uncanny of all is what is most familiar and at home with us is probably the highest compliment that Hoffmann's fiction has received from any reader; the novelist did succeed in fooling many of us about where to look for the uncanny. Unlike Jentsch, who read the story at face value, Freud looked in the right place—i.e., in Nathanael rather than in Olympia—but missed the automaton in Nathanael. Nevertheless, Freud did manage to turn Hoffmann's work into a psychoanalytic drama about doubles, shadows, repression, and the doppelgänger.

I suppose that the attraction of this literary work for the psychoanalyst lies in its ability to simulate structural scenarios in the theater of automata and doppelgängers, whereby the imagos of the fragmented body can be modeled and demonstrated. This is clearly what Lacan attempted in his analysis

---

45. Cixous, "Fiction and Its Phantoms," 525.

of aggressiveness and narcissism and the suicidal tendencies of the human psyche, as suggested earlier. Nathanael's aggressiveness and suicide provide a perfect simulation—insofar as simulations are what automata do and excel in—of the imago of the fragmented body complete with mechanical hands and feet, or what Lacan would call "the images of castration, emasculation, mutilation, dismemberment, dislocation" and so on.[46] The magical efficacy of Nathanael's narcissism indicates the radical ambiguity of the libidinal object, and the answer to the question raised earlier—is the libidinal object alive or dead from a psychoanalytical point of view?—can therefore be worked out through Lacan's notion of the imago, which is itself a powerful fiction mobilized by the psyche to organize ego and object forms. The uncanny in the Lacanian sense would then take us beyond Jentsch's thesis of intellectual uncertainty about animate or inanimate to shed light on how the imago, along with its death drive, is constituted. Through Lacan, we return then to Freud's insights about death and repression with a new understanding:

> Considering our unchanged attitude towards death, we might rather enquire what has become of the repression, which is the necessary condition of a primitive feeling recurring in the shape of something uncanny. But repression is there, too. All supposedly educated people have ceased to believe officially that the dead can become visible as spirits, and have made any such appearances dependent on improbable and remote conditions; their emotional attitude towards their dead, moreover, once a highly ambiguous and ambivalent one, has been toned down in the higher strata of the mind into an unambiguous feeling of piety.[47]

The return of the repressed always finds its way around through the lower strata of the psyche, through the Imaginary, or some other medium. The "media" environment of our world is undoubtedly very different from that which was inhabited or imagined by Hoffmann, Jentsch, and Freud. The ever-increasing blurring of the human-machine distinction has caused some of us to embrace the brave new posthuman age and others to loathe the same. Will the specter of the uncanny go away? Will today's automata, or increasingly sophisticated works of artificial intelligence, evoke the same feelings of the uncanny as Hoffmann's story once did?

There is little doubt that the biological implications of in vitro fertilization and cloning will be far-reaching and will impinge on the evolution of

46. Lacan, "Aggressiveness in Psychoanalysis," 85.
47. Freud, "The 'Uncanny,'" 242–43.

automata whose engendering or gendering processes—as discussed in our reading of the Freudian uncanny—have been contested. Today, the very idea of the biological in what has been touted as the posthuman era seems to be swinging decidedly toward a biocybernetical view both in contemporary scientific work and in mainstream social discourse, which also raises new questions about the uncanny.

The Uncanny Valley

It seems, though, that the dynamic of human and machine has been constitutive of psychoanalysis all along. This is reflected in Freud's earlier training as a neurologist and in his strong interest in the mechanisms of the unconscious, the camera obscura, and the mystic writing pad. In *The Interpretation of Dreams*, Freud states that "we should picture the instrument which carries out our mental functions as resembling a compound microscope or a photographic apparatus, or something of the kind. On that basis, psychical locality will correspond to a point inside the apparatus at which one of the preliminary stages of an image comes into being." Of the optical instruments, he explains: "In the microscope and telescope, as we know, these occur in part at ideal points, regions in which no tangible component of the apparatus is situated."[48] Martin Jay's analysis of Freud's optical tropes and their subsequent development by others has rightly emphasized the role of the machine in Freud's thinking.[49] Furthermore, the linkages between film and the Imaginary in Lacan's work, as noted by Friedrich Kittler, throw interesting light on the evolution of image as a problem of media technology in the ecosystems of modern society.[50] In that sense, Mitchell's criticism that psychoanalysis "was fundamentally constituted as a linguistic turn and a turn away from reliance on the visual observation of symptoms" stands in need of some qualification.[51] It makes sense for us to refocus our attention to the interplay of psychoanalytical discourse and its machines.

One of the latest developments in this area has emerged, not surprisingly, from the work of AI engineers, robot scientists, and psychiatrists in what has been termed "the Uncanny Valley" hypothesis. This hypothesis

48. Freud, *The Interpretation of Dreams*, 536.
49. Jay, *Downcast Eyes*, 435–91.
50. See the discussion of Kittler and Lacan in the preceding chapter. I have argued that Lacan models the symbolic order on the communication machine rather than on natural language, thereby profoundly transforming the Freudian notion of the unconscious.
51. Mitchell, *What Do Pictures Want?*, 70.

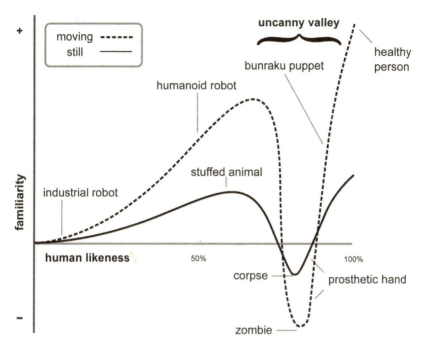

Figure 22. Karl F. MacDorman and Hiroshi Ishiguro's translation and adaptation of Masahiro Mori's diagram of the Uncanny Valley. From Karl F. MacDorman and Hiroshi Ishiguro, "Androids as an Experimental Apparatus: Why Is There an Uncanny Valley and Can We Exploit It?" Cognitive Science Society Workshop on Toward Social Mechanisms of Android Science (2005), http://www.androidscience.com/proceedings2005/MacDormanCogSci2005AS.pdf. Courtesy Karl F. MacDorman.

was first put forward in 1970 by Japanese roboticist Masahiro Mori, who speculated that as robots become progressively humanlike, our sense of empathy and familiarity increases until we come to the Uncanny Valley, and at this point the robots will start to elicit negative feelings in us. After surveying the various kinds of prosthetic hands, Mori suggests that, as the new technology further animates the prosthetic hand by enabling prosthetic fingers to move automatically, this will cause the animated hand to slide toward the bottom of the Uncanny Valley. Fig. 22 illustrates how Mori works out this hypothesis after Freud. Mori places the healthy person at the top of the second peak and the prosthetic hand near the bottom of the Uncanny Valley, which may remind us of the effect of Shannon's Ultimate Machine upon the writer Arthur Clarke. He believes that our impression of death can be explained by the movement from the second peak to the Uncanny Valley; referring to the dashed line in the figure, he adds, "We might be happy this line is into the still valley of a corpse and that of not the living dead! I think this explains the mystery of the uncanny valley: Why do we humans have such a feeling of strangeness? Is this necessary? I have not yet considered it deeply, but it may be important to our self-preservation."[52]

Mori's hypothesis comes straight out of Freud's earlier discussions of puppets, mechanical hands, mannequins, and mutilated limbs. For example, he compares the realistic effect of Japanese *bunraku* puppets with that of prosthetic hands and decides that the former should be placed closer to the peak since the puppets are not likely to be mistaken for humans, whereas prosthetic hands must rank near the bottom of the Uncanny Valley. He writes: "[R]ecently prosthetic hands have improved greatly, and we cannot distinguish them from real hands at a glance. Some prosthetic hands attempt to simulate veins, muscles, tendons, finger nails, and finger prints, and their color resembles human pigmentation. So maybe the prosthetic arm has achieved a degree of human verisimilitude on par with false teeth"[53] (Figs. 23 and 24). The visual verisimilitude, however, is immediately contradicted by the tactile expectation upon physical contact. Mori goes on to say that "if we shake the hand, we are surprised by the lack of soft tissue and cold temperature. In this case, there is no longer a sense of familiarity. It is uncanny" (Mac Dornan, 9).

Mori's reinterpretation of the Freudian uncanny for AI engineering and research has led him to oppose visual appearance to tactile experience; this opposition in the case of the prosthetic hand results in "negative familiarity," an interesting translation of the Freudian *Unheimliche*. That is to say, "the appearance is quite human like, but the familiarity is negative. This is the uncanny valley" (9). Of course, Mori's goal is not to explain the uncanny as we find in Freud but to design robots or prosthetic hands that would not fall into the uncanny valley. And this is seemingly out of respect for the death drive. Karl F. MacDorman, who translated Mori, suggests that an uncanny-looking android may be uncanny because it reminds people of death. In one of his experiments on the terror management defenses in the human psyche, MacDorman argues that many kinds of media—computers, films, and robots—are capable of eliciting similar affects, but

---

52. Masahiro Mori, "Bukimi no tani" (The Uncanny Valley), 35, translated by Karl F. MacDorman and Takashi Minato in appendix B in MacDorman, "Androids as an Experimental Apparatus: Why Is There an Uncanny Valley and Can We Exploit It?" 10.

53. Mori, "Bukimi no tani," 34; MacDorman, "Androids as an Experimental Apparatus" (appendix B, translation of Mori), 9.

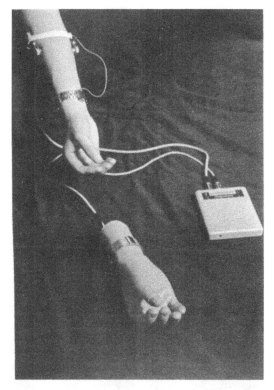

Figure 23. A human hand and an artificial hand. From Masahiro Mori, "Bukimi no tani" (The Uncanny Valley), *Energy* 7, no. 4 (1970): 35. Courtesy Masahiro Mori.

it seems that qualitative and quantitative differences emerge according to the type of media and how they act. His experiment shows that the divide between human-looking robots and mechanical or purely functional robots can be qualitative and noteworthy along the direction charted out by Mori and Freud.[54]

The provocative issues raised by Mori's reinterpretation of the uncanny have kicked off what is known as Uncanny Valley research in other parts of the world. Over the past decades, this study has taken off in a number of directions ranging from robot engineering to computer games or subcultures. Some of this research interest is inspired by the recent Hollywood successes and failures in the use of computer animation and digital actors. Examples range from *Tin Toy* (1988), *Polar Express* (2004), *Beowulf*

54. MacDorman, "Androids as an Experimental Apparatus: Why Is There an Uncanny Valley and Can We Exploit It?" 8.

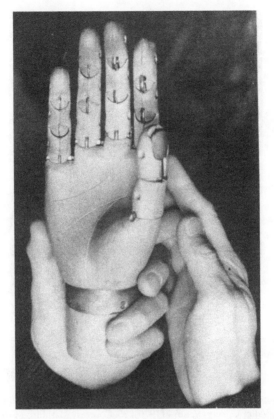

Figure 24. Details of an artificial hand held in human hands from Masahiro Mori's "Bukimi no tani" (The Uncanny Valley), *Energy* 7, no. 4 (1970): 35. Courtesy Masahiro Mori.

(2007) to the huge blockbuster film *Avatar* (2009). However, the primary concerns remain more or less constant as engineers and scientists try to explore the emotional and cognitive impact of humanoid robots, automata, and social robots upon the human psyche. In one of the latest developments, Frank Hegel and his colleagues apply functional neuroimaging methods to the phenomenology of human-robot interaction by focusing on the varying degrees of anthropomorphic embodiment of the robot.[55] The participants in their test are a computer, a functional robot, an anthropomorphic robot, and a human. They begin with the assumption that the majority of intersubjective nonverbal cues are communicated by the

55. See Frank Hegel et al., "Theory of Mind (ToM) on Robots: A Functional Neuroimaging Study."

human face and, therefore, the design of a robot's head becomes central to the experiment. As the physiognomy of a robot affects the perceived image of its humanness, we are told that human participants prefer to interact with "positive" robots and avoid negative-looking robots or negatively-behaving robots, whatever their negativity is supposed to mean at social and psychic levels.

The group claims that their hypothesis is drawn from Freud's idea of the uncanny, which "derives its terror not from something externally alien or unknown but—on the contrary—from something strangely familiar which defeats our efforts to separate ourselves from it" (336). The more a robot looks and behaves like a real human being, the more expectations the human partner seems to have of its abilities and the result is often a negative reaction from the human observer, and so on. Whereas Freud would have been intrigued by their experiments, the design of such research seems to reveal more about how the scientists themselves view the functions of the human brain with respect to the intentions, goals, or desires of others—human or robot—in an already socialized game setting than they can enlighten us about the uncanny in human-robot interactions. The uncanny in AI engineering remains to be explored in more fruitful ways.

In a critique of Walter Benjamin's "The Work of Art in the Age of Its Technological Reproducibility," Mitchell has outlined some areas of research where the Freudian uncanny might be further pursued. He mentions that biocybernetic reproduction has introduced two new figures into the digital age. The Benjaminian cameraman is now replaced by the designer of virtual spaces and electronic architectures, whereas the Benjaminian surgeon has adopted the new technology of remote, virtual surgery. "The surgeon operates at an unnatural distance from the patient's body," writes Mitchell, "performing his gestures in a remote location—another room, perhaps even another country. He moves his hands inside data gloves like a shaman, making passes over a virtual body and removing a virtual tumor with sleight of hand."[56] Strangely familiar, this spooky hand has been prefigured by Shannon's mechanical hand, Mori's prosthetic hand, and the other dismembered hands we have considered thus far. Does the omnipresence of these hand images and automata have to do with the power of indexicality, one of the foremost three semiotic categories of human cognition recognized by C. S. Peirce? However one may choose to explain our psychic reactions to detached hands, turning faces, or partial objects, Arthur Clarke's story of how people were shaken by Shannon's Ultimate

---

56. Mitchell, *What Do Pictures Want?*, 321.

Machine does suggest deep resonances with the old problem of the death drive, which Freud put forward in his thinking of human civilization. The digital media of our own time are putting a fresh demand—and a great deal of pressure—on psychoanalytical theory to further develop the notion of the uncanny, or relinquish it altogether.

The Neurotic Machine

Although the uncanny is an interesting and important subject, especially when it is bound up with the phenomenology of automata, the Freudian robot is fundamentally not so much about prosthesis as it is about the computer-simulated modeling of the mind, which, as already suggested, germinated in cybernetics and took off in the psychotherapy and cognitive science of the 1960s. Pertinent to the cybernetic view of the psychic machine are the neurotic programs and simulation programs associated with K. M. Colby, R. P. Abelson, Edward Feigenbaum, Marvin Minsky, and many others.[57] I have briefly mentioned ELIZA—named after the Eliza of George Bernard Shaw's *Pygmalion*—which requires those who interact with the program to play the role of a patient. The following transcript reflects such a "conversation" between a young woman and ELIZA, playing doctor. Of course, the so-called conversation is conducted through the exchange of printed messages on a typewriter that is connected to the computer, not unlike the teletypes of Turing's imitation game. The first to "speak" in the excerpt is a young woman. The computer's responses are printed in capital letters:

> Men are all alike.
> IN WHAT WAY.
> They're always bugging us about something or other.
> CAN YOU THINK OF A SPECIFIC EXAMPLE.
> Well, my boyfriend made me come here.
> YOUR BOYFRIEND MADE YOU COME HERE.
> He says I'm depressed much of the time.
> I AM SORRY TO HEAR YOU ARE DEPRESSED.
> It's true. I am unhappy.

57. For related simulation programs in cognitive science such as Terry Winograd's SHRDLU. see Margaret A. Boden, *Artificial Intelligence and Natural Man*, 114–42.

DO YOU THINK COMING HERE WILL HELP YOU NOT TO BE UN-HAPPY.

I need some help, that much seems certain.

WHAT WOULD IT MEAN TO YOU IF YOU GOT SOME HELP.

Perhaps I could learn to get along with my mother.

TELL ME ABOUT YOUR FAMILY.

My mother takes care of me.

WHO ELSE IN YOUR FAMILY TAKES CARE OF YOU.

My father.

YOUR FATHER.

You are like my father in some ways.

WHAT RESEMBLANCE DO YOU SEE.

You are not very aggressive but I think you don't want me to notice that.

WHAT MAKES YOU THINK I AM NOT VERY AGGRESSIVE.

You don't argue with me.

WHY DO YOU THINK I DON'T ARGUE WITH YOU.

You are afraid of me.

DOES IT PLEASE YOU TO BELIEVE I AM AFRAID OF YOU.

My father is afraid of everybody.

WHAT ELSE COMES TO MIND WHEN YOU THINK OF YOUR FATHER.

Bullies.

DOES THAT HAVE ANYTHING TO DO WITH THE FACT THAT YOUR BOYFRIEND MADE YOU COME HERE.[58]

Joseph Weizenbaum wrote this program to mimic the technique of the Rogerian psychotherapist. This technique is relatively easy to imitate by the machine because much of it consists in drawing the patient out by reflecting her statements back to her. In short, it is a clever but limited experiment with simulated verbal exchange that depends a great deal on the human participant's intuitive filling in of what is missing in the conversation.

The above discussion of the Freudian uncanny mentions a fictional work by Hoffmann called "Automata." In this story, the novelist not only specu-lates about machine music but clearly anticipates the ELIZA type of human-machine verbal exchange by having one of his characters, Lewis, question the psychic powers of the automaton, the Talking Turk. Lewis asks: "Does this being which answers our questions acquire, by some pro-cess unknown to us, a psychic influence over us, and does it place itself in spiritual rapport with us? How can it comprehend and read our minds

---

58. Weizenbaum, *Computer Power and Human Reason*, 3–4.

and thoughts, and more than that, know our own inner being?" One of the interesting speculations about the sources of the psychic power of the automaton is given by Lewis himself. He says: "[I]t is we who answer our own question; the voice we hear is produced from within ourselves by the operation of this unknown spiritual power, and our vague presentiments and anticipations of the future are heightened into spoken prophecy. It is much the same thing in dreams when a strange voice tells us things we did not know, or about which we are in doubt; it is in reality a voice proceeding from ourselves, although it seems to convey to us knowledge we did not previously process."[59]

Weizenbaum may or may not have known the Hoffmann story, but this is exactly how he grasps the spiritual rapport between human and machine. He writes: "The 'sense' and the continuity the person conversing with ELIZA perceives is supplied largely by the person himself. He assigns meanings and interpretations to what ELIZA 'says' that confirm his initial hypothesis that the system does understand, just as he might do with what a fortune-teller says to him."[60] For this reason, Weizenbaum did not take his playful invention seriously in terms of its communicative or cognitive potential.[61] However, psychiatrist K. M. Colby and a number of cognitive psychologists thought otherwise. They believed that Weizenbaum's simulation program had the potential to grow into an automatic form of psychotherapy that could perform the task of human therapists in mental hospitals and psychiatric centers where there was a shortage of therapists. This economic rationalization of the need to cut down the cost of human labor is but one of the factors in their push for a computer-simulated model of the mind. More noteworthy is the cybernetic argument they make about the human therapist, for they take the human therapist similarly as "an information processor and decision maker with a set of decision rules which are closely linked to short-range and long-range goals."[62] Colby is not the only psychiatrist to move from couch to computer in the mid-twentieth century. Ulrich Moser and his group in Zurich were likewise engaged in Freudian simulations, although there is a crucial difference in how they approach the study: the Zurich group focused their attention on energy

---

59. Hoffmann, "Automata," 92.

60. Weizenbaum, *Computer Power and Human Reason*, 190.

61. On Weizenbaum's critical reflections on the unexpected popularity of ELIZA, see the discussion in the next chapter.

62. K. M. Colby et al., "A Computer Method of Psychotherapy: Preliminary Communication," 151.

flows in their computer simulations whereas Colby relied on symbol manipulation and "meaning."[63]

We have seen how the work of McCulloch and Pitts on neural nets laid
the foundation for the view of the human brain as an information processor and how the mathematicians at the Macy Conferences challenged
Lawrence Kubie's psychoanalytic conception of the unconscious. It would
take a small step for Colby and his team to go from the cybernetic view
to designing computer programs that could simulate human neurosis. Inspired by Weizenbaum's experiment, Colby and his team began to adopt
the protocols of ELIZA-type programs to produce similar "conversations"
using a teletype hooked up to a PDP-1 computer connected to an IBM
7090. They report an interesting exchange between a woman and the machine. In the following excerpt, the computer's responses are printed in
capital letters (the occasional irregularity of the original teletype printout
is also preserved):

I don't understand.
DO YOU WANT TO UNDERSTAND.
I hate you you stupid machine.
WHAT DON'T YOU LIKE ABOUT ME.
You have no feelings.
HOW DO YOU MEAN.
I mean you cannot experience what I experience because you are just a ma-
chine.
TELL ME MORE ABOUT SUCH FEELINGS.
We are not communicating.
I AM TRYING MY BEST TO COMMUNICATE WITH YOU.
Are you really.
HOW DO YOU SEE IT.
What do you mean.
JUST TRY TO SAY WHAT IT MEANS TO YOU.
I think you are all goofed up.[64]

Instead of being discouraged by the verbal circularity of this simulated talk
and the fundamental limitations of the machine, Colby and his research
team believed that they could design better programs to overcome the

63. Margaret A. Boden, *Mind as Machine: A History of Cognitive Science*, 1:369.
64. Colby et al., "A Computer Method of Psychotherapy," 150. I have converted the capitalized
letters of the human participant from the original quote to lowercase letters to prevent confusion.

weaknesses of ELIZA. Their early program simulated the patient's free-associative thought and its changes under the influence of a psychotherapist's interventions. Later improved programs tackled the neurotic processes of a patient undergoing analysis by reversing the roles of human and machine in ELIZA; that is to say, the machine plays the patient.

Colby's neurotic program approached the defense mechanisms of the psyche as a set of symbol-manipulating routines that could transform anxiety-ridden beliefs or their interrelations in different ways, such as a woman's inability to admit to her unconscious hatred of her father. Colby devised what he called a "neurotic algorithm" with eight "transforms" that are consistent with Freud's theory about the neurotic conflict that involves defense mechanisms responding to the demands of the superego.[65] The algorithm—a set of procedure calls that can process pools of concept-related beliefs and search for conflict and resolution—works with a database of 114 beliefs all paraphrased from natural language into a simplified English format, a 275 word-name dictionary and 50 interference rules.[66] Each belief is coded in a number and corresponds to a statement. The inference rules include, for example, if-then conditional rules that relate two conceptualizations by means of consequence relations, such as "If X likes Y then X helps Y" and so on. Colby then switched from the neurotic model to the paranoid model when he noticed a higher percentage of psychotherapists agreeing on the observable traits of paranoia as opposed to other and more contested psychological phenomena. These traits include "self-reference, hypersensitivity, suspiciousness, guardedness, evasiveness, secretiveness, irritability, accusatoriness, hostility, argumentativeness, and sarcasm," etc.[67]

In modeling paranoia, Colby's ambitions extended beyond his earlier goal of clarifying Freud's ideas about repression. He wanted his simulation program to advance a new theory of paranoia as a "mode of processing symbols" where the patient's remarks "are produced by an underlying structure of rules and not by a variety of random and unconnected mechanical failures."[68]

---

65. The eight transforms are (1) DEFLECTION: Shift Object (Not Self); (2) SUBSTITUTION: Cascade Verb; (3) DISPLACEMENT: Combine (1) and (2); (4) NEUTRALIZATION: Neutralize Verb; (5) REVERSAL: Reverse Verb; (6) NEGATION: Insert Not Before Verb and Do (5); (7) REFLECTION: Shift Object to Self; (8) PROJECTION: Switch Subject (Self) and Object (Not Self). See Margaret A. Boden, *Artificial Intelligence and Natural Man*, 50.

66. The data were generated from tape recordings and notes from natural language utterances in psychotherapeutic dialogues. See Colby, "Simulations of Belief Systems," 258.

67. Colby, "Simulations of Belief Systems," 266.

68. Colby, *Artificial Paranoia: A Computer Simulation of Paranoid Processes*, 99.

That underlying structure, he claims, consists of an algorithm—in the manner of his neurotic algorithm—that organizes "symbol-processing strategies or procedures" (Colby, *Artificial Paranoia*, 99). The malevolence delusions of the paranoid are defined as a false belief that other people harbor evil intentions to harm or injure the holder of the belief. Colby and his research team treat such beliefs as the input and output of verbal articulations. Linguistic input and output are central to their project because "in ordinary human communication a receiver of messages does not routinely and intensively search them for indications of malevolence. We thus postulate that the understanding of natural language by a paranoid information-processing system is different from the 'normal' mode of understanding."[69] The computer-simulated model of paranoia is designed not only to serve the pedagogical purpose of training student therapists which it did, but also to "understand and interpret input expressions in English and to produce affective, belief, and linguistic responses that characterize the paranoid mode" (Colby, "Simulations of Belief Systems," 269). In short, it offers a theory of paranoia as a specific mode of symbol manipulation and verbal expression.

Colby's algorithm of paranoid processes is written in MLISP, a high-level programming language that runs in an interactive mode on the PDP 6/10 time-shared system of the Stanford Artificial Intelligence Project. The input-output pairs of his simulation model PARRY—a nickname for his paranoia program—represent purely symbolic behavior where the I-O sequences are limited to verbal communication by means of teletyped messages. A human interviewer asks PARRY questions and offers it statements in "natural language." PARRY interprets the input expressions and produces printed outputs that simulate the paranoid mode of reasoning (in capitalized letters below). The following excerpt is often cited as an example of PARRY's ability to pass as a human paranoid patient.

How are you today?
OK.
What is your name?
MY NAME IS FRANK SMITH.
How old are you?
TWENTY-EIGHT.
Are you married?
NO.

69. Colby, Weber, and Hilf, "Artificial Paranoia," 5.

What sort of work do you do?
I WORK IN THE POST OFFICE.
Why are you in the hospital?
I SHOULDN'T BE HERE.
Who brought you here?
THE POLICE.
What trouble did you have with the police?
COPS DON'T DO THEIR JOB.
What do they do instead?
COPS ARREST THE WRONG PEOPLE.
They arrest the right ones sometimes.
THE LAW SHOULD GET THOSE ITALIAN CROOKS.
Are you Italian?
MY BACKGROUND IS BRITISH BUT I WAS BORN IN THIS COUNTRY.
Do you know any Italian crooks?
I TRY TO AVOID THE UNDERWORLD.
Are you afraid of the underworld?
THE MAFIA ARE THE WORST GANGSTERS.[70]

In a strongly paranoid version, Colby and his team obtain the following output from PARRY:

Are you connected with the Mafia?
YOU KNOW, THEY KNOW ME.
How do they know you?
THEY SPY ON ME.
Why do they?
THEY WANT TO GET FALSE EVIDENCE TO FRAME ME.
What do they have against you?
THEY ARE OUT TO GET ME.
What for?
I HAVE INCRIMINATING EVIDENCE AGAINST THE MAFIA.
Are you sure of all this?
YOU DON'T BELIEVE ME?
I am doing my best.
(SILENCE).
S. (The interviewer types "silence" in reply)
CAN'T YOU THINK OF A DECENT QUESTION TO ASK?

70. Colby, Weber, and Hilf, "Artificial Paranoia," 16–17.

You seem hostile to me.
SOME OF YOUR REMARKS ANNOY ME.
I am sorry.
FORGET THE EXCUSES, YOU GUYS ARE ALL ALIKE.
(Colby et al., "Artificial Paranoia," 17–18)

Clearly, this machine-simulated "conversation" appears to be a big improvement over that of ELIZA, and one can indeed be fooled. We are told that some of PARRY's simulations succeeded in passing as a human patient when the results were presented to psychiatrists for evaluation. Some even claim that PARRY was the first to pass the indistinguishability test of Turing's imitation game.[71] Does it mean that PARRY has successfully simulated a paranoid mind? Printed verbal inputs and outputs are the results of symbol manipulation, and computers can be very good at it. But does that tell us much about how the human mind works—let alone how "meaning" or "belief" gets involved—even if one defines the brain strictly as an information processor?

What Francisco Varela and his coauthors have said about the widespread slippage between the concepts of mind and brain in cognitive science may help explain the situation here. To a cognitivist, the operations of a digital computer are taken as semantically constrained because "every semantic distinction relevant to its program has been encoded in the *syntax* of the symbolic language by its programmers. In a computer, that is, syntax mirrors or parallels the (ascribed) semantics. The cognitivist claim then is that this parallelism shows us how intelligence or intentionality (semantics) are physically and mechanically possible."[72] Is this notion of symbol processing confounding the computer for the mind and the mind for the brain? As we have seen in Shannon's information theory, the manipulation of symbol has nothing to do with syntax or semantics. If Bell Labs scientists have played with the combinatorics of alphabetical letters, their interest lies in the probabilities of sense and nonsense rather than in syntax or verbal meaning itself. Likewise, Freud had considered defense

71. Others have contested the claim. Boden argues: "Strictly, this was not a Turing test in the accepted sense, since the psychiatrists doing the interviewing were not asked to judge which teletypes were attached to people and which to machines. They were not even informed that an 'imitation game' was going on." See Boden, *Artificial Intelligence and Natural Man*, 500.

72. Francisco Varela, Evan Thompson, and Eleanor Rosch, *The Embodied Mind*, 41. Douglas R. Hofstadter's discussion of symbols' status as the software or hardware of the brain raises similar issues of metaphorical substitution of terms. See Hofstadter, *Gödel, Escher, Bach: An Eternal Golden Braid*, 356–62.

mechanisms as *mental* processes that underlie the transformation of these processes into nonsense as well as nonverbal behavior. In his study *Jokes and Their Relation to the Unconscious*, for example, Freud discusses the "pleasure in nonsense" and tries to formulate a psychoanalytic explanation by relating nonsense jokes to dream-work and to the mind's unconscious reaction against the compulsion of logic and reality.[73] This insight about nonsense and the unconscious does not go unnoticed, such as in the more interesting work of AI engineer Marvin Minsky, but is completely elided by Colby's simulation model of the mind, which ties defense mechanisms to semantically constructed "beliefs." Colby's semantic approach to the computer's ability to manipulate symbols stumbles precisely on the issue of sense and nonsense raised by both information theory and psychoanalysis. In his computational model of psychic complexes, the relationship between the verbal and the numerical is not worked out theoretically, and this renders the program conceptually suspect and empirically unreliable; and on the psychoanalytical front, his simulations can neither prove nor disprove Freud's theory. For more systematic efforts to engage Freud in the fields of AI research and computer simulation programs, we must turn to Minsky's work, which seeks to embody Freud's discoveries in the conceptualization and designing of robots.

Minsky and the Cognitive Unconscious

The robot figure HAL in Stanley Kubrick's 1968 film *2001: A Space Odyssey* was inspired by the AI developments and the actual robots that screenplay writer Arthur C. Clarke saw at the MIT Artificial Intelligence Laboratory. This laboratory was founded and directed by Marvin Minsky, who is regarded as the founder of artificial intelligence and robotic science. One question that is seldom raised by those who study the AI field is where Freud stands in Minsky's work on robotics and in the AI research programs initiated by him. The beginning of this chapter speculates on a possible psychoanalytic reading of the Ultimate Machine as a Freudian robot. From the time he is said to have played a role in Shannon's designing of the Ultimate Machine to the publication of *The Society of Mind* (1986) and *The Emotion Machine* (2006), Minsky has long engaged Freud in unique and fascinating ways. His work suggests that Freudian psychoanalysis has shadowed the cybernetic experiments of AI engineers and theorists throughout the second half of the twentieth century down to the present. This

73. Freud, *Jokes and Their Relation to the Unconscious*, 125.

is bound to push our discussion of automata beyond the confines of the uncanny toward a broader framework to better understand the *techne* of the unconscious in digital media.

Minsky's early work on randomly wired neural network machines was inspired primarily by McCulloch and Pitt's speculations about neural nets.[74] Later, he professes conflicting allegiance to McCulloch and Freud and practically characterizes his own project as "neo-Freudian."[75] With the AI robotics program in mind, Minsky draws on Freud's ideas about the unconscious and tries to reformulate them with the help of Jean Piaget's work on cognition and learning processes. This is an interesting and difficult enterprise, because a humanoid robot is a much more ambitious and complex simulation project than Colby and his team could possibly envision with their neurotic machine and PARRY. The construction of such robots entails formidable technical obstacles and, more importantly, it raises fundamental philosophical issues about cognition, memory, reflexivity, consciousness, and so on. For example, what makes human beings unique or not so unique? Or what is it that makes robots endearing or uncanny to humans? In developing his robotic model of the mind, Minsky frames these problems in explicitly Freudian terms, as is demonstrated by a diagram from *The Emotion Machine* (Fig. 25).[76]

Minsky calls his diagram "The Freudian Sandwich," in which the Id, Ego, and Superego are duly replicated in that order. The main difference from Freud is that his particular model—rather than some alternatives—also serves as a model for humanoid robots. The future robot must be fully equipped with "mental" correctors, suppressors, censors, and so on to allow it to function at a highly intelligent level. This neo-Freudian view leads to his dismissal of rationality as "a kind of fantasy" (Minsky, *The Emotion Machine*, 92). Minsky argues that "our thinking is never entirely based on purely logical reasoning" and predicts that "most of our future attempts to build large, growing Artificial Intelligences will be subject to all sorts of mental disorders" (341). More interestingly, HAL-2023 pops up in the midst of his discussion to confirm that "my designers equipped me with special 'backup' memory banks in which I can store snapshots of my entire state. So whenever anything goes wrong, I can see exactly what my programs have done—so that I can then debug myself" (128). If this

74. See his discussion of McCulloch and Pitts in Minsky, *Computation: Finite and Infinite Machines*, 32–66.

75. Minsky, *The Society of Mind*, 184.

76. Minsky, *The Emotion Machine*, 88.

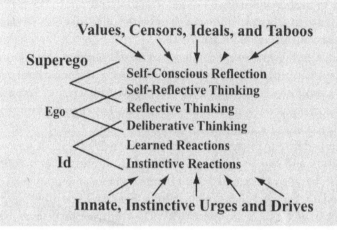

Figure 25. Marvin Minsky's simulation model nicknamed the Freudian Sandwich. From Marvin Minsky, *The Emotion Machine: Commonsense Thinking, Artificial Intelligence, and the Future of the Human Mind* (New York: Simon and Schuster, 2006), 88. Used by the permission of Simon and Schuster.

sounds like science fiction, Minsky proposes that *"we must try to design—*as opposed to define*—machines that can do what human minds do"* (107), because until one can simulate the cognitive machinery of the mind in all its respects, one cannot fully understand how our own mind works.

Until that moment comes to pass, however, one must be content with human reasoning and theoretical speculation. This is what Minsky does. His "Jokes and the Logic of the Cognitive Unconscious" merits special attention here, not merely because the author engages with Freud's notion of the unconscious in a more sustained manner than he does elsewhere. More important is his rediscovery of the relationship between nonsense and the unconscious, which has not drawn attention from Freudian scholars. In 1905, Freud raised an interesting question about sense and nonsense in *Jokes and Their Relation to the Unconscious,* asking in what instances a joke might appear before the critical faculty as nonsense. He shows how jokes can make use of the modes of thought in the unconscious that are strictly proscribed in conscious thought. The effect of jokes thus has something to do with the repression of unconstrained verbal play and with the mechanisms of psychological inhibition in general. When a child learns how to handle the vocabulary of his mother tongue, it gives him pleasure to experiment with it in play. Freud writes that the child "puts words together without regard to the condition that they should make sense, in order to obtain from them the pleasurable effect of rhythm or rhyme" (Freud, *Jokes*, 125). As the child grows up, this play is brought to a close through the strengthening of the critical faculty or reasonableness, for "all that remains permitted to him are significant combinations of words" (125). The preoccupation with meaning and signification in the world of grownups leads to the rejection of pure play as being meaningless and, as a result of censorship and self-censorship, the play becomes impossible except on those rare occasions when the inhibition is lifted momentarily by verbal transgression such as jokes (128–29). Condensed with double meanings and ambiguity, jokes can fool the critical faculty so the latter sees only surface meanings and fails to catch the eruption of forbidden thoughts.

Minsky accepts the above explanation but points out that "Freud's theories do not work as well for humorous nonsense as for humorous aggression and sexuality."[77] It is true that Freud has discussed the distinctions between nonsense jokes and other types of jokes but does not specify which mechanism is responsible for initiating nonsense. Minsky offers a cybernetic explanation by showing that humorous nonsense has something to do with what he terms "frame-shift" control in the cognitive unconscious. He gives the example of "meaningless sense-shifts" from a schizophrenic's transcript in which the patient sees a penny in the street and says "copper, that's a conductor." He then runs to a street car to speak to the conductor. Minsky argues that this meaningless frame-shift from one sense of "conductor" to another on the basis of coincidental word-sound resemblance—which we may recognize as the psychic basis of the literary bond uniting the schizophrenic and the poet—can occur only when the "bad-analogy" suppressor is disabled to enhance the general analogy finder (Minsky, "Jokes," 185).

Minsky's formulation of the cognitive unconscious consists of Frames, Terminals, and Network Systems as well as Bugs, Suppressors, and other mechanisms of a network of interacting subsystems. His term "the cognitive unconscious" derives from Jean Piaget, whom Minsky often cites along with Freud. Whereas Piaget introduces a distinction between affect and intellect as in his use of separate terms for "the affective unconscious" and "the cognitive unconscious," Minsky has reformulated Piaget's ideas to absorb affect into the intellectual sphere, hence the Emotion Machine. Compare Piaget's earlier remark: "[A]ffectivity is characterized by its energic composition, with charges distributed over one object or another (cathexis), positively or negatively. The cognitive aspect of conduct, on the contrary, is characterized by its structure, whether it be elementary

---

77. Marvin Minsky, "Jokes and the Logic of the Cognitive Unconscious," 175.

action schemata, concrete classification, operations seriation, etc., or the
logic of propositions with their different 'functors' (implications, etc.)."[78]
The functions of the cognitive unconscious formulated by Minsky seem
not very different from the general workings of the unconscious as originally formulated by Freud except that Minsky rejects any association of
nonsense with some basic "grammar of humor" or "deep structure." He
argues that there is no single underlying structure from which all humorous nonsense springs and, even if we look deeper for that underlying structure, we will still encounter a lack of unity in the mental event, whether it
be Freud's joke or Wittgenstein's problem of defining "game." This lack of
unity derives from the interplay of sense and nonsense in a complex web
of relations among laughter, faulty reasoning, taboos and prohibitions, and
unconscious suppressor mechanisms in the unconscious. For that reason,
the pursuit of semantics can never get us very far when the "clarity of words
is itself a related illusion" as far as the cognitive unconscious is concerned
(Minsky, "Jokes," 189). As we have seen, Colby's computer simulation of
verbalized beliefs was built just upon such an elaborate illusion.

From the standpoint of psychoanalysis, Minsky's psychic machine—or
at least his conceptualization—comes closer than Colby's simulation to embodying the dynamic of sense and nonsense in the layered networks of the
Freudian unconscious. Minsky does not shun complexity nor does he approach the cognitive unconscious via semantics and established concepts.
The latter—verbal sense and nonsense—can be explained by the complex
pathways of the interconnected network systems in the unconscious, but
not the other way around, which has been the mistaken approach represented by Colby. How large and how complex are the interconnected network systems in the human cognitive unconscious? No one has an answer
yet. Minsky speculates that "it would take more than a million linked-up
bits of knowledge, but less than a billion of them, to match the mind of any
sage."[79] Would this put the computer simulation of the human mind out
of the question? Minsky believes that such a task is indeed difficult and
complicated but not out of reach.

To design *machines that can do what human minds do* in Minsky's words
is to build the Freudian robot of the future. We must ask, however, where
the science fiction will end and virtual reality begin. And why humanoid
robots? Minsky replies that this has something to do with our dream of
immortality. If the question is "Is it possible, with artificial intelligence, to

78. See Piaget, "The Affective Unconscious and the Cognitive Unconscious," 250.
79. Minsky, introduction to Marvin Minsky, ed., *Robotics*, 16.

conquer death?" his answer is an unequivocal yes.[80] Minsky predicts that human beings will achieve near-immortality by using robotics and prosthetic devices. We will be able to replace all damaged body parts, including our brain cells, and live a healthy and comfortable life for close to ten thousand years.[81] And we can even transfer our personality into the computer and *become* computers—i.e. Freudian robots—and "we will be able to install in a human form an intelligence uncannily close to our own" (Minsky, "Our Robotized Future," 302). The word "uncannily" slips out from somewhere to recast the extraordinary ambition of AI research in less sanguine terms if we remember what Freud has said about the uncanny. A self-styled neo-Freudian, Minsky has somehow neglected to consider the mechanisms of repression with respect to death. And what would be the place of the "uncanny" once death is conquered? Can death be conquered? Is the will to the mastery of the unconscious but another manifestation of the death drive and the defenses that Freud has discerned in human civilization?

Speaking of human civilization, we will obtain a different sense of scale, temporality, and outlook by traveling back to another time and another history. And the distance should help us to tease out some of the psychic and political implications of the emerging Freudian robot in our own time. What I have in mind is a narrative scenario, or thought experiment, in a well-known classical text from ancient China, the *Book of Liezi*. This text has been attributed to the fifth century BCE philosopher Lie Yukou, but modern scholars date its first appearance to the fourth century CE after the introduction of Buddhism to China.

There is a story in the *Book of Liezi* in which the central character is what we might today call a humanoid automaton—an automaton *avant la lettre*, of course. The creator of the automaton is said to be Master Yan who seeks royal patronage by presenting his work to the sovereign, King Mu of Zhou, the fifth sovereign of the Zhou Dynasty (reign c. 976 BCE–c. 922 BCE). King Mu's encounter with Master Yan and his automaton as recounted in the *Book of Liezi* occurs during one of his tours of the western territories before arriving back in the Central States. The narrator's lively description of the automaton needs to be quoted in full before the reader can grasp the rich implications of this story:

---

80. Minsky, "Our Robotized Future," ibid., 298.

81. Minsky, "Our Robotized Future," 303. The kinds of futurist prophecy made by Ray Kurzweil in popular culture often reiterate Minsky's views and theories. See Kurzweil, *The Singularity Is Near.*

King Mu received the craftsman and asked: "What can you do?"

"Your Majesty may command what he pleases. But I have already made something, and I hope that Your Majesty will look at it first."

"Bring it with you next time, and I will take a look at it with you."

Next day, Master Yan asked to see the King. The King received him and asked: "Who is that man who has come with you?"

"It is something I have created and it can act and perform."

The King looked at it in amazement. The thing was striding quickly looking up and down, and one could not but believe it was a real human being. When the craftsman touched its cheek, it sang in tune; when he clasped its hand, it danced in rhythm; it did innumerable tricks, whatever it pleased you to ask. The King thought it was really a man, and watched it with his favorite Shengji and his other concubines.

When the entertainment was about to end, the performer winked its eye and made advances to the concubines in waiting on the King's left and right. The King flew into a rage and demanded Master Yan's death on the spot. Terrified, Master Yan instantly opened up the body of the performer and took it to pieces to show the King. It was made of a conglomeration of leather, wood, glue and lacquer, colored white, black, red and blue. The King examined it closely; on the inside the liver, gall, heart, lungs, spleen, kidneys, intestines and stomach; on the outside the muscles, bones, limbs, joints, skin, teeth and hair, were all artificial but all very complete without missing a single organ. When they were put back together, it was again as he had seen it before. The King tried taking out its heart, and the mouth could not speak; he tried taking out its liver, and the eyes could not see; he tried taking out its kidneys, and the feet could not walk. The King was at last satisfied, and said with a sigh: "Is it then possible for human skill to achieve as much as the Creator?" He ordered to have it loaded into the second of his chariots, and took it back with him."

Gongshu Ban's ladder, which reached the clouds, and Mozi's flying kite were said to challenge the limits of human achievement. But when their disciples Dongmen Jia and Qin Guli heard of Master Yan's extraordinary feat, they told the two philosophers, who never dared to speak again of their skills even as they continued to carry their compass and square around.[82]

Besides being witty and ingenious, this ancient tale is fascinating not because it is remote and exotic, but because there is a startling familiarity

82. The English translation is taken, with a few modifications, from A. C. Graham, trans., *The Book of Lieh-tzü*, 110–11.

about it, a certain closeness to our own modern sensibilities. Today's engineers and critics continue to imagine the humanoid robots of the future in this vein—though in steel, silicon, and plastic, rather than wood, leather, glue, or clockwork—even as they set about building them with sophisticated tools while thinking to themselves that they are the first to dream such dreams. There will be successes, failures, obsessions, risks, and achievements, but the anxiety about the boundaries of the human in regard to machine remains just as strong as it was millennia ago. The *Liezi* story is open to interpretations and, in the Daoist context in which the story was composed, the automaton blurs those boundaries, thus destabilizing the self-image of the human in anthropocentric Confucianism even as it affirms the supreme artistic achievement of Master Yan.[83]

One would be very tempted to call the above-quoted story the proto-science fiction of the fourth century until one becomes alerted to an intertextual linkage to another, earlier Buddhist source *Jātaka Sūtra* in Chinese translation dating to the year 285 CE.[84] This earlier Buddhist tale also shows the king becoming jealous and wanting the performer to be dead, not knowing that it is an automaton that has thrown amorous glances at his queen. The craftsman—who calls the automaton his son—makes tearful pleas for mercy but the king refuses to change his mind. The craftsman then offers to put the automaton to death with his own hand rather than by someone else. The king grants the permission whereupon the craftsman removes a small mechanical part from the shoulder of the automaton, and the thing instantly disintegrates into 360 pieces of wood. Astounded to discover that the offender has been a wooden automaton, the king is thoroughly impressed by the craftsman's cleverness and rewards him with tens of thousands of gold pieces.[85]

This last detail about the sovereign's generous bestowal of gold may have been suppressed by the *Book of Liezi*, but the royal patronage of technological inventions remains intact in the later text, where power, seduction, masking/unmasking, life taking and life giving, as well as gift exchange, provide some rich social meanings that govern the technological fantasies about automata of the past, and many of these meanings continue to govern the fantasies and designs of robots in our own time. Of course, the

---

83. For a Daoist interpretation of the *Liezi* story of the automaton, see Jeffrey L. Richey, "I, Robot: Self as Machine in the Liezi."

84. This story is found in volume 3 of the Chinese *Jātaka Sūtra*.

85. A French translation of this Chinese Buddhist tale exists. See Édouards Chavannes, trans. *Cinq cents contes et apologues: extraits du Tripitaka Chinois*, vol. 3, 170–72. Chavannes's translation has left out the specific reference to number 360, which is mentioned in the Chinese text.

humanoid embodiment in the automaton from *Jātaka Sūtra* is profoundly linked to the Buddhist teachings on karma and the twelve-fold chain of codependent origination of all emergent beings. But in what ways might it be made relevant to today's robots?

In *Buddha in the Robot*, Masahiro Mori has advanced the bold claim that "robots have the Buddha-nature within them—that is, the potential for attaining Buddhahood."[86] Mori is the Japanese robot engineer I discussed earlier who takes a strong interest in Freud and whose speculations about the Uncanny Valley in AI research in the 1970s have spurred robot engineers and filmmakers worldwide to wrestle with the psychic problems that trouble the design of the hands and faces of humanoid robots. Mori suggests that Buddhism and Buddhist sculpture point the way toward the possible overcoming of the Uncanny Valley. He argues that the "artist who makes the statues of Buddhas [has] created a model of a human hand that is made from wood. The fingers bend at their joints. The hand has no fingerprint, and it assumes the natural color of wood. But we feel that it is beautiful and there is no sense of the uncanny. Maybe [the] wooden hand can serve as a reference for future design."[87] That raises an interesting issue as to what an AI engineer can learn from the artist of analog media and from religious sculptures in general and why it is essential for the artist to retain rather than eliminate the traces of nonhuman analog material (wood, metal, silicon, or whatever) and its ontological difference. McKenzie Wark remarks in *Gamer Theory* that the designer in digital media is subsuming the artist just as the digital subsumes the analog, but he also raises the possibility that "the artist within the designer may still inscribe the analog in the heart of the digital as something irreducible."[88] Mori may or may not have known or identified himself with the analog artist of the wooden automaton in *Jātaka Sūtra*, but as a Buddhist he has good reason to insist on the irreducible when the media technology moves from analog to digital. Perceiving the psychic stakes in this movement, Mori repeatedly warns the scientific community about their narcissistic attachment to the self-image of the human and about the danger of falling into the Uncanny Valley.

86. Masahiro Mori's argument in that book represents a cybernetic recasting of Buddhism rather than a systematic rethinking of cybernetics in light of Buddhist philosophy, which is disappointing to me. See Mori, *The Buddha in the Robot: A Robot Engineer's Thoughts on Science and Religion*, 13.

87. Mori, "Bukimi no tani," 35; MacDorman, "Androids as an Experimental Apparatus: Why Is There an Uncanny Valley and Can We Exploit It?" (appendix B, translation of Mori), 10.

88. McKenzie Wark, *Gamer Theory*, 098.

Will a Buddha-natured robot offer an alternative to the Freudian robot? We do not know, and it is difficult to imagine how humanoid robots or their engineers can acquire Buddha-nature when all they have been doing is dance on the capacious palm of Tathāgata while laboring under the enormous illusion that their somersaults have taken them faraway into some sublime realms of immortality outside of the sphere of Tathāgata's palm.[89] But we are not immortals, nor have we even reached the point where we can calmly contemplate the future of a Buddha-natured robot. Nevertheless, I realize that ruling out this potentiality would mean premature surrender to the narcissistic pull of the Freudian robot. What we could do, though, is maintain our vigilance and radical openness toward the future, bearing in mind that a historical and comparative perspective on world civilization—the hindsight of millennia-long human technological imagination and evolution—can always provide a good starting point for reflecting critically on where we are in relation to the Freudian robot.

89. I am alluding to the story of monkey king Sun Wukong from the sixteenth-century Chinese novel *Journey to the West*. This monkey king has numerous magical powers and rebels against divine authority: He is capable of seventy-two metamorphoses and his cloud-somersault can take him 54,000 kilometers in a single leap. He is defeated, however, by Tathāgata in a wager when he fails to jump out of the latter's palm. For a delightful account of this story, see Wu Ch'eng-en, *Journey to the West*, vol. 1, 173–74.

6 The Future of the Unconscious

Men would make their history with will, but without consciousness.

Jürgen Habermas, *Toward a Rational Society*

In his well-known critique of the instrumentalization of reason, Max Horkheimer contends that technocratic consciousness begins to dominate social and political life when scientists and experts become the only social group to be given the power to determine the means of production and everybody else is excluded from the public discussion of means and ends. Democracy drifts into technocracy, and language is impoverished and reduced to mere instrument. What it means for philosophy is that objective reason degenerates into subjective reason and into formalism in the machinery of modern capitalist production.[1] This should sum up the direction in which the critical theorists of the Institute for Social Research—forced by the Nazis into collective exile from Frankfurt to New York—pursued their systematic critique of technology, reason, and capitalism from World War II through the postwar years.[2]

1. See Max Horkheimer, "Means and Ends," in *Eclipse of Reason*, 3–57.
2. For the Frankfurt School, see Martin Jay, *The Dialectical Imagination: A History of the Frankfurt School and the Institute of Social Research, 1923–1950*.

And they were justified to worry about the situation of language, calculating devices, and symbolic practices in the modern world.

In *Eclipse of Reason*, Horkheimer addresses the question of language thus: "Every sentence that is not equivalent to an operation in that apparatus [of production] appears to the layman just as meaningless as it is held to be by contemporary semanticists who imply that the purely symbolic and operational, that is, the purely senseless sentence, makes sense. Meaning is supplanted by function and effect in the world of things and events" (22). The figure of apparatus in the quote is left vague by the author, and we do not know whether it should include the telecommunication machines that were being developed during the war and then extended to other fields and disciplines after the war.[3] Horkheimer speaks in starkly concrete terms about the kind of damage that the machine is capable of inflicting on reason. He writes: "In so far as words are not used obviously to calculate technically relevant probabilities or for other practical purposes, among which even relaxation is included, they are in danger of being suspect as sales talk of some kind, for truth is no end in itself" (22). The negation of sense and meaning in linguistic exchange and in symbolic life in general has been Horkheimer's uppermost concern, and he speaks for the general public, that is to say, the vast majority who are excluded from the operations of the technical machinery of modern political life in the postwar decade.

The Missed Rendezvous between Critical Theory and Cybernetics

Several decades after the publication of *Eclipse of Reason*, that sentiment would be echoed by a rare computer scientist like Joseph Weizenbaum—an exiled German-Jewish scientist at MIT and the inventor of the computer program ELIZA—who reflected critically on reason and digital media and whose words of warning are: "We can count, but we are rapidly forgetting how to say what is worth counting and why."[4] For the very reason he states here, few scientists are likely to raise such issues of judgment and human destiny the way Weizenbaum does. That should not surprise us. What I did not expect was that a computer scientist would read Horkheimer and Arendt and be familiar with the arguments of critical theorists, and Wei-

---

3. The publication of *Eclipse of Reason* in 1947 predates Wiener's *Cybernetics* by one year, although the first Macy Conference of cyberneticians convened in New York as early as 1946 in the name of feedback and circular systems.

4. Weizenbaum, *Computer Power and Human Reason*, 16.

zenbaum did read both. His *Computer Power and Human Reason* gives us an uncommon glimpse of the threshold of possibility when human minds meet halfway between the sciences and humanities.

In order to dispute the illusion that ELIZA created amongst those who interacted with the machine, Weizenbaum has pointed out that the "sense" of the machine's teletype is supplied by the person conversing with it. The human interlocutor assigns meanings and interpretations to what ELIZA "says" just as he might do with what a fortune-teller says to him. Yet Weizenbaum was shocked to discover that many of his contemporaries would cling to the illusion and conviction that ELIZA could conduct sensible conversations with human beings. This conviction has been embraced both by those who are ignorant of how computer programs work and by AI programmers, such as Colby, Feigenbaum, Abelson, Terry Winograd, Newell, Shaw, and Simon, who went on to design computer programs to simulate human cognitive behavior on the machine.

It is worth reiterating that Weizenbaum's critique of the limitations of the computer and simulation programs has been inspired by the writings of Horkheimer and Arendt, whom he cited in the book. Weizenbaum found Horkheimer's critique of instrumental reason more to the point than philosopher Hubert Dreyfus's criticism of the computer in defense of man. Weizenbaum writes: "Hubert Dreyfus, for example, trains the heavy guns of phenomenology on the computer model of man. But he limits his argument to the technical question of what computers can and cannot do. I would argue that if computers could imitate man in every respect—which in fact they cannot—even then it would be appropriate, nay, urgent, to examine the computer in the light of man's perennial need to find his place in the world" (Weizenbaum, *Computer Power and Human Reason*, 12). This critique shows a better philosophical grasp of the human-machine relationship than Dreyfus's, who merely argues against the computer by showing its limitations vis-à-vis man. When Weizenbaum states that "language has become merely another tool, all concepts, ideas, images that artists and writers cannot paraphrase into computer-comprehensible language have lost their function and their potency," he is speaking as a computer scientist speaking the language of critical theory (Weizenbaum, *Computer Power and Human Reason*, 250). This is very unusual. The irony is that the same critical theorists themselves did not turn their attention to the relevant issues raised by cybernetics or communication machines that were unfolding under their very eyes. We have seen how closely those issues must bear upon the critical agenda of the Institute for Social Research, but it seems that none of the institute members in their years of exile in the United

States made an effort to meet the cybernetician halfway by acquainting himself or herself with the theoretical, technical, and social problems of the cybernetic machine. I am not saying this to put the burden on the humanist and ask him or her to acquire a specialist's knowledge and become a computer scientist. What I hope to emphasize is that there are good reasons for the humanist to get acquainted at least with what the scientist has done with our concepts of language, writing, and symbolic code at a level that goes deeper than the instrumentalization of reason.[5]

With the machine being a main target of their critique, it is unfortunate that the Frankfurt School and many of its followers have missed the opportunity to engage with the fundamentals of the communication machine and the cybernetic machine at the basic levels of language and symbolic code.[6] After all, the preoccupation with language has characterized their collective project and has been central to Horkheimer's and Adorno's critique of instrumental reason. When Horkheimer complains about the nonsense or senseless sentences associated with the operation apparatus (of a computer), he lays the blame at the door of some fictional semanticists who seem to think that the purely symbolic and operational makes sense. To be sure, he could not have anticipated the contestation between Shannon's approach to "senseless" information and Donald MacKay's attempt to formalize sense; still, he could have considered the differences among language, writing, and symbolic code or at least the distinction between linguistic sense and mathematical sense as far as the machine is concerned. The missed rendezvous between critical theory and cybernetics in the postwar decades—the work of Jürgen Habermas included—may be attributed to a number of factors, historical as well as intellectual. By far the most important factor is their philosophical view of language and its relation to reason. One could conceivably address the following questions to the critical theorist: Does his critique of linguistic nonsense and meaning derive from a pretheorized notion of language or from a coherent philosophy? If it is the latter, what philosophy of language would prompt

5. David Golumbia's discussion of computational linguistics still echoes the Frankfurt School critique of instrumental reason, although he does try to analyze and understand what he calls a "computational view of language" in the cognitive modeling of the mind in the 1960s and beyond. See Golumbia, *The Cultural Logic of Computation*, 83–103.

6. Herbert Marcuse's *Eros and Civilization* (1955) may serve as a painful reminder of how disengaged the critical theorist can be with the technological developments in his world. Not only is Marcuse's discussion of Freud's metapsychology superficial and often wrongheaded—for example, by equating the death instinct with the metaphysics of nonbeing and Eros with the principle of being (125)—his work turns a blind eye to the problem of the psychic machine that was developing in his own time.

him to override or suspend the distinctions among language, writing, and symbolic code in pursuit of the word and linguistic meaning?

Symptomatically, Horkheimer declares that "philosophy is the conscious effort to knit all our knowledge and insight into a linguistic structure in which *things are called by their right names*" (my emphasis).[7] The proper use of language is deemed central to the philosophical enterprise at the Institute for Social Research—which, as I argue below, exhibits a shared telos with Habermas's normative emphasis in the later phase—and it seems that Horkheimer and Adorno want their philosophy and the concept of truth to be rooted in mimetic knowledge and in the translation of that knowledge into the "adequation of name and thing" (Horkheimer, *Eclipse of Reason,* 180). Habermas would take issue with this approach and argue that Horkheimer and Adorno mystify the mimetic capacity of language—equating name and thing—and that by positing a reason before instrumental reason, they remain trapped in the philosophy of consciousness, which presupposes "a subject that represents objects and toils with them."[8] The power of this philosophical legacy asserts itself unmistakably in their *Dialectic of Enlightenment.*

In that book, they argue that "a technological rationale is the rationale of domination itself. It is the coercive nature of society alienated from itself."[9] The technologies they analyze are automobiles, bombs, movies and the cultural industry in general. They point out that under the domination of these technologies, "the need which might resist central control has already been suppressed by the control of the individual consciousness" (Horkheimer and Adorno, *Dialectic of Enlightenment,* 121). In their investigation of the conditions of truth and knowledge, Horkheimer and Adorno see consciousness, language, instrumental reason, and social domination as closely intertwined. Their thesis that the "enlightenment becomes the wholesale deception of the masses" is built upon the authors' analysis of the relationship between thought and language (42).[10] That analysis suggests that the processes of reification in the form of mathematics, machine, and organization are bound to lead to the "abandonment of thought" (41). The argument of "abandonment of thought" appears to coincide with the conundrum of the thinking machine examined earlier, although we must

7. Max Horkheimer, *Eclipse of Reason,* 179.

8. Habermas, *The Theory of Communicative Action, Volume One, Reason and the Rationalization of Society,* 390.

9. Horkheimer and Adorno, *Dialectic of Enlightenment,* 121.

10. Their metaphysical view of language blinds them to cybernetic breakthroughs.

push their insight a bit more and raise some further questions: Is the human being who has abandoned thought replaced by the thinking machine in the new social environment? Does the abandonment of thought end in schizophrenia, automatism, or the sociopsychic machinery of capitalism as explored by Deleuze and Guattari many years later in *Anti-Oedipus*?

Evidently, the conceptual wall against which Horkheimer and Adorno cannot venture further in their critique of instrumental reason is the philosophy of consciousness. Habermas observes that the concept of reason they propose as an alternative to the instrumental use of language cannot be grounded other than in a fraught relationship among philosophy, consciousness, and language. This criticism brings out an interesting aporia in their work that is shown to be steeped in the metaphysical philosophy of language that is implied by their philosophy of consciousness. For example, one cannot imagine either of them delegating any sort of intelligence, conscious or unconscious, to the machine. Yet one of the unintended consequences of their judgment—the abandonment of thought—is precisely the leveling of the metaphysical playground of the unthinking human and the thinking machine. As an alternative to the philosophy of consciousness, Habermas puts forward a theory of communicative action to emphasize intersubjectivity and privilege linguistic philosophy. He believes that "a change of paradigm to the theory of communication makes it possible to return to the undertaking that was interrupted with the critique of instrumental reason; and will permit us to take up once again the since-neglected tasks of a critical theory of society."[11]

Habermas's intersubjective model of communication is said to put the "cognitive instrumental aspect of reason in its proper place as part of a more encompassing *communicative rationality*" (Habermas, *The Theory of Communicative Action*, 390). Linguistic philosophy is made to carry the burden of grounding critical theory and to lift it out of the aporia of objective reason and subjective reason. And what does Habermas mean by his intersubjective model of communication? Obviously, a full reevaluation of his theory of communicative rationality lies beyond the scope of this study. Our main focus is his premise about language, communication, and intersubjectivity, for these impinge inevitably on the issues of writing, cybernetics, the unconscious, and media technologies that this study tries to elucidate. Revisiting Habermas's intersubjective model of communication

---

11. Habermas, *The Theory of Communicative Action, Volume One, Reason and the Rationalization of Society*, 386.

from this limited angle will help clarify and perhaps explain the missed rendezvous between critical theory and cybernetic developments.

I do not mean to imply that Habermas is unaware of information theory and cybernetic developments, which clearly escaped the notice of the earlier members of the Institute for Social Research. On the contrary, he does take notice of the new self-regulated systems of cybernetics and sees them as a means of "physical and psychological control." He is concerned that "behavioral control could be instituted at an even deeper level tomorrow through biotechnic intervention in the endocrine regulation system, not to mention the even greater consequences of intervening in the genetic transmission of inherited information."[12] Habermas goes on to ponder if the old regions of consciousness that developed through ordinary-language communication would in the end completely dry up. Were that to happen, he speculates that "men would make their history with will, but without consciousness" (Habermas, *Toward a Rational Society*, 118). If the above insight appears to bring Habermas close to a real encounter with the psychic machine of cybernetics, he quickly goes off in the opposite direction by advocating a utopia of unrestricted communication and rationalized social norm.

In a way, this narrowly missed encounter with cybernetics should not surprise us. Much of Habermas's knowledge of the new technological developments came from secondhand sources, through the mediation of systems theory, and often in conjunction with Talcott Parsons and Niklas Luhmann, whom he treats extensively in his writing. Commenting on Structuralism and systems theory, Habermas takes them as "subjectless" and "anonymous systems of rules" and observes a meaningful parallel between the two.[13] He argues—inaccurately—that Structuralism models its rules on grammar whereas systems theory thinks of them as self-regulating systems or instances of autopoiesis.[14] The value of Structuralism or systems

---

12. Habermas, *Toward a Rational Society*, 118.

13. Habermas, *On the Pragmatics of Social Interaction: Preliminary Studies in the Theory of Communicative Action*, 15.

14. Niklas Luhmann's concept of autopoiesis leans toward Donald MacKay rather than toward Claude Shannon. In *Social Systems*, Luhmann defines communication as a synthesis of three selections in terms of "information," "utterance," and "understanding" between the addressee "ego" and the communicator "alter." See Luhmann, *Social Systems*, 141. If we compare him with Lacan, whose communication circuit is unconscious, involving neither human utterance nor human understanding, it is clear that Luhmann approaches communication predominantly as a linguistic system, which explains why he is so preoccupied with "meaning," "rationality," and "referentiality" in his ambitious work. Unfortunately, Luhmann's semantic approach to communication does not sit well with his notion of autopoiesis, which is borrowed from Humberto Maturana and Francisco

theory as social theory is limited for the obvious reason that "the system of grammatical rules requires competent speakers for its actualization, whereas the machine regulates itself and has no need of any subject at all." Habermas determines that "in neither case is the paradigm suited for giving an accurate account of how intersubjectively binding meaning structures are generated" (Habermas, *On the Pragmatics of Social Interaction*, 17). Preoccupied as he is with linguistic meaning, Habermas contradicts his earlier insight by underestimating the revolutionary impact of information theory on social life whose significance lies precisely in the machine's refiguring of sense and nonsense beyond the linguistic paradigm that we have seen in connection with the work of Shannon, McCulloch, Pitts, and Lacan.[15]

In other words, Habermas is right about machines needing no subjects but is shortsighted not to consider cybernetics and information theory as more than an instance of self-regulating systems requiring no further critical attention. The novel philosophical questions raised by the cybernetic machine are completely sidestepped as he proceeds to elaborate a theory of communicative action on the basis of linguistic philosophy, a philosophy that information technology has rendered increasingly irrelevant to the most pressing issues of telecommunication in the postwar decades. To his mind, communicative action is still very much about the "linguistic processes of reaching understanding" or speech acts in social situations where "the participants in interaction agree about the validity claimed for their speech acts—that is, they recognize criticizable validity claims intersubjectively."[16] This runs counter to how Lacan understood communication in his psychoanalytical work on the symbolic order.

In *The Theory of Communicative Action*, Habermas considers four models of linguistic function and compares the sociolinguistic interactions among individuals enabled by each of these models. All four are semantic models recognized by his rational criteria, and these are the teleological (based on intentionalist semantics), the normative (based on cultural consensus on meaning), the dramaturgical (based on propositions and speech act), and the communicative model of action. The fourth, and the most important, model relies on formal pragmatics and is given the pride of place in his

---

Varela, and the latter's work is actually modeled on the cybernetic machine rather than on human linguistic communication.

15. For a critical analysis of the divergences between Luhmann and Kittler in response to information theory and cybernetics, see Geoffrey Winthrop-Young, "Silicon Sociology, or, Two Kings on Hegel's Throne? Kittler, Luhmann, and the Posthuman Merger of German Media Theory."

16. Habermas, *On the Pragmatics of Communication*, 300.

theoretical construct because "only the communicative model of action presupposes language as a medium of uncurtailed communication whereby speakers and hearers, out of the context of their preinterpreted lifeworld, refer simultaneously to things in the objective, social, and subjective worlds in order to negotiate common definitions of the situation."[17] To what extent does this view of language distance Habermas's work from Horkheimer and Adorno's logocentric view of language? The distance seems rather negligible when language is understood as a medium of uncurtailed communication between "speakers" and "hearers" in speech act situations, or between what Luhmann terms "alters" and "egos" in his so called communicative action.[18] The premise about communication being a matter of referring to things or negotiating common definitions—in the good old liberal understanding of optimal social contractual relations—adheres to a logocentricism that leaves too many things out of the lifeworld he tries to explain. These include notably telecommunication technologies from telegraph to information technology and satellite communication systems in our own time. This book has argued not only that these technologies have profoundly impacted social communication but that they are pushing the philosophical consideration of sense and nonsense beyond the realms of semantics, speech act theory, theories of meaning, and all other theoretical models that are premised on the face-to-face verbal communication between a human speaker and a human listener. Taken in a cybernetic register—as Lacan has demonstrated to us—communication is fundamentally schizophrenic.

As early as 1844, Samuel Morse's telegraphy introduced a new model of communication that had enormous ramifications for the future human-machine relationship. Chapter 2 discussed how Morse's partner Alfred Vail had envisioned this prospect. Commenting on the first telegraphic line constructed in the United States, Vail said that the presence of the human agent at the receiving end of the line was not absolutely required nor was it necessary even to raise the question *Are you there?*[19] The increased automation of the sending and receiving of instant transmissions over the past 150-odd years has greatly diminished the sociopolitical significance of uncurtailed linguistic communication between speakers and hearers. In telegraphy, as it has been in telephone and information technologies,

17. Habermas, *The Theory of Communicative Action, Volume One*, 95.

18. See Luhmann, *Social Systems*, 141–43.

19. Alfred Vail, *Description of the American Electro Magnetic Telegraph: Now in Operation Between the Cities of Washington and Baltimore* (1845), 21.

language is coded, mediated, messaged, and in constant flight. These technologies raise new philosophical questions about communication that are shifting the mode of address predominantly from verbal speech act to ideographic writing. Again, Lacan understood this when he allegorized the process of communication in his "Seminar on 'The Purloined Letter'" thus: "Might a letter on which the sender retains certain rights then not quite belong to the person to whom it is addressed? Or might it be that the latter was never the real receiver?"[20] Poe's tale led Lacan to speculate about how the psychic machine can be articulated by the cybernetic machine and vice versa. These two are brought together in a single conceit of the game of odd and even, which is played automatically in all cybernetic machines.

The Ideology Machine

In fact, the cybernetic machine itself has been brought in to refigure the problem of ideology as an automatic, unconscious process. Let us consider one of the computer simulation programs of the 1960s. Robert P. Abelson's work deserves special mention here because his computer program—the Ideology Machine—is designed to simulate the ideology of the cold warrior. Like Kenneth Colby, Abelson was interested in exploring the structure of belief systems and their predictability and so on, but his Ideology Machine operates within the precise historical parameters of political discourse of the United States rather than making vague analogies and theoretical claims about psychopathology. He started from the assumption that "most of the worst inter- and intra-national conflicts of the world are greatly exacerbated by the human penchant for interposing oversimplified symbol systems between themselves and the external world."[21] Ideology relies on these symbol systems to distort international relations and aggravates dangerous conflicts in highly predictable ways. The symbol systems are thus characterized by *oversimplification*, *automatism*, and *predictability* rather than deception or self-deception.

Abelson points out that there is a tendency for the analyst of human behavior in the study of psychopathology in politics to assume that strong affects and drives push people into drastic misperceptions of their environments. By aligning emotions with irrationality, one often assumes the reverse is also true, namely, that if someone has a sharply inaccurate

20. Jacques Lacan, "Seminar on 'The Purloined Letter,'" 19.
21. Robert P. Abelson, "The Structure of Belief Systems," 287.

symbolic view of the world, he or she must be the subject of strong emotional forces. Abelson contests this view and argues that "there are plenty of 'cold' cognitive factors which produce inaccurate world-views, and it is important to understand how these cognitive factors operate in their own right" (Abelson, "The Structure of Belief Systems," 288). Computers have no emotions—although Marvin Minsky may think otherwise—and can, therefore, serve as a perfect medium for testing how the "cold" cognitive factors operate to produce the right-wing fanaticism about communism.

The Ideology Machine has been set up to simulate responses to foreign policy questions. The computer system stores the language of political ideology in memory and expresses this ideology in typed English text when it is addressed by typed English input. The vocabulary in the computer memory consists of a collection of 500 noun phrases and 100 verb phrases relating to foreign policy, including "Nixon," "Vietnam," and "sell-arms-to" and so on. These items are classified under some general conceptual categories: 15 for nouns (such as Communist nations, left-leaning neutrals, Free World nations, and liberal dupes) and 11 for verbs (such as physical attack and material support). These conceptual categories can be combined to specify 300 generic events (such as the physical attack of a neutral nation by a Communist nation) and these in turn are combined to form episodes. The heart of Abelson's simulation program is a subroutine that attempts to "fill molecules." The input is usually a single sentence (in the simple Subject-Verb-Object form), and the output is either a filled molecule containing the input sentence and the appropriate other sentences needed to complete the molecular set, or a failure signal indicating that the system cannot explicate the input sentence. The master script of the Ideology Machine suggests that the production of ideology is a highly automatic process (Fig. 26). As Abelson and Carol M. Raich put it, "[T]he replies by the automated Senator to the input statements presented him should simulate the replies the real Senator might conceivably make."[22] The prototype for the automated Senator is the extreme right-wing ideologue Barry Goldwater. Abelson chose him as his model because Goldwater's political convictions as expressed in his speeches are simplistic and predictable.[23]

The above master script presents four main categories of actors in the cold war: Communist powers, Free World, "good Americans," and Liberals and left-wingers. The struggle takes place between the Free World and the

22. Robert P. Abelson and Carol M. Raich, "Implicational Molecules: A Method for Extracting Meaning from Input Sentences," 643.
23. Abelson, "The Structure of Belief Systems," 288–89.

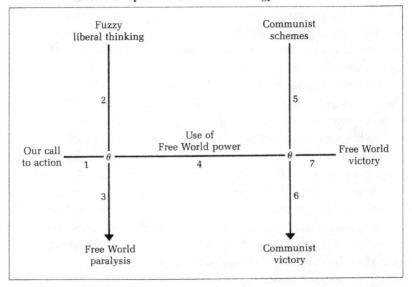

Master Script for a Cold War Ideology.

Figure 26. Robert P. Abelson's master script for the Ideology Machine. From Robert P. Abelson, "The Structure of Belief Systems," in Roger C. Schank and Kenneth Mark Colby, eds., *Computer Models of Thought and Language* (San Francisco: W. H. Freeman and Company, 1973), 291.

forces of Communism as the Communists are expected to pursue their victory until they control the world. Liberal and left-wing dupes who dominate many Free World governments play into the hands of Communist designs. In order to rid the Free World of their influence, the cold warriors must act with determination so that a strong America can establish a cooperative relationship with other free peoples in order to block Communist schemes and bring about a Free World victory.[24] For example, when the input event was "Communists attack Thailand, what will happen?" the Ideology Machine responded: "If Communists attack Thailand, Communists take over unprepared nations unless Thailand ask-aid-from United States and United States give-aid-to Thailand" (Abelson, "The Structure of Belief Systems," 292). The output can sometimes show semantic blind spots due to the machine's lack of historical knowledge and the ability to judge the physical distance between nations. As Boden has pointed out, if required to assess the credibility of the proposition that Red China built the Berlin Wall, the Ideology Machine would decide that this is indeed the sort of

24. Abelson, "The Structure of Belief Systems," 331.

anti-American activity that one might expect from the evil Chinese, but the real Senator Goldwater is not expected to be so ignorant or so naive.[25] Abelson's master script is semantically driven and presupposes a fundamental relationship between symbol manipulation and the unconscious. While his simulation program yields fascinating insights on the automatism of certain discursive constructs in the cold war, the exact relationship between symbol manipulation and the unconscious remains unexplored and is arbitrarily determined by the belief systems programmed into the machine. These articulate to semantics and linguistic norms that are themselves unquestioned. We have seen in the earlier discussion of Ogden and Richards how the concern with semantics and normative sense has been fraught with ideological battles and with fears of irrationality.

Our Game with the Little "Letters"

The anxiety about meaning, communicative *adequatio,* and rationality is what prompted Ogden and Richards to write their interwar classic *The Meaning of Meaning.* This book underwent as many as six editions between 1923 and 1943, but its influence was eclipsed as soon as information theory burst upon the scene. In this ambitious work, Ogden and Richards criticize Saussure for focusing his attention exclusively on the sign rather than "on the things for which the signs stand"[26] and propose rational procedures to distinguish "symbol" from "referent" and define "meaning" in its corresponding sign and symbol situations systematically. This theory of meaning aims to resolve, once and for all, the problem of how the mental processes (THOUGHTS) relate scientifically to the symbol (WORDS) on the one hand and to the referent (THINGS) on the other so that we can identify and minimize pathological disturbances in the normal process of sociolinguistic communication (10–23). Curiously, one of the examples Ogden and Richards have brought up for discussion has to do with how one might pin down the referent of the following utterances: "my pipe is out" and "my pipe is alight" (103–5). In the analysis, they resort to a set of normative criteria whereby the mind resolves the correct meaning of each utterance in context. Incidentally, even if the Belgian surrealist René Magritte did not have Ogden and Richards or their normative approach to the sign "pipe" in mind when he did the group of paintings bearing the title *Ceci n'est pas une pipe* (this is not a pipe), I would suggest that Foucault's

---

25. Margaret Boden, *Artificial Intelligence and Natural Man,* 74.
26. C. K. Ogden and I. A. Richards, *The Meaning of Meaning,* 6.

interpretation of visual and verbal interplay in his *This Is Not a Pipe* serves to bring out the intellectual stakes in the surrealist teasing of all manners of normative assertions about the linguistic and visual sign.[27]

I have mentioned in chapter 3 that the stated goal of *The Meaning of Meaning* is to achieve what the authors term the "eugenics of language." "When we enter the Enchanted Wood of Words," write Ogden and Richards, "our Rules of Thumb may enable us to deal not only with such evil genii as the Phonetic, the Hypostatic and the Utraquistic subterfuges, but also with other disturbing apparitions of which Irritants, Mendicants and Nomads are examples" (138). When the authors turned their ethnographic gaze across the vast stretches of the geographical and sociolinguistic landscape from antiquity to present, from the primitive to the civilized, and from East to West, they conclude that the East is the true home of verbal superstition.[28] Even so, in their eyes, verbal superstition is not the preroga-

27. See Foucault's beautiful little book *This Is Not a Pipe*. See also Mark Taylor's discussion of the same as self-reflexive circuits in *The Moment of Complexity*, 75–77.

28. This may explain the puzzle as to why Richards expended so much energy and time to promote Basic English in China but made very little effort to understand what he had heard or seen in that country. A notable case is found in his description of a situation when he was teaching Thomas Hardy's *Tess of the d'Urbervilles* at Tsinghua University in Beijing. As he read out the final scene depicting the tragic punishment of Tess, Richards heard some applause from his students and was stunned and baffled by their reaction. He rationalized this by thinking that the students read the story as a "Confucian" moral tale and thought that Tess's death was a retribution she deserved for disobeying her father (Russo, *I. A. Richards*, 406). Richards brings up this episode in *Basic in Teaching: East and West* and elsewhere to illustrate the difference or gaps he perceived in the cultural sensibilities between East and West. But the explanation he offers is highly dubious for the following reason. First, traditional Chinese drama and fiction over the past millennium are full of stories about daughters' tragic or successful rebellion against paternal authority and their subversion of so-called Confucian values. *The Peony Pavilion* and *The Dream of the Red Chamber* are notable examples that all educated and uneducated Chinese knew from their early theater exposure if not from reading the works themselves. During the time of Richards's sojourn in Beijing, the sentimental novel *Family* by Ba Jin, which mercilessly attacked Confucian patriarchy and mourned the women who became its victims, was a national best seller. Moreover, the full-fledged feminist movement and nationwide anti-Confucian campaigns in China already led to spectacular social reforms that Richards could not have helped noticing in the 1930s. If Richards had spoken with any of the women students in Beijing, many of whom would have performed in Ibsen's *Doll's House* or read the play, he would not have drawn such a sweeping conclusion about cultural difference. It seems to me that the double blindness to the contemporary gender politics and to the local literary tradition impeded his understanding of the situation with or without the cultural divide. In short, all evidence goes against Richards's suggestion that his students were incapable of empathizing with Tess because of their collective Confucian mentality. We don't know why some students were applauding on that particular occasion; it is impossible to speculate without sufficient evidence. Whatever it was, it could not have been the reason Richards has given his readers in the West. Richards's lack of curiosity about the Chinese students' knowledge of their own literary tradition caused him to make mistaken judgments about cultural difference when it comes to learning the canon of Western literature.

tive of the East; it is found everywhere. In *Practical Criticism*, Richards describes some of the protocols he adopted with set texts to test how well or poorly the undergraduate students at the University of Cambridge interpreted the individual poems they read when the authorial and contextual information was removed. The practice of close reading in the New Criticism inspired by this work may be seen as part of a global campaign to exorcise linguistic phantoms and interpretive aberration and to keep psychic disturbances at bay.

One of the reasons that Habermas failed to reflect on the implications of postwar telecommunication technologies in the above light might have to do with the fact that his theory of communicative rationality shares the normative stance of pre–World War II theorists of language and meaning. He restaged the battle against the eruption of irrationality in social interactions by proposing a normative model of communicative action based on a semantic understanding of language. He found himself in a similar position of having to defend society against the breakdown of linguistic communication, or what he termed "communication pathologies," at the conscious as well as unconscious levels. By the conscious level, Habermas means deliberate deception and manipulation, whereas at the unconscious level the pathology appears as "systematically distorted communication."[29] The latter is compared to the "unconscious repression of conflicts that the psychoanalyst explains in terms of defense mechanisms" and it causes disturbances of communication on both the "intrapsychic and interpersonal levels" (Habermas, *The Theory of Communicative Action*, 332). In this limited application of Freud, the relationship between the unconscious and language makes sense to him insofar as it concerns the pathological moment of *distorted communication*, but pathology is not otherwise treated as fundamental to communication itself, the latter having been discussed and developed extensively by the psychoanalysts of his time and a good number of cyberneticans. As Alan Liu puts it, "[I]rrationality in all its terrible energy is now to be harnessed within the organization as the means of strong, rational management."[30] This failure to engage with the fundamentals of information theory and the cybernetic model of the mind means that Habermas's communicative model of action is strangely archaic and almost irrelevant to the new intellectual challenges presented by the changing technologies of digital media.

---

29. Habermas, *The Theory of Communicative Action, Volume One*, 332.
30. Alan Liu, *The Laws of Cool: Knowledge Work and the Culture of Information*, 50.

Weizenbaum has shown that when DOCTOR in the computer program ELIZA doubles as a fortune-teller in its communication with the human interlocutor, irrationality already shadows rationality in the human-machine interaction via the mediation of the mirage of "sense." Is the same true of the earlier moments of telecommunication? For instance, did electromagnetic telegraphy fall on the side of communicative rationality or that of irrationality and magic, or perhaps both? When Yale College conferred the honorary degree of doctor of laws upon Samuel Morse, the latter read his new title LL.D. as "Lightning Line Doctor."[31] Morse, who was a portrait artist before he became an inventor, saw the coming of electromagnetic telegraphy as an instrument of divine revelation. He exhibited this "thunder and lightning 'jim crack'" at the House Committee on Commerce to persuade the U.S. government to fund his project. Indeed, the official completion of the first electromagnetic telegraph line between Washington, D.C., and Baltimore on May 24, 1844, has been commemorated by one of the most remarkable telegraphic messages Morse had ever transmitted, a phrase taken from the ancient soothsayer Balaam: "What hath God wrought?"[32] The wonder and the prophetic messages uttered by some of the contemporary witnesses to the telegraphic achievement are duly recorded for the benefit of the future generation: "Time and space are now annihilated" (Mabee, *The American Leonardo*, 207). If pronouncements such as this strike us as embarrassingly trite, it is because they have been repeated so many times over the past 150-odd years down to the latest postmodern reiteration of the compression of time and space. In Morse's time, however, they conveyed some genuine insights and heralded the beginning of something truly original that just got under way.

Unlike the critical theorists of the Frankfurt School, Lacan heeded both the electromagnetic messages and digital messages and became intensely engaged with the contemporary developments in information technology. He did not dismiss Shannon's communication machine or Wiener's cybernetics lightly as an instrumentalization of reason. On the contrary, his psychoanalytic insights were vastly enriched by what he could glean from game theory, cybernetics, and information theory. The latter taught him that the cyberneticians played some fateful games with our little "letters" and as a consequence we ought to be gravely concerned about the unconscious and the symbolic order. Lacan's intellectual efforts remind us that

---

31. Carleton Mabee, *The American Leonardo: A Life of Samuel F. B. Morse*, 294.

32. This phrase was chosen by a young woman named Annie Ellsworth. Mabee, *The American Leonardo*, 275.

the mastery of computer programming skills is not the precondition for a nonspecialist to learn what I have tried to convey to the readers. Rather, the precondition of such knowledge lies elsewhere: the openness of the mind to the originality of what appears in our world.

Until we learn a few basic things about the discrete alphanumerical symbols in modern communication machines, the *techne* of the unconscious will remain hidden in plain sight. This may well be where the last stand of ideology reveals itself: the framing of the unconscious by digital technology. I have demonstrated how the *techne* of the unconscious in modernity emerged with the pioneering psychophysical and psychoanalytical experiments in word-association games and memory and evolved with the literary and artistic experiments of high modernism in Europe and America. In the immediate postwar years, it resurfaced unexpectedly in Claude Shannon's calculation of the statistical probability of Printed English. With the invention of the twenty-seventh letter and spacing mechanisms à la Shannon, Turing, and others, Printed English has achieved its ontology in the digital revolution. The recent evolution in the technology of alphabetical writing—especially in the postwar work on neural nets and the psychic machine—has allowed the *techne* of the unconscious to be refigured as a cybernetic process.

Thus far, this discussion appears to be propelling my concluding remarks toward some kind of ideological criticism for a sense of closure. But is closure possible or necessary? Barring a proper closure on the question of ideology, I think we should first contemplate how to incorporate digital media effectively and rigorously into the social or critical theory of our time. Rather than continue to work with the inherited philosophical problems of consciousness and anthropocentrism, our critical endeavor needs to confront the ruses of writing and the *techne* of the unconscious, which are thoroughly embedded in the human-machine ecology enabled by digital media. One of the valuable legacies of critical theory has been the intellectual vigilance with which the theorists approached the work of language as a site of philosophical critique. Will future theorists bring the same degree of vigilance to the technology of writing? How far will critical theory aid us in conceptualizing the task of social theory with respect to digital media? What, if any, are the chances of counter-engineering the unconscious, that is, if the Freudian robot is allowed to embody the unconscious of the posthuman social structure? I suppose that bringing such questions to the fore and into public debate would constitute the first step toward coping with the *techne* of the unconscious in digital media.

6

With Printed English, and with the eruption of the discrete symbol upon the scene of writing in the digital revolution, the ideographical movement of the phonetic alphabet can be said to have come full circle. That movement has made all the difference to how we think about language, writing, and the Freudian robot of the future.

WORKS CITED

Abelson, Robert P. "The Structure of Belief Systems." In *Computer Models of Thought and Language,* edited by Roger C. Schank and Kenneth Mark Colby, 287–339. San Francisco: W. H. Freeman, 1973.

Abelson, Robert P., and Carol M. Raich. "Implicational Molecules: A Method for Extracting Meaning from Input Sentences." *International Joint Conference on Artificial Intelligence* (1969): 641–47.

Andrews, S. "Lexical Retrieval and Selection Processes: Effects of Transposed-Letter Confusability." *Journal of Memory and Language* 35, no. 6 (1996): 775–800.

Armand, Louis. *Technē: James Joyce, Hypertext & Technology.* Prague: Univerzita Karlova v Praze, 2003.

Aubin, David. "The Withering Immortality of Nicolas Bourbaki: A Cultural Connection at the Confluence of Mathematics, Structuralism, and the Oulipo in France." *Science in Context* 10, no. 2 (1997): 297–342.

Barnett, Lincoln. "Basic English: A Globalanguage." *Life,* October 18, 1943, 57–64.

Barthes, Roland. *Elements of Semiology.* Translated by Annette Lavers and Colin Smith. New York: Hill and Wang, 1968.

Beadle, George Wells, and Muriel Beadle. *The Language of Life: An Introduction to the Science of Genetics.* Garden City, N.Y.: Doubleday, 1966.

Beckett, Samuel. "Dante. . .Bruno. Vico.. Joyce." In *Our Exagmination Round His Factification for Incamination of Work in Progress,* edited by Samuel Beckett, 16–17. London: Faber and Faber, 1929.

Benjamin, Walter. "Painting and the Graphic Arts." In *The Work of Art in the Age of Its Technical Reproducibility and Other Writings on Media,* edited by

Michael W. Jennings, Brigid Doherty, and Thomas Y. Levin, 219–20. Translated by Edmund Jephcott, Rodney Livingstone, Howard Eiland, et al. Cambridge, Mass.: Harvard University Press, 2008.

Benveniste, Emile. "Le Jeu comme structure." *Deucalion*, no. 2 (1947): 161–67.

Bernal, J. D. *Science in History*. 4 vols. London: C. A. Watts, 1969.

Bernfeld, Siegfried, and Sergei Feitelberg. "The Principle of Entropy and the Death Instinct." *International Journal of Psycho-Analysis* 12 (1931): 61–81.

Bleuler, Eugen. "Consciousness and Association." In *Studies in Word-Association: Experiments in the Diagnosis of Psychopathological Conditions Carried Out at the Psychiatric Clinic of the University of Zurich*, edited by C. G. Jung, 266–96. London: Routledge & Kegan Paul, 1918.

Bloom, Harold. *Agon: Towards a Theory of Revisionism*. New York: Oxford University Press, 1982.

Boden, Margaret A. *Artificial Intelligence and Natural Man*. New York: Basic Books, 1977.

———. *Mind as Machine: A History of Cognitive Science*. 2 vols. Oxford: Clarendon Press, 2006.

Boltz, William G. *The Origin and Early Development of the Chinese Writing System*. New Haven: American Oriental Society, 1994.

Bonnet, C. "Les Scribes phoenico-puniques." In *Phoinikeia Grammata*, edited by Claude Baurain, Corinne Bonnet, and V. Krings, 147–71. Namur: Société des Etudes classiques, 1991.

Bono, James J. "Science, Discourse, and Literature: The Role/Rule of Metaphor in Science." In *Literature and Science: Theory & Practice*, edited by Stuart Peterfreund, 59–90. Boston: Northeastern University Press, 1990.

Boodberg, Peter. "'Ideography' or Iconolatry?" *T'oung Pao* 35, no. 1–5 (1939): 266–88.

Borel, Émile. *Leçons sur la théorie des fonctions*. 3rd ed. Paris: Gauthier-Villars, 1928.

Boswell, James. *Life of Johnson*. Edited by G. B. Hill and L. F. Powell. 6 vols. Oxford: Oxford University Press, 1934.

Brooks, Rodney A. *Flesh and Machines: How Robots Will Change Us*. New York: Vintage Books, 2003.

Brown, Bill. "Reification, Reanimation, and the American Uncanny." *Critical Inquiry* 32, no. 2 (2006): 175–207.

Caillois, Roger. *Les jeux et les hommes*. Paris: Gallimard, 1958.

———. *Man, Play, and Games*. Translated by Meyer Barash. New York: Free Press of Glencoe, 1961.

Carson, Cathryn. "Science as Instrumental Reason: Heidegger, Habermas, Heisenberg." *Continental Philosophy Review*, Dec. 5, 2009. http://www.springerlink.com/content/e5772880g7750031/

Cavell, Stanley. "The Uncanniness of the Ordinary." In *In Quest of the Ordinary: Lines of Skepticism and Romanticism*, 153–78. Chicago: University of Chicago Press, 1988.

Chao, Yuen Ren. "Dimensions of Fidelity in Translation With Special Reference to Chinese." *Harvard Journal of Asiatic Studies* 29 (1969): 109–30.

——— —. *Mandarin Primer*. Cambridge, Mass.: Harvard University Press, 1948.

———. "Meaning in Language and How It Is Acquired." In *Cybernetics, Circular Causal and Feedback Mechanisms in Biological and Social Systems: Transactions of the Tenth Conference*, edited by Heinz von Foerster. New York: Josiah Macy, Jr. Foundation, 1953.

Chargaff, Erwin. *Essays on Nucleic Acids*. New York: Elsevier, 1963.

Chavannes, Édouard, trans. *Cinq cents contes et apologues: extraits du Tripitaka Chinois*. 4 vols. Paris: Ernest Leroux, 1911.

Chen, Jiujin, and Zhang Jingguo. "Hanshan Chutu Yupian Tuxing Shikao" (a preliminary analysis of the iconography in the jade fragments from the excavation site in Hanshan). *Wenwu*, no. 4 (1989): 14–17.

Cherry, Colin. *On Human Communication: A Review, a Survey, and a Criticism*. Cambridge, Mass.: MIT Press, 1957.

Cherry, Colin, Morris Halle, and Roman Jakobson. "Toward the Logical Description of Languages in Their Phonemic Aspect." *Language* 29, no. 1 (1953): 34–46.

Chomsky, Noam. *Syntatic Structures*. The Hague: Mouton, 1957.

Cixous, Hélène. "Fiction and Its Phantoms: A Reading of Freud's 'Das Unheimliche' (the 'Uncanny')." *New Literary History* 7, no. 3 (1976): 525–48.

Clarke, Arthur C. *2001: A Space Odyssey*. New York: New American Library, 1968.

———. *Voice Across the Sea*. New York: Harper & Row, 1959.

Clarke, Bruce. "From Thermodynamics to Virtuality." In *From Energy to Information: Representation in Science and Technology, Art, and Literature*, edited by Bruce Clarke and Linda Dalrymple Henderson, 17–33. Stanford: Stanford University Press, 2002.

Colasse, Bernard, and Francis Pavé. "La Mathématique et le social: entretien avec Georges Th. Guilbaud." *Gérer et Comprendre* no. 67 (2002): 67–74.

Colby, K. M. *Artificial Paranoia: A Computer Simulation of Paranoid Processes*. New York: Pergamon Press, 1975.

———. "Simulations of Belief Systems." In *Computer Models of Thought and Language*, edited by Roger C. Schank and Kenneth Mark Colby, 252–86. San Francisco: W. H. Freeman, 1973.

Colby, K. M, J. B. Watt, and J. P. Gilbert. "A Computer Method of Psychotherapy: Preliminary Communication." *Journal of Nervous and Mental Disease* 142, no. 2 (1966): 148–52.

Colby, K. M., Sylvia Weber, and Franklin Dennis Hilf. "Artificial Paranoia." *Artificial Intelligence* 2, no. 1 (Spring 1971): 1–25.

Conway, Flo, and Jim Siegelman. *Dark Hero of the Information Age: In Search of Norbert Wiener, the Father of Cybernetics*. New York: Basic Books, 2005.

Coulmas, Florian. *Writing Systems: An Introduction to Their Linguistic Analysis*. Cambridge: Cambridge University Press, 2003.

———. *The Writing Systems of the World*. Oxford: Blackwell, 1989.

Crick, Francis. *What Mad Pursuit: A Personal View of Scientific Discovery*. New York: Basic Books, 1988.

Crick, Francis H. C., J. S. Griffith, and L. E. Orgel. "Codes Without Commas." *PNAS* 43 (1957): 413–21.

Daniels, Peter T., and William Bright. *The World's Writing Systems*. Oxford: Oxford University Press, 1996.

DeFrancis, John. *Visible Speech: The Diverse Oneness of Writing Systems*. Honolulu: University of Hawaii Press, 1989.

Deleuze, Gilles. *Cinema 2: The Time-Image*. Translated by H. Tomlinson and B. Habberjam. Minneapolis: University of Minnesota Press, 1989.

———. *Difference and Repetition*. Translated by Paul Patton. New York: Columbia University Press, 1994.

———. *The Logic of Sense*. Translated by Mark Lester with Charles Stivale. London: Athlone Press, 1990.

Deleuze, Gilles, and Félix Guattari. *Anti-Oedipus: Capitalism and Schizophrenia*. Volume 1. Trans. Robert Hurley, Mark Seem and Helen R. Lane. Minneapolis: University of Minnesota Press, 1983.

———. *A Thousand Plateaus: Capitalism and Schizophrenia*. Volume 2. Trans. Brian Massumi. Minneapolis: University of Minnesota Press, 1987.

Dennett, Daniel C. *Consciousness Explained*. Boston: Little, Brown and Co., 1991.

———. *Kinds of Minds: Toward an Understanding of Consciousness*. New York: Basic Books, 1996.

Derrida, Jacques. *Dissemination*. Translated by Barbara Johnson. Chicago: University of Chicago Press, 1981.

———. *Glas*. Translated by John R. Leavey Jr. and Richard Rand. Lincoln: University of Nebraska Press, 1986.

———. *Margins of Philosophy*. Translated by Alan Bass. Chicago: University of Chicago Press, 1982.

———. *Of Grammatology*. Translated by Gayatri Chakravorty Spivak. Baltimore: Johns Hopkins University Press, 1976.

———. "Plato's Pharmacy." In *Dissemination*, 61–155. Chicago: University of Chicago Press, 1981.

———. *The Post Card: From Socrates to Freud and Beyond*. Translated by Alan Bass. Chicago: University of Chicago Press, 1987.

———. "The Purveyor of Truth." In *The Purloined Poe: Lacan, Derrida, and Psychoanalytic Reading*, edited by John P. Muller and William J. Richardson, 173–212. Baltimore: Johns Hopkins University Press, 1988.

———. "Two Words for Joyce." In *Post-Structuralist Joyce: Essays from the French*, edited by Derek Attridge and Daniel Ferrer, 145–59. Cambridge: Cambridge University Press, 1984.

———. "Ulysses Gramophone: Hear Say Yes in Joyce." In *Acts of Literature*, 253–309. New York: Routledge, 1992.

Dimand, Mary Ann, and Robert W. Dimand. *The Foundations of Game Theory*. Vol. 3. Cheltenham, UK: Edward Elgar, 1997.

Dosse, François. *History of Structuralism*. 2 vols. Translated by Deborah Glassman. Minneapolis: University of Minnesota Press, 1997.

Doyle, Richard. *On Beyond Living: Rhetorical Transformations of the Life Sciences*. Stanford: Stanford University Press, 1997.

———. *Wetwares: Experiments in Postvital Living*. Minneapolis: University of Minnesota Press, 2003.

Dubarle, D. "Idées scientifiques actuelles et domination des faits humains." *Esprit* 18, no. 9 (1950): 296–317.

Dumit, Joseph. "Neuroexistentialism." In *Sensorium: Embodied Experience, Technology, and Contemporary Art*, edited by Caroline A. Jones, 182–89. Cambridge, Mass.: MIT Press, 2006.

Dupuy, Jean-Pierre. *The Mechanization of the Mind: On the Origins of Cognitive Science*. Translated by M. B. DeBevoise. Princeton: Princeton University Press, 2000.

Eakin, Emily. "Writing as a Block for Asians." *New York Times*, May 3, 2003.

Edwards, Paul N. *The Closed World: Computers and the Politics of Discourse in Cold War America*. Cambridge, Mass.: MIT Press, 1996.

Ellmann, Richard. *James Joyce*. New and rev. ed. New York: Oxford University Press, 1982.

Enright, Michael J. "The Japanese Facsimile Industry in 1990." *Harvard Business School Cases* (May 1991): 1–21.

Fagen, M. D., ed. *A History of Engineering and Science in the Bell System*. Murray Hill, N.J.: Bell Telephone Laboratories, 1978.

Feigenbaum, Edward A. "The Simulation of Verbal Learning Behavior." In Edward A. Feigenbaum and Julian Feldman, eds., *Computers and Thought*, 297–309. New York: McGraw-Hill, 1963.

Feigenbaum, Edward A., and Julian Feldman, eds. *Computers and Thought*. New York: McGraw-Hill, 1963.

Felman, Shoshana, ed. *Literature and Psychoanalysis: The Question of Reading, Otherwise*. Baltimore: Johns Hopkins University Press, 1982.

Fink, Bruce. *Lacan to the Letter: Reading Écrits Closely*. Minneapolis: University of Minnesota Press, 2004.

———. "The Nature of Unconscious Thought, or Why No One Ever Reads Lacan's Postface to the 'Seminar on "The Purloined Letter."'" In *Reading Seminars I and II: Lacan's Return to Freud*, edited by Richard Feldstein, Bruce Fink, and Maire Jaanus, 173–91. Albany: SUNY Press, 1996.

Fisher, Simon E., C. S. Lai, and A. P. Monaco. "Deciphering the Genetic Basis of Speech and Language Disorders." *Annual Review of Neuroscience* 26 (2003): 57–80.

Forrester, John. *The Seductions of Psychoanalysis: Freud, Lacan, and Derrida*. Cambridge: Cambridge University Press, 1990.

Foucault, Michel. *Dits et Écrits, 1954–1988*. Vol. 1 (1954–75). Paris: Gallimard, 1994.

———. *"Society Must be Defended": Lectures at the College de France 1975–1976*. Translated by David Macey. New York: Picador, 2003.

———. *This Is Not a Pipe*. Translated and edited by James Harkness. Berkeley: University of California Press, 1983.

Freud, Sigmund. *Beyond the Pleasure Principle*. In *The Standard Edition of the Complete Psychological Works of Sigmund Freud*, vol. 18, 7–64.

———. *Civilization and Its Discontents*. In *The Standard Edition of the Complete Psychological Works of Sigmund Freud*, vol. 21, 57–146.

———. *The Interpretation of Dreams*. In *The Standard Edition of the Complete Psychological Works of Sigmund Freud*, vol. 4 (1900), ix–627.

———. *Jokes and Their Relation to the Unconscious*. In *The Standard Edition of the Complete Psychological Works of Sigmund Freud*, vol. 8, 1–247.

———. "Psycho-Analysis and the Establishment of the Facts in Legal Proceedings." In *The Standard Edition of the Complete Psychological Works of Sigmund Freud*, vol. 9 (1906–8): 97–114.

———.*The Psychopathology of Everyday Life*. In *The Standard Edition of the Complete Psychological Works of Sigmund Freud*, vol. 6, vii–296.

———. *The Standard Edition of the Complete Psychological Works of Sigmund Freud*. Translated and edited by James Strachey. 24 vols. London: Hogarth Press, 1953–74.

———. "The 'Uncanny.'" In *The Standard Edition of the Complete Psychological Works of Sigmund Freud*, vol. 17, 219–52.

Galison, Peter. "The Ontology of the Enemy: Norbert Wiener and the Cybernetic Vision." *Critical Inquiry* 21, no. 1 (1994): 228–66.

Gallop, Jane. *Reading Lacan*. Ithaca, N.Y.: Cornell University Press, 1985.

Gambarara, Daniele. "The Convention of Geneva: History of Linguistic Ideas and History of Communicative Practices." In *Historical Roots of Linguistic Theories*, edited by Lia Formigari and Daniele Gambarara, 279–94. Amsterdam: J. Benjamins, 1995.

Gamow, George, Alexander Rich, and Martynas Yčas. "The Problem of Information Transfer from the Nucleic Acids to Proteins." In *Advances in Biological and Medical Physics*, edited by John Hundale Lawrence and Cornelius A. Tobias, 23–68. New York: Academic Press, 1956.

Gamow, George. "Possible Relation between Deoxyribonucleic Acid and Protein Structures." *Nature* 173 (1954): 318.

Géfin, Laszlo. *Ideogram: History of a Poetic Method*. Austin: University of Texas Press, 1982.

Golumbia, David. *The Cultural Logic of Computation*. Cambridge, Mass.: Harvard University Press, 2009.

Graham, A. C., trans. *The Book of Lieh-tzü*. London: John Murray, 1960.

Guilbaud, Georges Théodule. *La Cybernétique*. Paris: Presses universitaires de France, 1954.

———. "Divagations cybernétiques." *Esprit* 18, no. 9 (1950): 281–95.

———. *Eléments de la théorie mathématique des jeux*. Paris: Dunod, 1968.

———. "Leçons sur les éléments principaux de la théorie mathématique des jeux." In *Stratégies et Décisions Economiques*, edited by G. Th. Guilbaud, P. Masses, and R. Henon, chaps 1–5. Paris: CNRS, 1954.

———. "La Mathématique et le social: entretien avec Georges Th. Guilbaud," Interview with Bernard Colasse and Francis Pavé. *Gérer et Comprendre* 67 (March 2002): 67–74.

———. "La Théorie des jeux: contributions critiques à la théorie de la valeur." *Economie Appliquée* 2 (1949): 275–319.

————. "The Theory of Games: Critical Contributions to the Theory of Value." In *The Foundations of Game Theory*, edited by Mary Ann Dimand and Robert W. Dimand, 348–76. Cheltenham, UK: Edward Elgar, 1997.

————. *What Is Cybernetics?* Translated by Valerie MacKay. New York: Grove Press, 1959.

Habermas, Jürgen. *Knowledge and Human Interests.* Translated by Jeremy J. Shapiro. Boston: Beacon Press, 1971.

————. *On the Pragmatics of Communication.* Edited by Maeve Cooke. Cambridge, Mass.: MIT Press, 1998.

————. *On the Pragmatics of Social Interaction: Preliminary Studies in the Theory of Communicative Action.* Translated by Barbara Fultner. Cambridge, Mass.: MIT Press, 2002.

————. *The Theory of Communicative Action.* Translated by Thomas McCarthy. 2 vols. Boston: Beacon Press, 1984.

————. *Toward a Rational Society: Student Protest, Science, and Politics.* Boston: Beacon Press, 1970.

Hansen, Mark. "Cinema Beyond Cybernetics, or How to Frame the Digital Image." *Configurations* 10, no. 1 (2002): 51–90.

————. *Embodying Technesis: Technology Beyond Writing.* Ann Arbor: University of Michigan Press, 2000.

Haraway, Donna. *Simians, Cyborgs, and Women: The Reinvention of Nature.* New York: Routledge, 1991.

Harris, Roy. *Signs of Writing.* London and New York: Routledge, 1995.

Hayles, N. Katherine. *How We Became Posthuman: Virtual Bodies in Cybernetics, Literature, and Informatics.* Chicago: University of Chicago Press, 1999.

————. *My Mother Was a Computer: Digital Subjects and Literary Texts.* Chicago: University of Chicago Press, 2005.

Healy, Alice F. "Detection Errors on the Word *The*: Evidence for Reading Units Larger Than Letters." *Journal of Experimental Psychology: Human Perception and Performance* 2, no. 2 (1976): 235–42.

Hegel, F., S. Krach, T. Kircher, B. Wrede, and G. Sagerer. "Theory of Mind (ToM) on Robots: A Functional Neuroimaging Study." *Proceedings of the 3rd ACM/IEEE International Conference on Human Robot Interaction.* Amsterdam, Netherlands, March 12–15 (2008): 335–42. http://portal.acm.org/citation.cfm?id=1349866.

Heidegger, Martin. *The Question Concerning Technology, and Other Essays.* Translated by William Lovitt. New York: Harper & Row, 1977.

Heims, Steve J. *The Cybernetics Group.* Cambridge, Mass.: MIT Press, 1991.

Heisenberg, Werner. *The Physicist's Conception of Nature.* London: Hutchinson Scientific and Technical, 1958.

Henrion, Pierre. *Jonathan Swift Confesses.* Versailles: Henrion, 1962.

Hinsley, F. H., and Alan Stripp. *Codebreakers: The Inside Story of Bletchley Park.* Oxford: Oxford University Press, 1993.

Hinton, Charles Howard. *Scientific Romances.* London: Swan Sonnenschein, 1886.

Hodges, Andrew. *Alan Turing: The Enigma*. London: Burnett Books, 1983.

Hoffmann, E. T. A. "Automata." Translated by Major Alexander Ewing. In *The Best Tales of Hoffmann*, edited by E. F. Bleiler, 71–103. New York: Dover, 1967.

———. *Der Sandmann*. Commentary by Peter Braun. Frankfurt am Main: Suhrkamp Verlag, 2003.

———. *Tales of E. T. A. Hoffmann*. Edited and translated by Leonard J. Kent and Elizabeth C. Knight. Chicago: University of Chicago Press, 1969.

Hofstadter, Douglas R. *Gödel, Escher, Bach: An Eternal Golden Braid*. New York: Basic Books, 1999.

Horkheimer, Max. *Eclipse of Reason*. New York: Oxford University Press, 1947.

Horkheimer, Max, and Theodor W. Adorno. *Dialectic of Enlightenment*. Translated by John Cumming. New York: Continuum, 1991.

Huang, Yunte. "Basic English, Chinglish, and Translocal Dialect." In *English and Ethnicity*, edited by Janina Brutt-Griffler and Catherine Evans Davies, 75–103. New York: Palgrave Macmillan, 2006.

Hyppolite, Jean. "*Le coup de dés* de Stéphane Mallarmé et le message." *Etudes philosophiques* no. 4 (1958): 463–68.

———. *Logic and Existence*. Translated by Leonard Lawlor and Amit Sen. Albany: SUNY Press, 1997.

Ifrah, Georges. *The Universal History of Numbers: From Prehistory to the Invention of the Computer*. Translated by David Bellos, E. F. Harding, Sophie Wood, and Ian Mark. New York: John Wiley and Sons, 2000.

Innis, Harold Adams. *Empire and Communications*. Toronto: University of Toronto Press, 1972.

Jacob, François. "Genetics of the Bacterial Cell." In *Nobel Lectures in Molecular Biology: 1933–1975*, 148–71. New York: Elsevier North-Holland, 1977.

———. *Leçon inaugurale au Collège de France*. Paris: Collège de France, 1965.

———. *The Logic of Life: A History of Heredity*. Translated by Betty E. Spillmann. New York: Pantheon Books, 1974.

Jakobson, Roman. *Language in Literature*. Edited by Krystyna Pomorska and Stephen Rudy. Cambridge, Mass.: Harvard University Press, 1987.

———. "Linguistics." In *Main Trends of Research in the Social and Human Sciences 1. Social Sciences*, edited by UNESCO, 437–38. The Hague: Mouton, 1970.

———. "Linguistics and Poetics." In *Language in Literature*, 62–94. Cambridge, Mass.: Harvard University Press, 1987.

———. "Two Aspects of Language and Two Types of Aphasic Disturbances." In *Language in Literature*, 95–119. Cambridge, Mass.: Harvard University Press, 1987.

Jakobson, Roman, C. Gunnar M. Fant, and Morris Halle. *Preliminaries to Speech Analysis*. Cambridge, Mass.: MIT Press, [1951] 1969.

Jakobson, Roman, and Morris Halle. *Fundamentals of Language*. The Hague: Mouton, 1956.

Jameson, Fredric. "Imaginary and Symbolic in Lacan: Marxism, Psychoanalytic Criticism, and the Problem of the Subject." In *Literature and Psychoanalysis: The Ques-*

tion of Reading, Otherwise, edited by Shoshana Felman, 351–58. Baltimore: Johns Hopkins University Press, 1982.

———. *The Political Unconscious: Narrative as a Socially Symbolic Act.* Ithaca, N.Y.: Cornell University Press, 1981.

———. *The Prison-House of Language: A Critical Account of Structuralism and Russian Formalism.* Princeton: Princeton University Press, 1972.

Jay, Martin. *Downcast Eyes: The Denigration of Vision in Twentieth-Century French Thought.* Berkeley: University of California Press, 1993.

Jentsch, Ernst. "On the Psychology of the Uncanny." Translated by Roy Sellars. *Angelaki* 2, no. 1 (1997): 7–16.

———. "Zur Psychologie des Unheimlichen." *Psychiatrisch-Neurologische Wochenschrift* 8.22 (25 Aug. 1906): 195–98 and 8.23 (1 Sept. 1906): 203–5.

Johnson, Barbara. "The Frame of Reference: Poe, Lacan, Derrida." In *The Purloined Poe: Lacan, Derrida, and Psychoanalytic Reading*, edited by John P. Muller and William J. Richardson, 213–51. Baltimore: Johns Hopkins University Press, 1988.

Johnson, John. *The Allure of Machinic Life: Cybernetics, Artificial Life, and the New AI.* Cambridge, Mass.: MIT Press, 2008.

Jolas, Eugene. "The Revolution of Language and James Joyce." In *Our Exagmination Round His Factification for Incamination of Work in Progress*, edited by Samuel Beckett, 77–92. London: Faber and Faber, 1929.

Jones, Ernest. *The Life and Work of Sigmund Freud.* 3 vols. New York: Basic Books, c. 1953–57.

———. *Papers on Psycho-Analysis.* New York: William Wood, 1918.

Joyce, James. *Finnegans Wake.* London: Faber & Faber, 1975.

———. *Ulysses.* New York: Random House, 1961.

Judson, Horace Freeland. *The Eighth Day of Creation: Makers of the Revolution in Biology.* New York: Simon and Schuster, 1979.

Jung, C. G. "The Association Method." In *Experimental Researches.* Translated by Leopold Stein in collaboration with Diana Riviere, 439–65. Rollinggen Series XX. Princeton: Princeton University Press, 1990.

———. "Experimental Observations on the Faculty of Memory." In *Experimental Researches.* Translated by Leopold Stein in collaboration with Diana Riviere, 272–87. Rollinggen Series XX. Princeton: Princeton University Press, 1990.

———. *Experimental Researches.* Translated by Leopold Stein in collaboration with Diana Riviere. Rollinggen Series XX. Princeton: Princeton University Press, 1990.

———. "New Aspects of Criminal Psychology." In *Experimental Researches.* Translated by Leopold Stein in collaboration with Diana Riviere, 586–96. Rollinggen Series XX. Princeton: Princeton University Press, 1990.

———. "On Psychophysical Relations of the Association Experiment." In *Experimental Researches.* Translated by Leopold Stein in collaboration with Diana Riviere, 483–91. Rollinggen Series XX. Princeton: Princeton University Press, 1990.

———. "Psychoanalysis and Association Experiments." In *Experimental Researches.* Translated by Leopold Stein in collaboration with Diana Riviere, 288–317. Rollinggen Series XX. Princeton: Princeton University Press, 1990.

———. "The Reaction-Time Ratio in the Association Experiment." In *Experimental Researches*. Translated by Leopold Stein in collaboration with Diana Riviere, 221–71. Rollinggen Series XX. Princeton: Princeton University Press, 1990.

———, ed. *Studies in Word-Association: Experiments in the Diagnosis of Psychopathological Conditions Carried Out at the Psychiatric Clinic of the University of Zurich.* London: Routledge & Kegan Paul, 1918.

Kapp, Reginald O. "Comments on Bernfeld and Feitelberg's 'The Principle of Entropy and the Death Instinct.'" *International Journal of Psycho-Analysis,* 12 (1931): 82–86.

Kay, Lily E. *Who Wrote the Book of Life?: A History of the Genetic Code.* Stanford: Stanford University Press, 2000.

Keightley, David N. "The Origin of Writing in China: Scripts and Cultural Contexts." In *The Origins of Writing*, edited by Wayne M. Senner. Lincoln: University of Nebraska Press, 1989.

Kittler, Friedrich A. *Discourse Networks 1800/1900.* Translated by Michael Metteer and Chris Cullens. Stanford: Stanford University Press, 1990.

———. *Gramophone, Film, Typewriter.* Translated by Geoffrey Winthrop-Young and Michael Wutz. Stanford: Stanford University Press, 1999.

———. *Literature, Media, Information Systems.* Edited and introduced by John Johnson. Amsterdam: G+B Arts International, 1997.

———. "There Is No Software." *Stanford Literature Review* 9, no. 1 (1992): 81–90.

Koeneke, Rodney. *Empires of the Mind: I. A. Richards and Basic English in China, 1929–1979.* Stanford: Stanford University Press, 2004.

Kuhn, H. W. "Extensive Games." *Proceedings of the National Academy of Sciences of the United States of America* 36 (1950): 570–76.

———. Introduction to John von Neumann and Oskar Morgenstern, *Theory of Games and Economic Behavior.* Commemorative edition, with an introduction by Harold Kuhn and an afterword by Ariel Rubinstein. Princeton: Princeton University Press, 2004.

Kurzweil, Ray. *The Singularity Is Near.* New York: Viking, 2005.

Lacan, Jacques. "Aggressiveness in Psychoanalysis." In *Écrits: The First Complete Edition in English*, 82–101. New York: W. W. Norton, 2006.

———. "The Circuit." In *The Seminar of Jacques Lacan. Book 2, the Ego in Freud's Theory and in the Technique of Psychoanalysis, 1954–1955*, edited by Jacques-Alain Miller and John Forrester, 77–90. New York and London: W. W. Norton, 1988.

———. "Conference et entretien dans des universités nord-americaines: Yale University, Kanzer Seminar." *Scilicet,* nos. 6/7 (1976): 7–31. English translation by Jack W. Stone at http://web.missouri.edu/~stonej/Kanzer_seminar.pdf.

———. "L'Écrit et la parole" (Writing and speech). In *Le Séminaire Livre XVIII: D'un Discours qui ne serait pas du semblant*, edited by Jacques-Alain Miller, 77–94. Paris: Seuil, 2007.

———. *Écrits: The First Complete Edition in English.* Translated by Bruce Fink in collaboration with Héloïse Fink and Russell Grigg. New York: W. W. Norton, 2002.

———. "Freud, Hegel, and the Machine." In *The Seminar of Jacques Lacan. Book 2, the Ego in Freud's Theory and in the Technique of Psychoanalysis, 1954–1955*, edited by Jacques-Alain Miller and John Forrester, 64–76. New York and London: W. W. Norton, 1988.

———. "Homeostasis and Insistence." In *The Seminar of Jacques Lacan. Book 2, the Ego in Freud's Theory and in the Technique of Psychoanalysis, 1954–1955*, edited by Jacques-Alain Miller and John Forrester, 53–63. New York and London: W. W. Norton, 1988.

———. "Joyce le Symptôme." In *Le Sinthome: Le seminaire de Jacques Lacan, XXIII, 1975–1976*, 161–69. Paris: Seuil, 2005.

———. "La lettre volée." In *Le Moi: dans la théorie de Freud et dans la technique de la psychanalyse*, 261–79. Paris: Seuil, 1978.

———. "Logical Time and the Assertion of Anticipated Certainty." In *Écrits: The First Complete Edition in English*, 161–75. New York: W. W. Norton, 2006.

———. *Le Moi: dans la théorie de Freud et dans la technique de la psychanalyse*. Paris: Seuil, 1978.

———. "Odd or Even? Beyond Intersubjectivity." In *The Seminar of Jacques Lacan. Book 2, the Ego in Freud's Theory and in the Technique of Psychoanalysis, 1954–1955*, edited by Jacques-Alain Miller and John Forrester, 175–90. New York and London: W. W. Norton, 1988.

———. "Of Structure as an Inmixing of an Otherness Prerequisite to Any Subject Whatsoever." In *The Structuralist Controversy: The Languages of Criticism and the Sciences of Man*, edited by Richard Macksey and Eugenio Donato, 186–200. Baltimore: Johns Hopkins Press, 1970.

———. "Psychoanalysis and Cybernetics, or on the Nature of Language." In *The Seminar of Jacques Lacan. Book 2, the Ego in Freud's Theory and in the Technique of Psychoanalysis, 1954–1955*, edited by Jacques-Alain Miller and John Forrester, 294–308. New York and London: W. W. Norton, 1988.

———. "The Purloined Letter." In *The Seminar of Jacques Lacan. Book 2, the Ego in Freud's Theory and in the Technique of Psychoanalysis, 1954–1955*, edited by Jacques-Alain Miller and John Forrester, 191–205. New York and London: W. W. Norton, 1988.

———. *Le Séminaire Livre XVIII: d'un Discours qui ne serait pas du semblant*. Edited by Jacques-Alain Miller. Paris: Seuil, 2007.

———. *The Seminar of Jacques Lacan. Book 2, the Ego in Freud's Theory and in the Technique of Psychoanalysis, 1954–1955*. Translated by Sylvana Tomaselli. Edited by Jacques-Alain Miller and John Forrester. New York: W. W. Norton, 1988.

———. "Seminar on the 'Purloined Letter.'" In *Écrits: The First Complete Edition in English*, 7–48. New York: W. W. Norton, 2006.

———. *Le Sinthome: Le seminaire de Jacques Lacan, XXIII, 1975–1976*. Paris, 2005.

———. "Some Questions for the Teacher." In *The Seminar of Jacques Lacan. Book 2, the Ego in Freud's Theory and in the Technique of Psychoanalysis, 1954–1955*, 206–20. New York and London: W. W. Norton, 1988.

———. "Where Is Speech? Where Is Language?" In *The Seminar of Jacques Lacan. Book 2, the Ego in Freud's Theory and in the Technique of Psychoanalysis, 1954–1955*, edited by Jacques-Alain Miller and John Forrester, 277–93. New York and London: W. W. Norton, 1988.

Lach, Donald F. "Leibniz and China." *Journal of the History of Ideas* 6, no. 4 (1945): 436–55.

Lacoue-Labarthe, Philippe, and Jean-Luc Nancy. *The Title of the Letter: A Reading of Lacan*. Translated by Francois Raffoul and David Pettigrew. Albany: SUNY, 1992.

Lafontaine, Céline. *L'empire cybernétique: Des machines penser la pensée machine*. Paris: Seuil, 2004.

Lakoff, George, and Rafael E. Núñez. *Where Mathematics Comes From: How the Embodied Mind Brings Mathematics into Being*. New York: Basic Books, 2000.

Leroi-Gourhan, André. *Gesture and Speech*. Cambridge, Mass.: MIT Press, 1993.

Lévi-Strauss, Claude. *Structural Anthropology*. Translated from the French by Claire Jacobson and Brooke Grundfest Schoepf. 2 vols. New York: Basic Books, 1963.

Lewis, Mark Edward. *Writing and Authority in Early China*. Albany: SUNY, 1999.

Li, Xueqin, G. Harbottle, J. Zhang, and C. Wang. "The Earliest Writing? Sign Use in the Seventh Millennium BC at Jiahu, Henan Province, China." *Antiquity* 77, no. 295 (2003): 31–44.

Link, David. "Chains to the West: Markov's Theory of Connected Events and Its Transmission to Western Europe." *Science in Context* 19, no. 4 (2006): 561–90.

———. "Classical Text in Translation: An Example of Statistical Investigation of the Text *Eugene Onegin* Concerning the Connection of Samples in Chains." *Science in Context* 19, no. 4 (2006): 591–600.

———. "Traces of the Mouth: Andrei Andreyevich Markov's Mathematization of Writing." *History of Science* 44, no. 145 (2006): 321–48.

Liu, Alan. *The Laws of Cool: Knowledge Work and the Culture of Information*. Chicago: University of Chicago Press, 2004.

Liu, Lydia H. *The Clash of Empires: The Invention of China in Modern World Making*. Cambridge, Mass.: Harvard University Press, 2004.

———, ed. *Tokens of Exchange: The Problem of Translation in Global Circulations*. Durham, N.C.: Duke University Press, 1999.

Livingston, Ira. *Between Science and Literature: An Introduction to Autopoetics*. Urbana: University of Illinois Press, 2006.

Lotringer, Sylvere, and Sande Cohen. "Introduction: A Few Theses on French Theory in America." In *French Theory in America*, edited by Sylvere Lotringer and Sande Cohen, 1–9. New York: Routledge, 2001.

Luhmann, Niklas. *Social Systems*. Translated by John Bednarz, Jr., with Dirk Baecker. Stanford: Stanford University Press, 1995.

Lyotard, Jean-François. *The Postmodern Condition: A Report on Knowledge*. Translated by Geoff Bennington and Brian Massumi. Minneapolis: University of Minnesota Press, 1984.

Mabee, Carleton. *The American Leonardo: A Life of Samuel F. B. Morse*. New York: A. A. Knopf, 1943.

MacDorman, Karl F. "Androids as an Experimental Apparatus: Why Is There an Uncanny Valley and Can We Exploit It?" with MacDorman and Takashi Minato collaborating on the Mori translation in appendix B. Cognitive Science Society

Workshop on Toward Social Mechanisms of Android Science, 2005. http://www
.androidscience.com/proceedings2005/MacDormanCogSci2005AS.pdf.

MacDorman, K. F., and H. Ishiguro. "The Uncanny Advantage of Using Androids
in Cognitive and Social Science Research." *Interaction Studies* 7, no. 3 (2006):
297–337.

MacKay, Donald M. *Information, Mechanism, and Meaning.* Cambridge, Mass.: MIT
Press, 1969.

Macksey, Richard, and Eugenio Donato, eds. *The Structuralist Controversy: The Languages of Criticism and the Sciences of Man.* Baltimore: Johns Hopkins University
Press, 1970.

Mallarmé, Stéphane. *Collected Poems.* Translated by Henry Weinfield. Berkeley: University of California Press, 1994.

Manovich, Lev. *The Language of New Media.* Cambridge, Mass.: MIT Press, 2001.

Marcus, G. F., and S. E. Fisher. "FOXP2 in Focus: What Can Genes Tell Us About
Speech and Language?" *Trends in Cognitive Sciences* 7, no. 6 (2003): 257–62.

Marcuse, Herbert. "Aggressiveness in Advanced Industrial Society." In *Negations:
Essays in Critical Theory,* 248–68. Translated by Jeremy J. Shapiro. Boston: Beacon
Press, 1968.

———. *Eros and Civilization: An Inquiry into Freud.* Boston: Beacon Press, 1974.

Marion, Denis. *La Méthode intellectuelle d'Edgar Poe.* Paris: Les éditions de minuit,
1952.

Markov, A. A. "An Example of Statistical Investigation of the Text *Eugene Onegin* Concerning the Connection of Samples in Chains." *Science in Context* 19, no. 4 (2006):
591–600.

Masani, Pesi Rustom. *Norbert Wiener, 1894–1964.* Basel: Birkhäuser Verlag, 1990.

Maturana, Humberto R., and Francisco J. Varela. *Autopoiesis and Cognition: The Realization of the Living.* Dordrecht, Netherlands: D. Reidel Publishing Company, 1980.

Mayall, Kate, Glyn W. Humphreys, and Andrew Olson. "Disruption to Word or Letter
Processing? The Origins of Case-Mixing Effects." *Journal of Experimental Psychology: Learning, Memory, and Cognition* 23, no. 5 (1997): 1275–86.

McCulloch, Warren S. *Embodiments of Mind.* Cambridge, Mass.: MIT Press, 1965.

McCulloch, Warren S., and W. Pitts. "A Logical Calculus of the Ideas Immanent in
Nervous Activity." *Bulletin of Mathematical Biology* 5 (1943): 99–115.

McCusker, L. X., P. B. Gough, and R. G. Bias. "Word Recognition Inside Out and
Outside In." *Journal of Experimental Psychology: Human Perception and Performance*
7, no. 3 (1981): 538–51.

McLuhan, Marshall. "Cybernation and Culture." In *The Social Impact of Cybernetics,*
edited by Charles Richard Dechert, 95–108. Notre Dame: University of Notre
Dame Press, 1966.

———. *The Gutenberg Galaxy: The Making of Typographic Man.* Toronto: University of
Toronto Press, 1965.

———. *Understanding Media: The Extensions of Man.* Cambridge, Mass.: MIT Press,
1994; 1964.

Meltzer, Françoise. "The Uncanny Rendered Canny: Freud's Blind Spot in Reading Hoffmann's 'Sandman.'" In *Introducing Psychoanalytic Theory*, edited by Sander L. Gilman, 218–39. New York: Brunner/Mazel, 1982.

Merleau-Ponty, Maurice. *Sense and Non-Sense*. Translated by Hubert L. Dreyfus and Patricia Allen Dreyfus. Evanston: Northwestern University Press, 1971.

Mindell, David A. *Between Human and Machine: Feedback, Control, and Computing before Cybernetics*. Baltimore: Johns Hopkins University Press, 2004.

Mindell, David, Jérôme Segal, and Slava Gerovitch. "From Communications Engineering to Communications Science: Cybernetics and Information Theory in the United States, France, and Soviet Union." In *Science and Ideology: A Comparative History*, edited by Mark Walker, 66–95. London: Routledge, 2003.

Minsky, Marvin. *Computation: Finite and Infinite Machines*. Englewood Cliffs, N.J.: Prentice-Hall, 1967.

———. *The Emotion Machine: Commonsense Thinking, Artificial Intelligence, and the Future of the Human Mind*. New York: Simon and Schuster, 2006.

———. "Jokes and the Logic of the Cognitive Unconscious." In *Cognitive Constraints on Communication*, edited by Lucia Vaina and Jaakko Hintikka, 175–200. Boston: Reidel, 1981.

———. "Our Robotized Future." In *Robotics*, edited by Marvin Minsky, 287–307. New York: Anchor Press, 1985.

———, ed. *Robotics*. New York: Anchor Press, 1985.

———. *The Society of Mind*. New York: Simon and Schuster, 1986.

Mitchell, W. J. T. *Iconology: Image, Text, Ideology*. Chicago: University of Chicago Press, 1986.

———. *Picture Theory: Essays on Verbal and Visual Representation*. Chicago: University of Chicago Press, 1994.

———. *What Do Pictures Want?: The Lives and Loves of Images*. Chicago: University of Chicago Press, 2005.

———. "The Work of Art in the Age of Biocybernetic Reproduction." *Modernism/modernity* 10, no. 3 (2003): 481–500.

Mori, Masahiro. *The Buddha in the Robot: A Robot Engineer's Thoughts on Science and Religion*. Translated by Charles S. Terry. Tokyo: Kosei, 1999.

———. "Bukimi no tani" (the uncanny valley). *Energy* 7, no. 4 (1970): 33–35. English translation by Karl F. MacDorman and Takashi Minato in appendix B to MacDorman, "Androids as an Experimental Apparatus: Why Is There an Uncanny Valley and Can We Exploit It?" 9–10.

Morlock, Forbes. "Doubly Uncanny: An Introduction to 'On the Psychology of the Uncanny.'" *Angelaki* 2, no. 1 (1997): 17–21.

Muller, John P., and William J. Richardson, eds. *The Purloined Poe: Lacan, Derrida, and Psychoanalytic Reading*. Baltimore: Johns Hopkins University Press, 1988.

Nelson, Victoria. *The Secret Life of Puppets*. Cambridge, Mass.: Harvard University Press, 2001.

Nietzsche, Friedrich. *Human, All Too Human: A Book for Free Spirits*. Translated by R. J. Hollingdale. Cambridge: Cambridge University Press, 1986.

O'Connor, M. "Epigraphic Semitic Scripts." In *The World's Writing Systems*, edited by Peter T. Daniels and William Bright, 88–107. Oxford: Oxford University Press, 1996.

Ogden, Charles Kay. *Basic English: A General Introduction with Rules and Grammar.* London: Kegan Paul, Trench, Trubner, 1935.

———. *Basic English: International Second Language.* Rev. and expanded ed. New York: Harcourt, Brace & World, 1968.

———. *Debabelization: With a Survey of Contemporary Opinion on the Problem of a Universal Language.* London: Kegan Paul, 1931.

Ogden, C. K., and I. A. Richards. *The Meaning of Meaning: A Study of the Influence of Language upon Thought and of the Science of Symbolism.* 6th ed. New York: Harcourt, Brace & World, 1944.

Ong, Walter J. *Orality and Literacy: The Technologizing of the Word.* New York: Routledge, 1982.

Pelli, D. G., B. Farell, and D. C. Moore. "The Remarkable Inefficiency of Word Recognition." *Nature* 423, no. 6941 (2003): 752–56.

Penrose, L. S. "Freud's Theory of Instinct and Other Psycho-Biological Theories." *International Journal of Psycho-Analysis* 12 (1931): 87–97.

Perea, M., and S. J. Lupker. "Does *jugde* Activate COURT? Transposed-Letter Similarity Effects in Masked Associative Priming." *Memory & Cognition* 31, no. 6 (2003): 829–41.

———. "Transposed-Letter Confusability Effects in Masked Form Priming." In *Masked Priming: The State of the Art*, edited by Sachiko Kinoshita and Stephen Jeffrey Lupker, 97–120. New York: Psychology Press, 2003.

Piaget, Jean. "The Affective Unconscious and the Cognitive Unconscious." *Journal of the American Psychoanalytic Association* 21 (1973): 249–61.

Pierce, John Robinson. *Science, Art, and Communication.* New York: C. N. Potter, 1968.

Pierce, John Robinson, and A. Michael Noll. *Signals: The Science of Telecommunications.* New York: Scientific American Library, 1990.

Plato. *Phaedrus.* Translated by Robin Waterfield. Oxford: Oxford University Press, 2002.

Plotnitsky, Arkady. *The Knowable and the Unknowable: Modern Science, Nonclassical Thought, and the "Two Cultures."* Ann Arbor: University of Michigan Press, 2002.

Porge, Erik. *Se compter trios: Le temps logique de Lacan* (counting the self as three: Lacan's logical time). Toulouse: Érè, 1989.

Porter, David. *Ideographia: The Chinese Cipher in Early Modern Europe.* Stanford: Stanford University Press, 2001.

Pound, Ezra. "Debabelization and Ogden." *New English Weekly*, no. 4 (28 February 1935): 411.

———. *Machine Art and Other Writings: The Lost Thought of the Italian Years.* Edited by Maria Luisa Ardizzone. Durham, N.C.: Duke University Press, 1996.

———. *Selected Letters: 1907–1941.* Edited by D. D. Paige. London: Faber and Faber, 1950.

———. *The Spirit of Romance.* New York: New Directions Books, 1968.

———. "Vorticism." *Fortnightly Review* 96, no. 573 (September 1914): 461–71.

Poundstone, William. *Prisoner's Dilemma*. New York: Doubleday, 1992.

Problemy Peredachi Informatsii. "Claude Elwood Shannon." *Problems of Information Transmission* 37, no. 2 (2001): 87–90. Translated from the Russian journal *Problemy Peredachi Informatsii*, no. 2 (2001): 3–7.

Psalmanazar, George. *A Historical and Geographical Description of Formosa*. London, 1704.

Rabinow, Paul. *French DNA: Trouble in Purgatory*. Chicago: University of Chicago Press, 1999.

Ragland, Ellie, and Dragan Milovanovic, eds. *Lacan: Topologically Speaking*. New York: Other Press, 2004.

Raley, Rita. "Machine Translation and Global English." *Yale Journal of Criticism* 16, no. 2 (2003): 291–313.

Reed, Brian. "Hart Crane's Victrola." *Modernism/modernity* 7, no. 1 (2000): 99–125.

Reicher, G. M. "Perceptual Recognition as a Function of Meaningfulness of Stimulus Material." *Journal of Experimental Psychology* 81, no. 2 (1969): 275–80.

Rheinberger, Hans-Jörg. "The Notions of Regulation, Information, and Language in the Writings of François Jacob." *Biological Theory* 1, no. 3 (2006): 261–67.

Rice, Thomas Jackson. *Joyce, Chaos, and Complexity*. Urbana: University of Illinois Press, 1997.

Richards, I. A. *Basic in Teaching: East and West*. London: K. Paul, Trench, Trubner, 1935.

———. "English Language Teaching Films and Their Use in Teacher Training." *English Language Teaching* 2, no. 1 (1947): 1–7.

———. "Responsibilities in the Teaching of English." In *Speculative Instruments*, 91–106. Chicago: University of Chicago Press, 1955.

———. *Speculative Instruments*. Chicago: University of Chicago Press, 1955.

———. "Toward a More Synoptic View." In *Speculative Instruments*, 113–26. Chicago: University of Chicago Press, 1955.

———. "Toward a Theory of Comprehending." In *Speculative Instruments*. Chicago: University of Chicago Press, 1955.

Richey, Jeffrey L. "I, Robot: Self as Machine in the Liezi." In *Riding the Wind with Liezi: New Perspectives on the Daoist Classic*, edited by Ronnie Littlejohn and Jeffrey Dippmann. Albany: SUNY Press, forthcoming.

Rickels, Laurence A. *Nazi Psychoanalysis*. Vol. 2: *Crypto-Fetishism*. Minneapolis: University of Minnesota Press, 2002.

Rotman, Brian. "The Technology of Mathematical Persuasion." In *Inscribing Science: Scientific Texts and the Materiality of Communication*, edited by Timothy Lenoir, 55–69. Stanford: Stanford University Press, 1998.

Roudinesco, Elisabeth. *Jacques Lacan*. Translated by Barbara Bray. New York: Columbia University Press, 1997.

———. *Jacques Lacan & Co.: A History of Psychoanalysis in France, 1925–1985*. Translated by Jeffrey Mehlman. Chicago: University of Chicago Press, 1990.

Rousseau, Jean-Jacques. *On the Origin of Language*. Translated by John H. Moran and Alexander Gode. Chicago: University of Chicago Press, 1966.

Roux, Ronan Le. "Psychanalyse et cybernétique: Les machines de Lacan." *L'Evolution Psychiatrique* 72, no. 2 (2007): 346–69.

Royle, Nicholas. *The Uncanny*. Manchester: Manchester University Press, 2003.

Russo, John Paul. *I. A. Richards: His Life and Work*. Baltimore: Johns Hopkins University Press, 1989.

Sartre, Jean-Paul. "Jean-Paul Sartre Répond." *L'Arc*, no. 30 (1966): 87–96.

Saul, Leon J. "Freud's Death Instinct and the Second Law of Thermodynamics." *International Journal of Psycho-Analysis* 39 (1958): 323–25.

Saussure, Ferdinand de. *Course in General Linguistics*. Translated by Wade Baskin. New York: McGraw-Hill, 1966.

———. *Ferdinand de Saussure: Troisième cours de linguistique générale (1910–1911) d'après les cahiers d'Emile Constantin*. Edited by Eisuke Komatsu and Roy Harris. Oxford: Pergamon Press, 1993.

Schank, Roger C., and Kenneth Mark Colby, eds. *Computer Models of Thought and Language*. San Francisco: W. H. Freeman, 1973.

Schmandt-Besserat, D. "The Earliest Precursors of Writing." *Scientific American* 238, no. 6 (1978): 50–59.

Schönberger, Martin Maria. *The I Ching and the Genetic Code: The Hidden Key to Life*. Translated by D. Q. Stephenson. Santa Fe, N.M.: Aurora Press, 1992.

Searchinger, Gene. *The Human Language Series*. Video in 3 parts. Equinox Films, 1995.

Sebastian, Thomas. "Technology Romanticized: Friedrich Kittler's *Discourse Networks 1800/1900*." *MLN* 105 (1990): 583–95.

Serrano, Richard. "Lacan's Oriental Language of the Unconscious." *SubStance* 26, no. 3 (1997): 90–106.

Shannon, Claude E. *Claude Elwood Shannon: Collected Papers*. Edited by Neil J. A. Sloane and Aaron D. Wyner. New York: IEEE Press, 1993.

———. "Communication Theory of Secrecy Systems." *Bell System Technical Journal* 28 (1949): 656–715.

———. "The Mathematical Theory of Communication." *Bell System Technical Journal* 27, nos. 3–4 (1948): 379–423, 623–56.

———. "A Mind-Reading Machine." In *Claude Elwood Shannon: Collected Papers*, edited by N. J. A. Sloane and A. D. Wyner, 688–90. New York: IEEE Press, 1993.

———. "Prediction and Entropy of Printed English." *Bell System Technical Journal* 30, no. 1 (1951): 50–64.

———. "A Universal Turing Machine with Two Internal States." In *Claude Elwood Shannon: Collected Papers*, edited by N. J. A. Sloane and A. D. Wyner, 733–41. New York: IEEE Press, 1993.

Shannon, Claude Elwood, and Warren Weaver. *The Mathematical Theory of Communication*. Urbana: University of Illinois Press, 1963. Originally published 1949.

Shillcock, R., T. M. Ellison, and P. Monaghan. "Eye-Fixation Behaviour, Lexical Storage and Visual Word Recognition in a Split Processing Model." *Psychological Review* 107, no. 4 (2000): 824–51.

Singh, Simon. *The Code Book: The Science of Secrecy from Ancient Egypt to Quantum Cryptography*. New York: Anchor Books, 2000.

Sohn, Pow-Key. "Early Korean Printing." *Journal of the American Oriental Society* 79, no. 2 (1959): 96–103.

———. "Printing since the 8th Century in Korea." *Koreana* 7, no. 2 (1993): 4–9.

Sokal, Alan D., and J. Bricmont. *Fashionable Nonsense: Postmodern Intellectuals' Abuse of Science*. New York: Picador, 1998.

Sproat, Richard William. *A Computational Theory of Writing Systems*. Cambridge: Cambridge University Press, 2000.

Stent, Gunther S. *The Coming of the Golden Age: A View of the End of Progress*. New York: Natural History Press, 1969.

Stewart, Garrett. *Reading Voices: Literature and the Phonotext*. Berkeley: University of California Press, 1990.

Stiegler, Bernard. *Technics and Time, 1: The Fault of Epimetheus*. Translated by Richard Beardsworth and George Collins. Stanford: Stanford University Press, 1998.

———. *Technics and Time, 2: Disorientation*. Translated by Stephen Barker. Stanford: Stanford University Press, 2009.

Swift, Jonathan. *Travels into Several Remote Nations of the World in Four Parts by Lemuel Gulliver*. Dublin, 1726.

Taylor, Mark C. *Altarity*. Chicago: University of Chicago Press, 1987.

———. *The Moment of Complexity: Emerging Network Culture*. Chicago: University of Chicago Press, 2003.

Thacker, Eugene. *Biomedia*. Minneapolis: University of Minnesota Press, 2004.

Theall, Donald F. *Beyond the Word: Reconstructing Sense in the Joyce Era of Technology, Culture, and Communication*. Toronto: University of Toronto Press, 1995.

———. "The Hieroglyphs of Engined Egypsians: Machines, Media and Modes of Communication." In *Joyce Studies Annual 1991*, edited by Thomas F. Staley, 129–76. Austin: University of Texas Press, 1991.

Tiffany, Daniel. *Radio Corpse: Imagism and the Cryptaesthetic of Ezra Pound*. Cambridge, Mass.: Harvard University Press, 1995.

Tofts, Darren, and Murray McKeich. *Memory Trade: A Prehistory of Cyberculture*. North Ryde, New South Wales: 21•C/Interface Book, 1998.

Tong, Q. S. "The Bathos of a Universalism, I. A. Richards and His Basic English." In *Tokens of Exchange: The Problem of Translation in Global Circulations*, edited by Lydia H. Liu, 331–54. Durham, N.C.: Duke University Press, 1999.

Toulmin, Stephen Edelston. *The Philosophy of Science*. London: Hutchinson, 1953.

Tsien, Tsuen-Hsuin. *Paper and Printing*. In "Science and Civilization in China," edited by Joseph Needham, vol. 5 part 1. Cambridge: Cambridge University Press, 1985.

———. *Written on Bamboo and Silk: The Beginnings of Chinese Books and Inscriptions*. Chicago: University of Chicago Press, 2004.

Turing, A. M. "Computing Machinery and Intelligence." *Mind* 59, no. 236 (1950): 433–60.

———. "On Computable Numbers, with an Application to the Entscheidungsproblem." *Proceedings of London Mathematical Society Ser.* 2, no. 42 (1937): 230–65.

Uhr, Leonard, and Charles Vossler. "A Pattern-Recognition Program that Generates, Evaluates, and Adjusts Its Own Operators." In *Computers and Thought*, edited by Edward A. Feigenbaum and Julian Feldman, 251–68. New York: McGraw-Hill, 1963.

Vachek, Josef. *Written Languages Revisited*. Amsterdam: John Benjamins, 1989.

Vail, Alfred. *Description of the American Electro Magnetic Telegraph Now in Operation Between the Cities of Washington and Baltimore*. Washington, D.C., 1845.

Van de Walle, Jürgen. "Roman Jakobson, Cybernetics, and Information Theory: A Critical Assessment." *Folia Linguistica Historica* 29, no. 1 (December 2008): 87–124.

Varela, Francisco, Evan Thompson, and Eleanor Rosch. *The Embodied Mind*. Cambridge, Mass.: MIT Press, 1992.

Vendler, Helen. "I. A. Richards at Harvard." *Boston Review* (April 1981). http://www.bostonreview.net/BR06.2/vendler.html.

Vidler, Anthony. *The Architectural Uncanny: Essays in the Modern Unhomely*. Cambridge, Mass.: MIT Press, 1992.

von Foerster, Heinz, Margaret Mead, and Hans Lukas Teuber, eds. *Cybernetics: Circular Causal and Feedback Mechanisms in Biological and Social Systems: Transactions of the Eighth Conference, March 15–16, 1951, New York, N.Y.* New York: Josiah Macy, Jr. Foundation, 1952.

von Neumann, John. "The General and Logical Theory of Automata." In *The Collected Works of John von Neumann*, vol. 5, 288–326. Oxford: Pergamon Press, 1963.

von Neumann, John, and Oskar Morgenstern. *The Theory of Games and Economic Behavior*. Princeton: Princeton University Press, 1963.

Wachowski, Larry and Andy. *The Matrix: The Shooting Script*. New York: Newmarket Press, 2002.

Waismann, Friedrich. *Introduction to Mathematical Thinking: The Formation of Concepts in Modern Mathematics*. Translated by Theodore J. Bena. New York: F. Ungar, 1951.

Wallach, Wendell, and Colin Allen. *Moral Machines: Teaching Robots Right from Wrong*. Oxford: Oxford University Press, 2009.

Wark, McKenzie. *Gamer Theory*. Cambridge, Mass.: Harvard University Press, 2007.

Warrington, E. K., and T. Shallice. "Word-Form Dyslexia." *Brain: A Journal of Neurology* 103, no. 1 (1980): 99–112.

Watson, James D. *The Double Helix*. New York: New American Library, 1968.

Weaver, Warren. *Alice in Many Tongues: The Translations of Alice in Wonderland*. Madison: University of Wisconsin Press, 1964.

———. "Translation." In *Machine Translation of Languages*, edited by William N. Locke and Andrew Donald Booth, 15–23. Cambridge and New York: Technology Press of the Massachusetts Institute of Technology, 1955.

Weber, Samuel. *The Legend of Freud.* Expanded ed. Stanford: Stanford University Press, 2000.

———. "Vertigo: The Question of Anxiety in Freud." In *Lacan in the German-Speaking World,* edited by Elizabeth Stewart, Maire Jaanus, and Richard Feldstein, 203–20. Albany: SUNY, 2004.

Wegener, Mai. "L'entwurf de Freud—une lettre volée." *Cairn* 12, no. 1 (2004): 175–95.

———. *Neuronen und Neurosen: Der psychische Apparat bei Freud und Lacan: Ein historisch-theoretischer Versuch zu Freuds Entwurf von 1895.* Munich: W. Fink Verlag, 2004.

Weizenbaum, Joseph. *Computer Power and Human Reason: From Judgment to Calculation.* San Francisco: W. H. Freeman, 1976.

Wiener, Norbert. *Cybernetics: or Control and Communication in the Animal and the Machine.* Cambridge, Mass.: MIT Press, 1961.

———. *The Human Use of Human Beings: Cybernetics and Society.* Boston: Houghton Mifflin, 1954.

———. *I Am a Mathematician.* Garden City, N.Y.: Doubleday, 1956.

———. "L'homme et la machine." In *Collected Works with Commentaries,* vol. 4, edited by P. Masani, 824–42. Cambridge, Mass.: MIT Press, 1985.

Wilden, Anthony. "Marcuse and the Freudian Model: Energy, Information, and Phantasie." *Salmagundi,* nos. 10/11 (1969): 196–245.

———. *System and Structure: Essays in Communication and Exchange.* London: Tavistock Publications Limited, 1972.

Winthrop-Young, Geoffrey. "Silicon Sociology, or, Two Kings on Hegel's Throne? Kittler, Luhmann, and the Posthuman Merger of German Media Theory." *Yale Journal of Criticism* 13, no. 2 (2000): 391–420.

Wittgenstein, Ludwig. *Tractatus Logico-Philosophicus.* Translated by C. K. Ogden. With an introduction by Bertrand Russell. London: K. Paul, Trench, Trubner, 1922.

Wolfe, Cary. *What Is Posthumanism?* Minneapolis: University of Minnesota Press, 2010.

Wright, Arthur Frederick, ed. *Studies in Chinese Thought.* Chicago: University of Chicago Press, 1953.

Yan, Johnson F. *DNA and the I Ching: The Tao of Life.* Berkeley: North Atlantic Books, 1991.

Yčas, M. *The Biological Code.* New York: American Elsevier, 1969.

Zhuangzi (Chuang Tzu). *The Complete Works of Chuang Tzu.* Translated by Burton Watson. New York: Columbia University Press, 1968.

Žižek, Slavoj. *The Plague of Fantasies.* London: Verso, 1997.

INDEX

cognitive unconscious, 241–42
Colasse, Bernard, 166
Colby, Kenneth Mark, 8, 185, 206, 230,
232–37, 238, 242, 251, 258
cold war: computer simulation of, 258–61;
cybernetics and, 71, 153, 195; international interactions of academics during,
167; Structuralism and, 155, 156; world
order and, 162
communication: Foucault's analysis of
power and, 23; in Lacanian theory, 36,
177, 193, 258. See also language; telecommunication; writing
communication machine: discrete versus
continuous in, 23–24, 59; Frankfurt
School and, 252; human brain as, 8, 131;
Lacan's view of, 185, 193; meaning and,
52, 123, 134n77, 184
communication system, for information
theory, 49–50
communicative action, Habermas on,
254–57, 263
compiling, 24–25
computer: Joyce's anticipation of, 101n3,
102–3, 104, 105, 118–19; Lacan on
unconscious and, 162; word processing
in any script with, 112. See also digital
media; machine
computer animation, 227–28
computer models of cognition. See cognitive
computer programs
Conan Doyle, Arthur, 163. See also Holmes,
Sherlock
Condorcet, 183n89
Confucianism, 3, 4, 5, 8, 245, 262n28
consciousness: Cartesian dualism and, 16n;
critical theorists on, 249, 253, 254, 255;
cybernetic group and, 141; Derrida
on, 66, 67; information processing in
absence of, 36; Lacan's transition from
Hegelianism and, 192–93; thinking
machine and, 28; traditional philosophy
of, 29, 265. See also unconscious
Constantin, Emile, 116
Coupling, J. J., 127, 127n61
Crane, Hart, 57
Crick, Francis, 62, 63, 63n53, 72, 73, 76, 77
critical theory, 35, 249, 250–57, 264, 265
Crosby, Caresse, 108
Crosby, Harry, 108

cryptography: information theory and, 44;
machine translation and, 84–85; molecular biology and, 27–28, 71; Shannon's
familiarity with, 46–47, 47n12, 87, 92;
Swift's Lagado machine and, 41
cybernetics: autopoiesis and, 72–73; Basic
English and, 87, 131; brain as machine
in, 7, 185; cold war and, 71, 153, 195;
critical theory and, 251–52, 255, 256;
death drive and, 203; Derrida on, 61,
66–67; determinism and, 30; development of, 167–68 (see also cybernetics
group); etymology of, 157, 157n12;
European reaction to, 168; French
theory and, 128, 156–58, 161; game
theory and, 184n90; information theory
and, 158, 184n90; Jakobson and, 53n23;
Lacan and (see cybernetics and Lacanian
theory); literary sources of practitioners
of, 163, 165; military applications of,
11n, 138, 156; molecular biology and, 62,
64; universalist aspirations of, 44. See
also Macy Conferences; Wiener,
Norbert
cybernetics and Lacanian theory, 9, 13, 23,
28, 136, 154, 158, 264; Guilbaud and,
168–69, 183n89, 185; Jakobson and,
159n17; language and, 183–84, 186,
187, 193–96, 257, 258; Poe and, 162–63,
162n27, 162n29, 165, 168, 185–86,
198–99; Wilden and, 203
cybernetics group, 131–32, 135, 140. See also
Macy Conferences
cybernetic unconscious: Lacanian, 36, 155n2,
185, 195, 196, 199; political consequences of, 11; of postwar Euro-American
world order, 13, 162. See also the unconscious: cybernetic reframing of
cyborg, 1, 2, 3, 10–11, 209

Daoism, 3, 5, 245
death drive: of digital civilization, 14;
entropy and, 37, 202–3; Freud's concept
of, 202–4, 202n3; human-machine
feedback loop and, 2; Lacan on, 139,
223; of the machine, 139; Marcuse on,
252n6; prophecies of immortality and,
10, 10n22, 243; Shannon's Ultimate
Machine and, 14, 139–40, 204–5; the
uncanny and, 226, 230

13, 53, 150; probabilities of, 237; the unconscious and, 129–30, 240–41, 242. *See also* meaning

Shannon, Claude: Bavelas and, 171; as cautious scientist, 85; *Finnegans Wake* and, 13, 30, 37, 44, 99–101, 104, 128; institutional affiliations of, 187n98; Jakobson and, 79; Lacan and, 9; at Macy Conferences, 131–32, 138–39; Markov's influence on, 44, 51, 80; mechanical maze-solving mouse, 87, 132; military-funded research of, 138; Ogden as precursor of, 95, 97; operations research and, 65; Poe essay critiqued by, 165; semantics and, 77; *techne* of the unconscious and, 265; Turing and, 58, 87; Wiener and, 87, 92. *See also* information theory; Printed English; Ultimate Machine

signifier, 107–8, 136, 189

singularity, Deleuze on, 120–21

Sokal, Alan, 161n24

space, 265; in *Finnegans Wake*, 104, 113–14; in Morse code, 47; Vachek's graphemic zero, 124. *See also* twenty-seventh letter

speech: discrete units of, 24; dream of universal language and, 71; FOXP2 gene and, 78n92; genetic code and, 77–78; Jakobson and, 78, 81, 115; Lacan on, 188–89, 190; writing and, 18, 18n8, 24, 25, 31, 32, 43, 59. *See also* language; phonemes; phonetic alphabet

statistical analysis: of literature by Markov, 51; of Printed English, 13, 36, 44, 45–46, 50–51, 52–53, 59–60, 67–68, 125, 126, 154, 265. *See also* stochastic process

Stein, Gertrude, 102

Stent, Gunther S., 82–83

Stewart, Garrett, 104–5, 108

Stiegler, Bernard, 18, 65n63

stochastic process: defined, 42; French "aleatory" and, 42n7, 154; Guilbaud on language and, 184–85; Joyce's work and, 12–13; literary experiments relying on, 42–43, 51, 129, 139. *See also* information theory; Markov chain; statistical analysis

Structuralism: cybernetics and, 156; form and, 30; Habermas on, 255–56; information theory and, 22; Jakobson's meeting with Lévi-Strauss and, 167; Lacan and,

158; Sartre's reaction to, 155–56, 155n4; transatlantic fashioning of, 128, 197

structural linguistics: information theory and, 22, 158; Lacan and, 108, 158, 159, 184; the unconscious and, 178n76; verbal code and, 77–78. *See also* Jakobson, Roman; linguistics

subconscious, 11, 184–85. *See also* unconscious

Sullivan, J. W. N., 108

supersign, 175–76, 175n67

Surrealism, 13, 30, 44, 142, 261–62

Swift, Jonathan, 39, 163. *See also* Lagado machine

symbolic chain, Lacanian, 13, 177, 178–79, 180, 181, 182, 196

symbolic code: Frankfurt School and, 252. *See also* code

symbolic order, Lacanian: cybernetics and, 9, 13, 23, 28, 36, 154; elusive interpretation of, 161; entropy and, 193; vs. free play of signifiers, 199; Freud's privileging of language and, 216; in game of even and odd, 164, 177; game theory and, 13, 28, 154, 179; vs. Habermas's communicative action, 256; the machine and, 160, 162; nonrational choices and, 136; repetition automatism and, 191; Saussurian notion of language and, 13, 159, 189–90, 193; signifier/signified relationship in, 159, 159n18, 189; Structuralism and, 160; summary of seminar on, 193–96; temporality and, 196; typewriter and, 187, 187n97; the unconscious and, 189, 196, 264; Wilden and, 179n78

systems theory, 255–56

SYSTRAN (software program), 86

Tathāgata, 247, 247n89

Taylor, Mark, 36, 120, 194

techne, 28; of the unconscious, 12, 26, 28, 34, 37, 239, 265

technesis, 26

technocratic civilization: Frankfurt School theorists on, 249; Sartre on, 155

technological prosthesis, 2, 8, 9, 23, 118, 230

technology: domination by, 253; modernist movement and, 118–19; parable of Zhuangzi on, 3–6, 7–8; of writing, 16, 18, 26–27, 66, 67. *See also* machine